A Chinese Fantasy

Fantasy

The Dragon King's Daughter

C O N T E N T S

Original Stories
[The Dragon King's Daughter] / [*Li Yǐ zhuàn*] By Li Chaowei
[The Story of How the Dragon Was Found] / [*Miscellaneous Morsels* from Youyang]

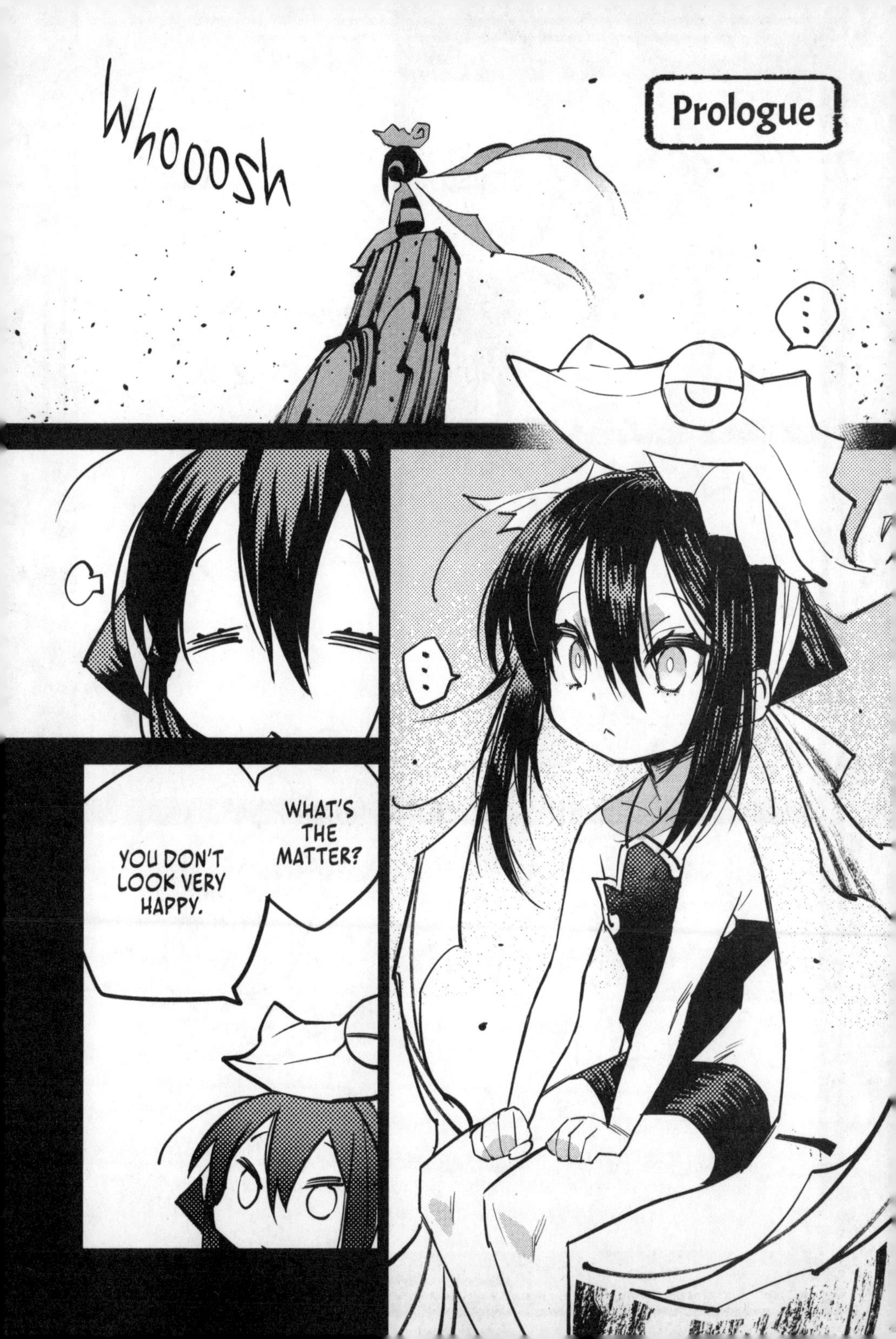
Prologue
Whooosh
...
...
WHAT'S THE MATTER?
YOU DON'T LOOK VERY HAPPY.

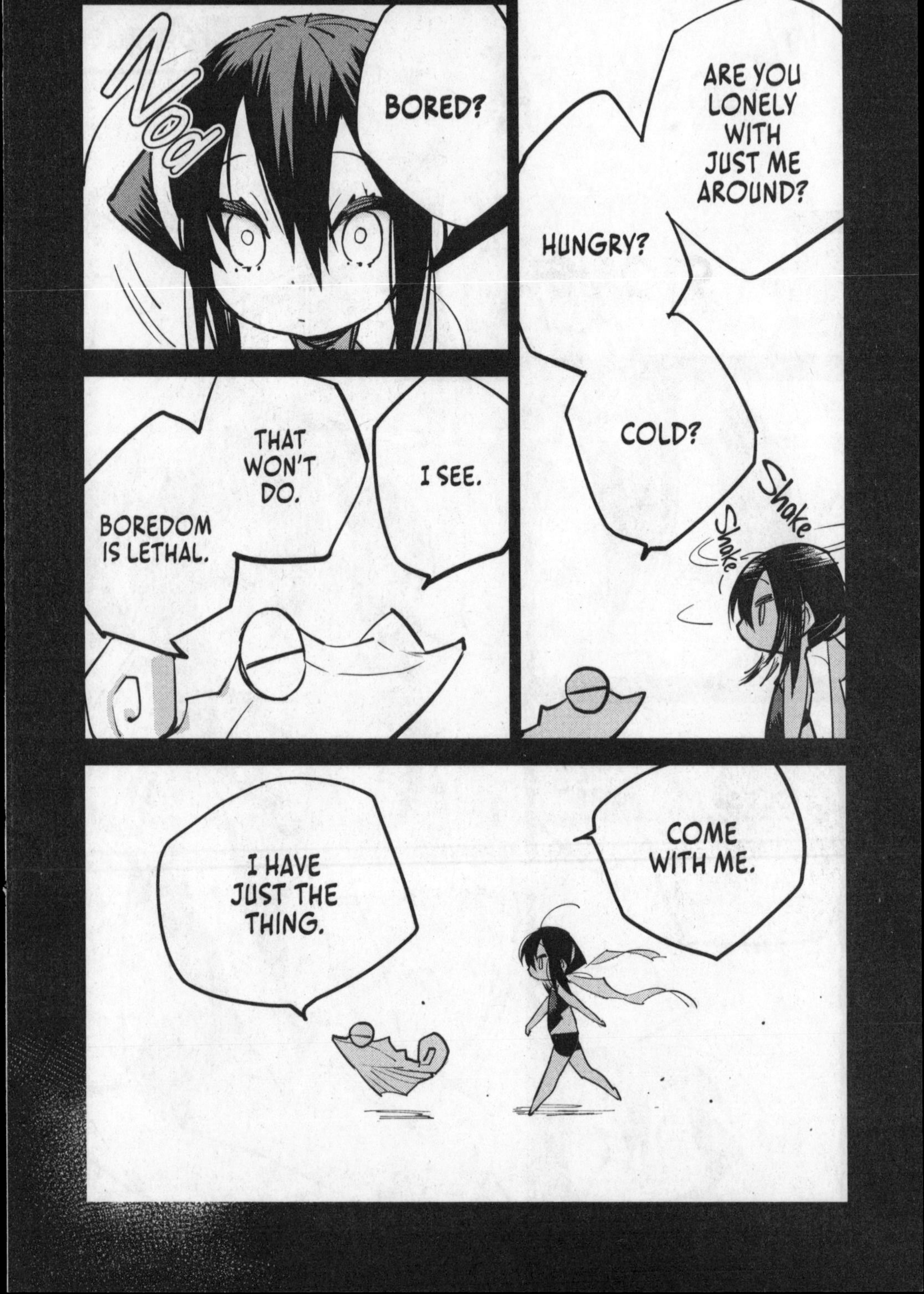
ARE YOU LONELY WITH JUST ME AROUND?
HUNGRY?
COLD?
Shake
Shake
BORED?
Nod
I SEE.
THAT WON'T DO.
BOREDOM IS LETHAL.
COME WITH ME.
I HAVE JUST THE THING.

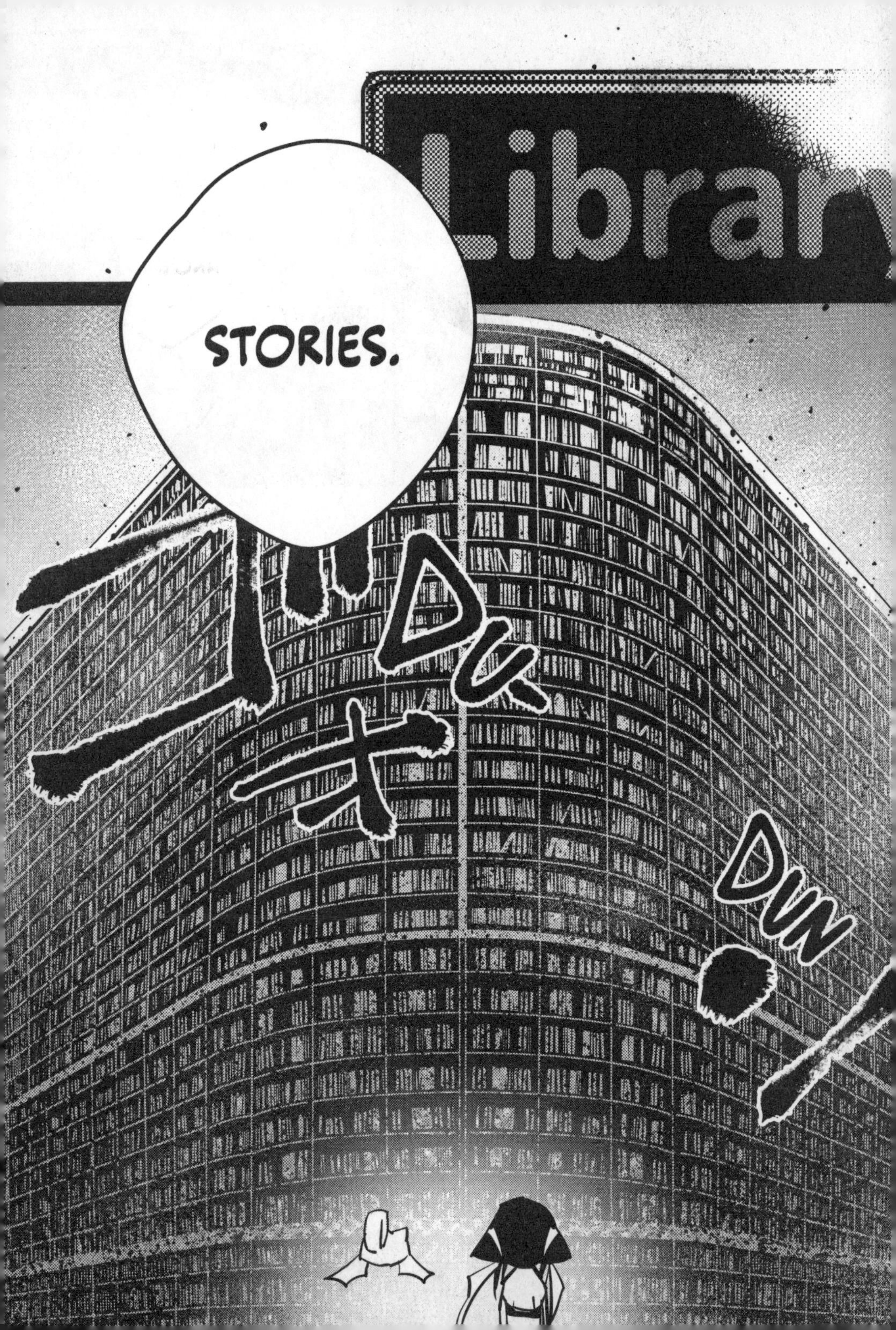
Librar
STORIES.
DU
DUN!

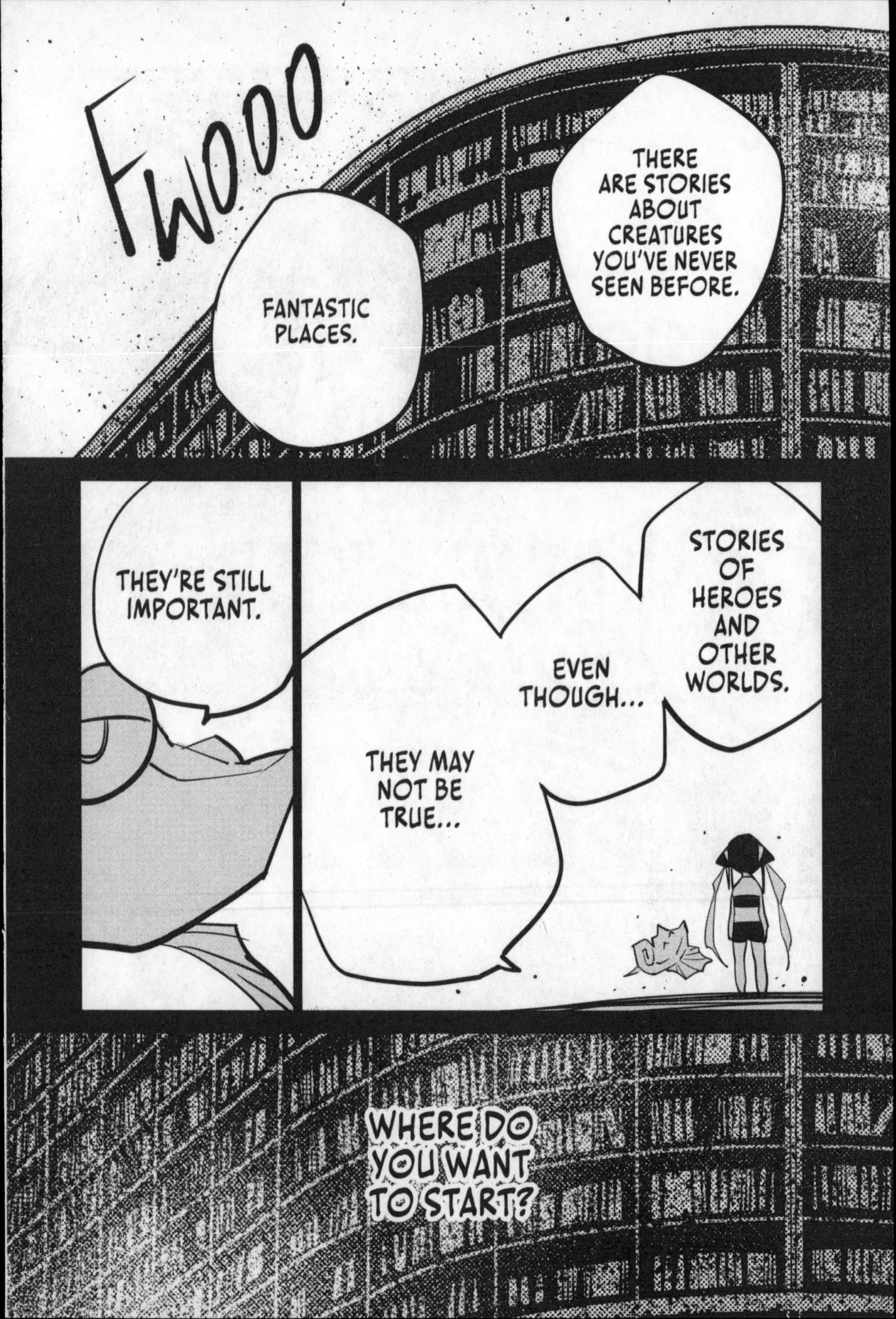
FWOOO
THERE ARE STORIES ABOUT CREATURES YOU'VE NEVER SEEN BEFORE.
FANTASTIC PLACES.
STORIES OF HEROES AND OTHER WORLDS.
EVEN THOUGH...
THEY MAY NOT BE TRUE...
THEY'RE STILL IMPORTANT.
WHERE DO YOU WANT TO START?

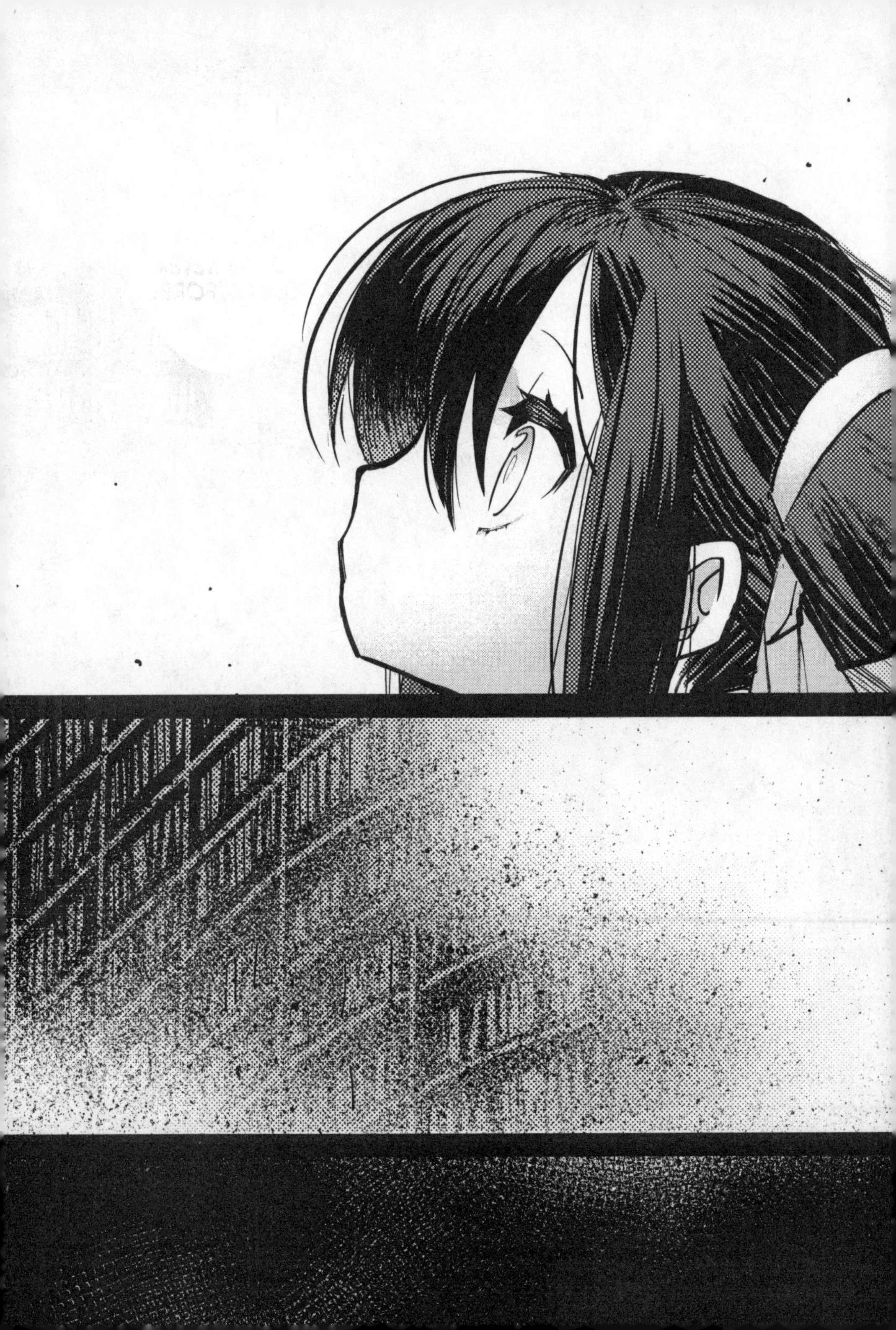

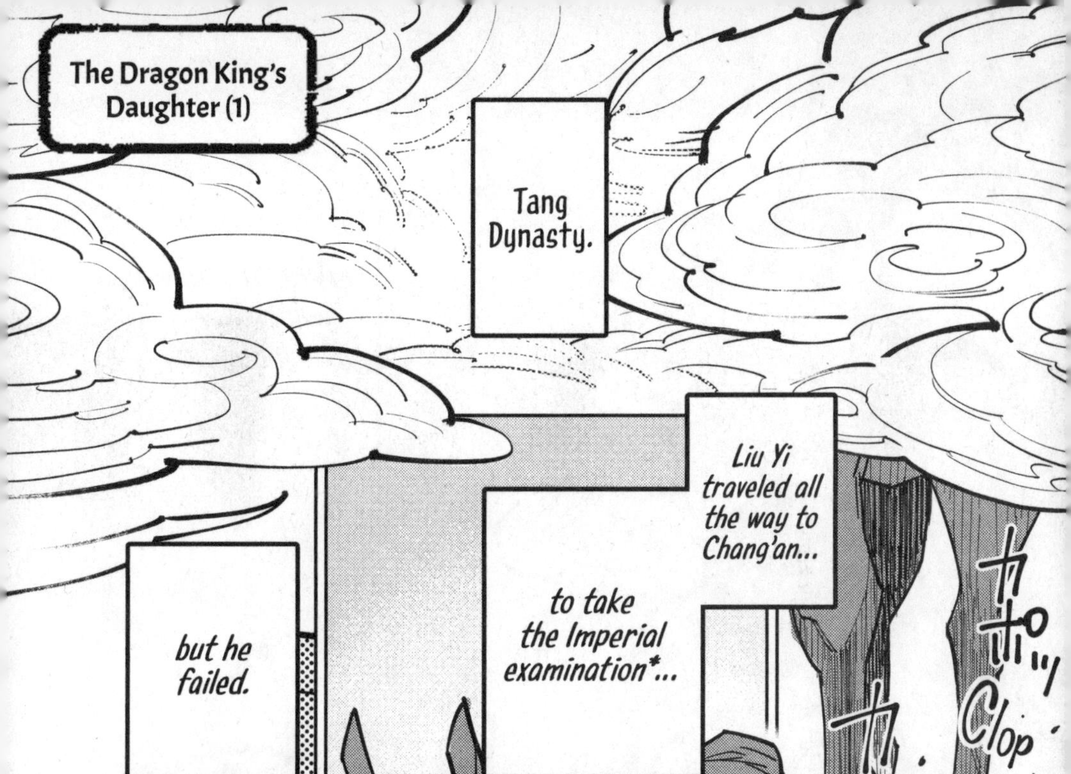
The Dragon King's Daughter (1)
Tang Dynasty.
Liu Yi traveled all the way to Chang'an...
to take the Imperial examination*...
but he failed.
カポッ
Clop
カポッ
Clop
カポッ
Clop

*A system of civil service exams for selecting state bureaucratic candidates in Imperial China.

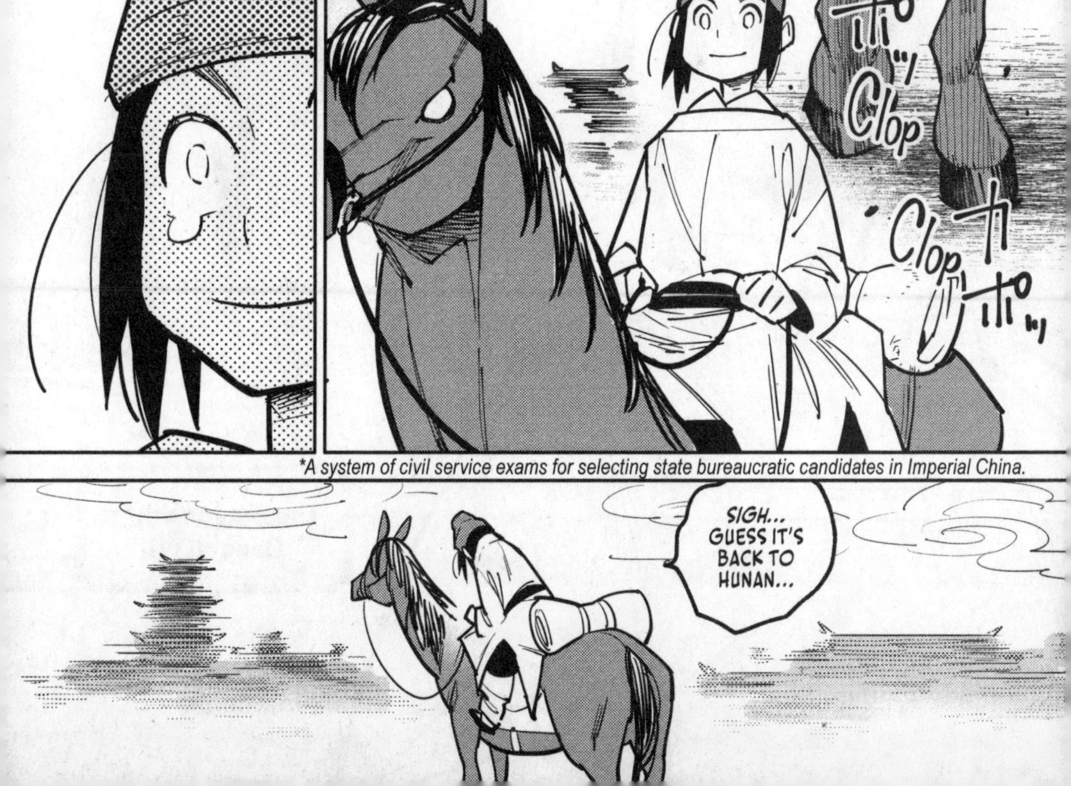
SIGH... GUESS IT'S BACK TO HUNAN...

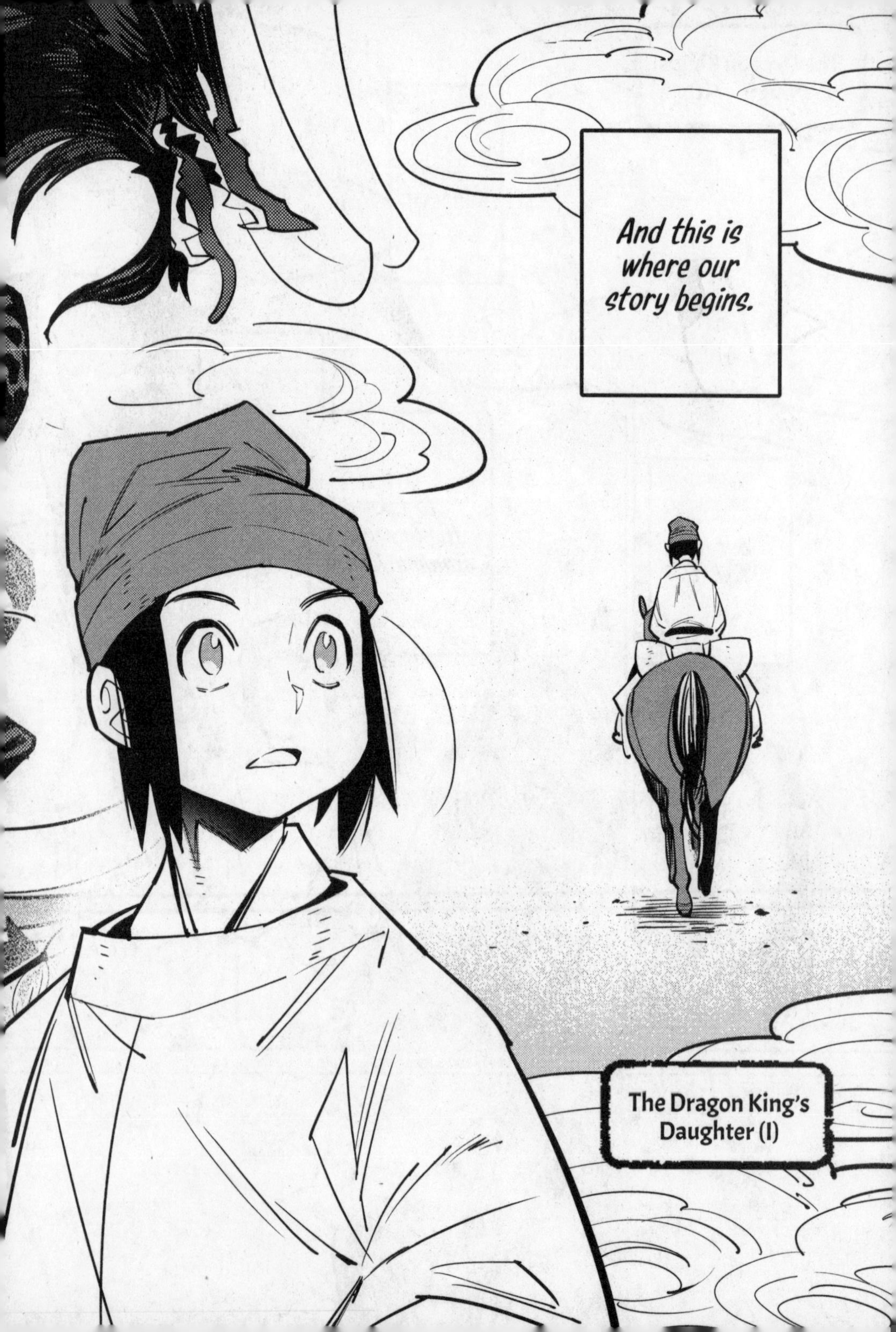
And this is where our story begins.
The Dragon King's Daughter (I)

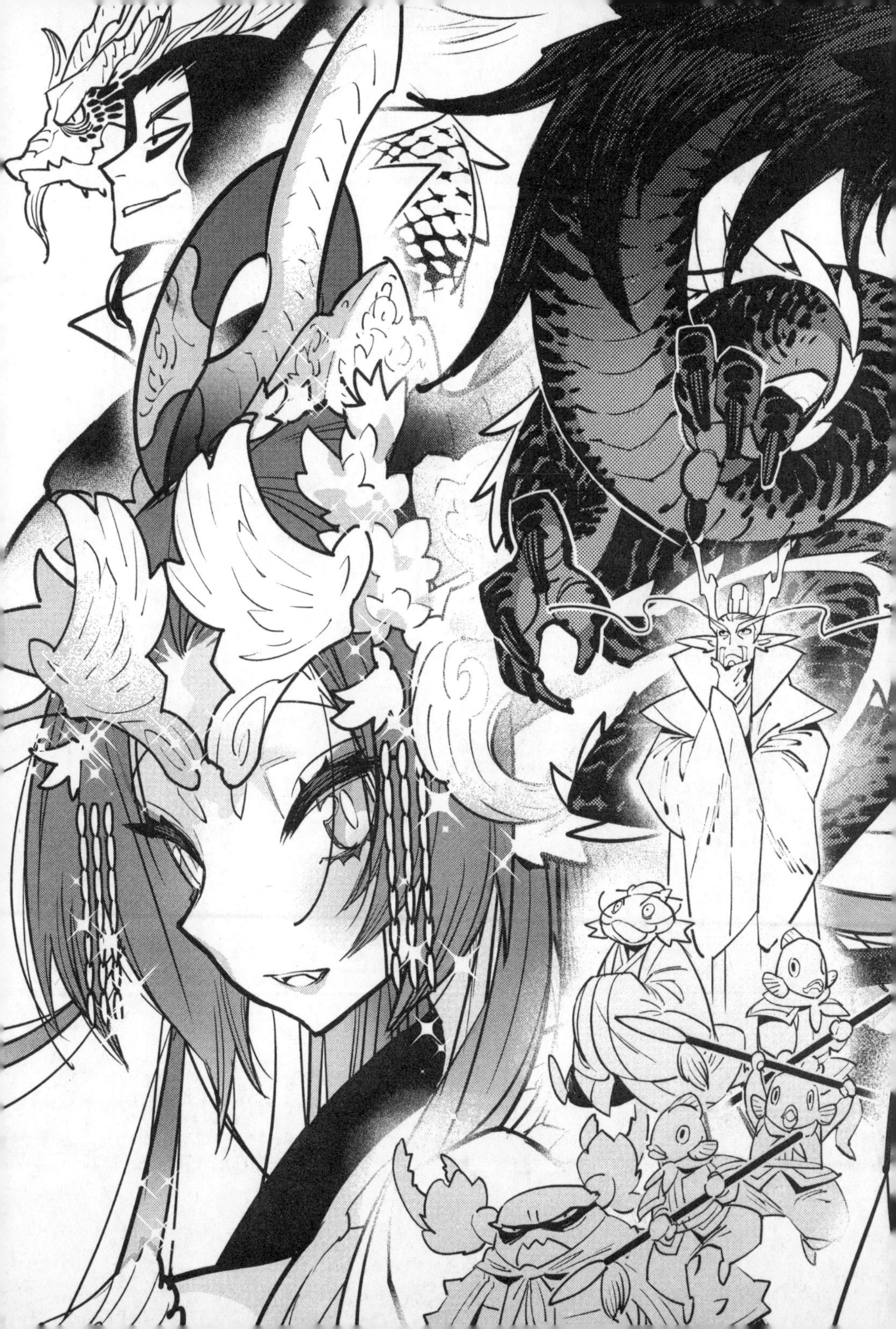

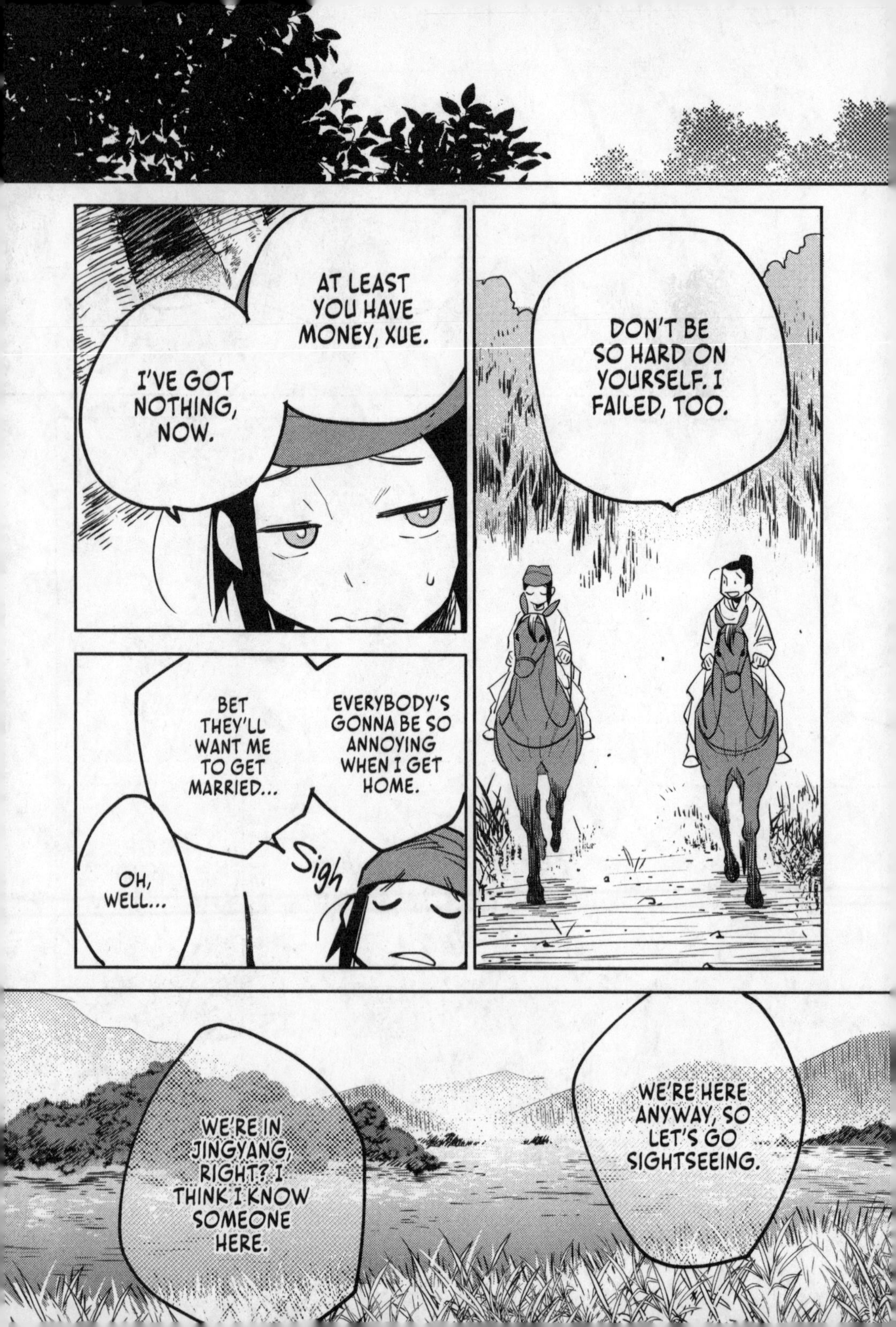
DON'T BE SO HARD ON YOURSELF. I FAILED, TOO.
AT LEAST YOU HAVE MONEY, XUE.
I'VE GOT NOTHING, NOW.
EVERYBODY'S GONNA BE SO ANNOYING WHEN I GET HOME.
BET THEY'LL WANT ME TO GET MARRIED...
Sigh
OH, WELL...
WE'RE HERE ANYWAY, SO LET'S GO SIGHTSEEING.
WE'RE IN JINGYANG, RIGHT? I THINK I KNOW SOMEONE HERE.

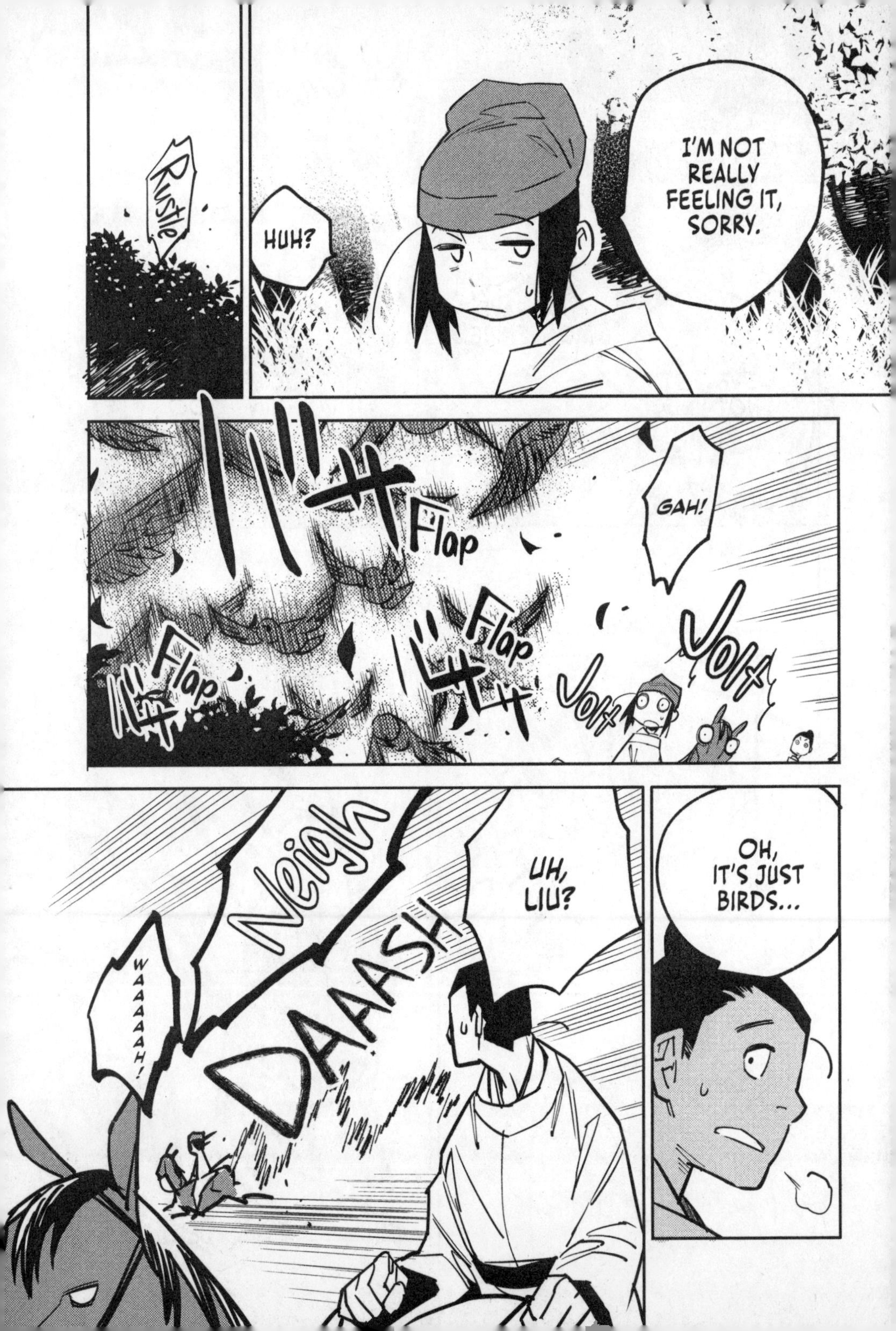
I'M NOT REALLY FEELING IT, SORRY.
HUH?
Rustle
GAH!
Flap
Flap
Flap
Jolt
Jolt
OH, IT'S JUST BIRDS...
UH, LIU?
Neigh
DAAASH
WAAAAAAH!

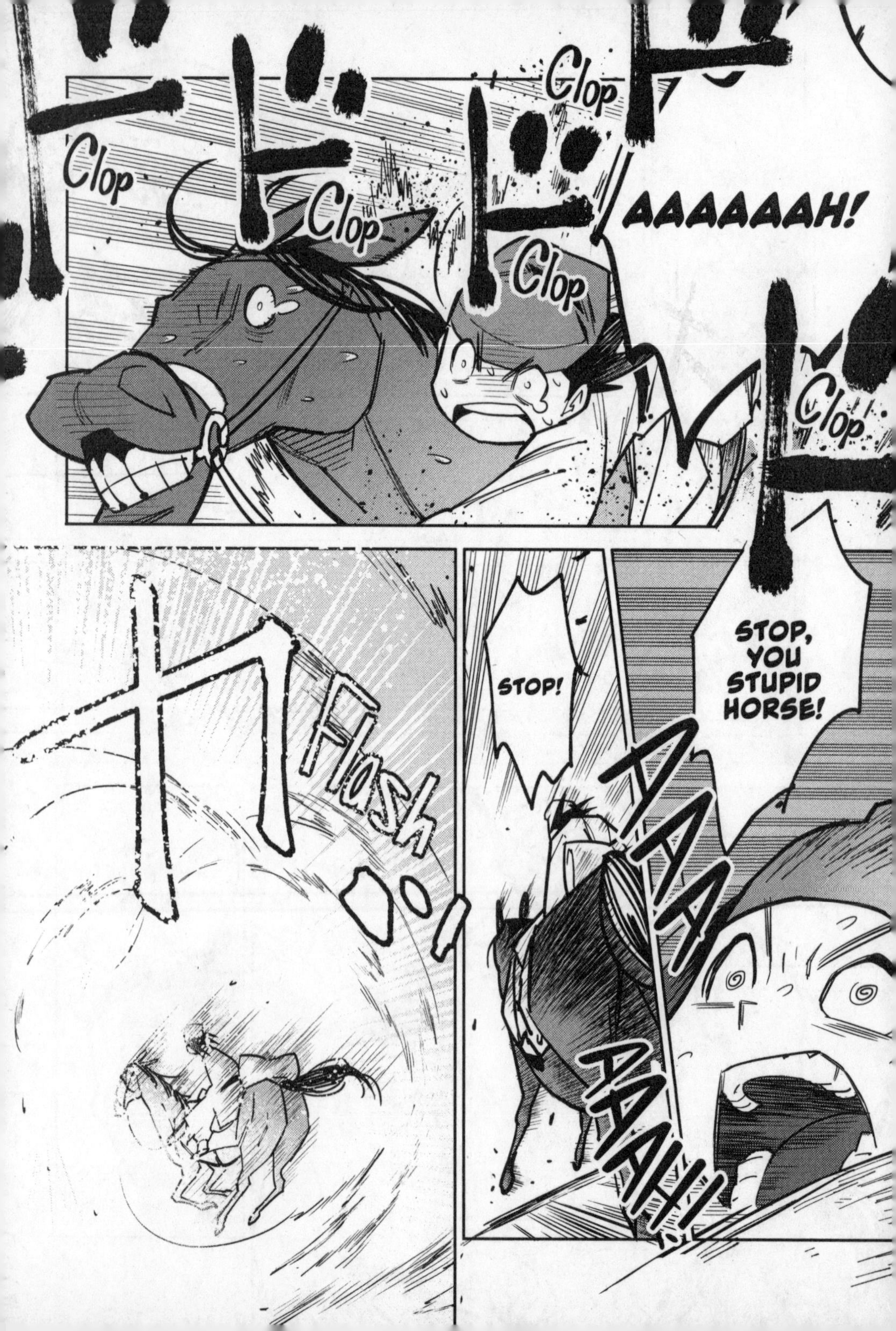
Clop
Clop
Clop
Clop
Clop
AAAAAAH!
Clop
STOP, YOU STUPID HORSE!
STOP!
AAAAAAAH!!
Flash

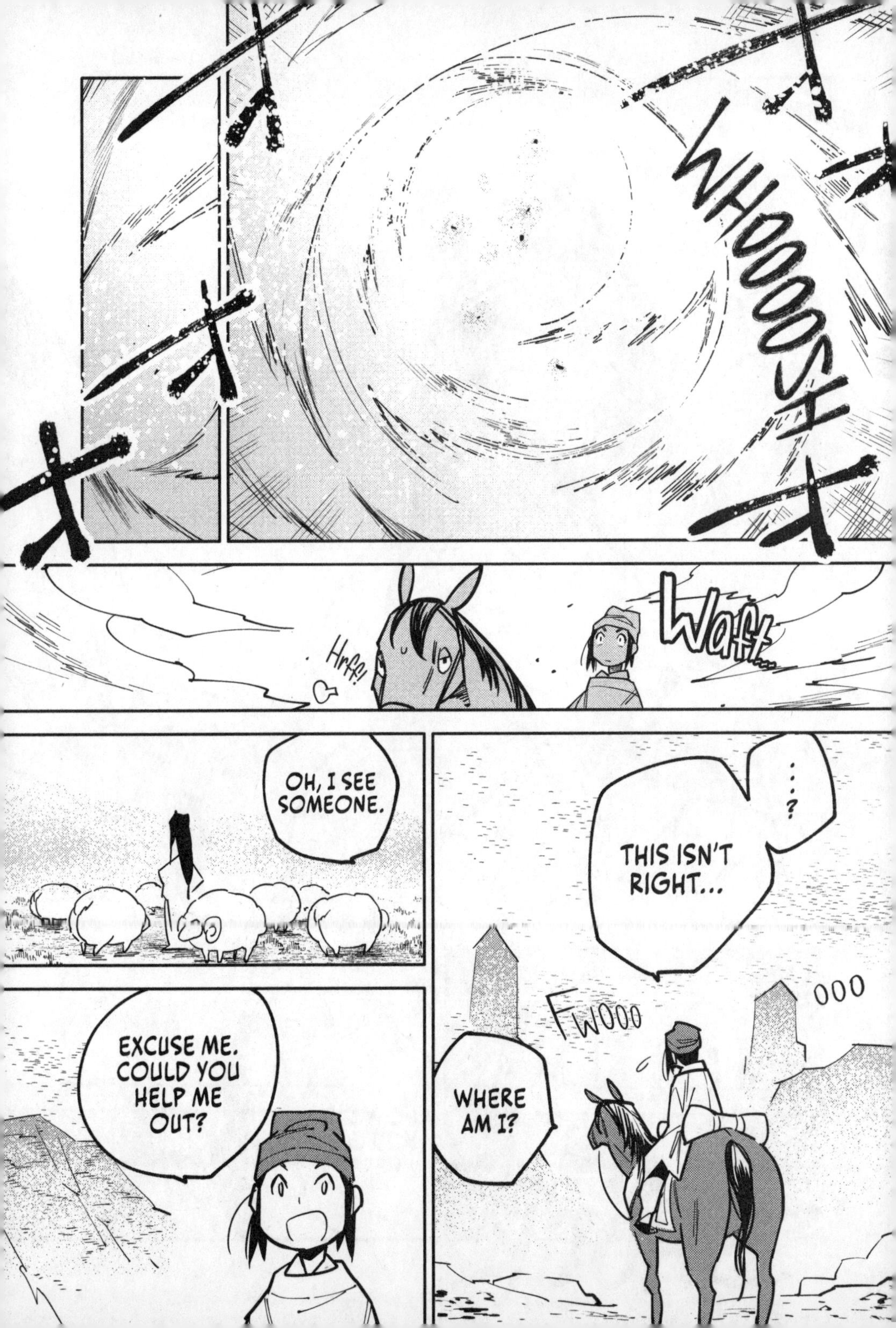
WHOOOOSH
Waft...
Hrff!
...?
THIS ISN'T RIGHT...
FWOOOOOO
WHERE AM I?
OH, I SEE SOMEONE.
EXCUSE ME. COULD YOU HELP ME OUT?

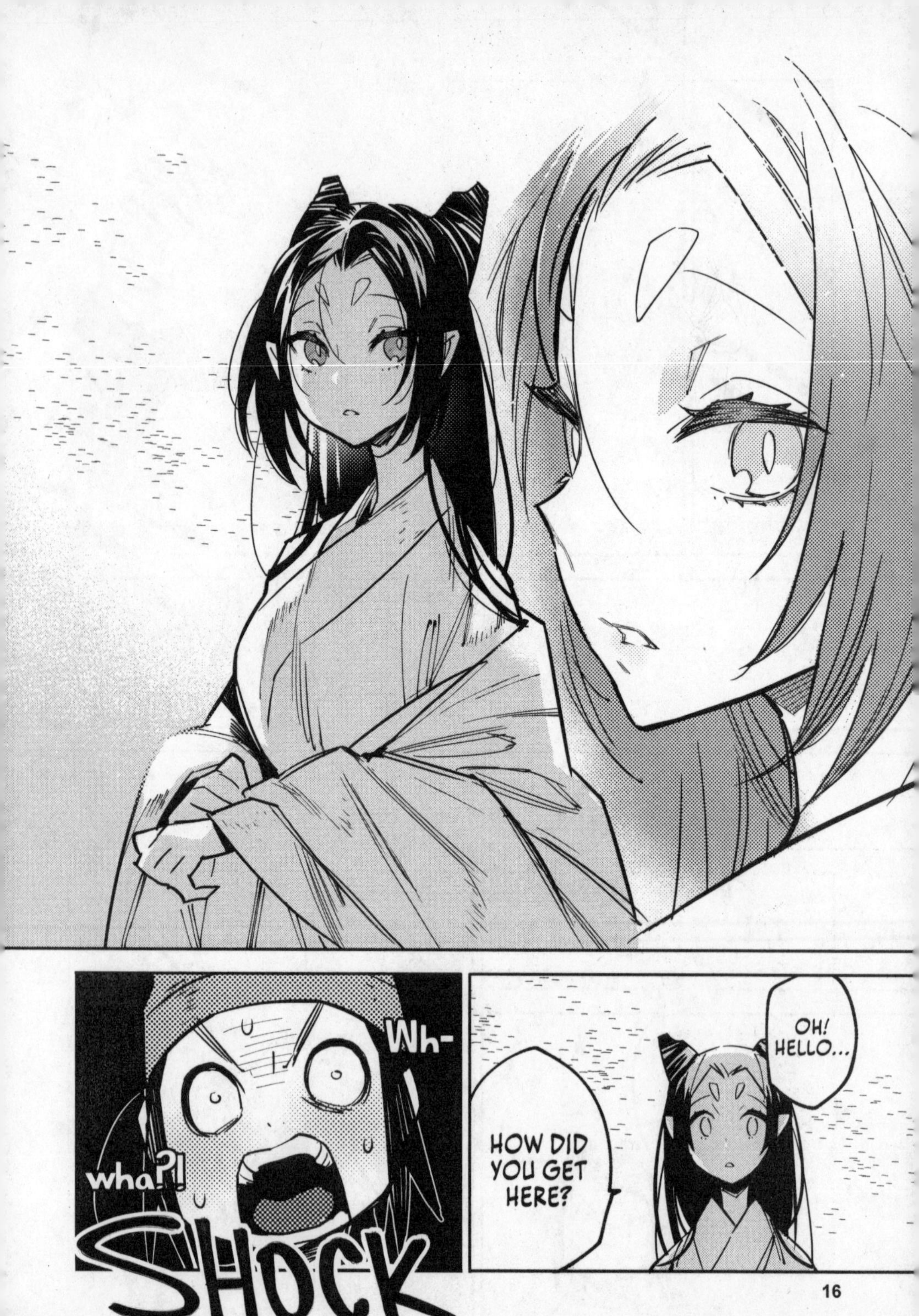
OH! HELLO...
HOW DID YOU GET HERE?
Wh- wha?!
SHOCK

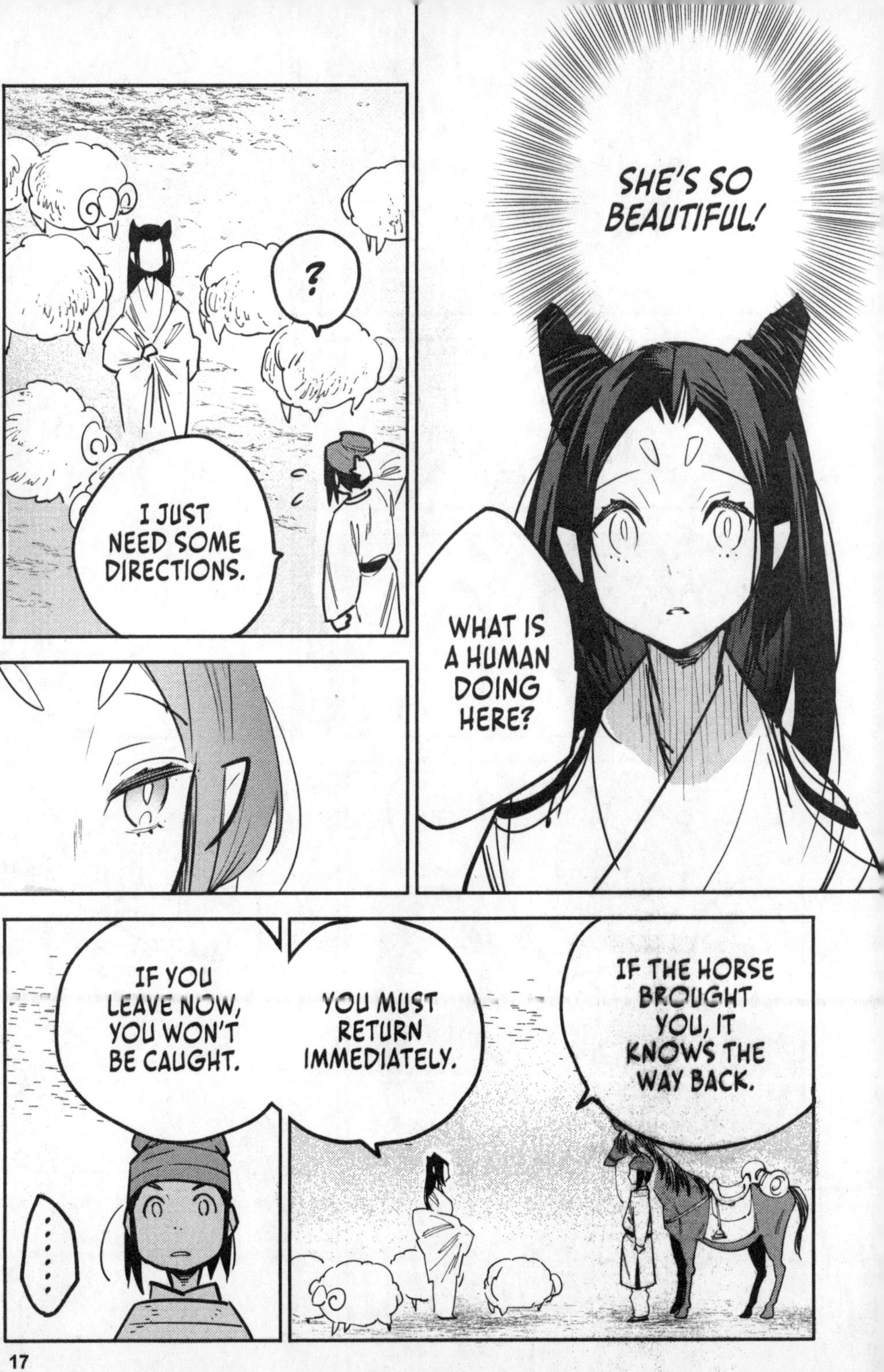

SHE'S SO BEAUTIFUL!
WHAT IS A HUMAN DOING HERE?
?
I JUST NEED SOME DIRECTIONS.
IF THE HORSE BROUGHT YOU, IT KNOWS THE WAY BACK.
YOU MUST RETURN IMMEDIATELY.
IF YOU LEAVE NOW, YOU WON'T BE CAUGHT.
......

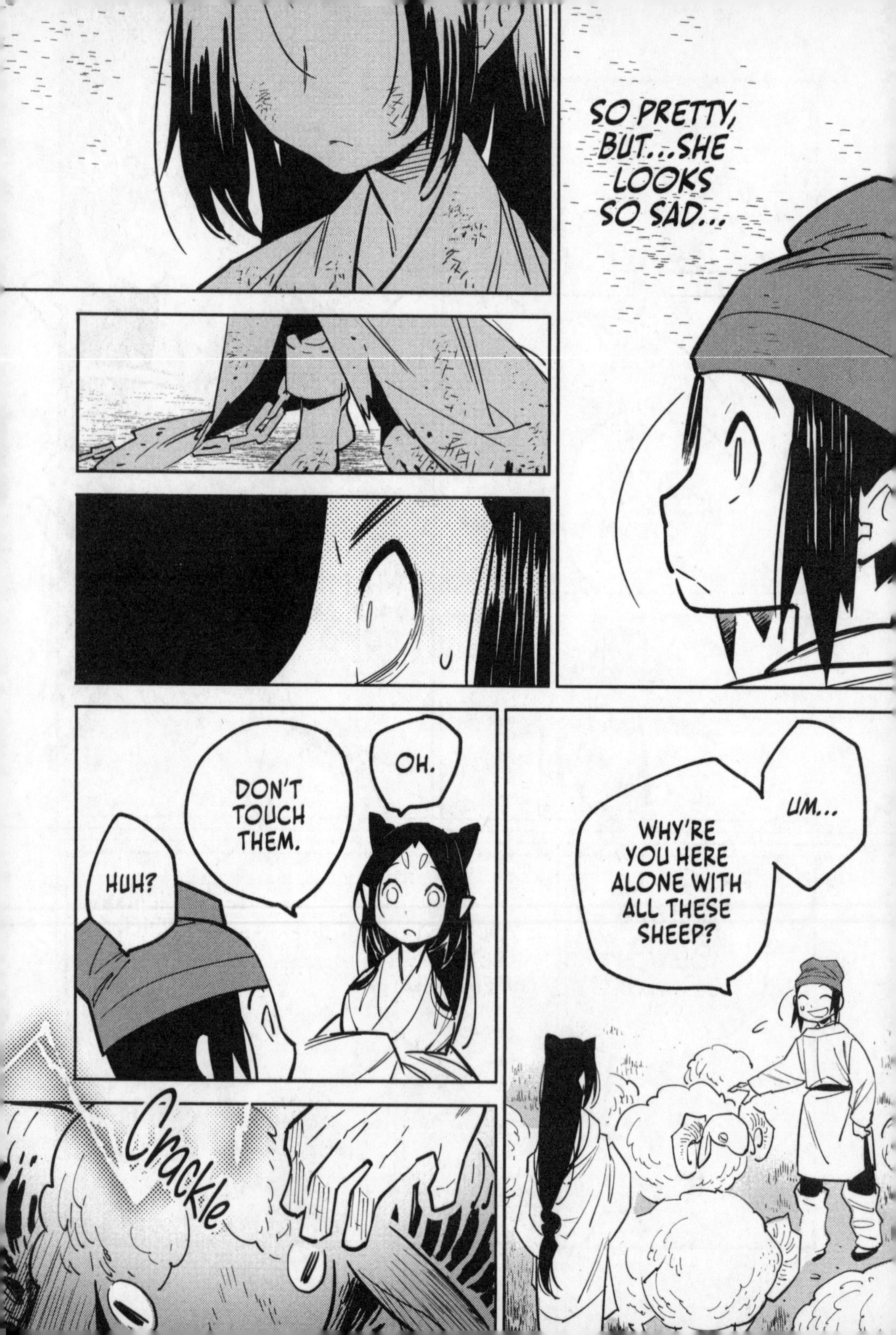
SO PRETTY, BUT...SHE LOOKS SO SAD...
UM...
WHY'RE YOU HERE ALONE WITH ALL THESE SHEEP?
OH.
DON'T TOUCH THEM.
HUH?
Crackle

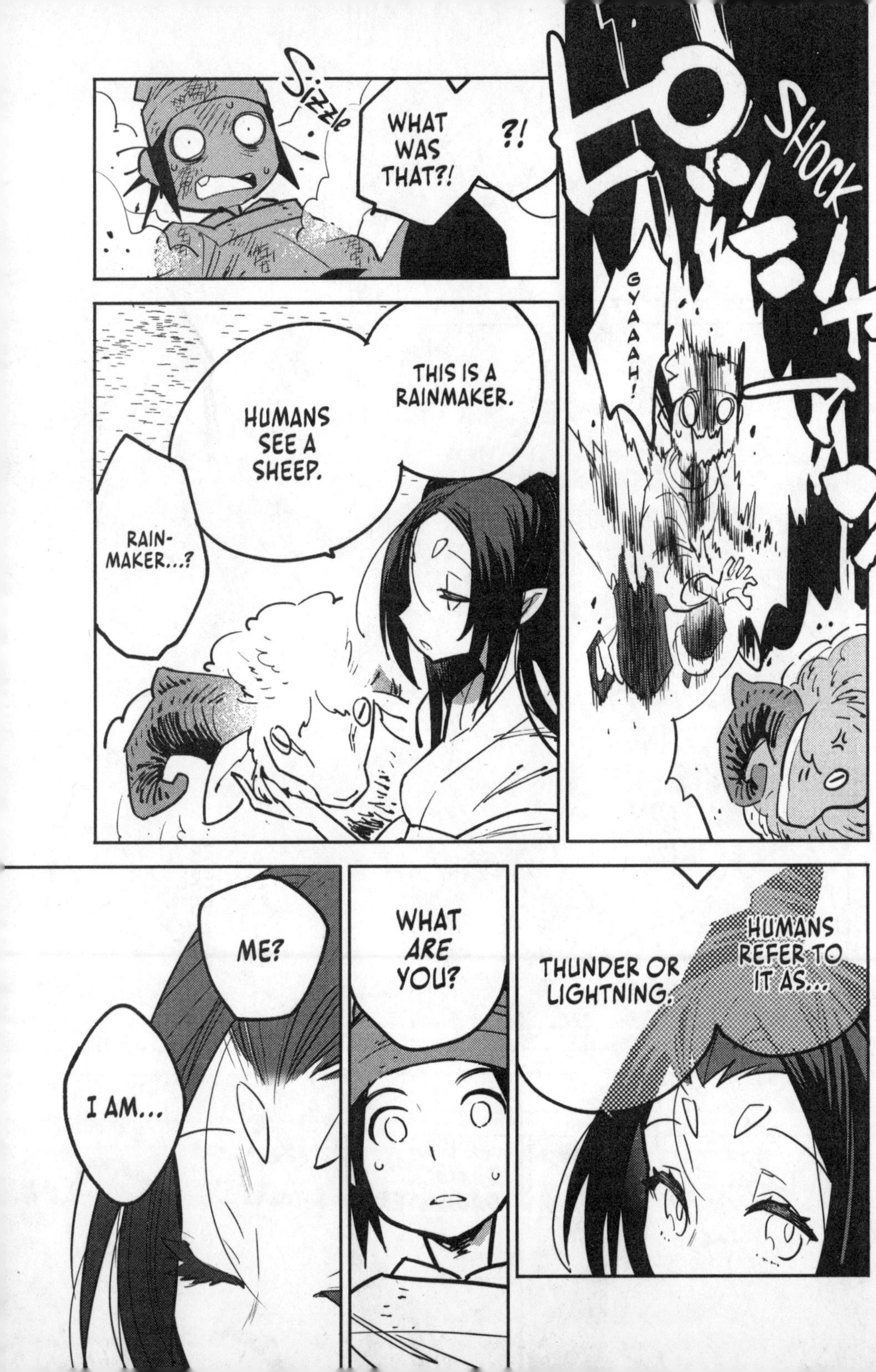
SHOCK
GYAAAH!
Sizzle
WHAT WAS THAT?!
?!
THIS IS A RAINMAKER.
HUMANS SEE A SHEEP.
RAIN-MAKER...?
HUMANS REFER TO IT AS...
THUNDER OR LIGHTNING.
WHAT ARE YOU?
ME?
I AM...

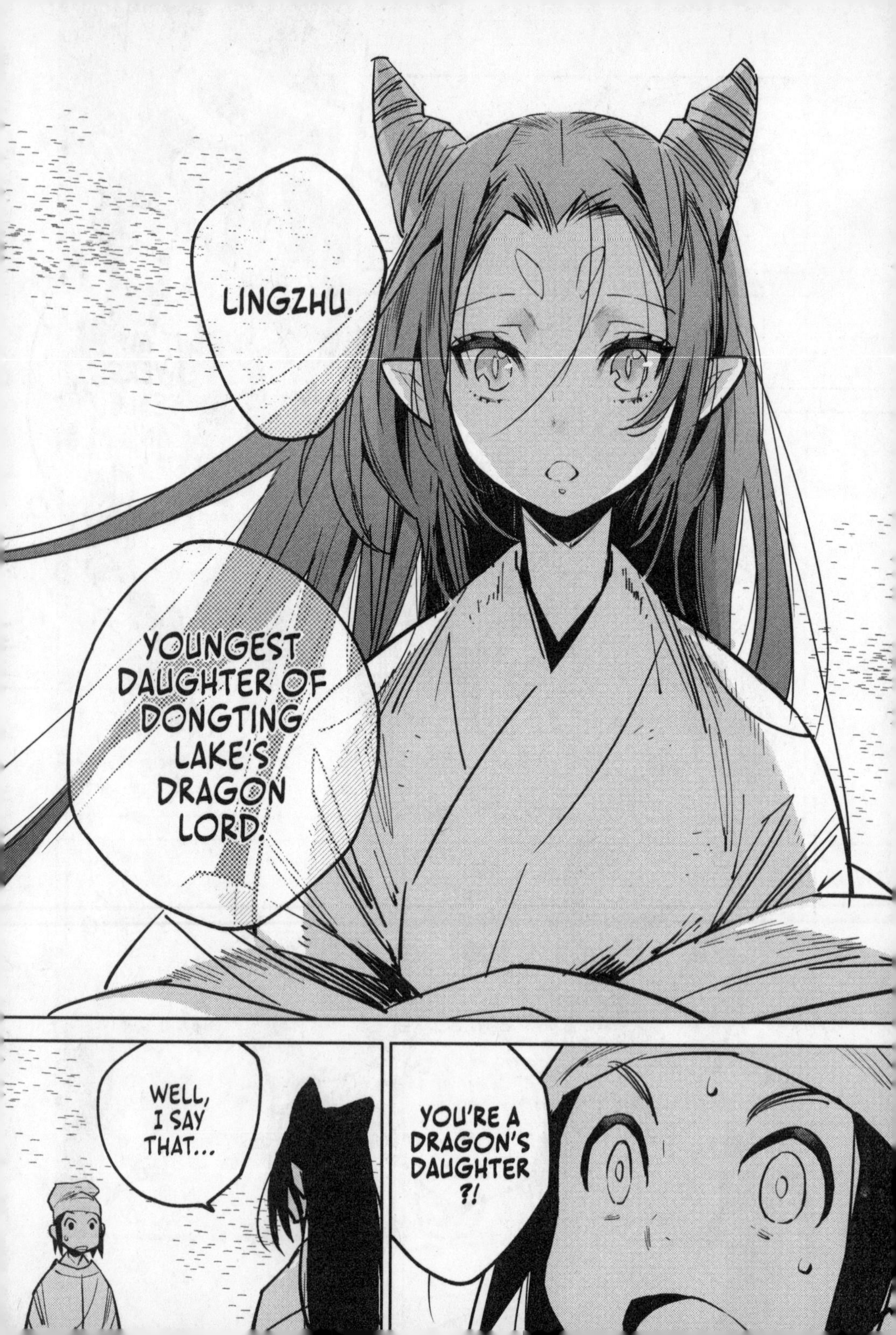
LINGZHU.
YOUNGEST DAUGHTER OF DONGTING LAKE'S DRAGON LORD.
YOU'RE A DRAGON'S DAUGHTER ?!
WELL, I SAY THAT...

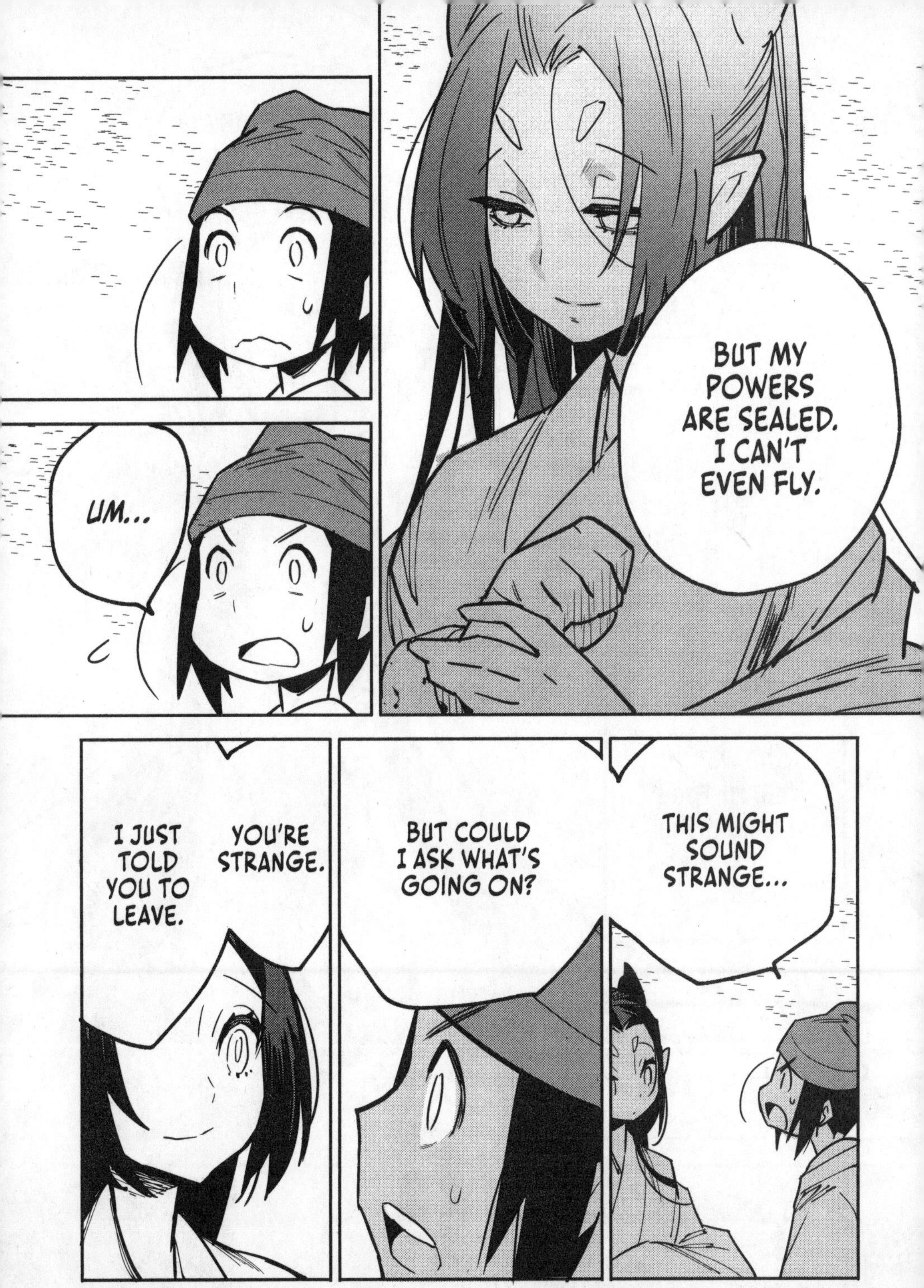
BUT MY POWERS ARE SEALED. I CAN'T EVEN FLY.
UM...
THIS MIGHT SOUND STRANGE...
BUT COULD I ASK WHAT'S GOING ON?
YOU'RE STRANGE.
I JUST TOLD YOU TO LEAVE.

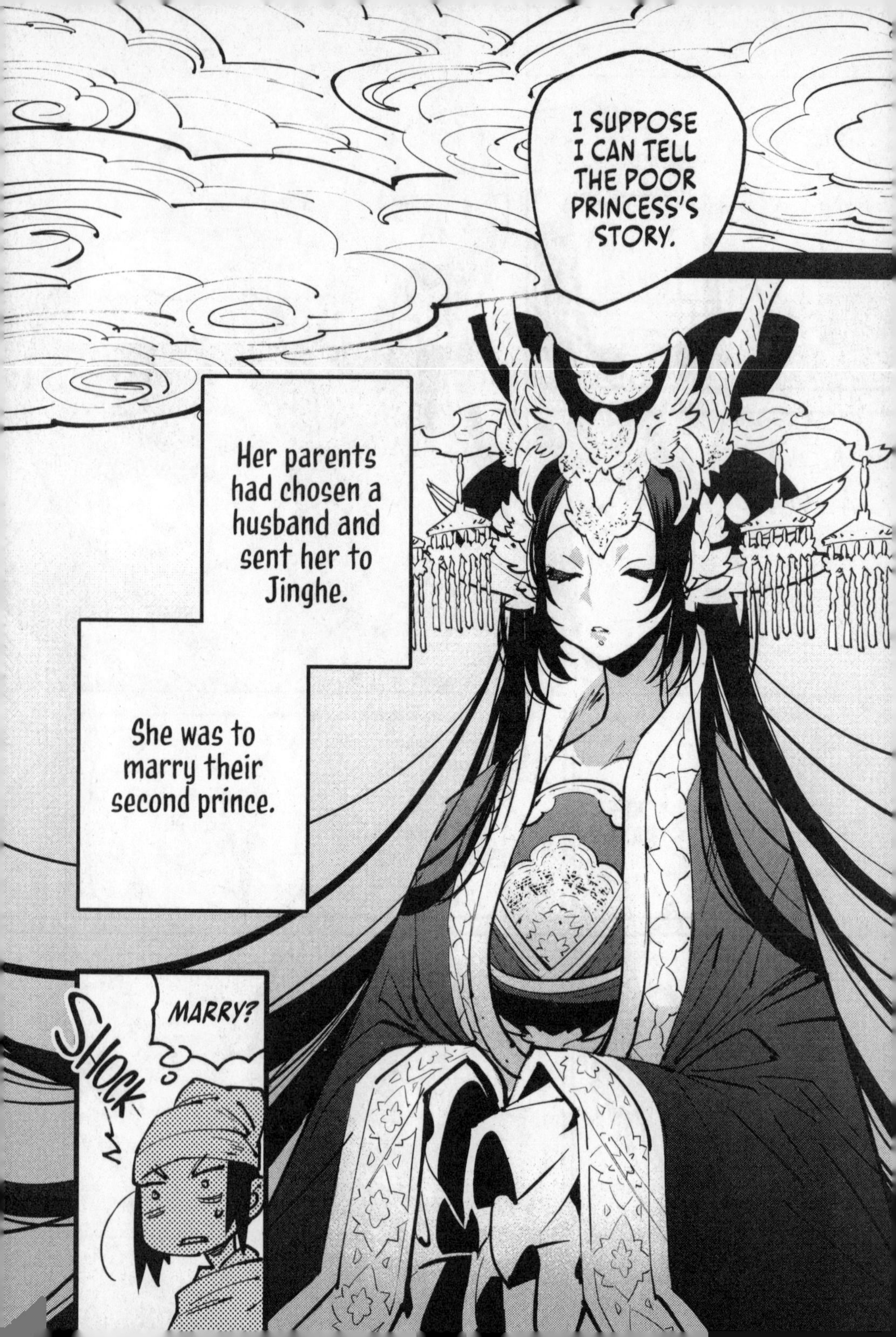
I SUPPOSE I CAN TELL THE POOR PRINCESS'S STORY.
Her parents had chosen a husband and sent her to Jinghe.
She was to marry their second prince.
MARRY?
SHOCK

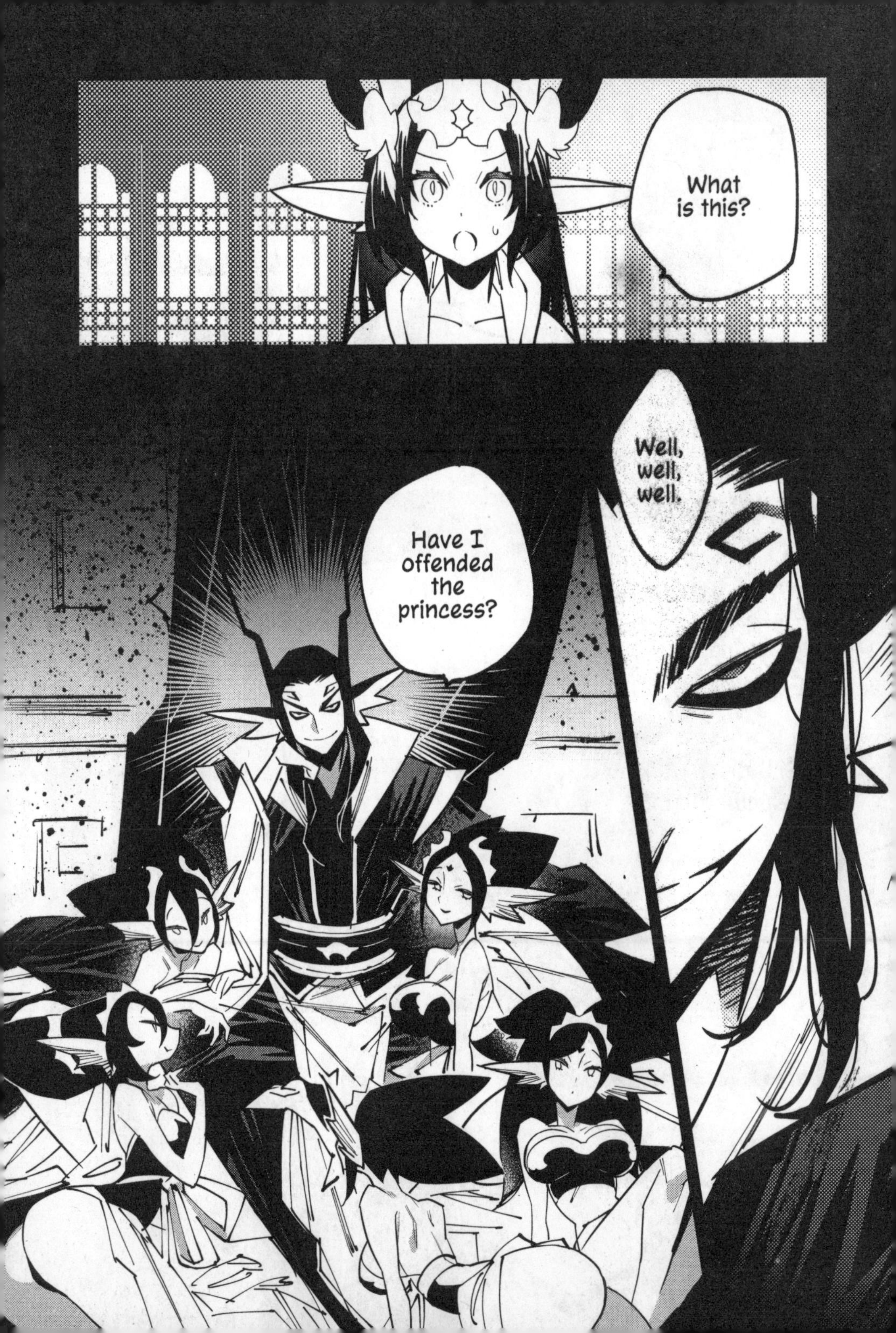
What is this?
Well, well, well.
Have I offended the princess?

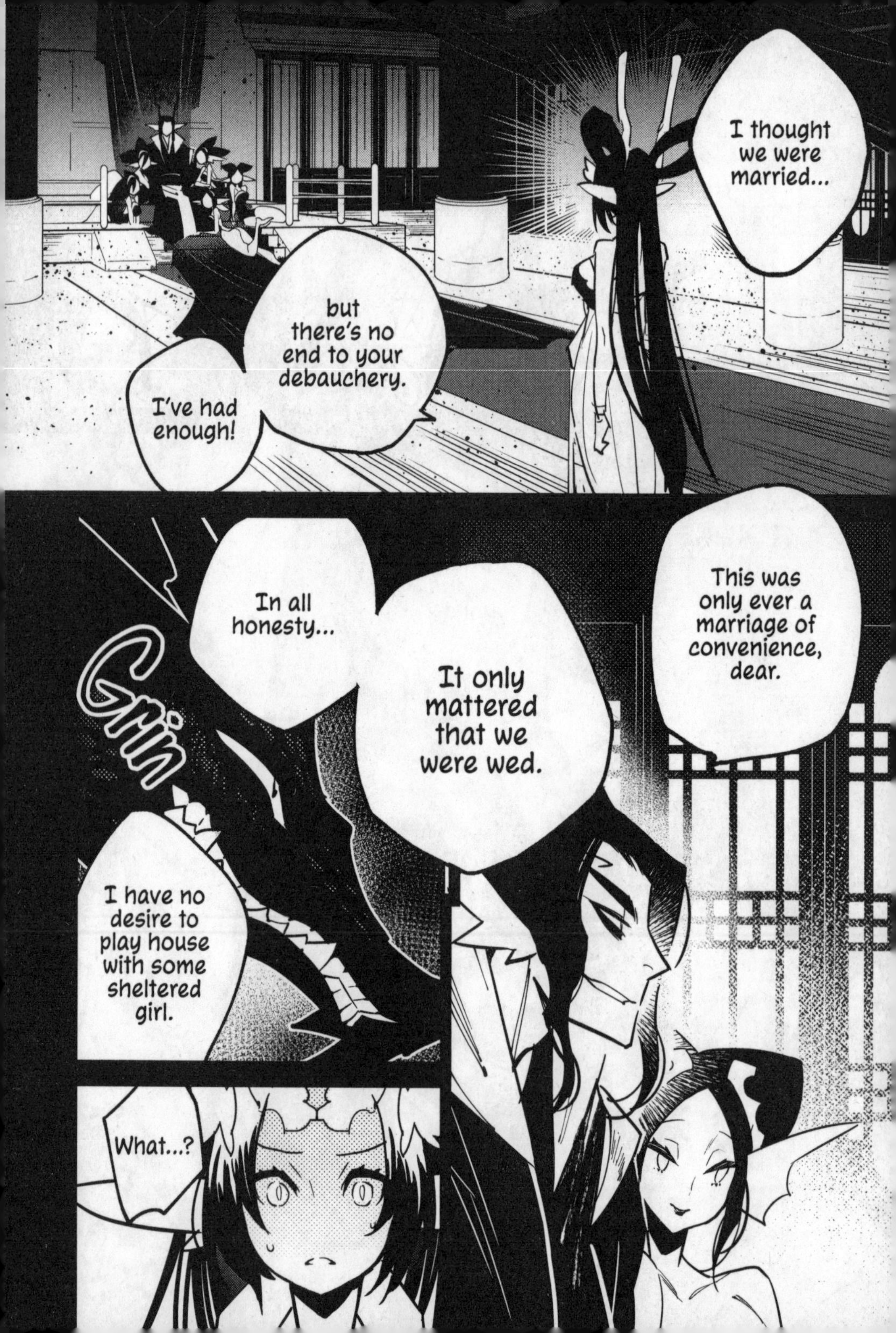
I thought we were married...
but there's no end to your debauchery.
I've had enough!
This was only ever a marriage of convenience, dear.
It only mattered that we were wed.
In all honesty...
Grin
I have no desire to play house with some sheltered girl.
What...?

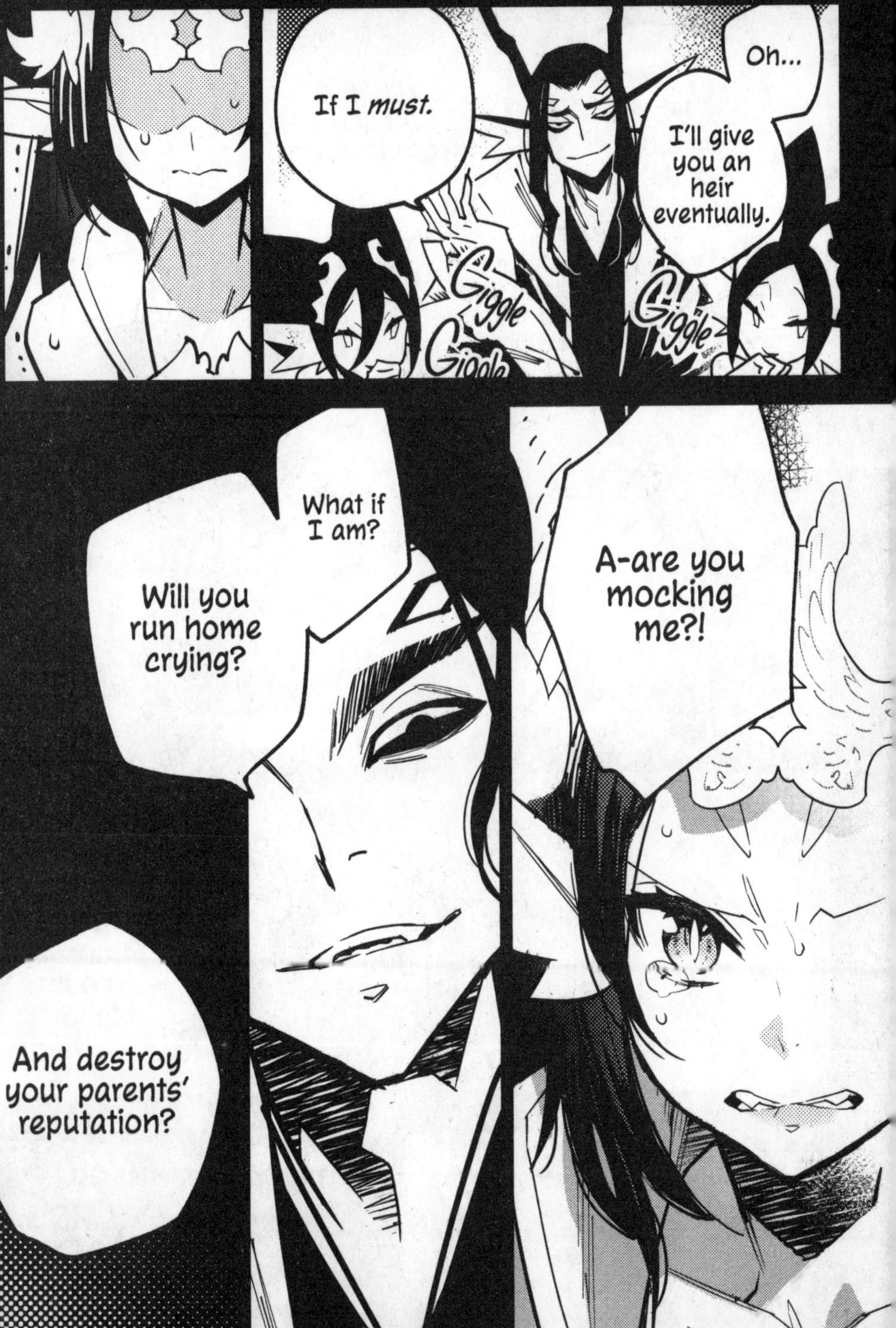
Oh...
I'll give you an heir eventually.
Giggle
Giggle
Giggle
If I must.
A-are you mocking me?!
What if I am?
Will you run home crying?
And destroy your parents' reputation?

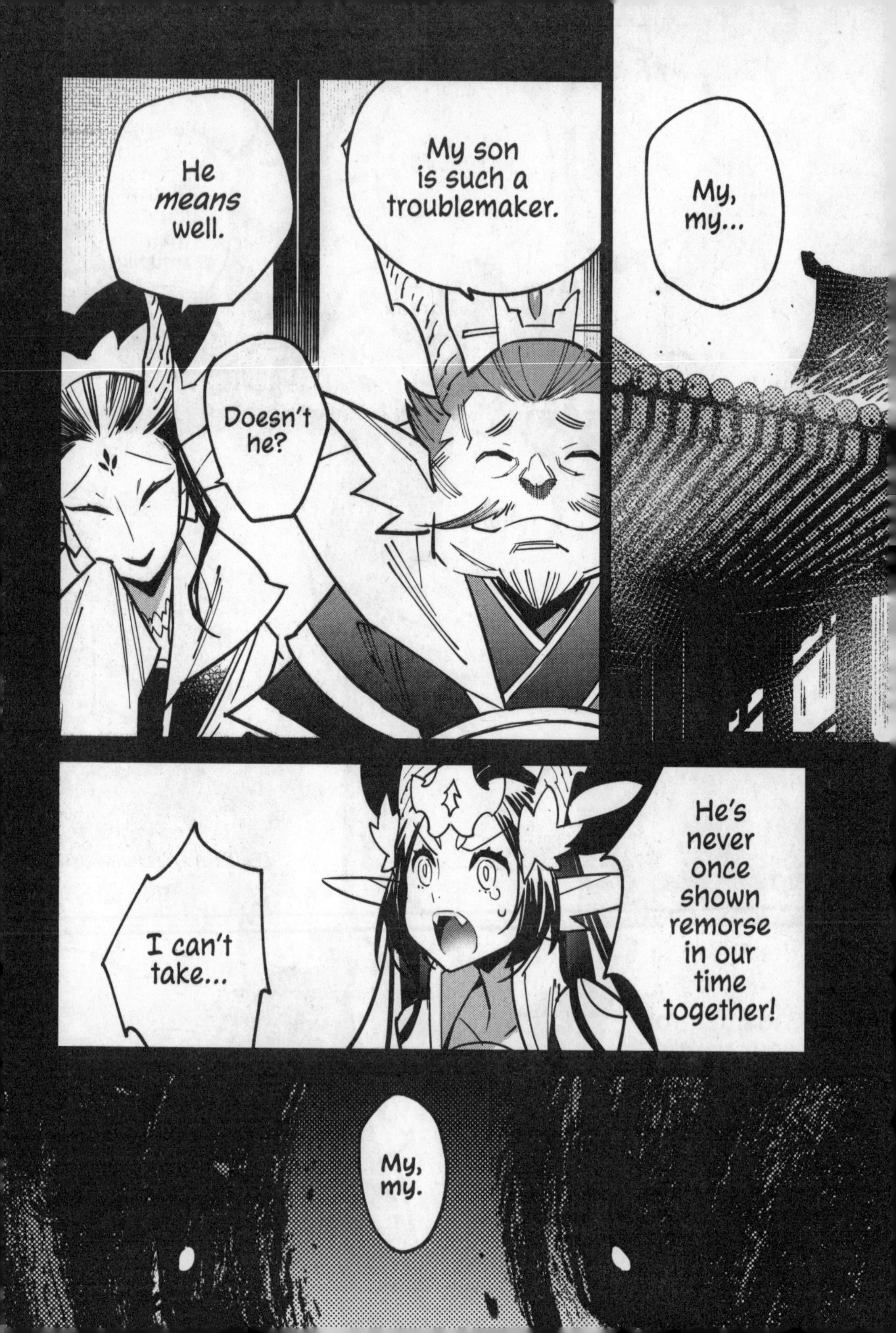
My, my...
My son is such a troublemaker.
He *means* well.
Doesn't he?
He's never once shown remorse in our time together!
I can't take...
My, my.

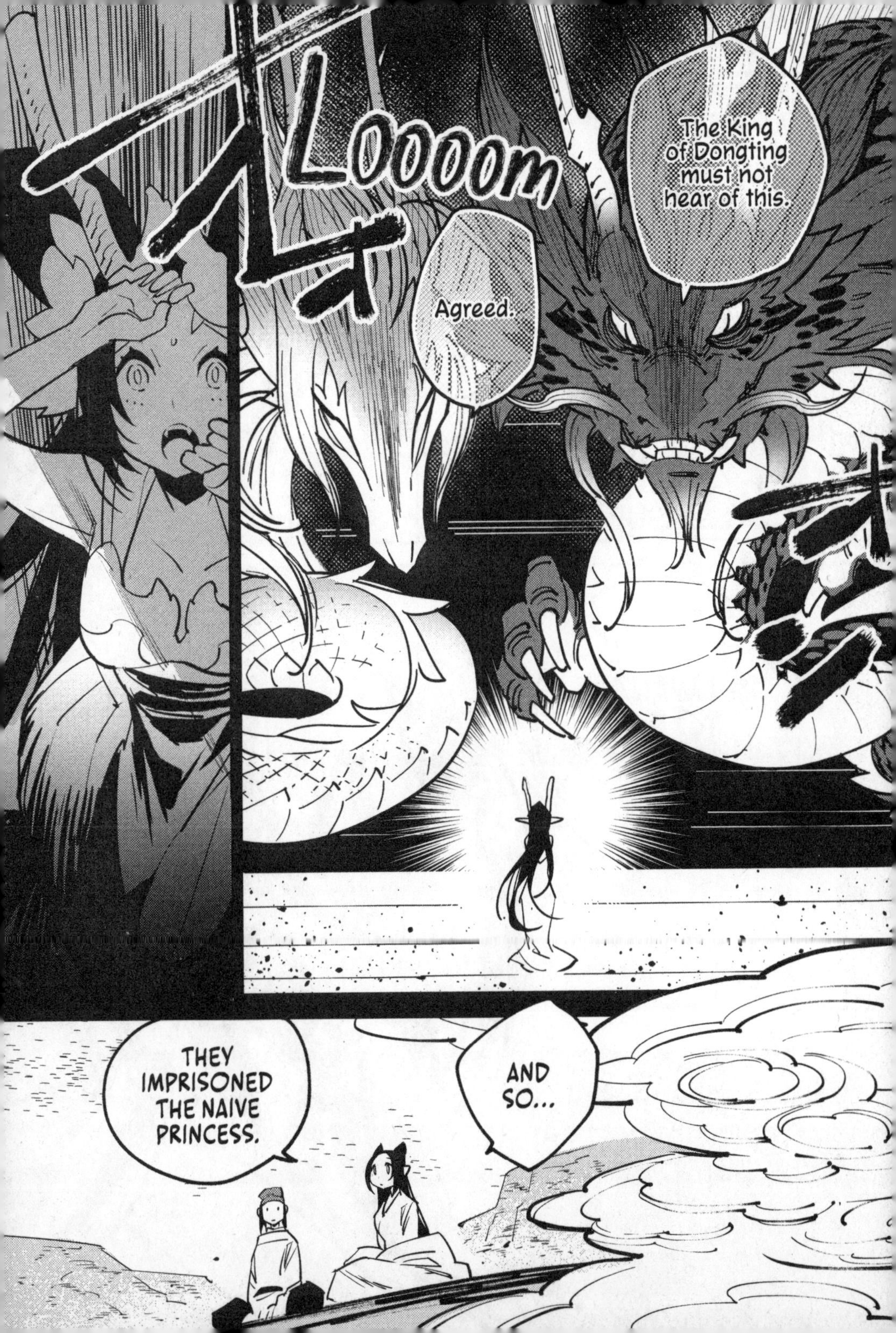
Looooom
The King of Dongting must not hear of this.
Agreed.
AND SO...
THEY IMPRISONED THE NAIVE PRINCESS.

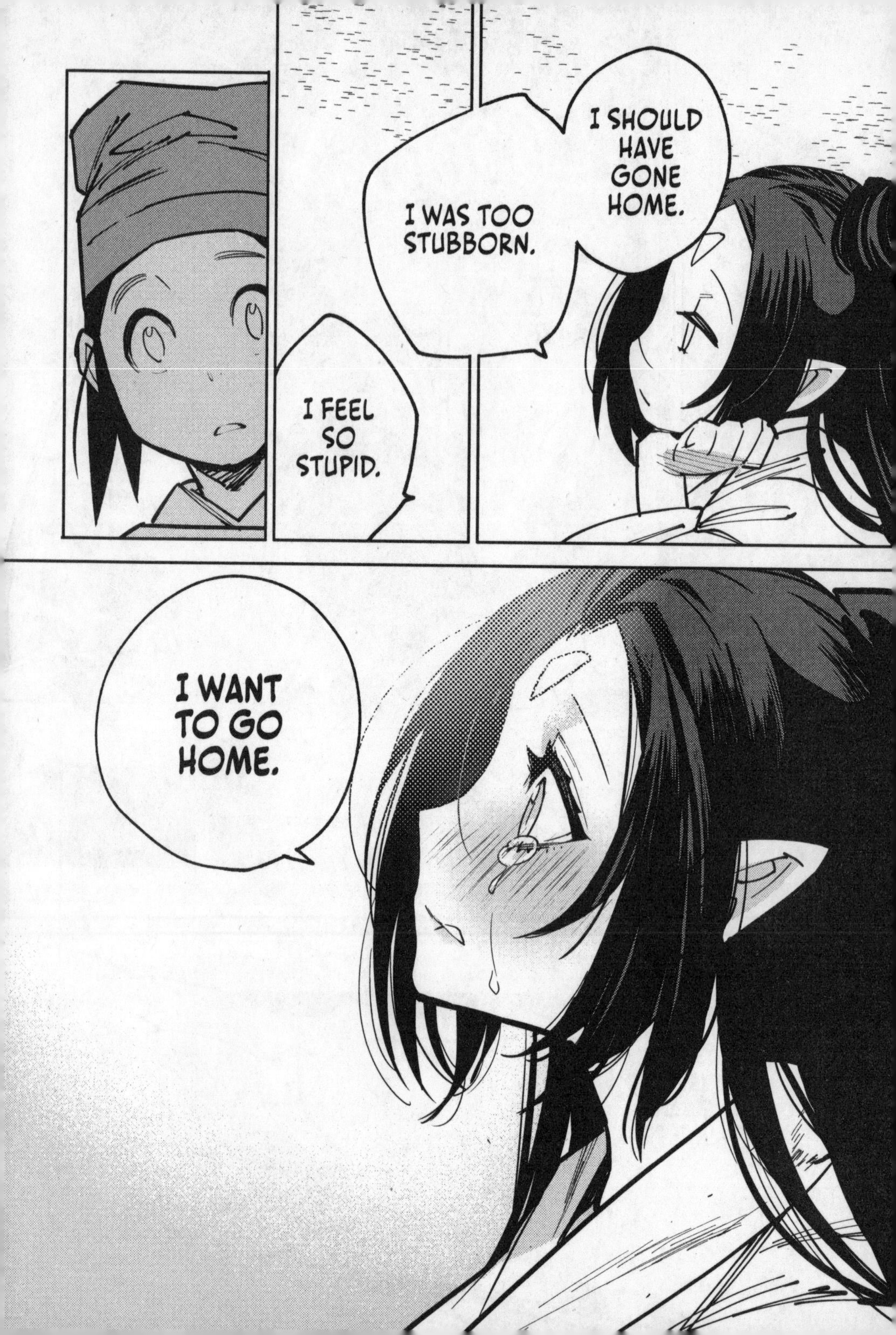
I SHOULD HAVE GONE HOME.
I WAS TOO STUBBORN.
I FEEL SO STUPID.
I WANT TO GO HOME.

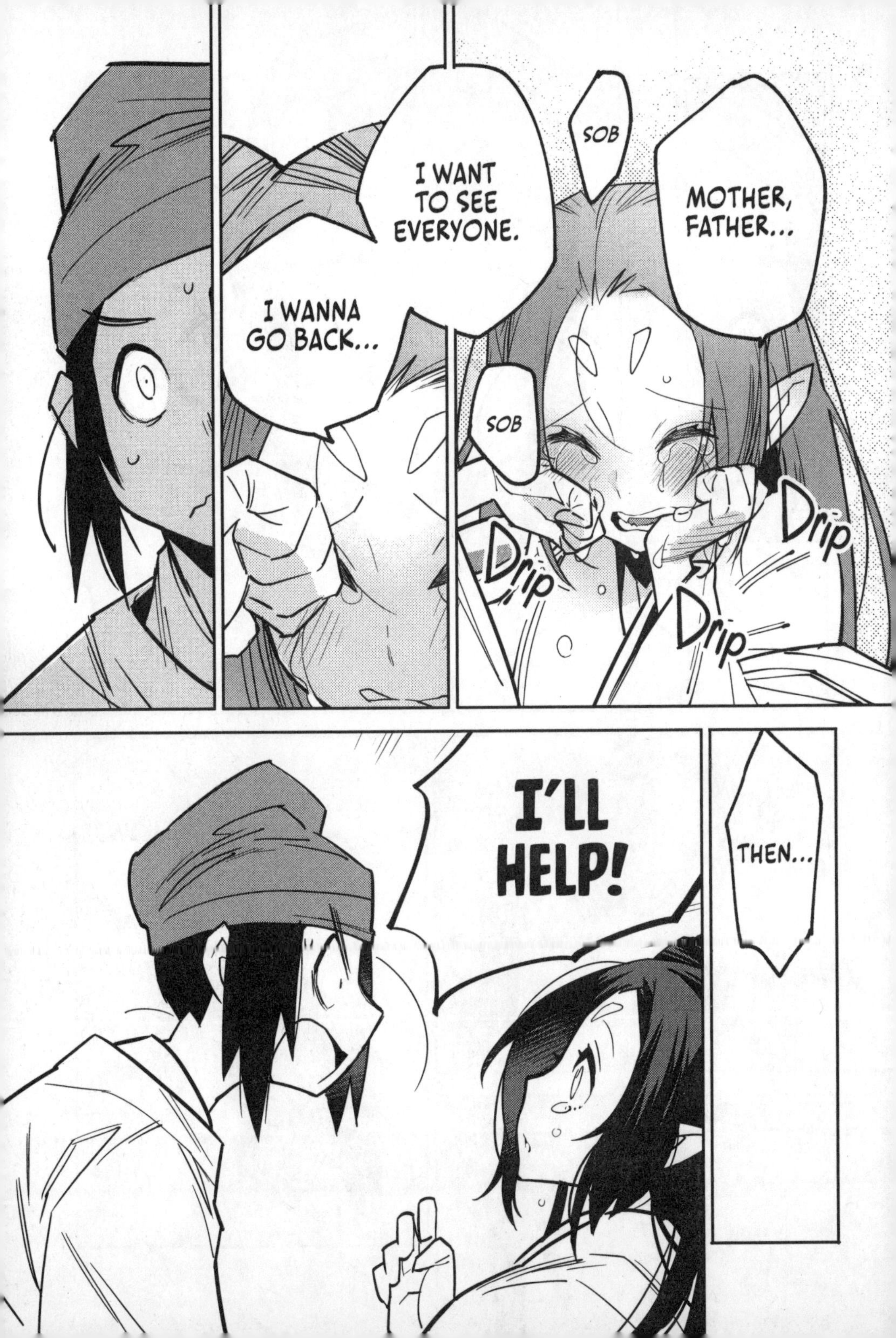
MOTHER, FATHER...
SOB
SOB
Drip
Drip
Drip
I WANT TO SEE EVERYONE.
I WANNA GO BACK...
THEN...
I'LL HELP!

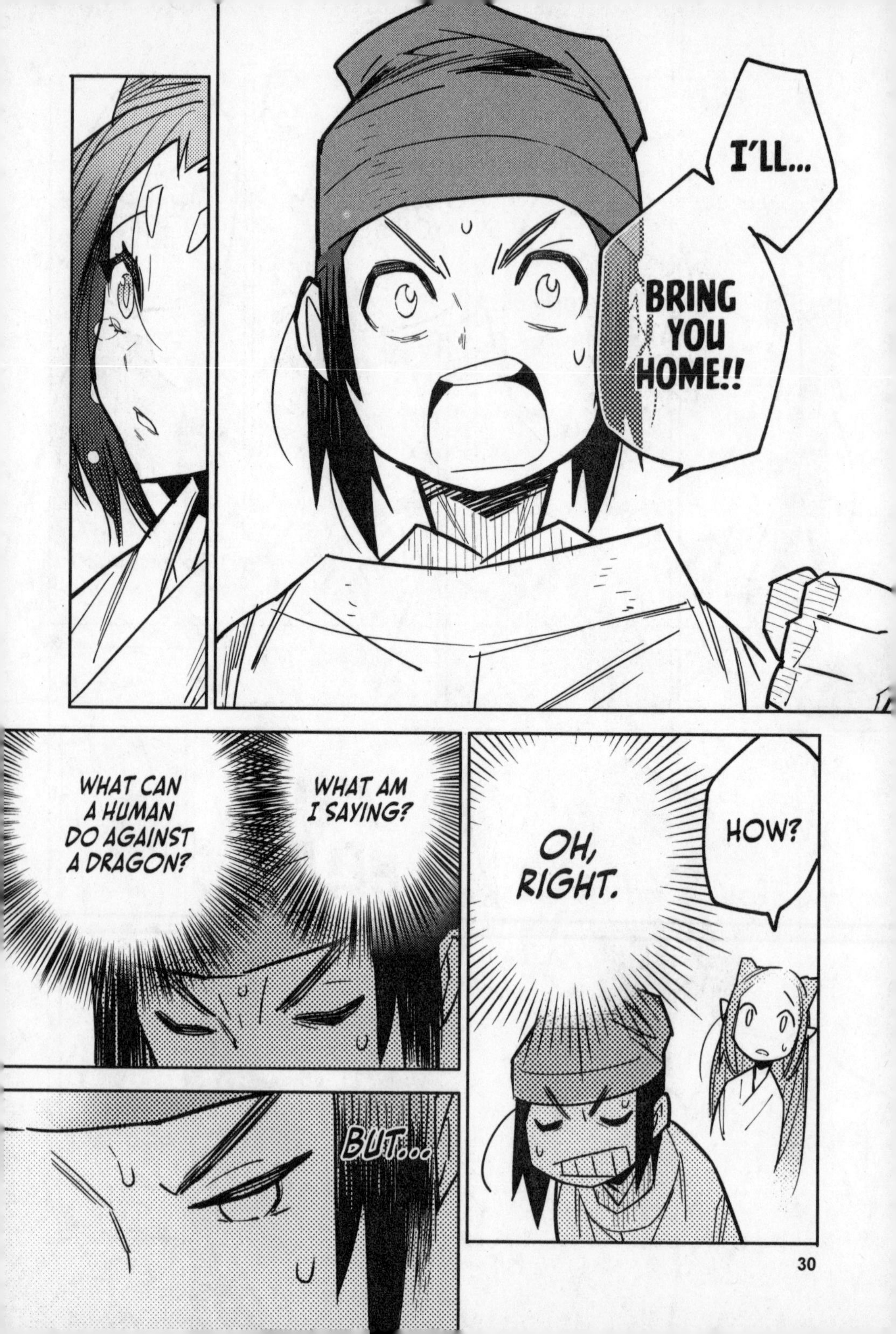
I'LL...
BRING YOU HOME!!
HOW?
OH, RIGHT.
WHAT AM I SAYING?
WHAT CAN A HUMAN DO AGAINST A DRAGON?
BUT...

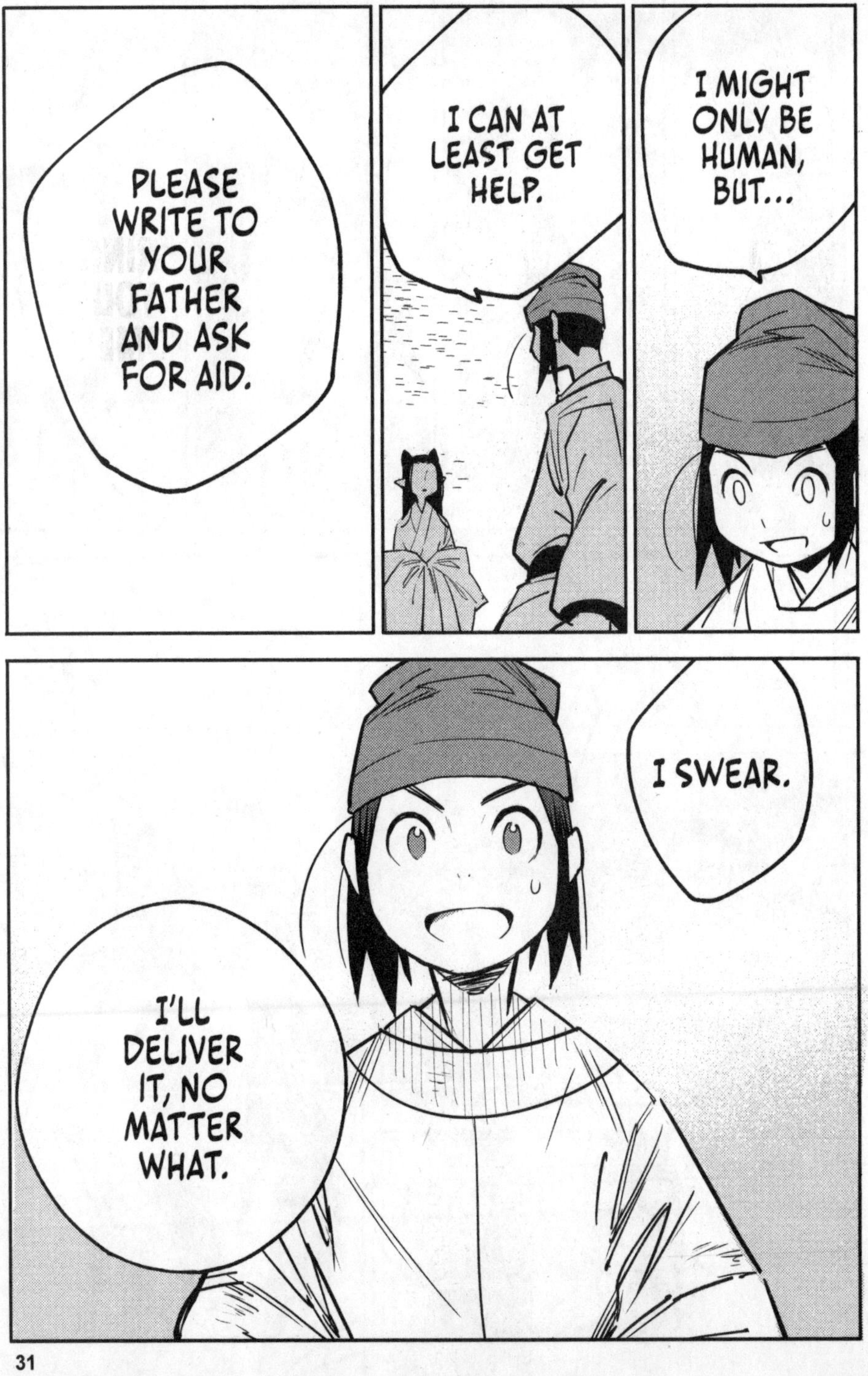
I MIGHT ONLY BE HUMAN, BUT...
I CAN AT LEAST GET HELP.
PLEASE WRITE TO YOUR FATHER AND ASK FOR AID.
I SWEAR.
I'LL DELIVER IT, NO MATTER WHAT.

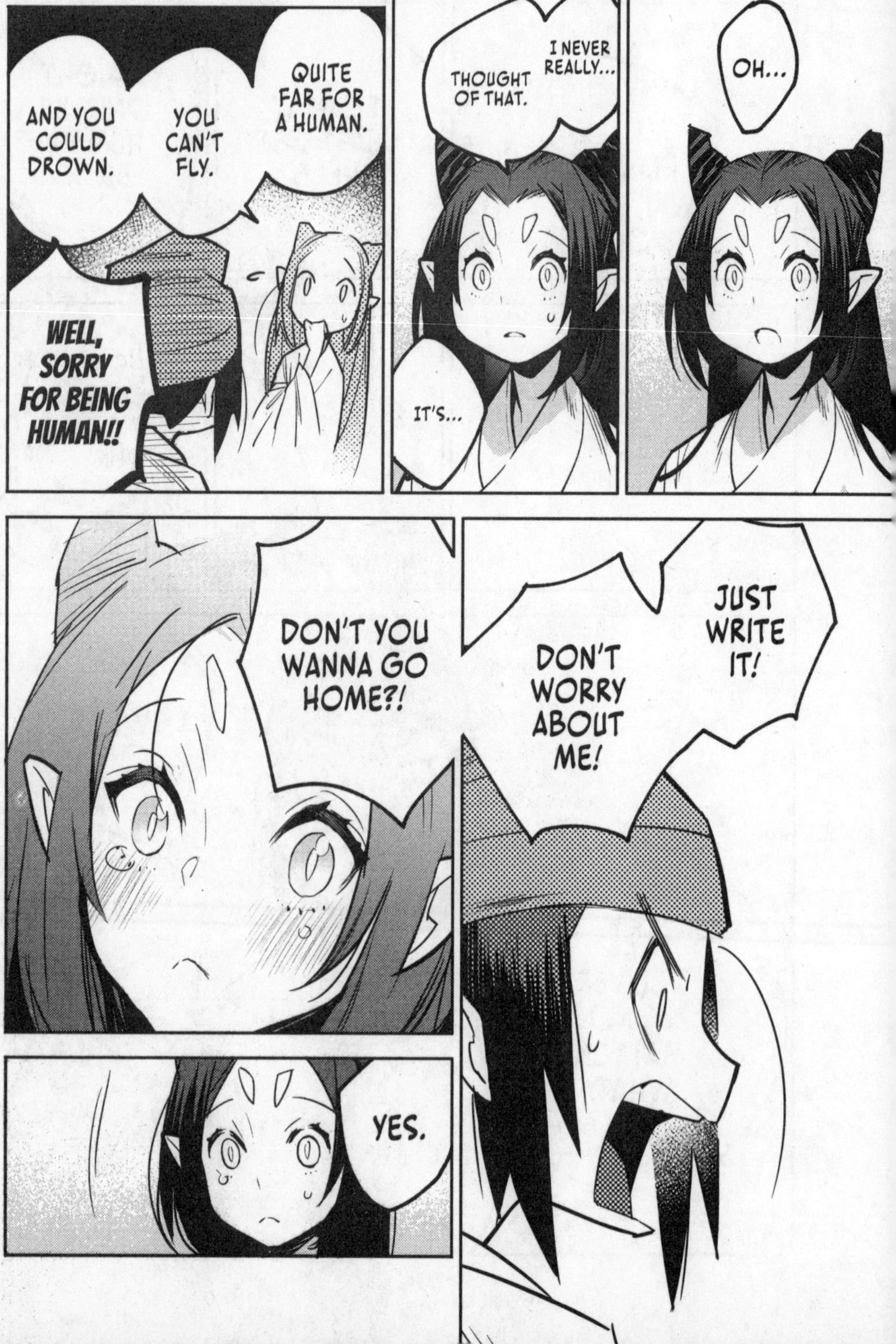
OH...
I NEVER REALLY...
THOUGHT OF THAT.
IT'S...
QUITE FAR FOR A HUMAN.
YOU CAN'T FLY.
AND YOU COULD DROWN.
WELL, SORRY FOR BEING HUMAN!!
JUST WRITE IT!
DON'T WORRY ABOUT ME!
DON'T YOU WANNA GO HOME?!
YES.

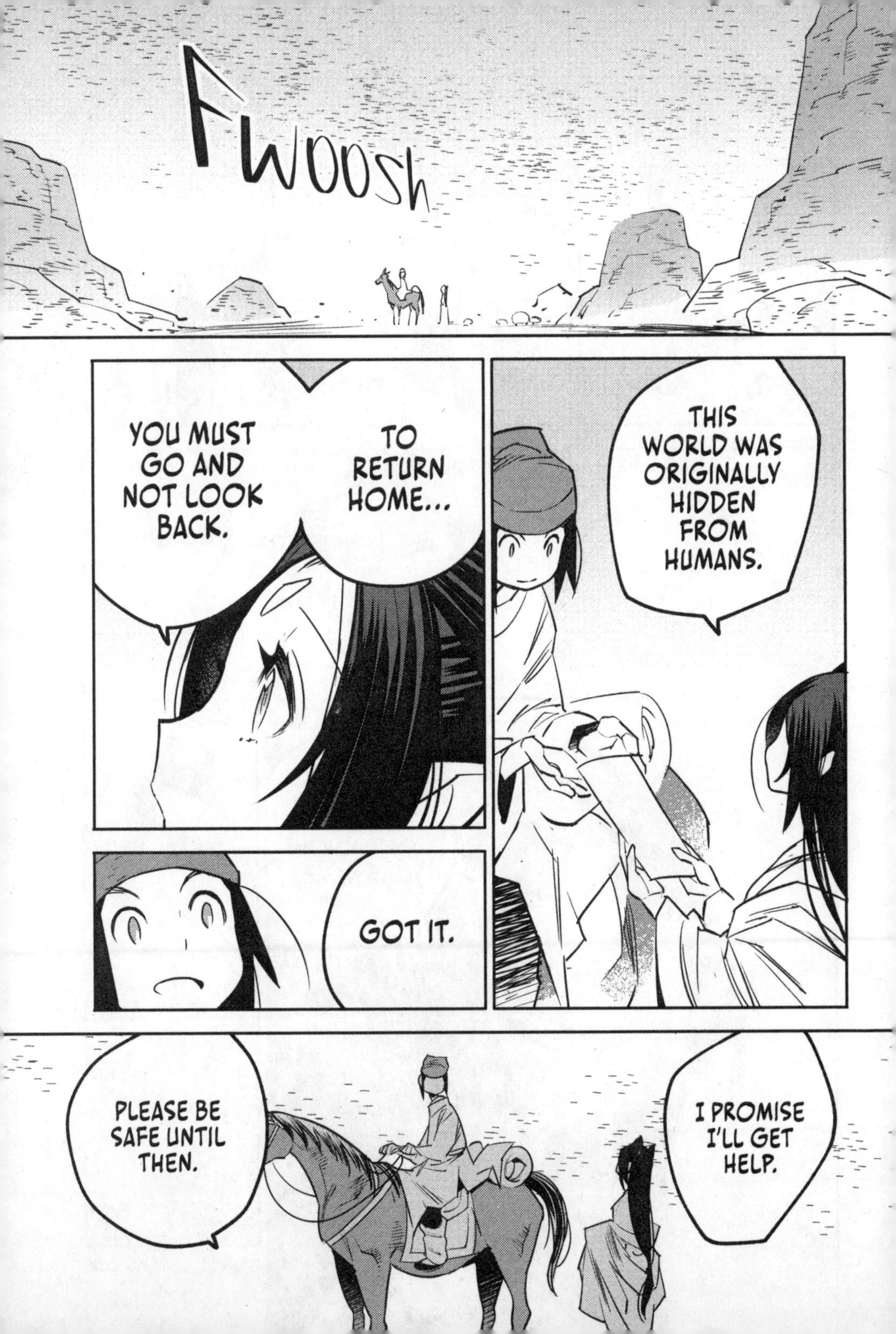
FWOOSH
THIS WORLD WAS ORIGINALLY HIDDEN FROM HUMANS.
TO RETURN HOME...
YOU MUST GO AND NOT LOOK BACK.
GOT IT.
I PROMISE I'LL GET HELP.
PLEASE BE SAFE UNTIL THEN.

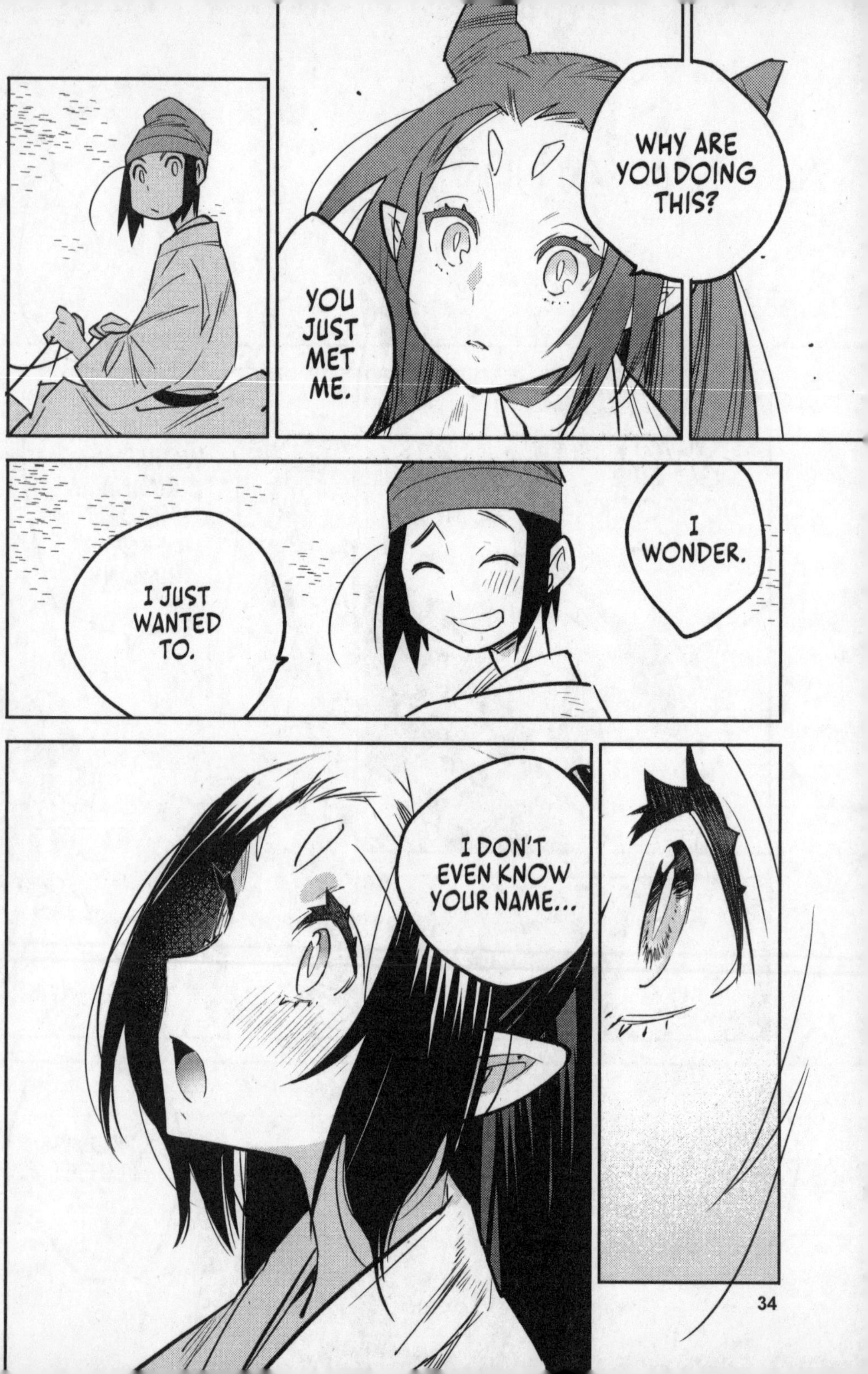
WHY ARE YOU DOING THIS?
YOU JUST MET ME.
I WONDER.
I JUST WANTED TO.
I DON'T EVEN KNOW YOUR NAME...

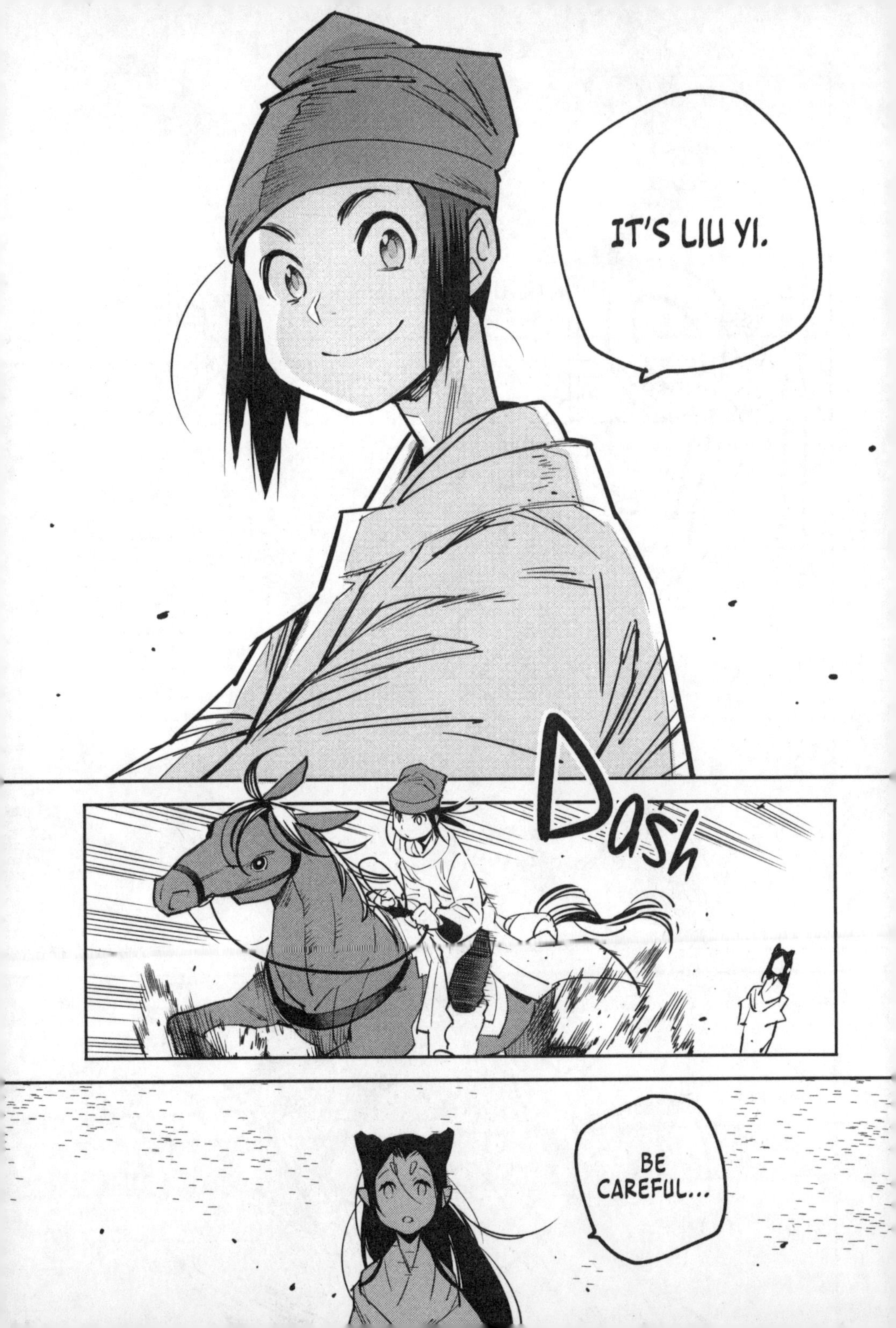
IT'S LIU YI.
DASH
BE CAREFUL...

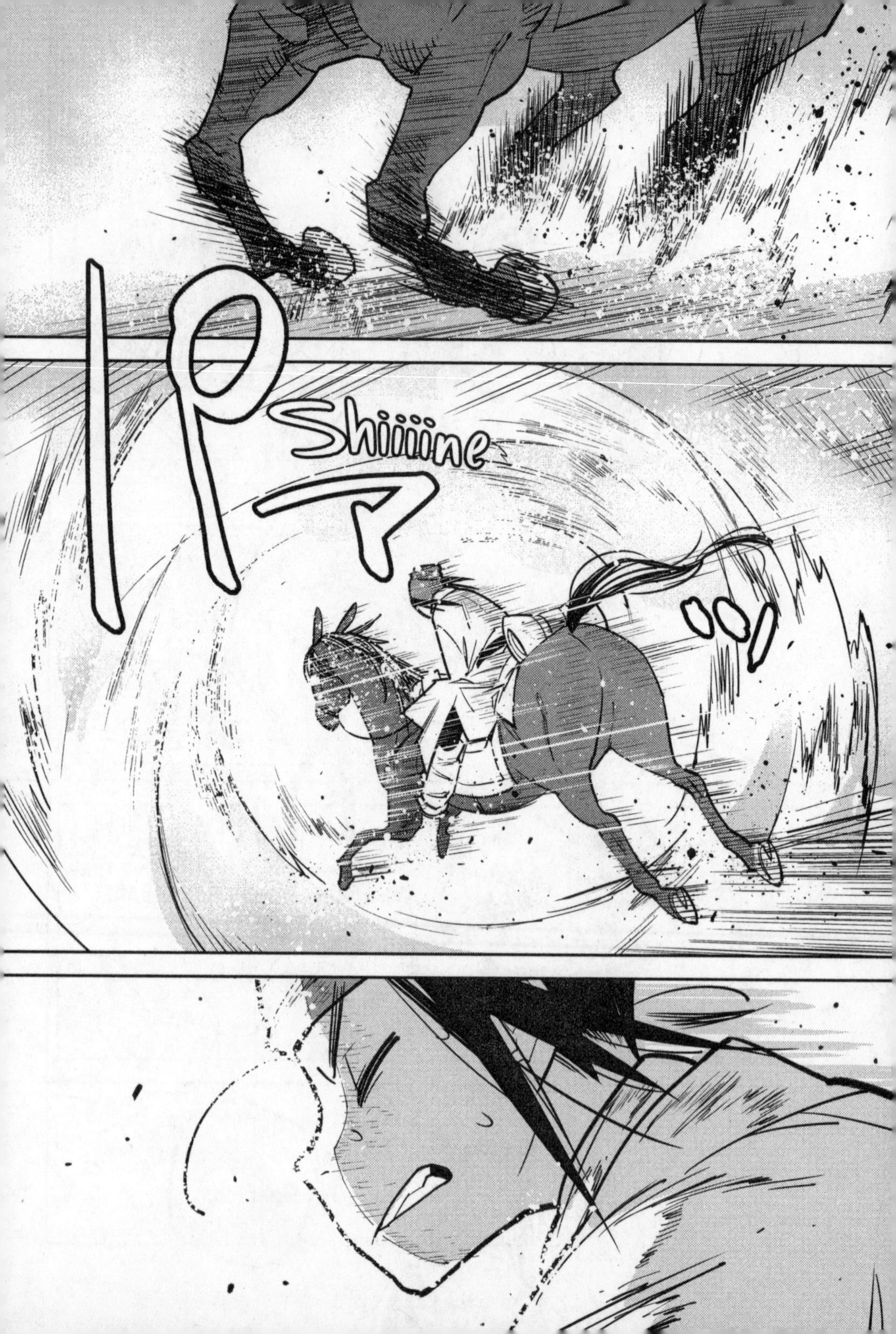
Shiiiine

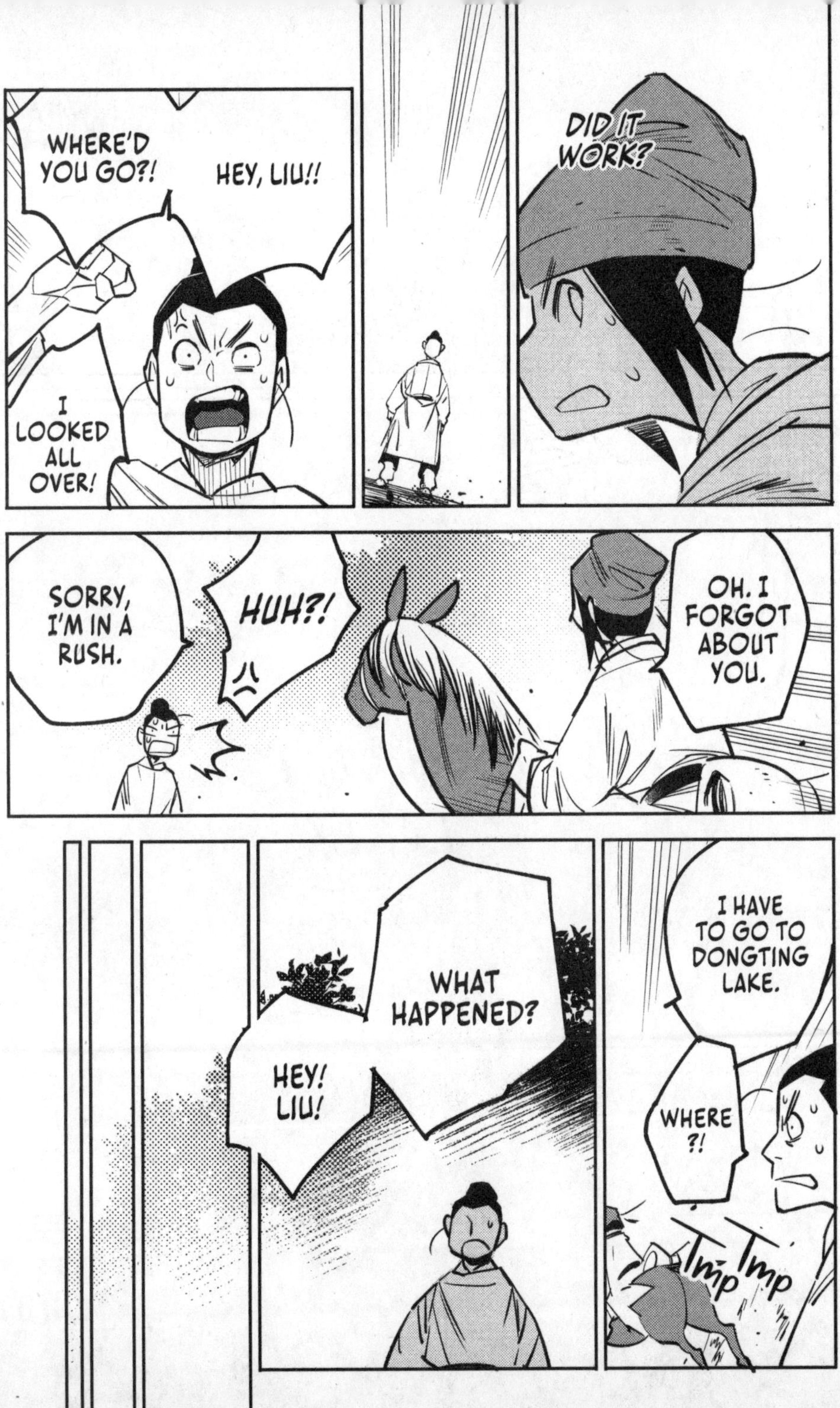
DID IT WORK?
HEY, LIU!!
WHERE'D YOU GO?!
I LOOKED ALL OVER!
OH. I FORGOT ABOUT YOU.
HUH?!
SORRY, I'M IN A RUSH.
I HAVE TO GO TO DONGTING LAKE.
WHERE ?!
Tmp Tmp
WHAT HAPPENED?
HEY! LIU!

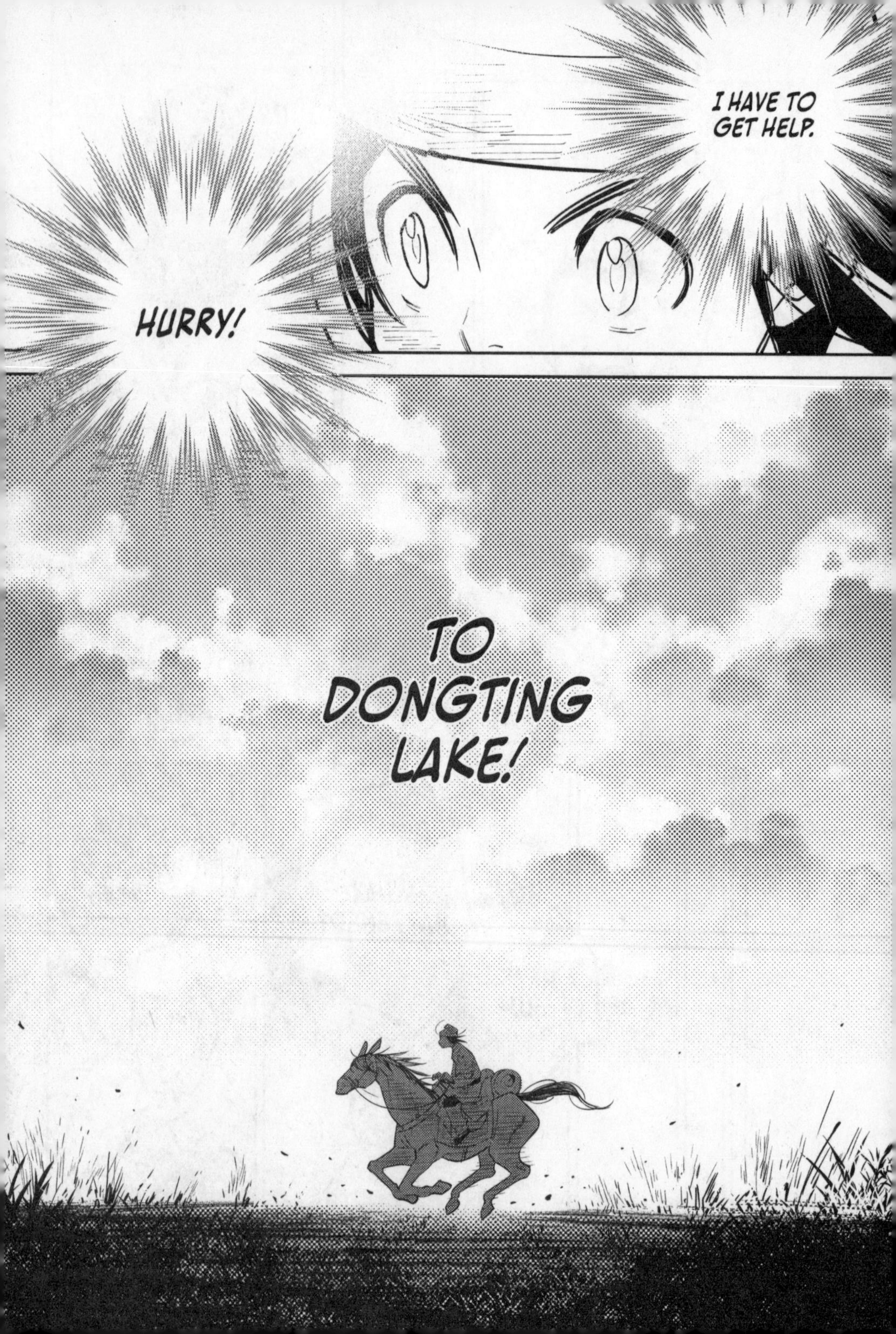

I HAVE TO GET HELP.
HURRY!
TO DONGTING LAKE!

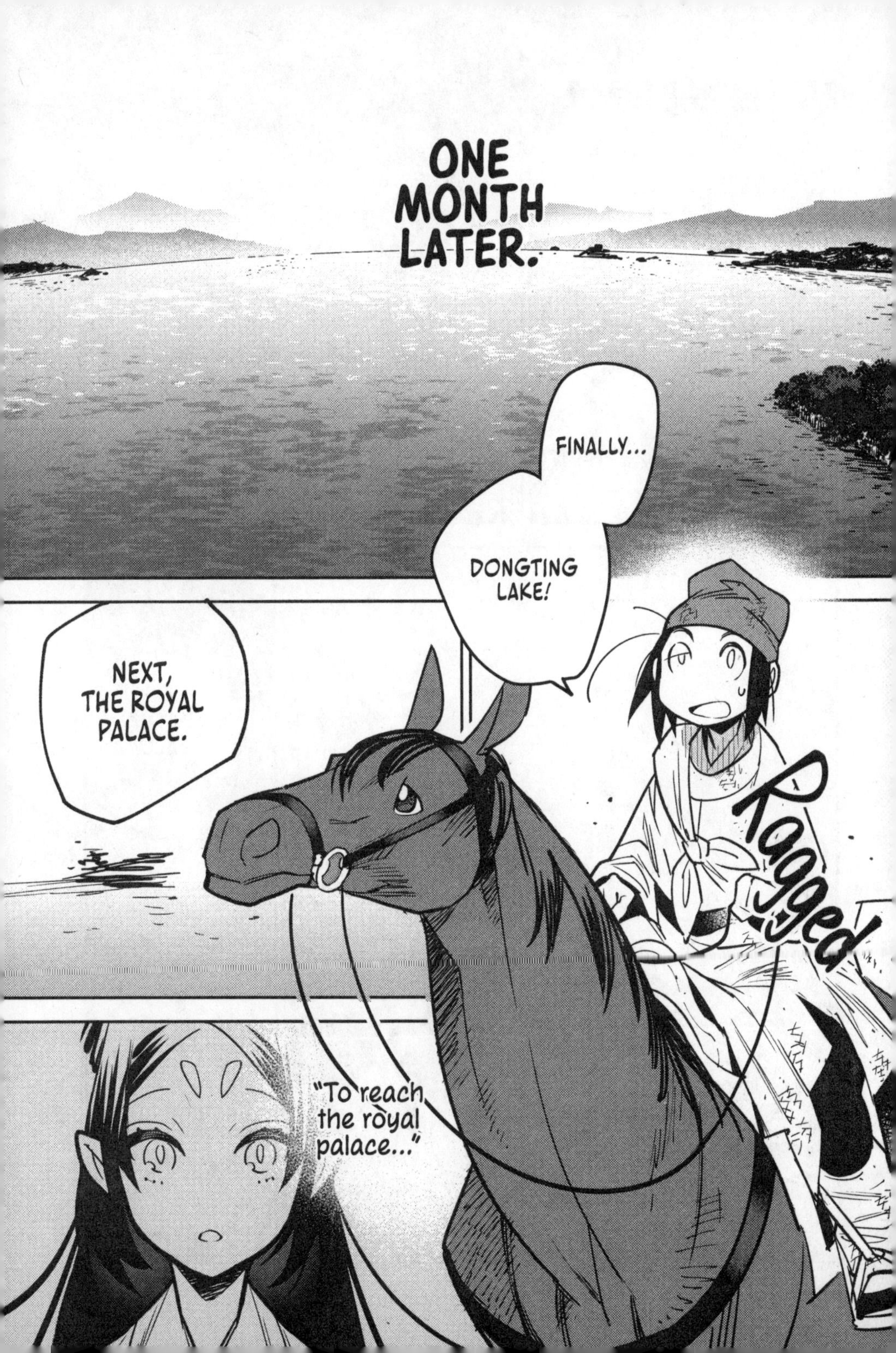
ONE MONTH LATER.
FINALLY...
DONGTING LAKE!
NEXT, THE ROYAL PALACE.
Ragged
"To reach the royal palace..."

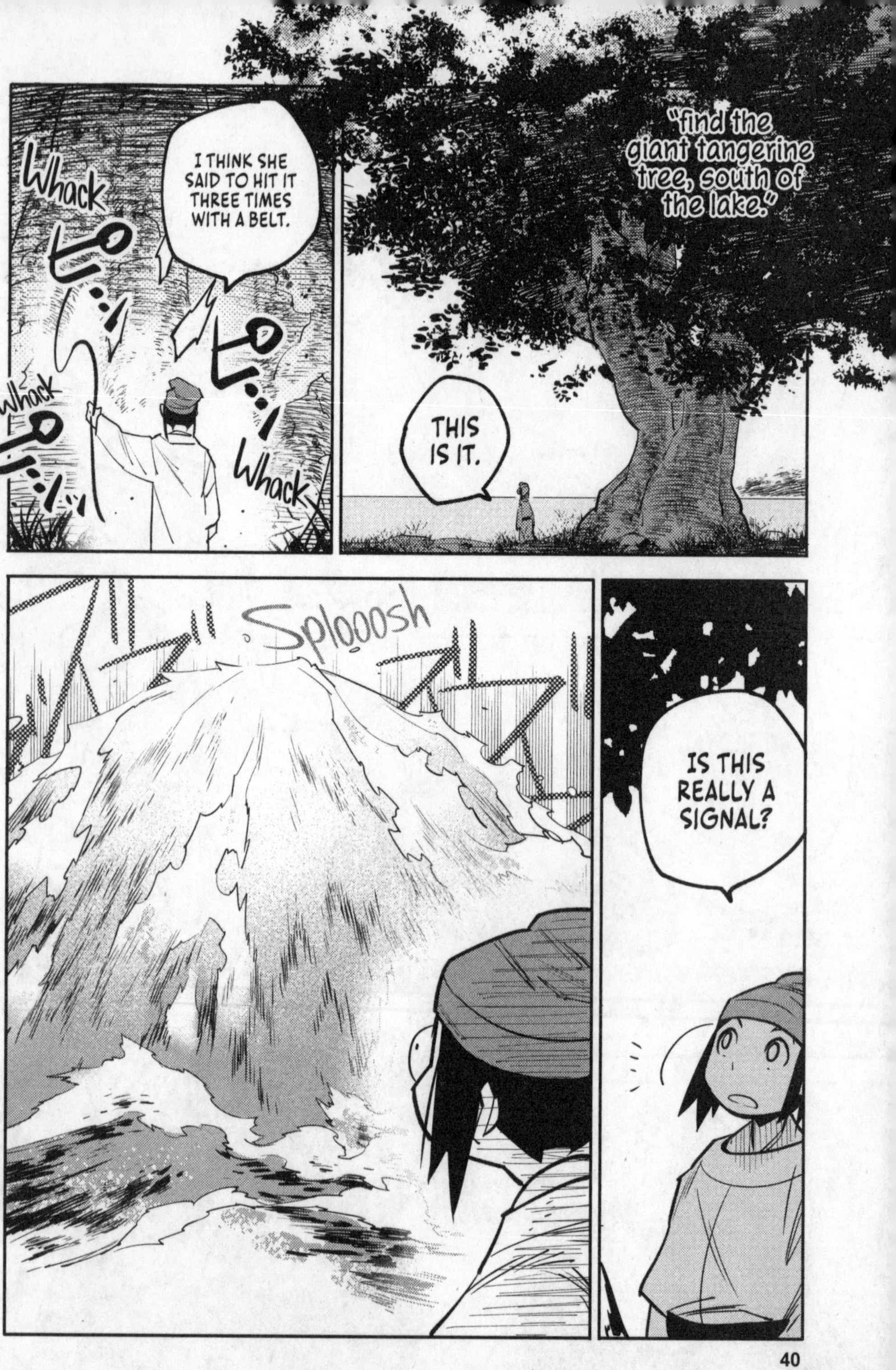
"find the giant tangerine tree, south of the lake."
THIS IS IT.
I THINK SHE SAID TO HIT IT THREE TIMES WITH A BELT.
Whack
Whack
Whack
IS THIS REALLY A SIGNAL?
Splooosh

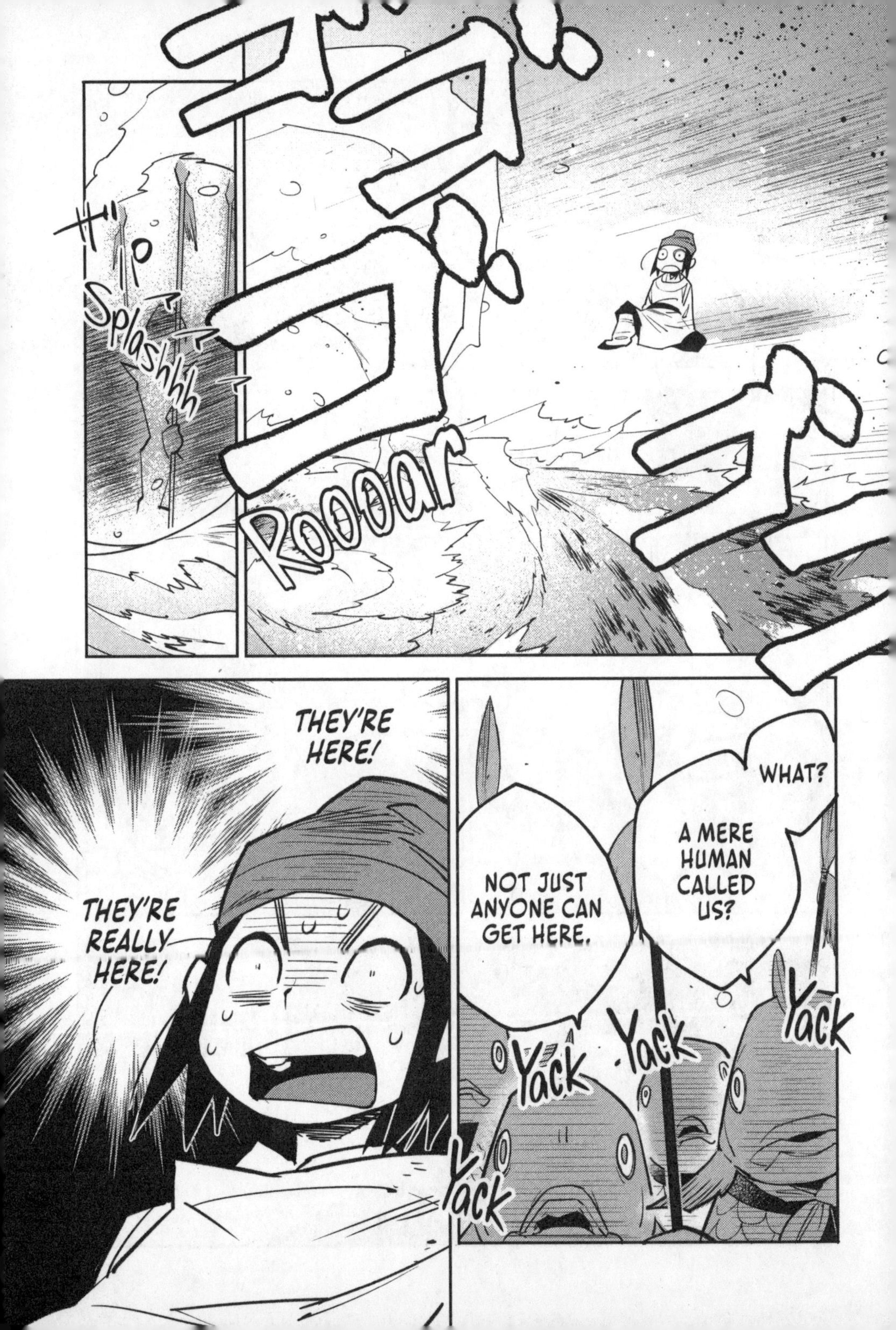
Rooooar
Splashhh
WHAT?
A MERE HUMAN CALLED US?
NOT JUST ANYONE CAN GET HERE.
Yack
Yack
Yack
Yack
THEY'RE HERE!
THEY'RE REALLY HERE!

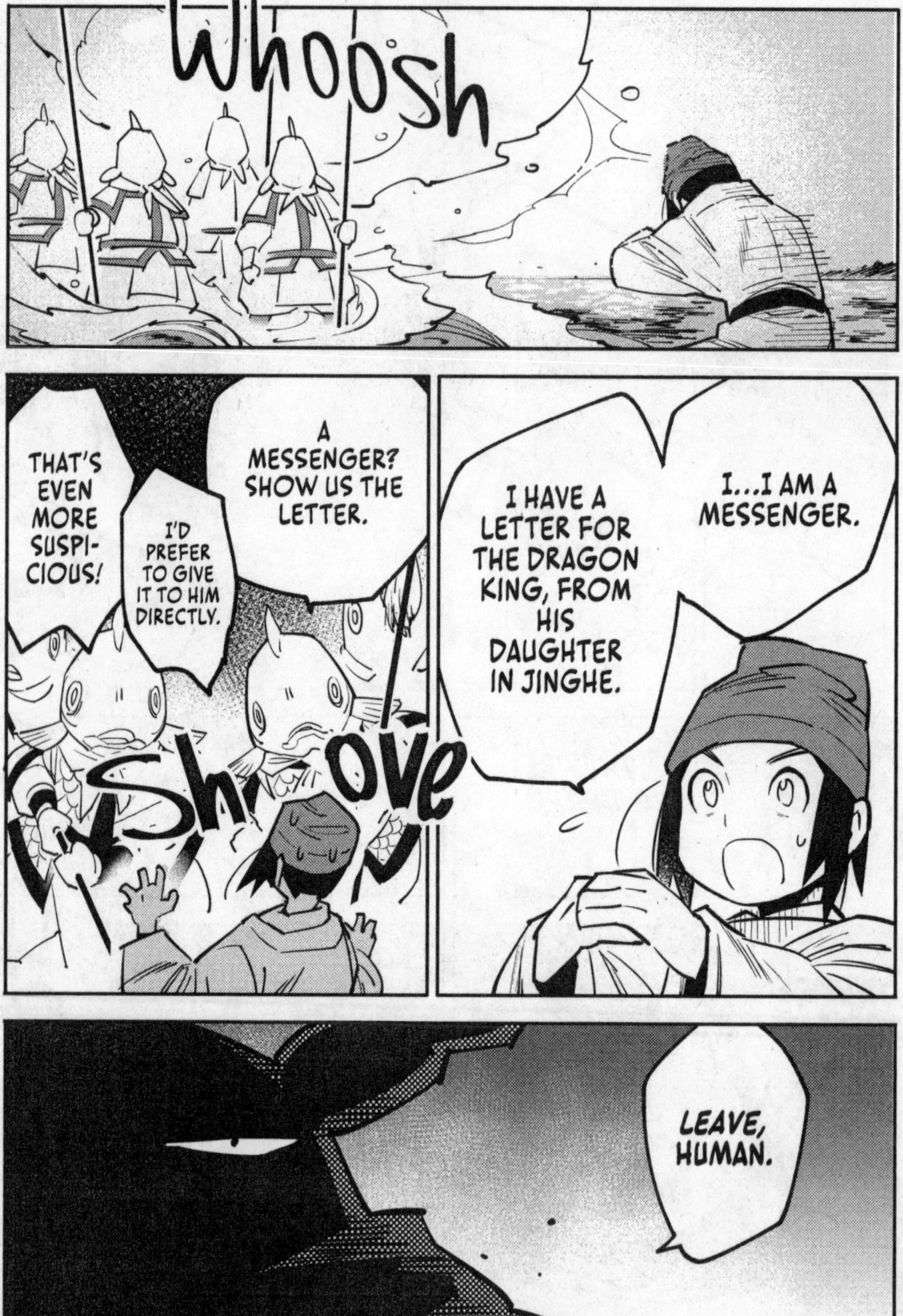
Whoosh
I...I AM A MESSENGER.
I HAVE A LETTER FOR THE DRAGON KING, FROM HIS DAUGHTER IN JINGHE.
A MESSENGER? SHOW US THE LETTER.
I'D PREFER TO GIVE IT TO HIM DIRECTLY.
THAT'S EVEN MORE SUSPI-CIOUS!
Shove
LEAVE, HUMAN.

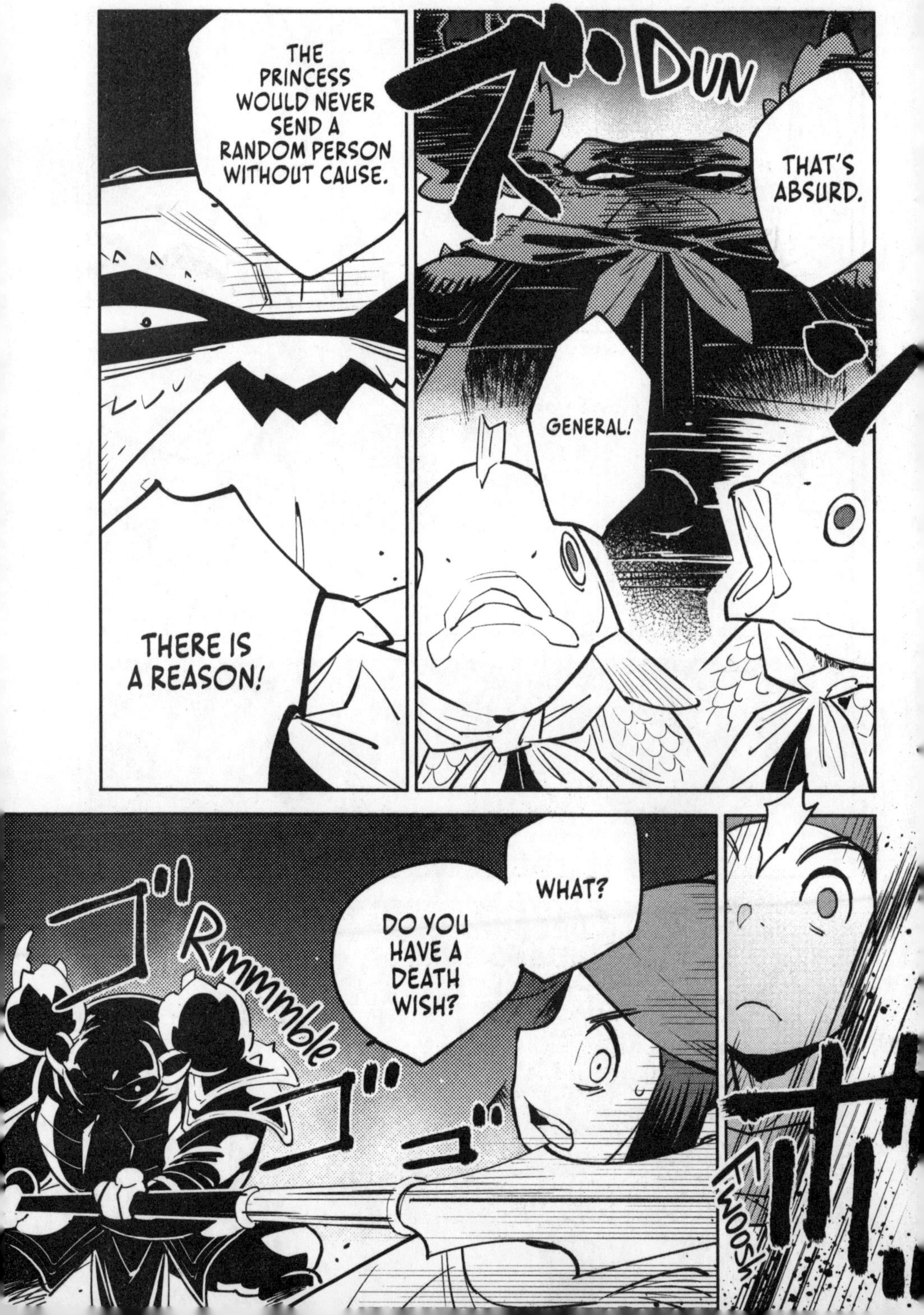
DUN
THAT'S ABSURD.
GENERAL!
THE PRINCESS WOULD NEVER SEND A RANDOM PERSON WITHOUT CAUSE.
THERE IS A REASON!
FWOOSH
WHAT?
DO YOU HAVE A DEATH WISH?
RMMMBLE

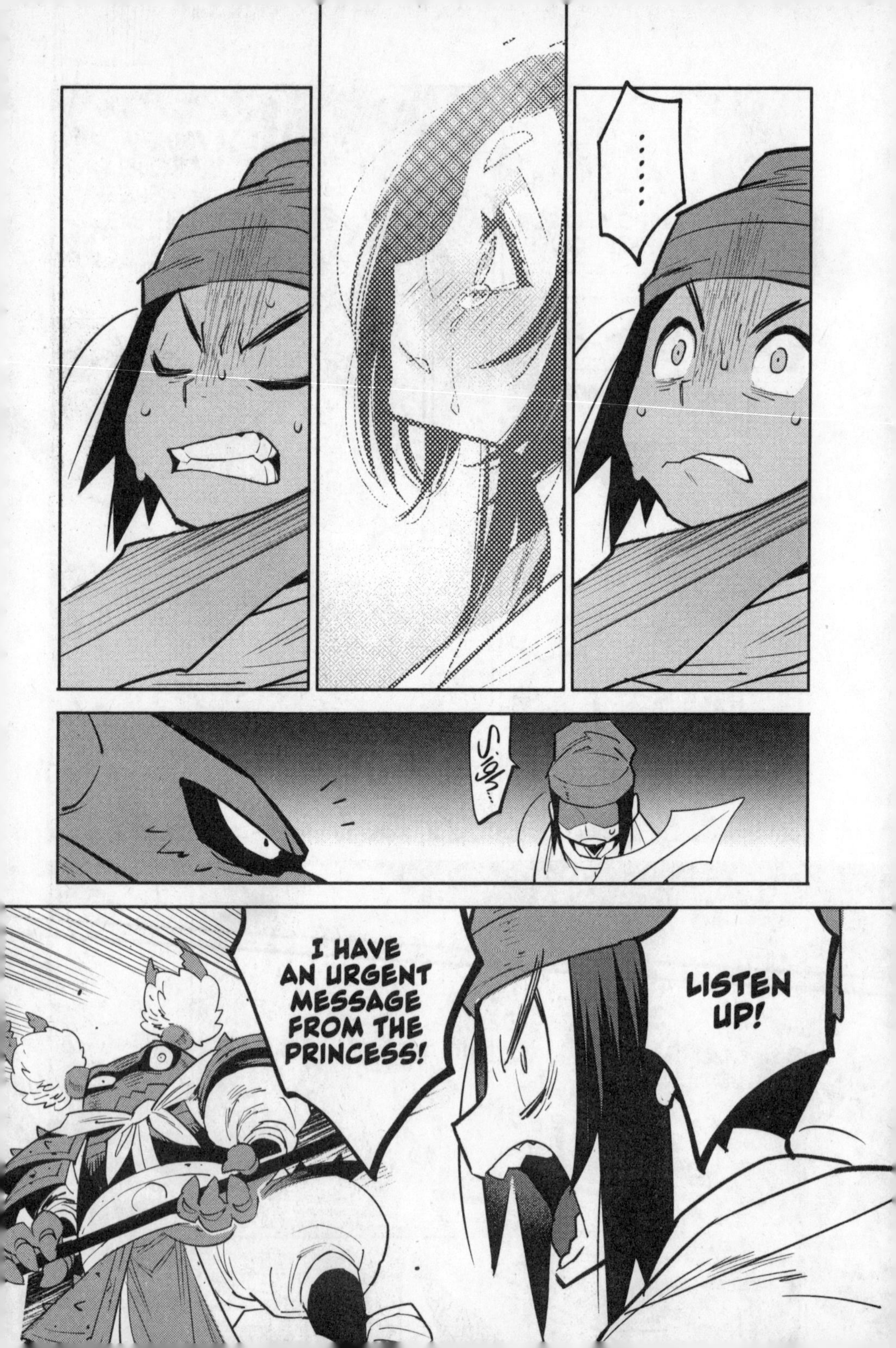
......
Sigh...
LISTEN UP!
I HAVE AN URGENT MESSAGE FROM THE PRINCESS!

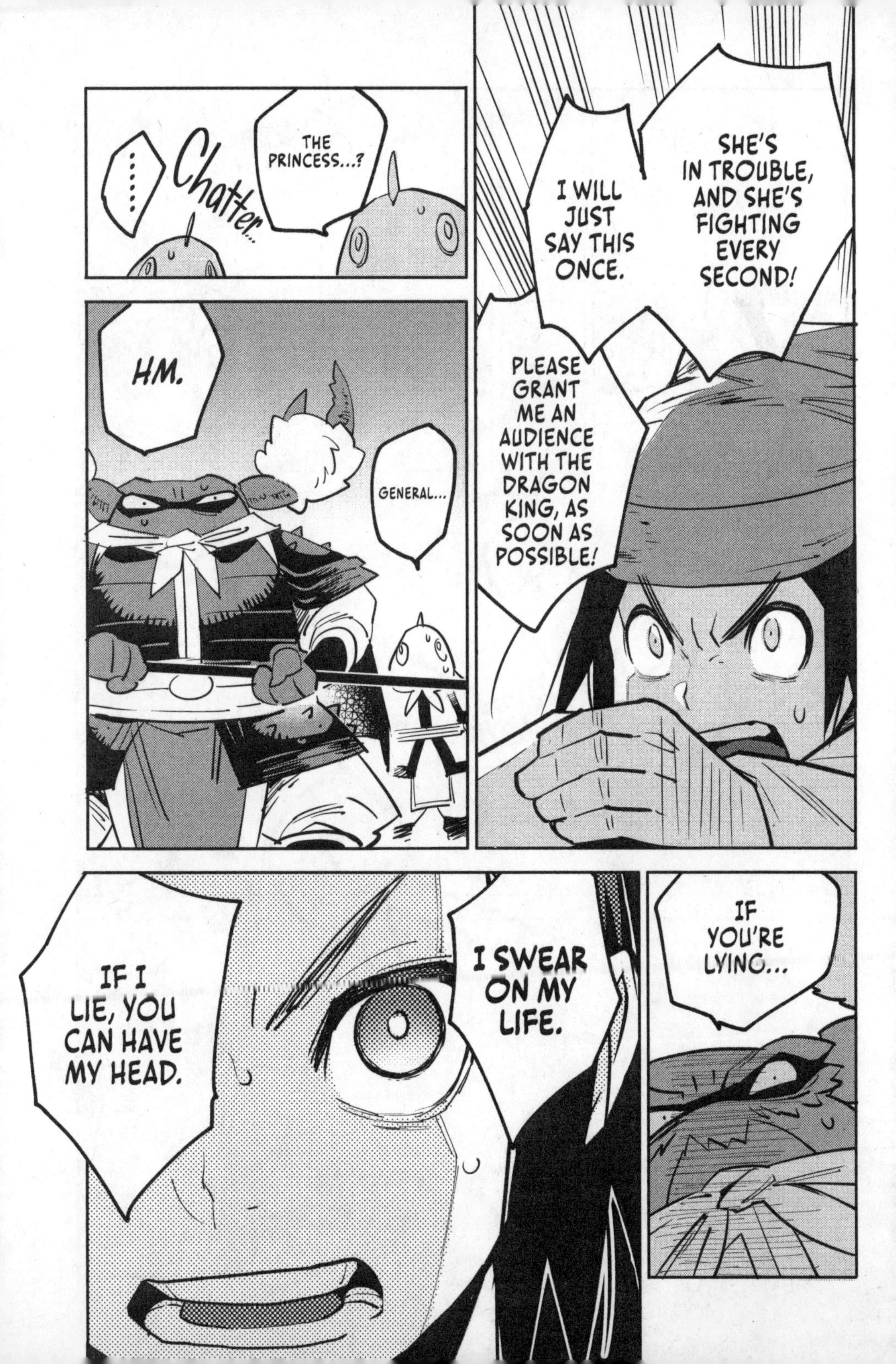
SHE'S IN TROUBLE, AND SHE'S FIGHTING EVERY SECOND!
I WILL JUST SAY THIS ONCE.
PLEASE GRANT ME AN AUDIENCE WITH THE DRAGON KING, AS SOON AS POSSIBLE!
THE PRINCESS...?
Chatter...
......
GENERAL...
HM.
IF YOU'RE LYING...
I SWEAR ON MY LIFE.
IF I LIE, YOU CAN HAVE MY HEAD.

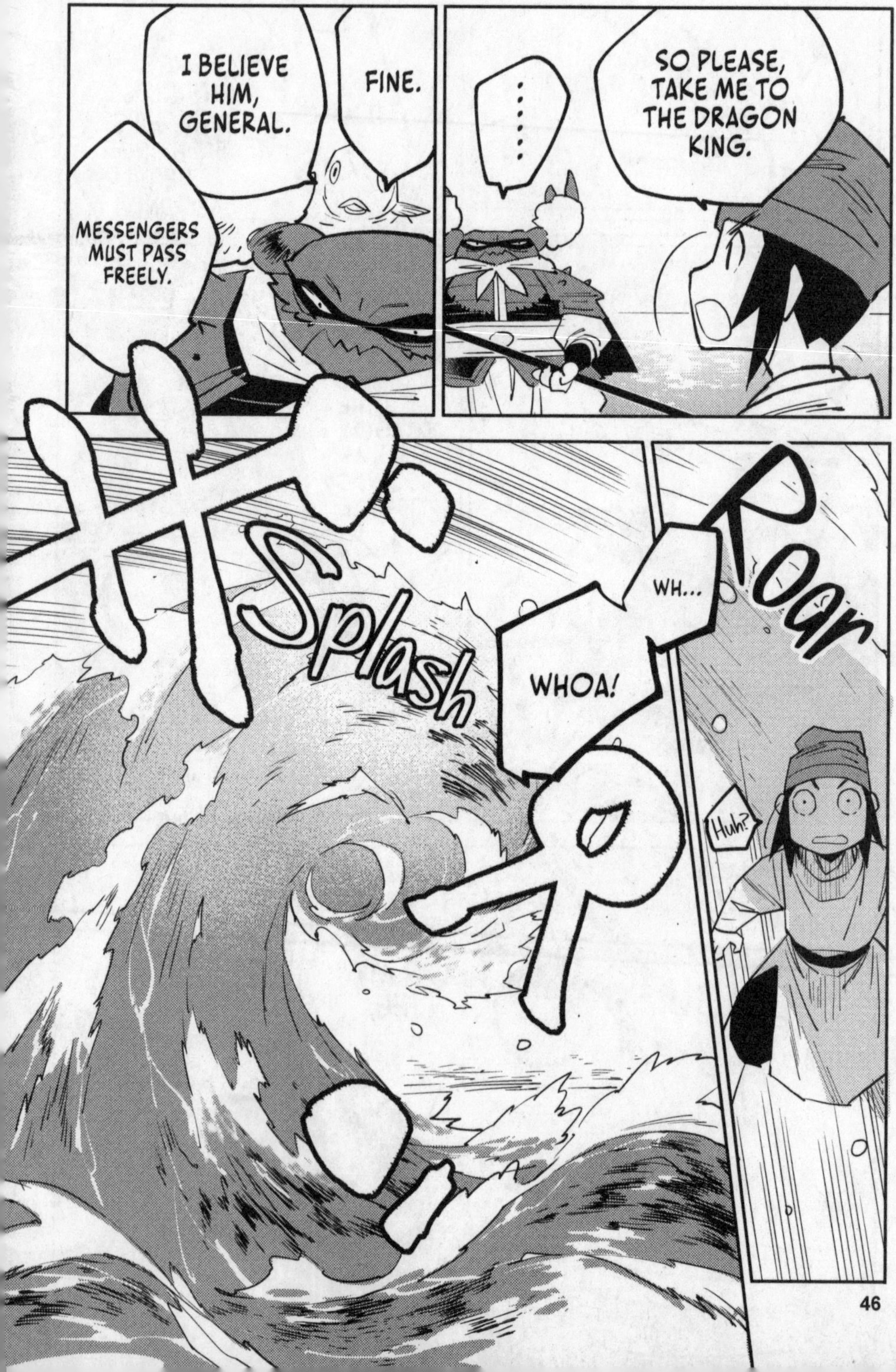
I BELIEVE HIM, GENERAL.
MESSENGERS MUST PASS FREELY.
FINE.
......
SO PLEASE, TAKE ME TO THE DRAGON KING.
Splash
WH...
WHOA!
Roar
Huh?

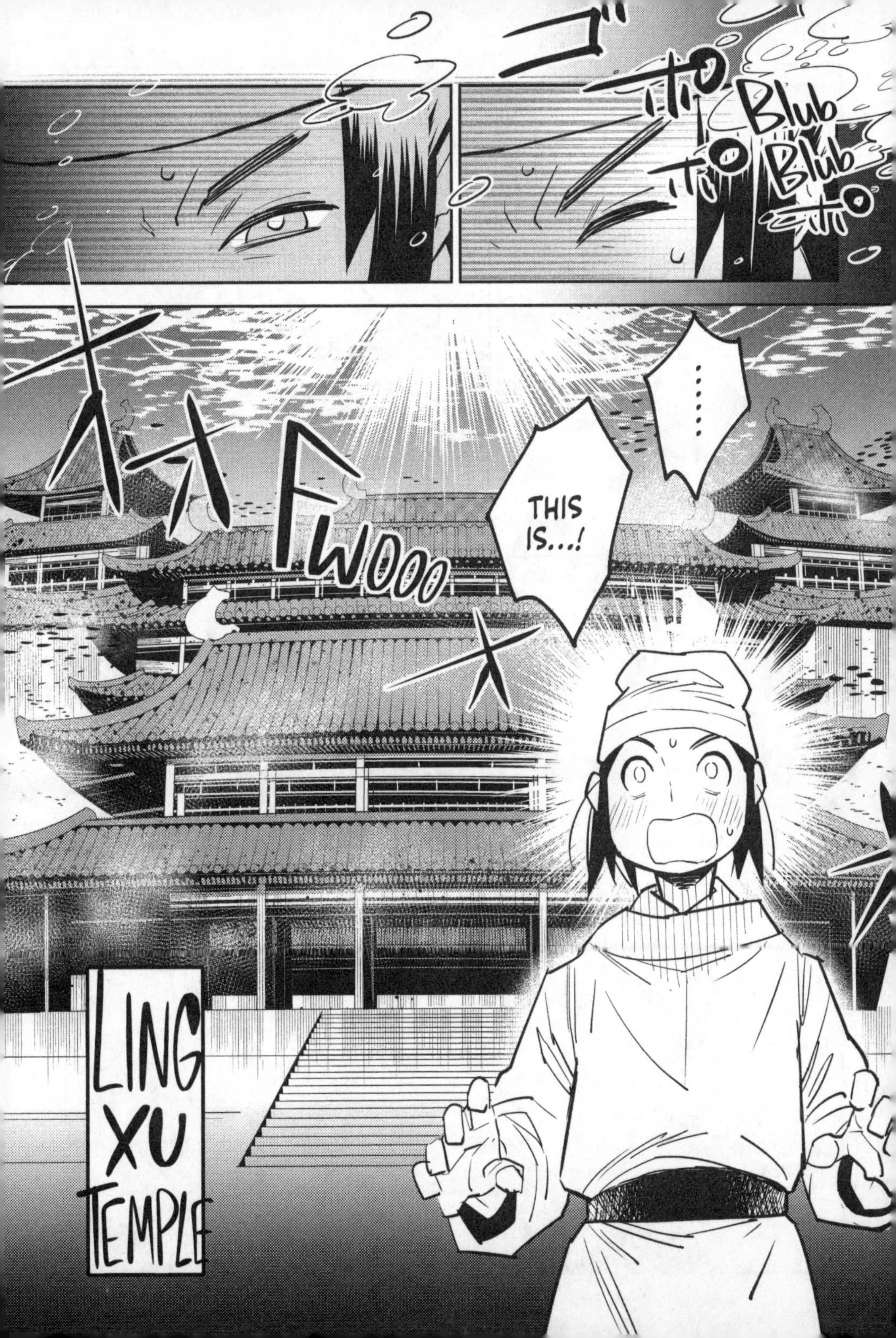
Blub
Blub
FWOOO
......
THIS IS...!
LING XU TEMPLE

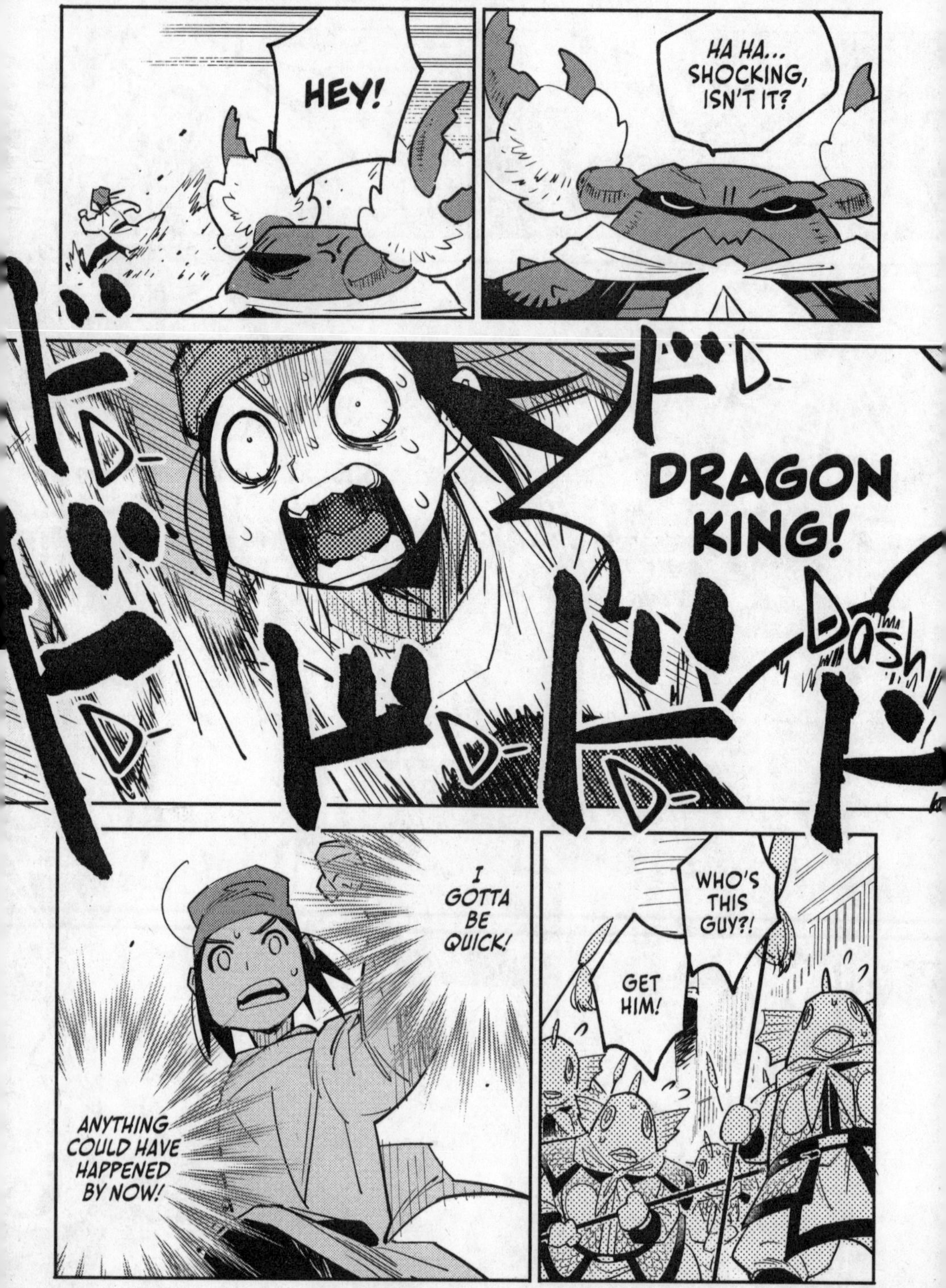
HA HA... SHOCKING, ISN'T IT?
HEY!
DRAGON KING!
Dash
WHO'S THIS GUY?!
GET HIM!
I GOTTA BE QUICK!
ANYTHING COULD HAVE HAPPENED BY NOW!

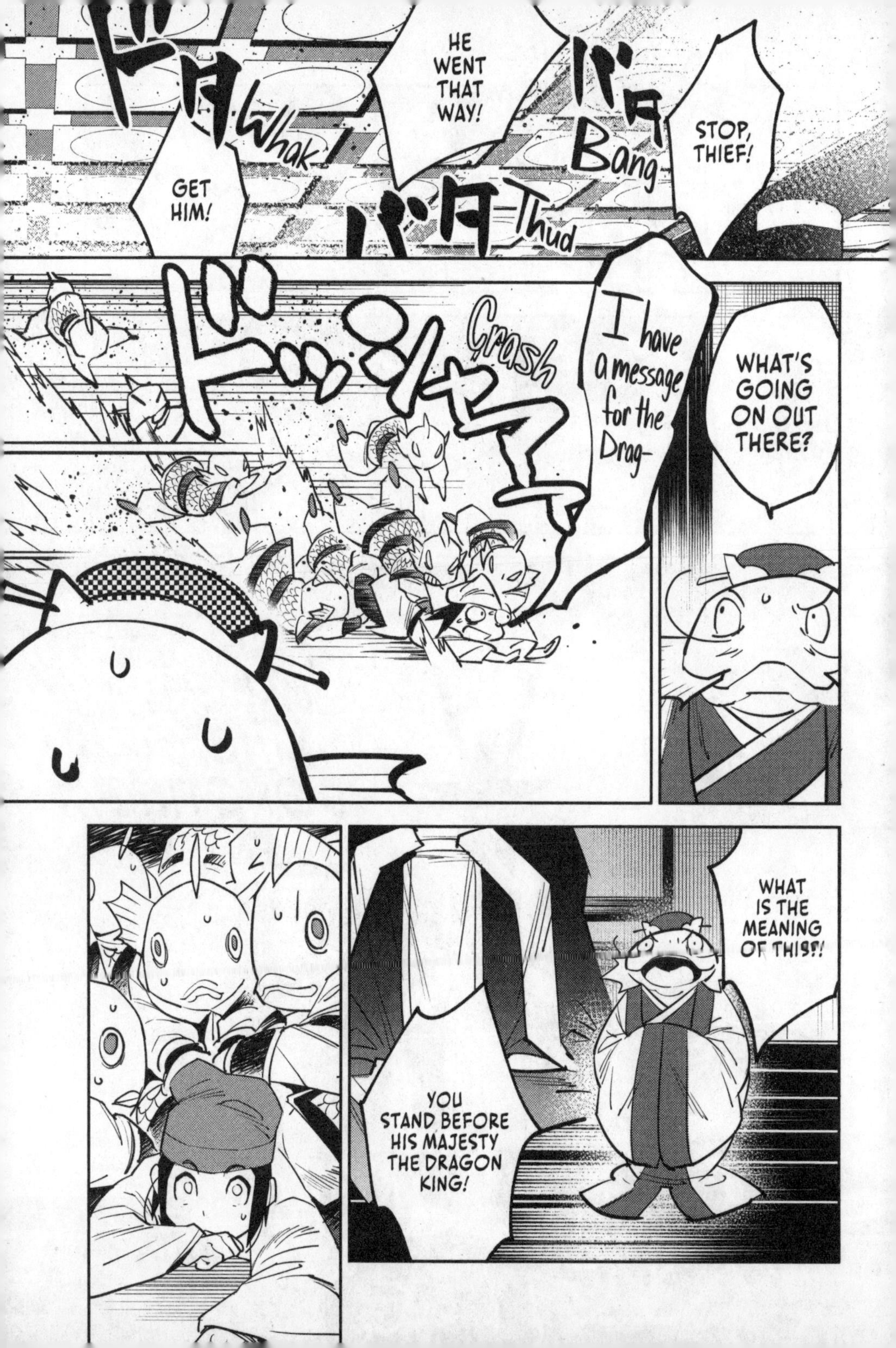
STOP, THIEF!
Bang
HE WENT THAT WAY!
Whak
GET HIM!
Thud
WHAT'S GOING ON OUT THERE?
I have a message for the Drag-
Crash
WHAT IS THE MEANING OF THIS?!
YOU STAND BEFORE HIS MAJESTY THE DRAGON KING!

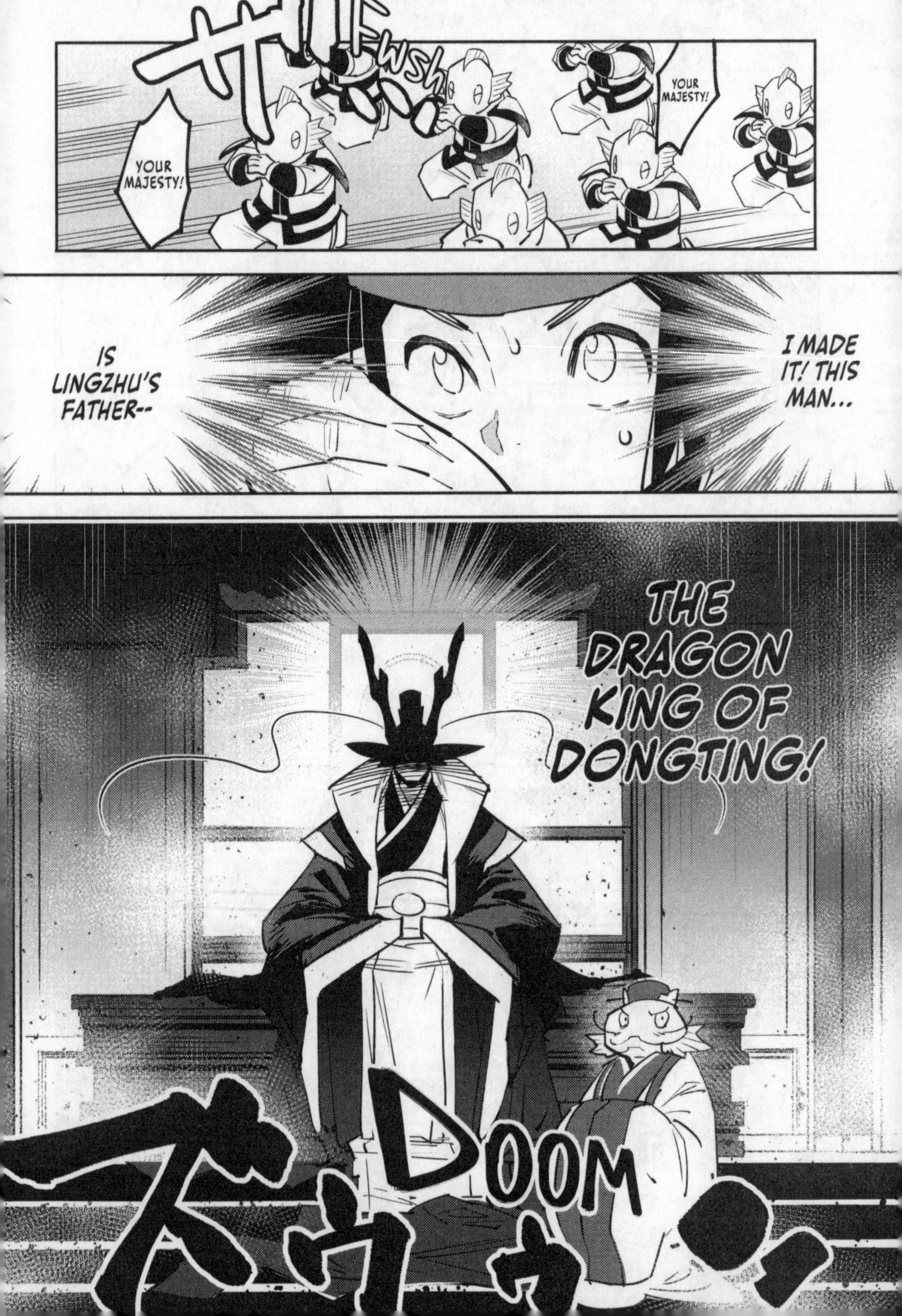
Fwsh
YOUR MAJESTY!
YOUR MAJESTY!
I MADE IT! THIS MAN...
IS LINGZHU'S FATHER--
THE DRAGON KING OF DONGTING!
DOOM

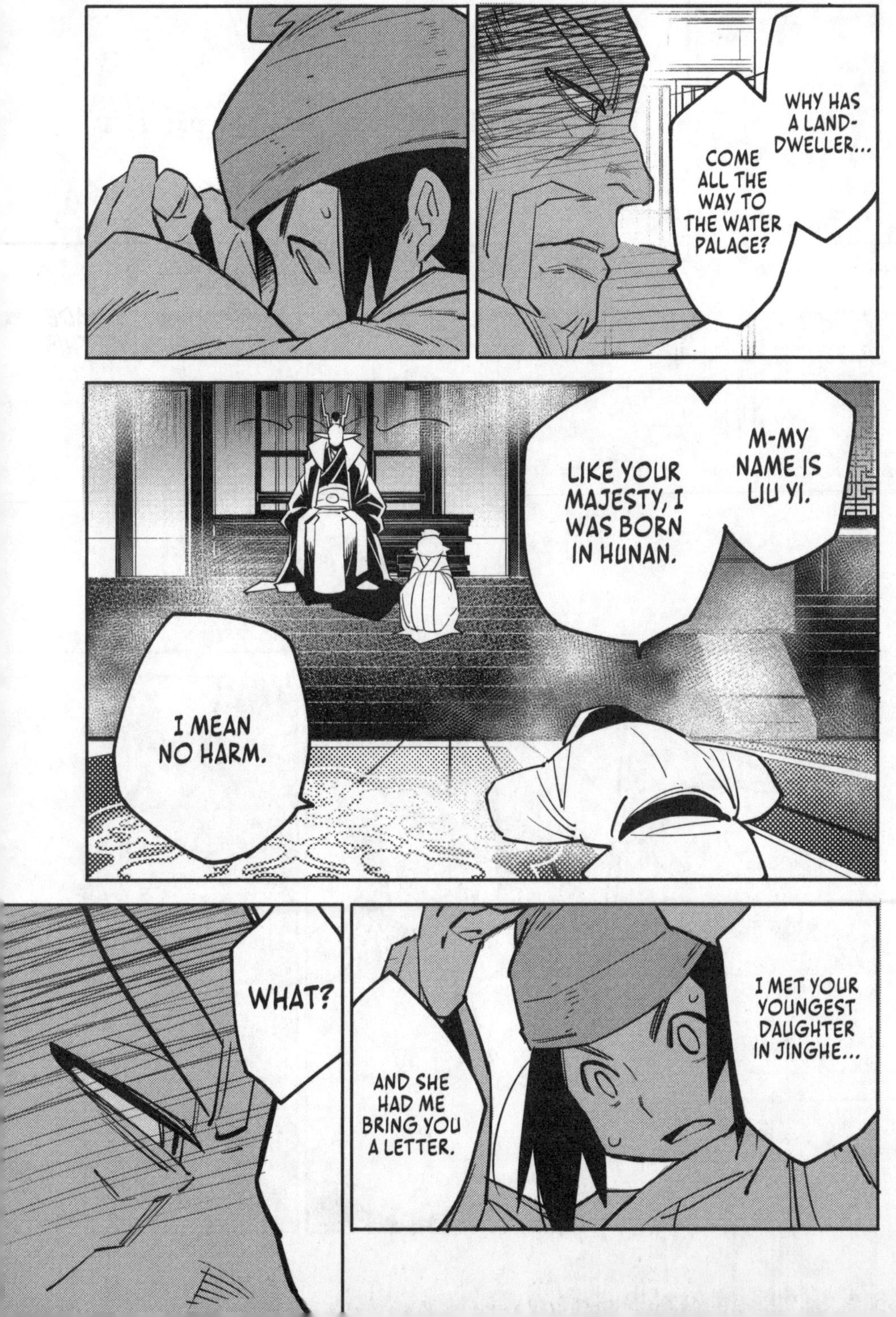
WHY HAS A LAND-DWELLER...
COME ALL THE WAY TO THE WATER PALACE?
M-MY NAME IS LIU YI.
LIKE YOUR MAJESTY, I WAS BORN IN HUNAN.
I MEAN NO HARM.
I MET YOUR YOUNGEST DAUGHTER IN JINGHE...
AND SHE HAD ME BRING YOU A LETTER.
WHAT?

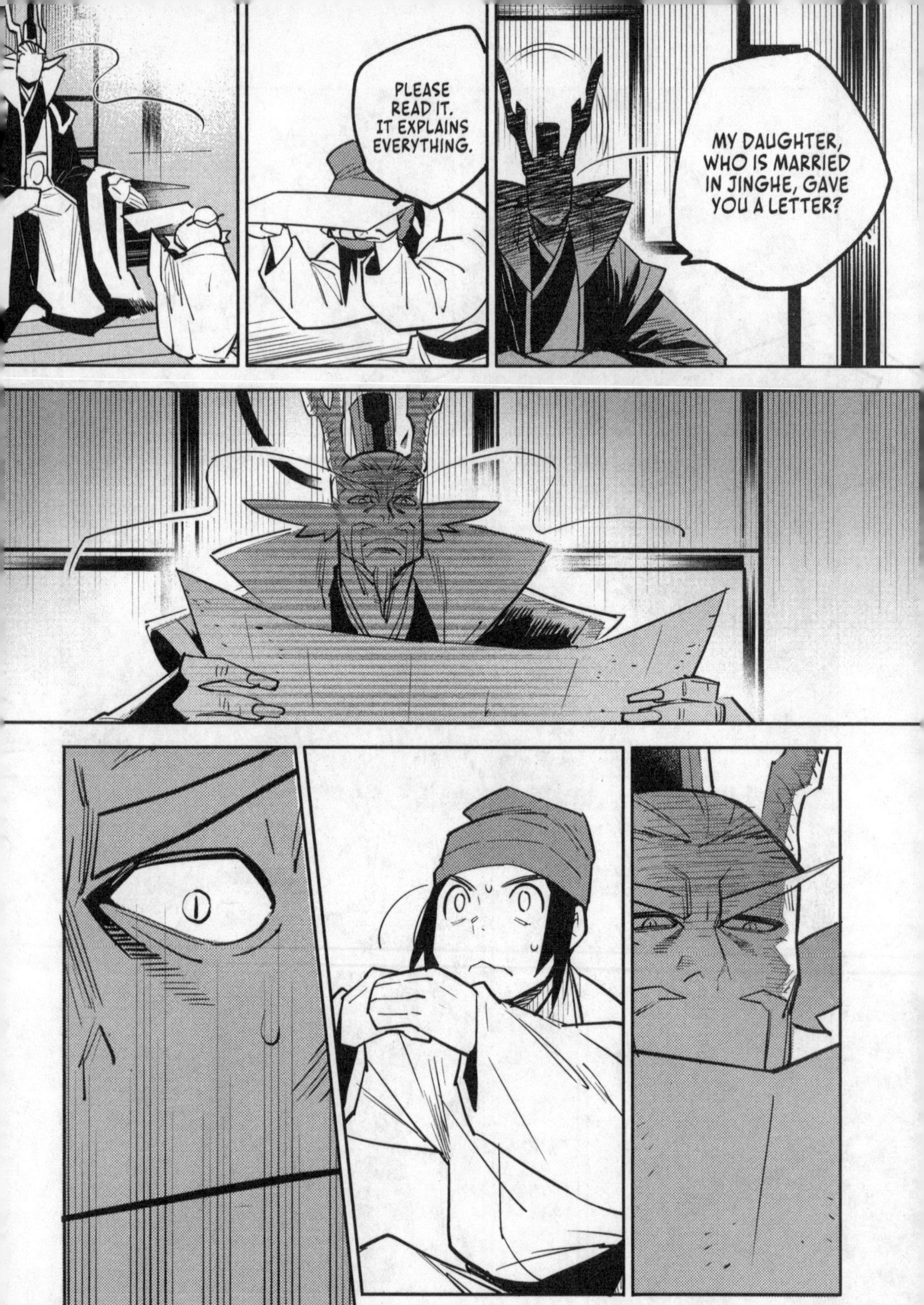
MY DAUGHTER, WHO IS MARRIED IN JINGHE, GAVE YOU A LETTER?
PLEASE READ IT. IT EXPLAINS EVERYTHING.

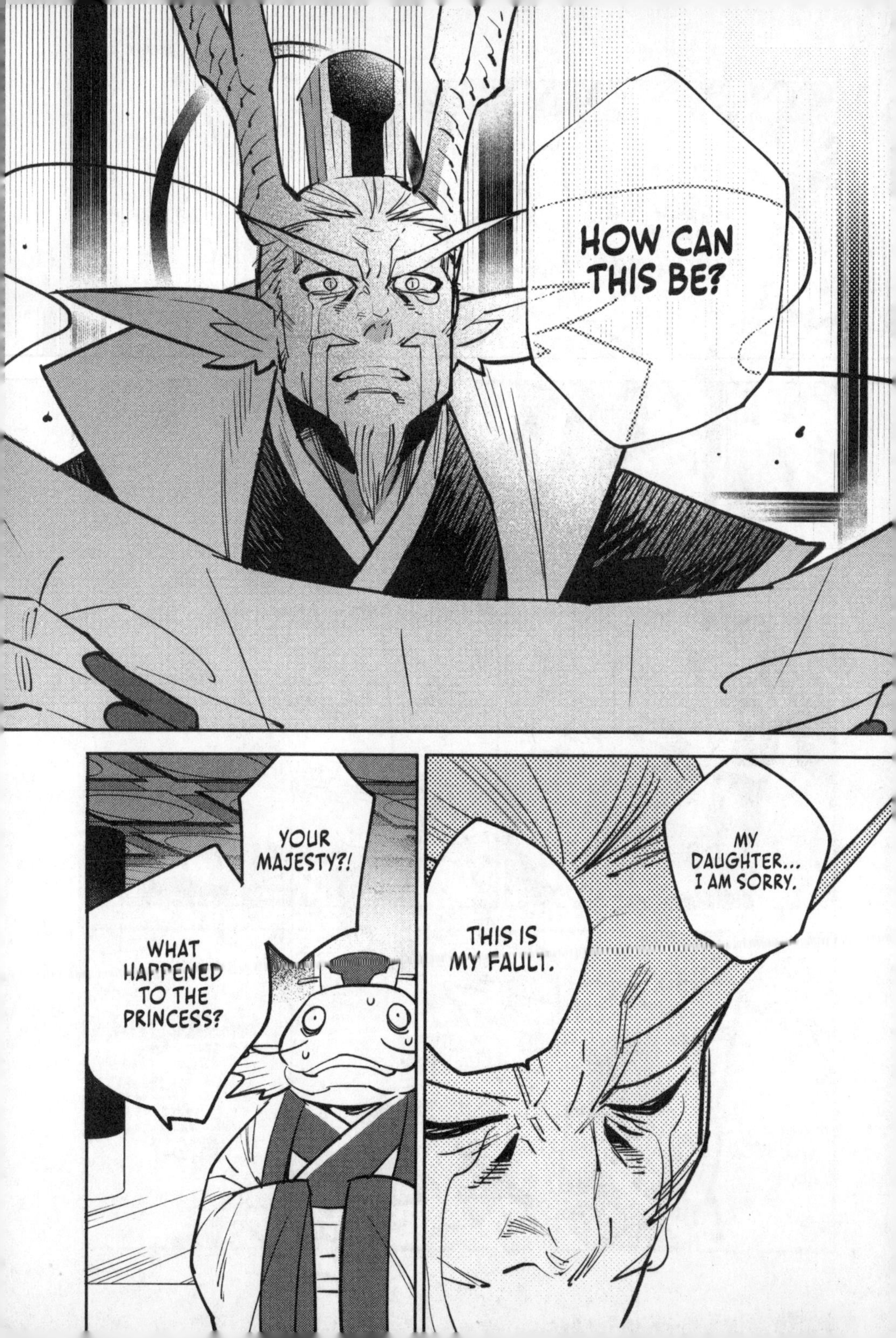
HOW CAN THIS BE?
MY DAUGHTER... I AM SORRY.
THIS IS MY FAULT.
YOUR MAJESTY?!
WHAT HAPPENED TO THE PRINCESS?

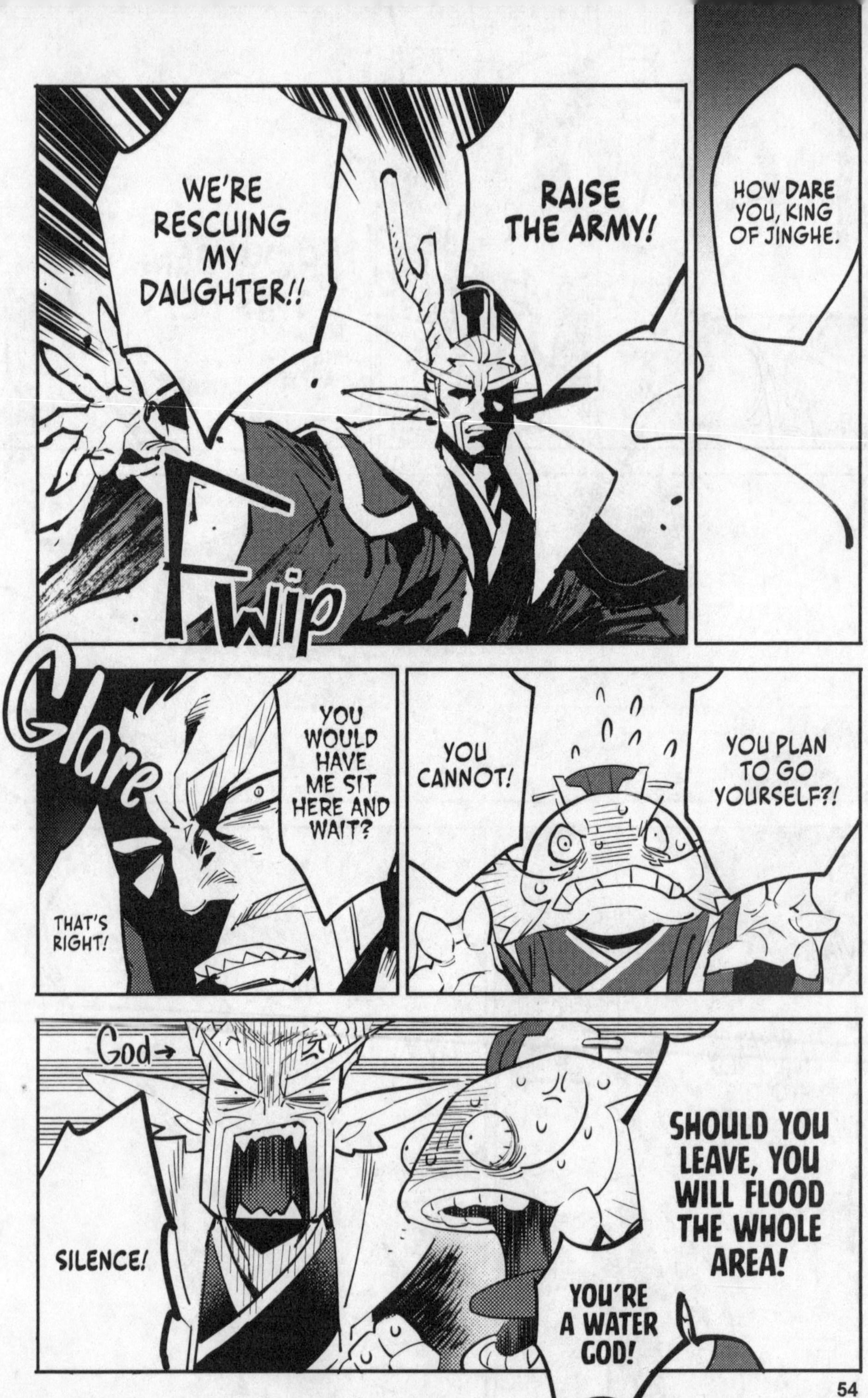
HOW DARE YOU, KING OF JINGHE.
RAISE THE ARMY!
WE'RE RESCUING MY DAUGHTER!!
Fwip
YOU PLAN TO GO YOURSELF?!
YOU CANNOT!
YOU WOULD HAVE ME SIT HERE AND WAIT?
THAT'S RIGHT!
Glare
SHOULD YOU LEAVE, YOU WILL FLOOD THE WHOLE AREA!
YOU'RE A WATER GOD!
SILENCE!
God→

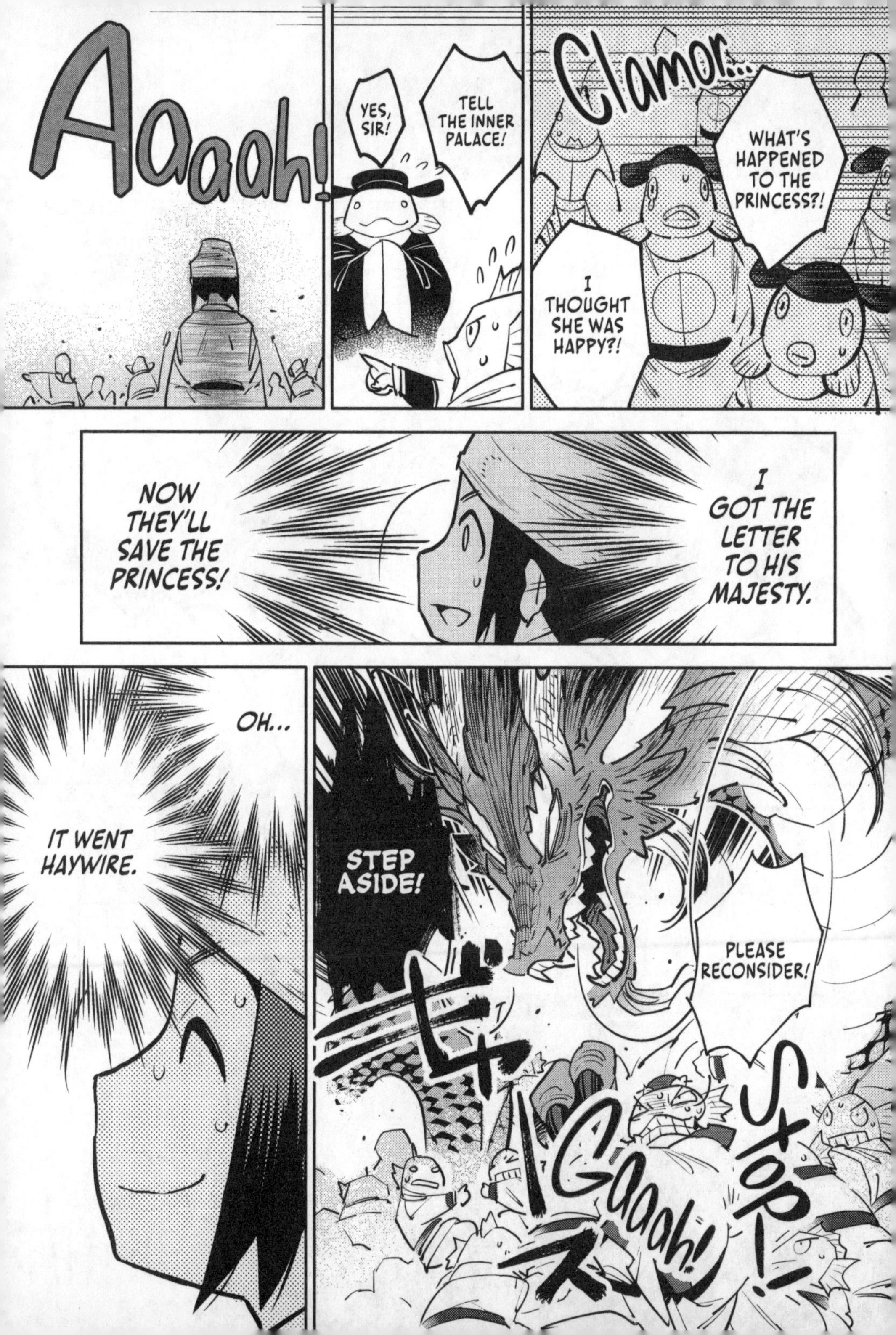
Clamor...
WHAT'S HAPPENED TO THE PRINCESS?!
I THOUGHT SHE WAS HAPPY?!
TELL THE INNER PALACE!
YES, SIR!
Aaaah!
I GOT THE LETTER TO HIS MAJESTY.
NOW THEY'LL SAVE THE PRINCESS!
PLEASE RECONSIDER!
STEP ASIDE!
Stop—!!
Gaaah!
OH...
IT WENT HAYWIRE.

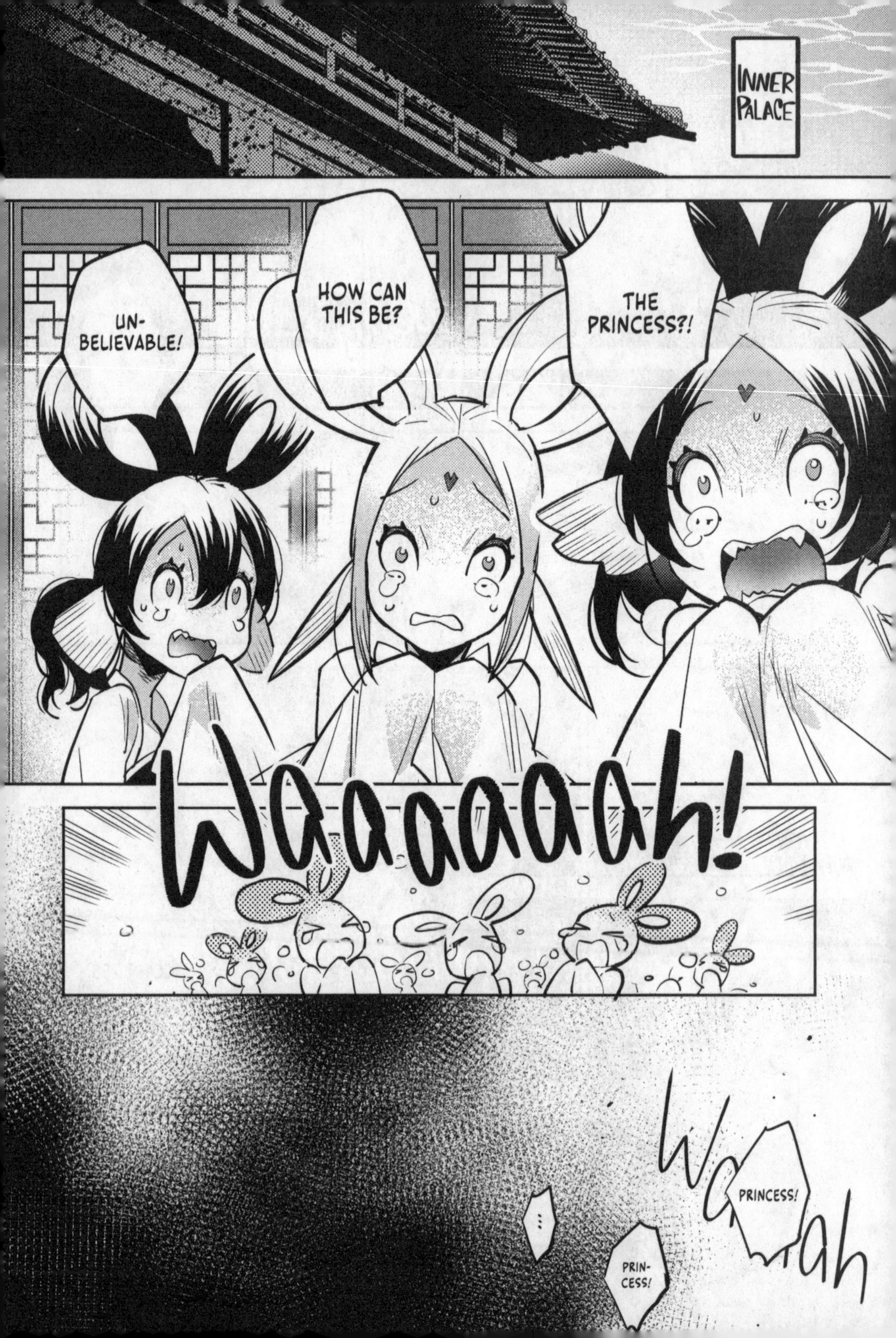
INNER PALACE
THE PRINCESS?!
HOW CAN THIS BE?
UN-BELIEVABLE!
Waaaaaah!
PRINCESS!
PRIN-CESS!
...

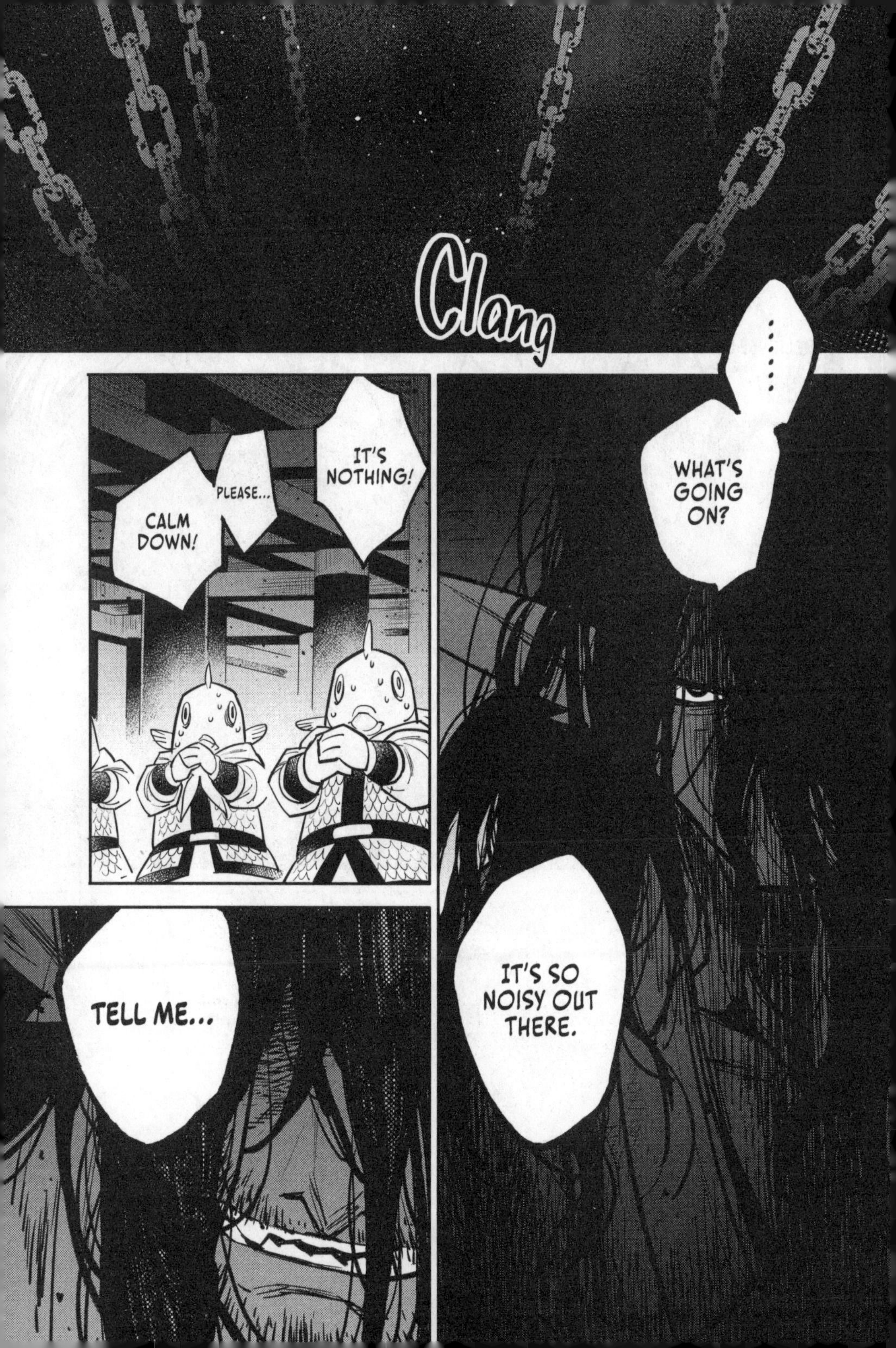
Clang
......
WHAT'S GOING ON?
IT'S SO NOISY OUT THERE.
IT'S NOTHING!
PLEASE...
CALM DOWN!
TELL ME...

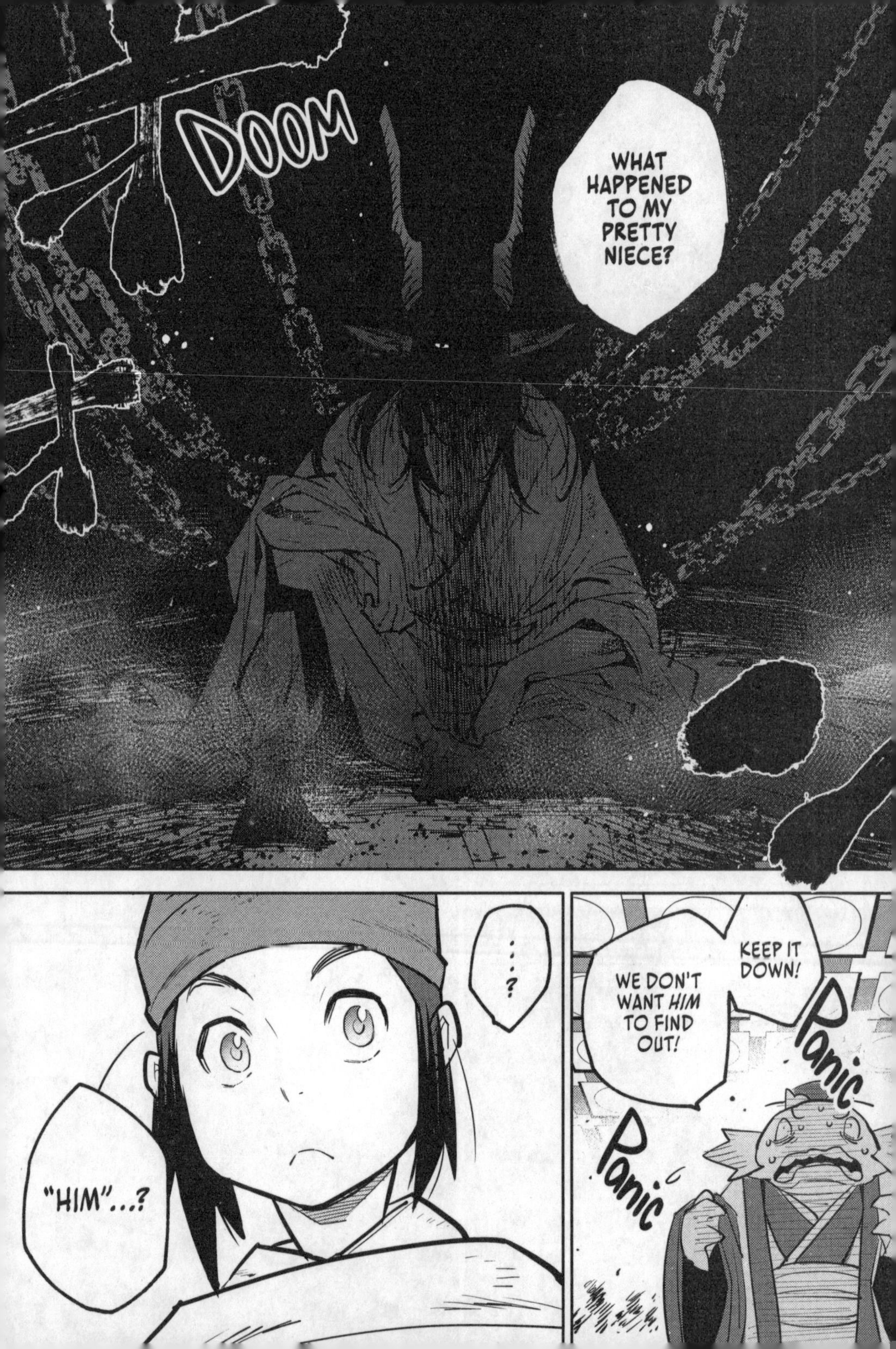
DOOM
WHAT HAPPENED TO MY PRETTY NIECE?
KEEP IT DOWN!
WE DON'T WANT *HIM* TO FIND OUT!
Panic
Panic
...?
"HIM"...?

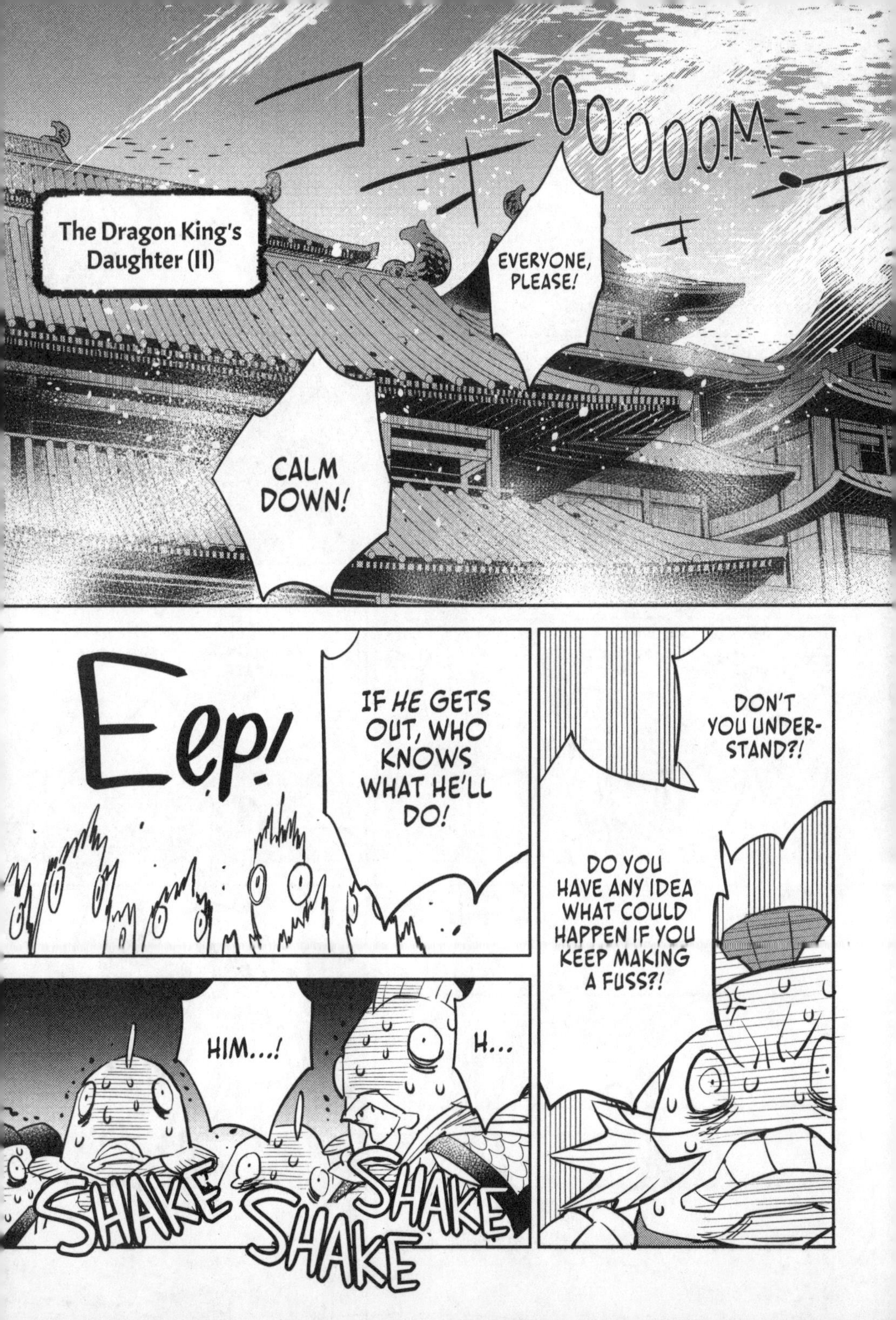

The Dragon King's Daughter (II)
DOOOOOM
EVERYONE, PLEASE!
CALM DOWN!
DON'T YOU UNDER-STAND?!
DO YOU HAVE ANY IDEA WHAT COULD HAPPEN IF YOU KEEP MAKING A FUSS?!
IF *HE* GETS OUT, WHO KNOWS WHAT HE'LL DO!
Eep!
H...
HIM...!
SHAKE
SHAKE
SHAKE

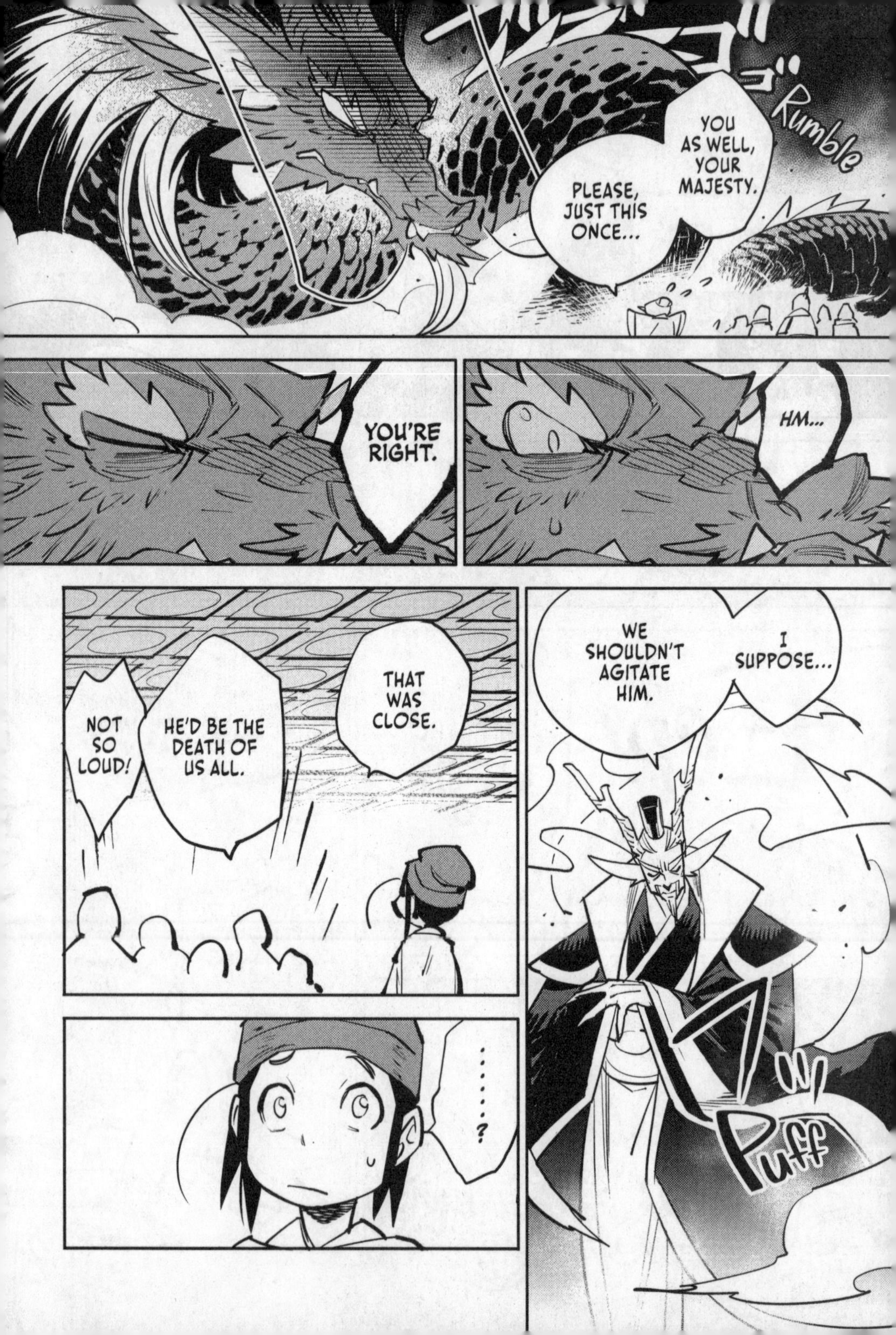
Rumble
YOU AS WELL, YOUR MAJESTY.
PLEASE, JUST THIS ONCE...
HM...
YOU'RE RIGHT.
I SUPPOSE...
WE SHOULDN'T AGITATE HIM.
Puff
THAT WAS CLOSE.
HE'D BE THE DEATH OF US ALL.
NOT SO LOUD!
......?

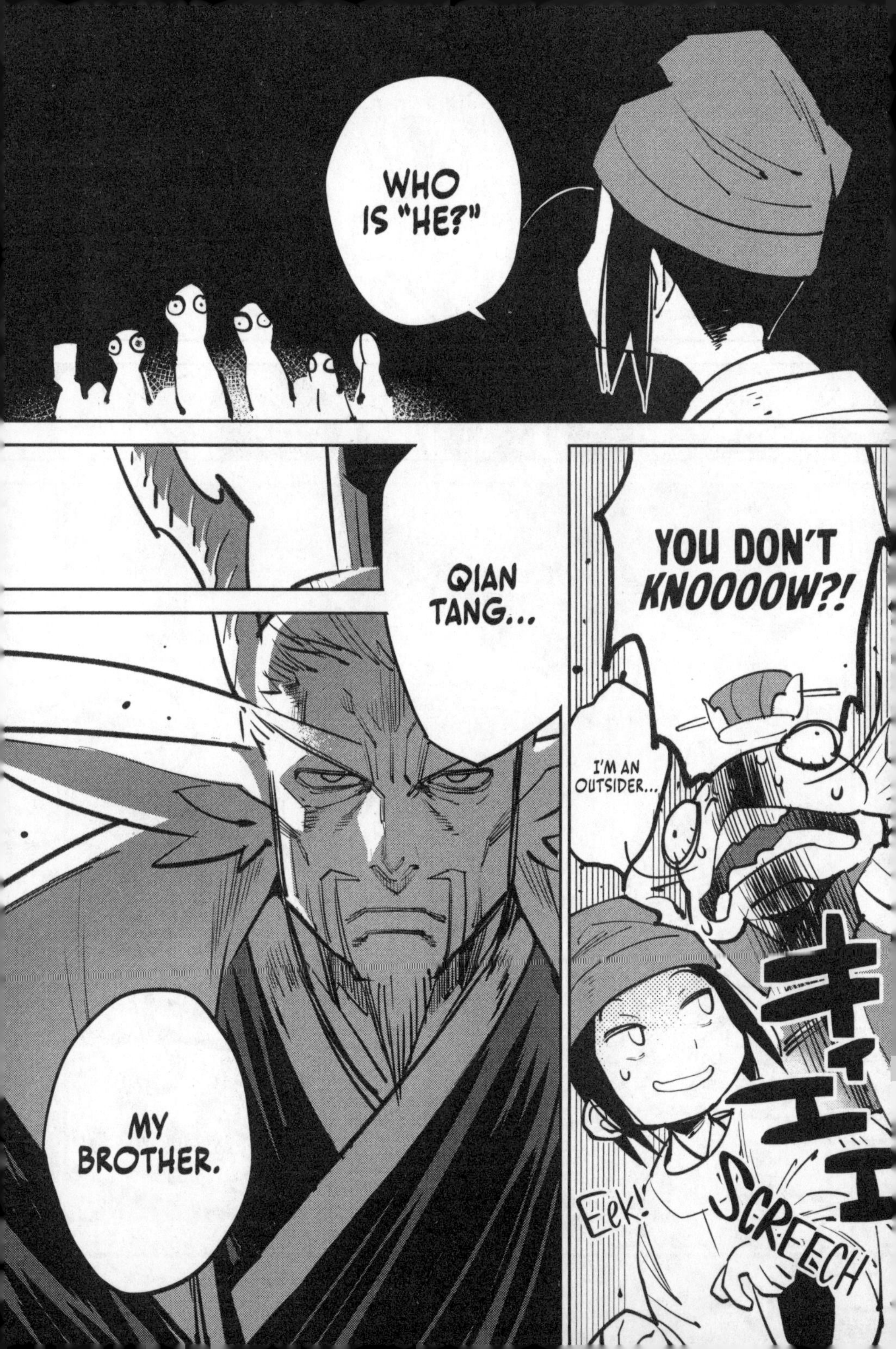
WHO IS "HE?"
YOU DON'T KNOOOOW?!
I'M AN OUTSIDER...
キィエエ
SCREECH
Eek!
QIAN TANG...
MY BROTHER.

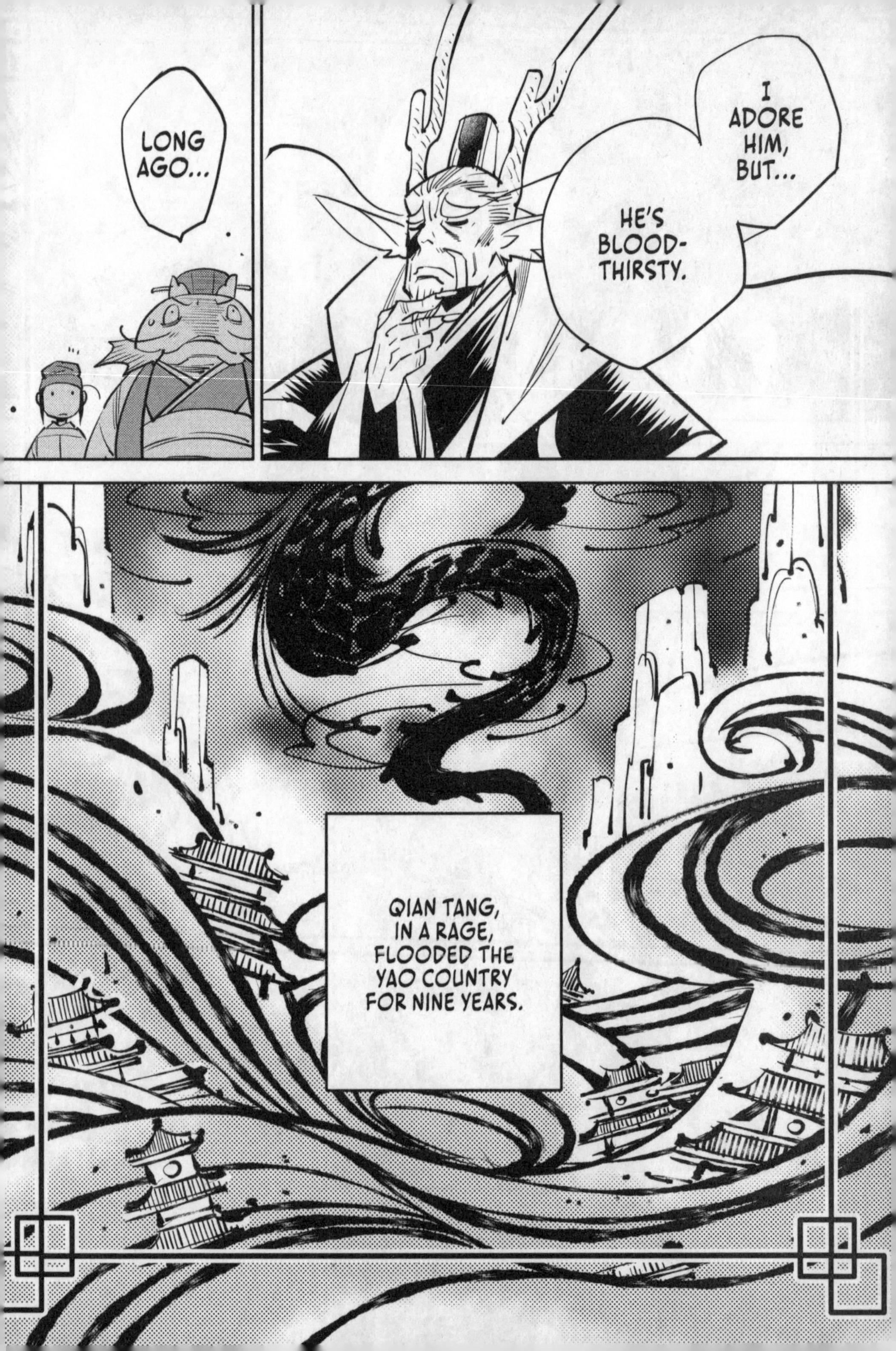
I ADORE HIM, BUT...
HE'S BLOOD-THIRSTY.
LONG AGO...
...
QIAN TANG, IN A RAGE, FLOODED THE YAO COUNTRY FOR NINE YEARS.

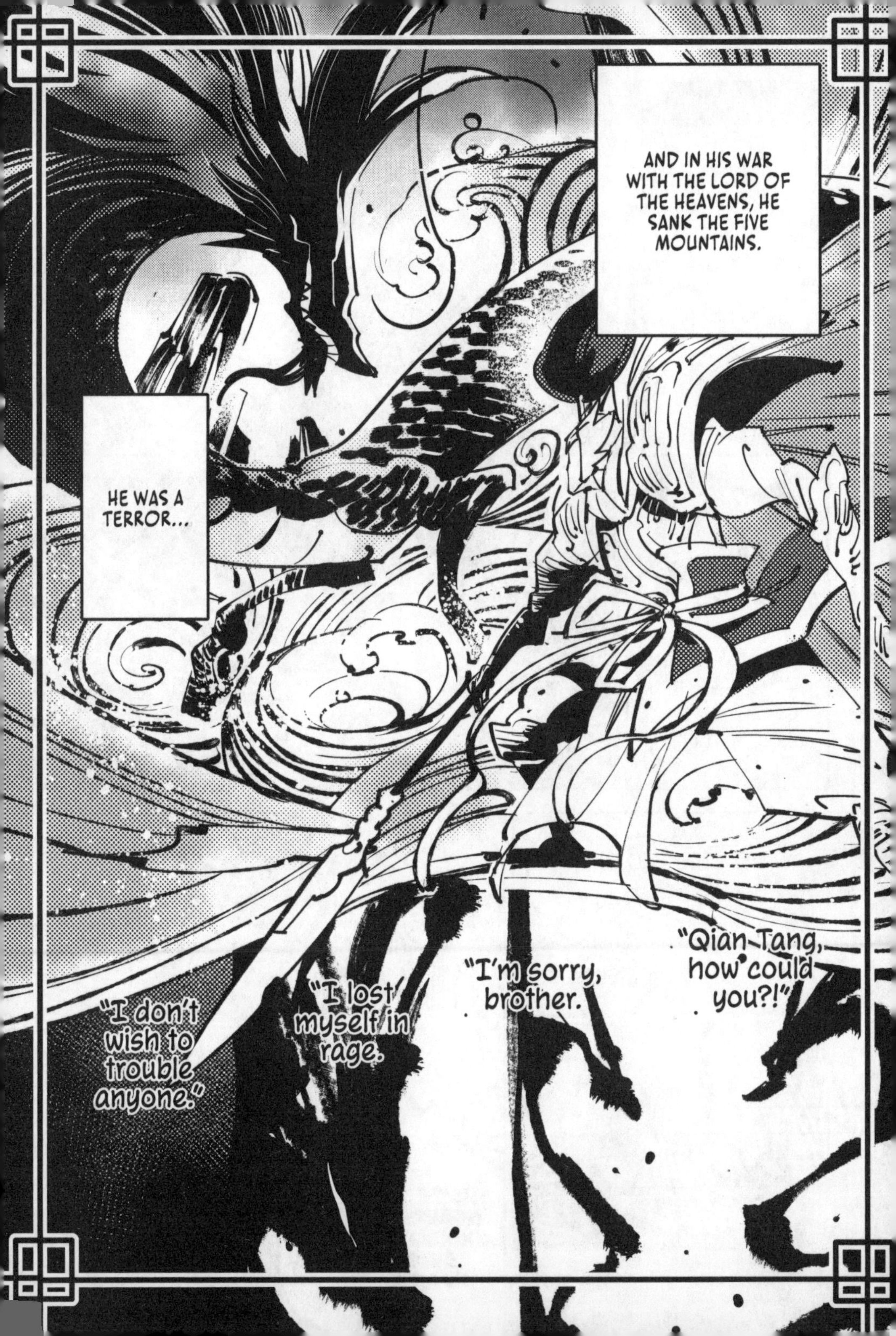
AND IN HIS WAR WITH THE LORD OF THE HEAVENS, HE SANK THE FIVE MOUNTAINS.
HE WAS A TERROR...
"Qian Tang, how could you?!"
"I'm sorry, brother.
"I lost myself in rage.
"I don't wish to trouble anyone."

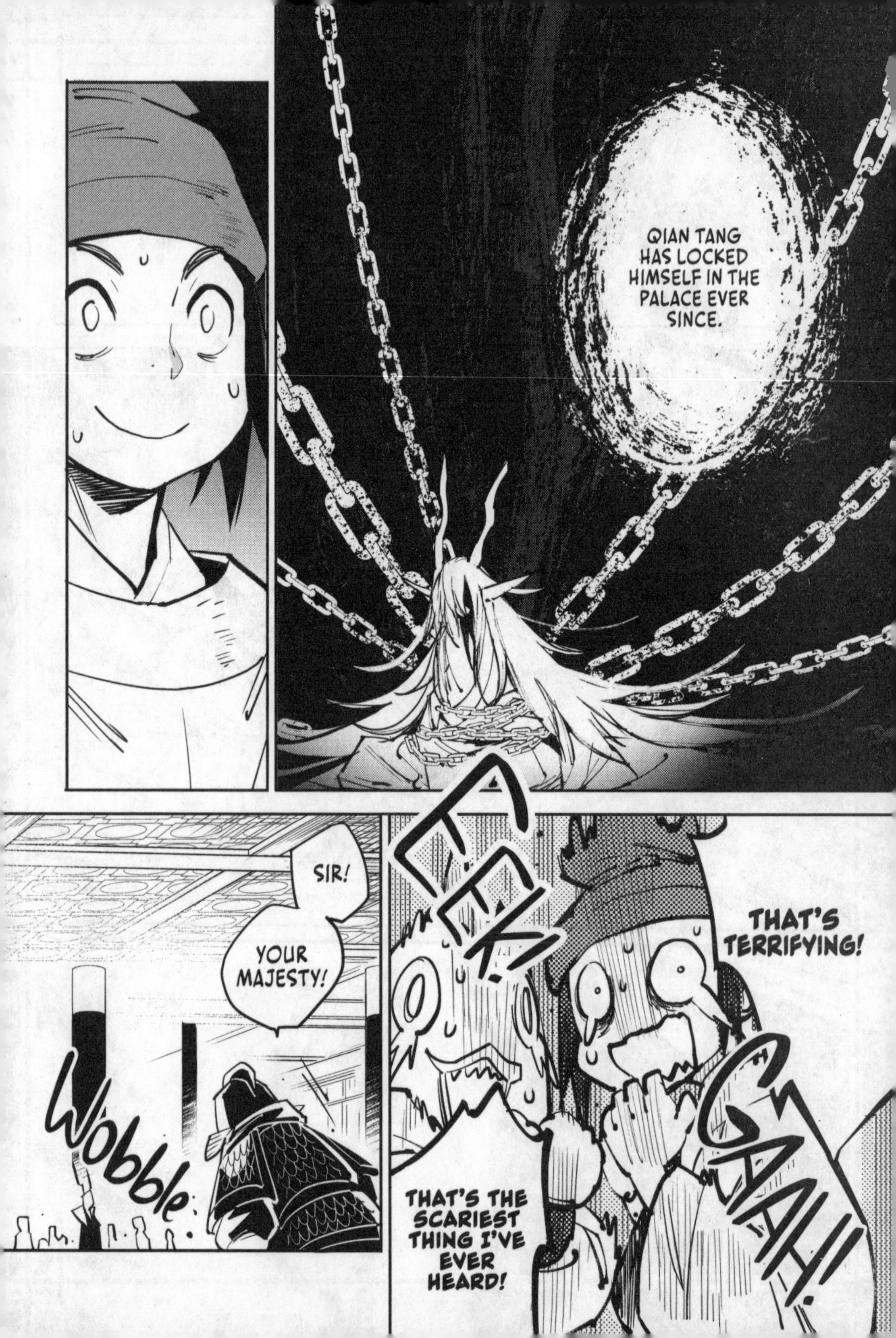
QIAN TANG HAS LOCKED HIMSELF IN THE PALACE EVER SINCE.
EEK!
THAT'S TERRIFYING!
GAAH!
THAT'S THE SCARIEST THING I'VE EVER HEARD!
SIR!
YOUR MAJESTY!
Wobble

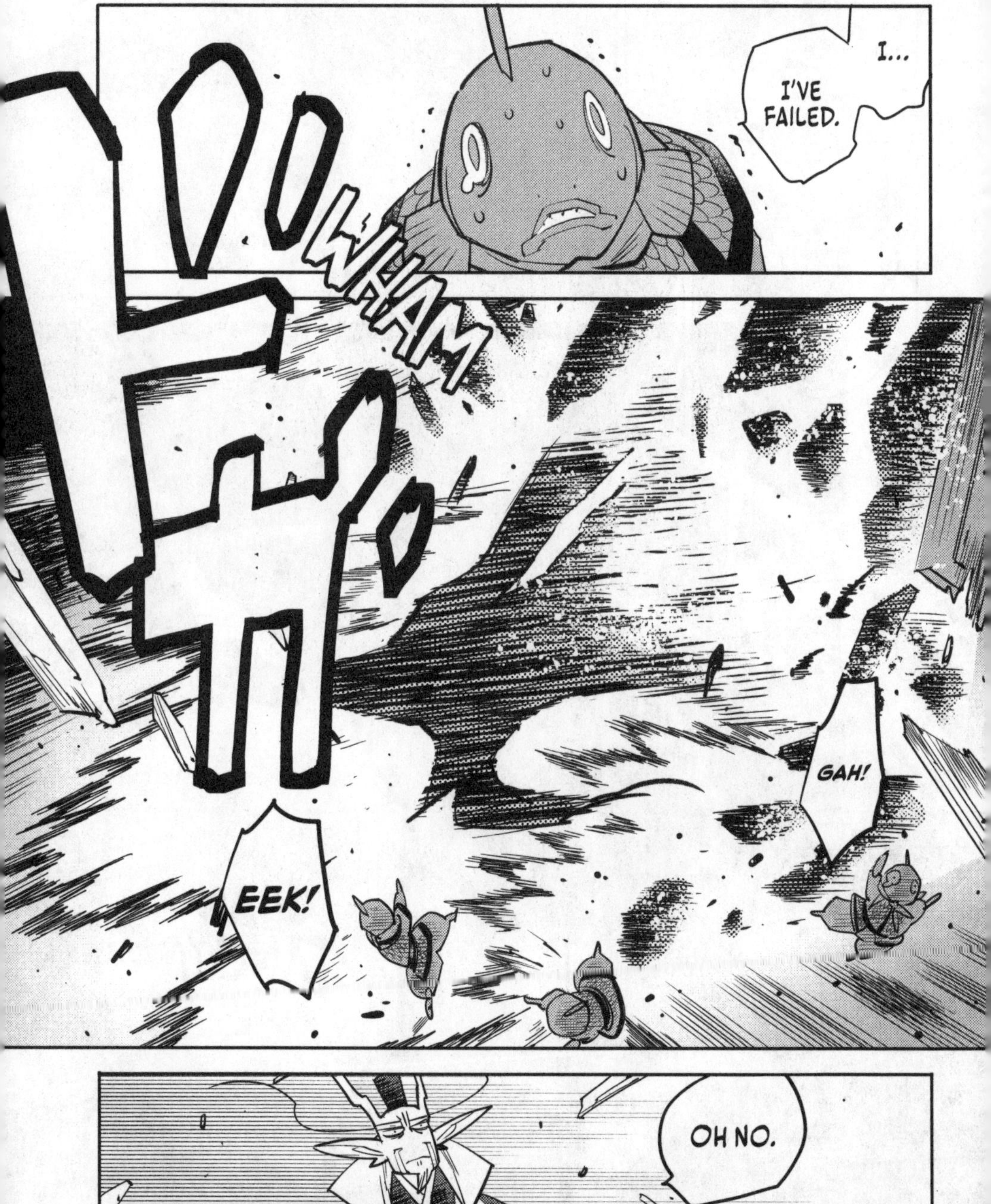
I...
I'VE FAILED.
WHAM
GAH!
EEK!
OH NO.

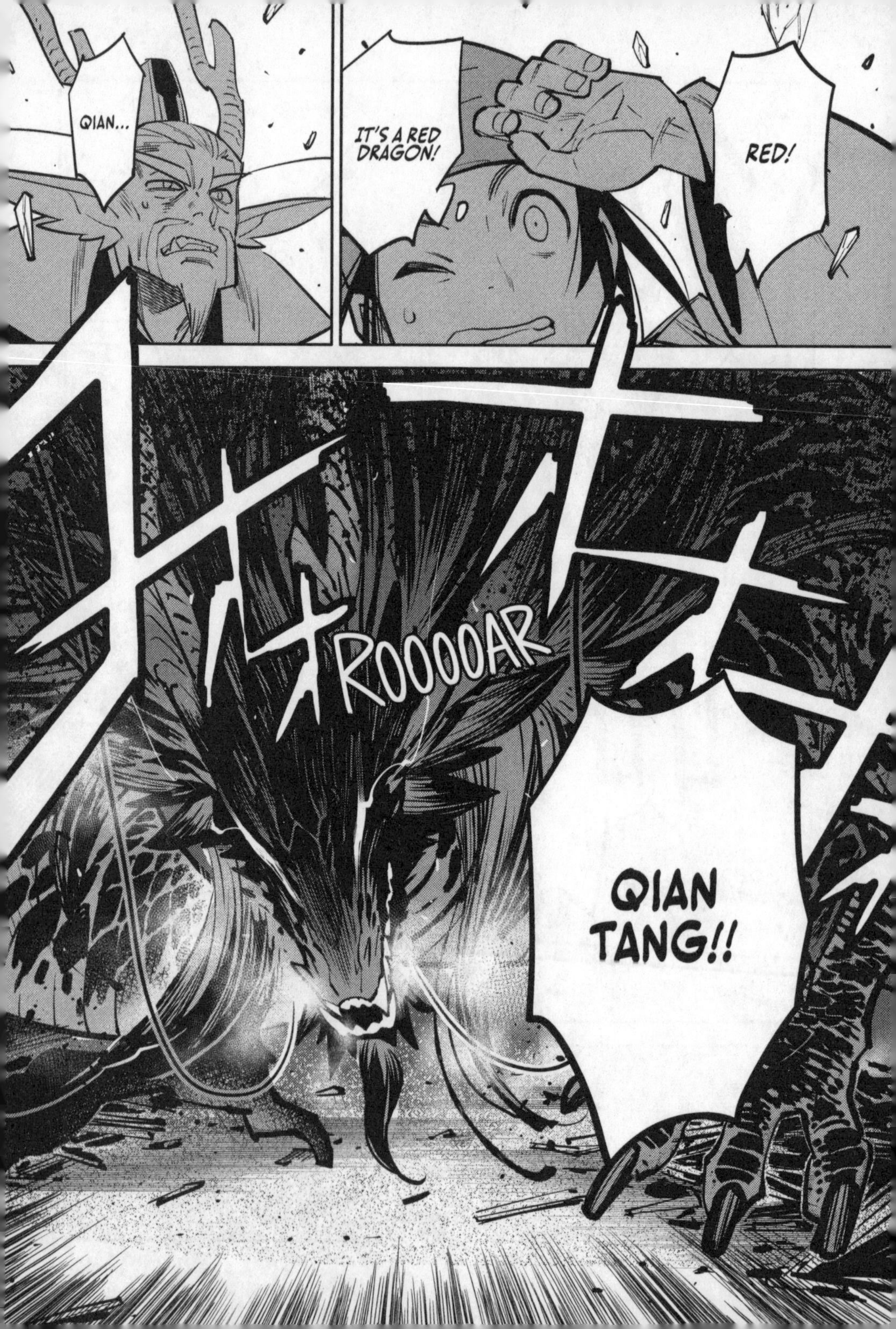
QIAN...
IT'S A RED DRAGON!
RED!
ROOOOAR
QIAN TANG!!

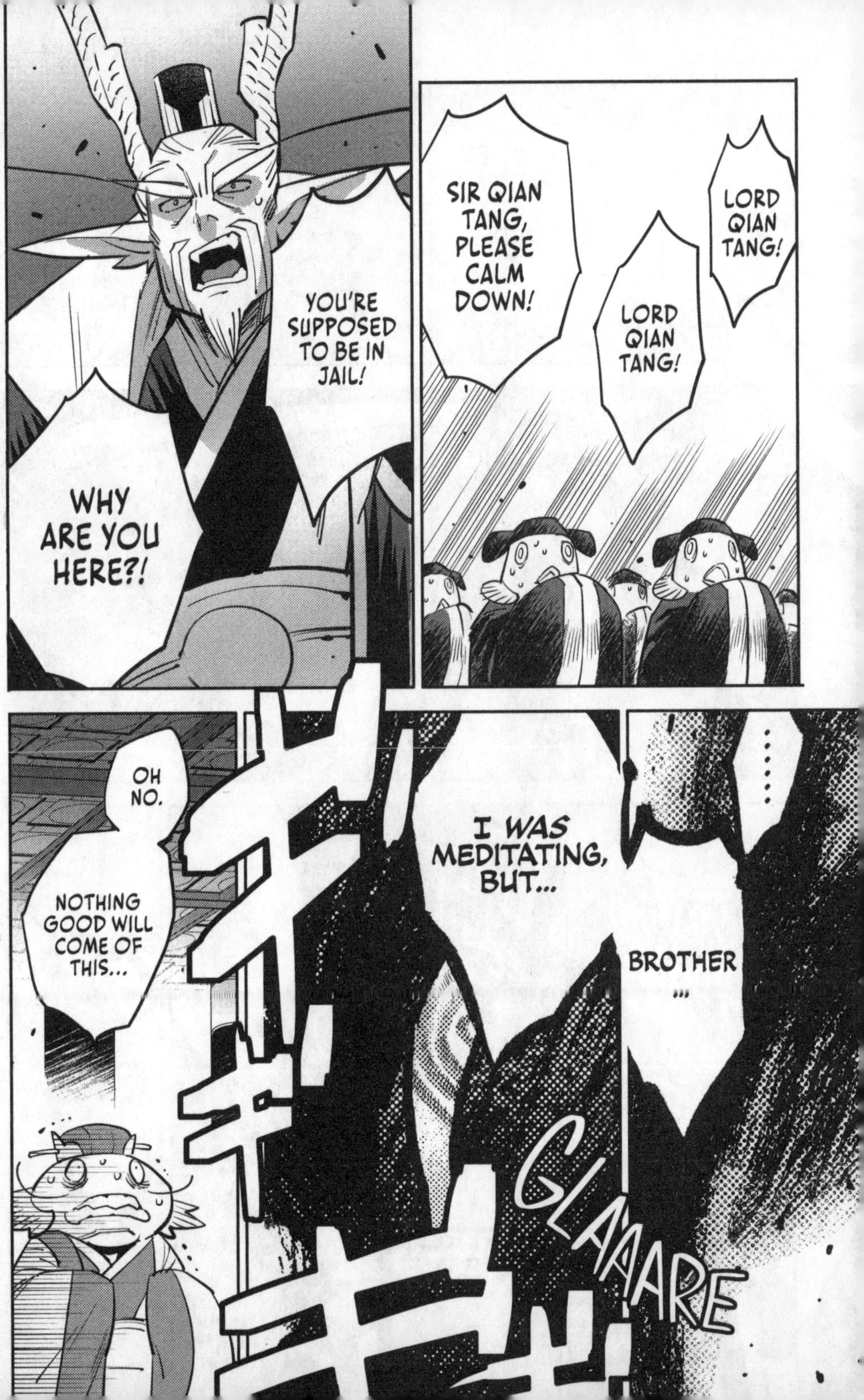

LORD QIAN TANG!
LORD QIAN TANG!
SIR QIAN TANG, PLEASE CALM DOWN!
YOU'RE SUPPOSED TO BE IN JAIL!
WHY ARE YOU HERE?!
......
I *WAS* MEDITATING, BUT...
BROTHER...
GLAAARE
OH NO.
NOTHING GOOD WILL COME OF THIS...

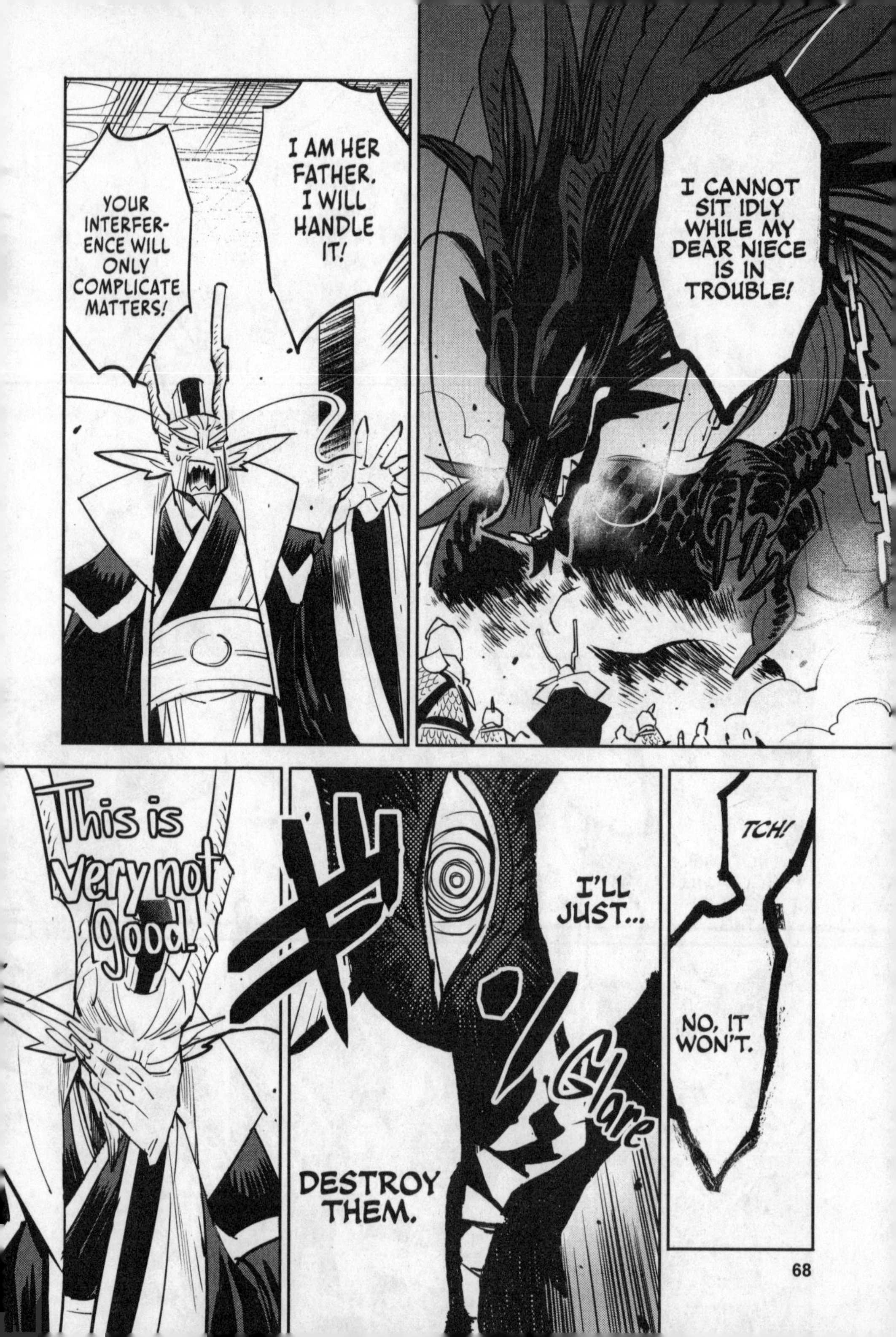

I CANNOT SIT IDLY WHILE MY DEAR NIECE IS IN TROUBLE!
I AM HER FATHER. I WILL HANDLE IT!
YOUR INTERFERENCE WILL ONLY COMPLICATE MATTERS!
TCH!
NO, IT WON'T.
I'LL JUST...
Glare
DESTROY THEM.
This is very not good.

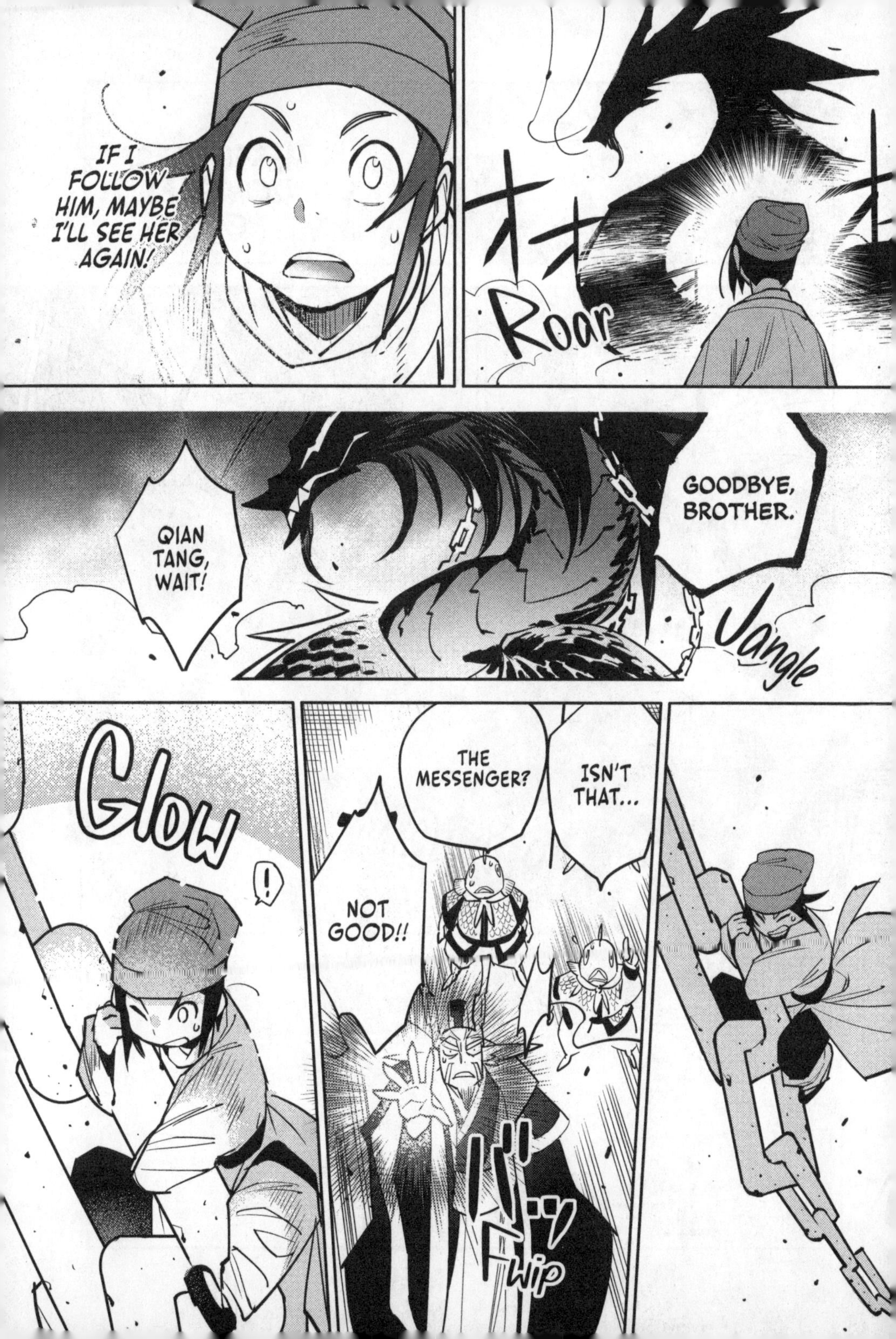
Roar
IF I FOLLOW HIM, MAYBE I'LL SEE HER AGAIN!
GOODBYE, BROTHER.
Jangle
QIAN TANG, WAIT!
ISN'T THAT...
THE MESSENGER?
NOT GOOD!!
Whip
Glow
!

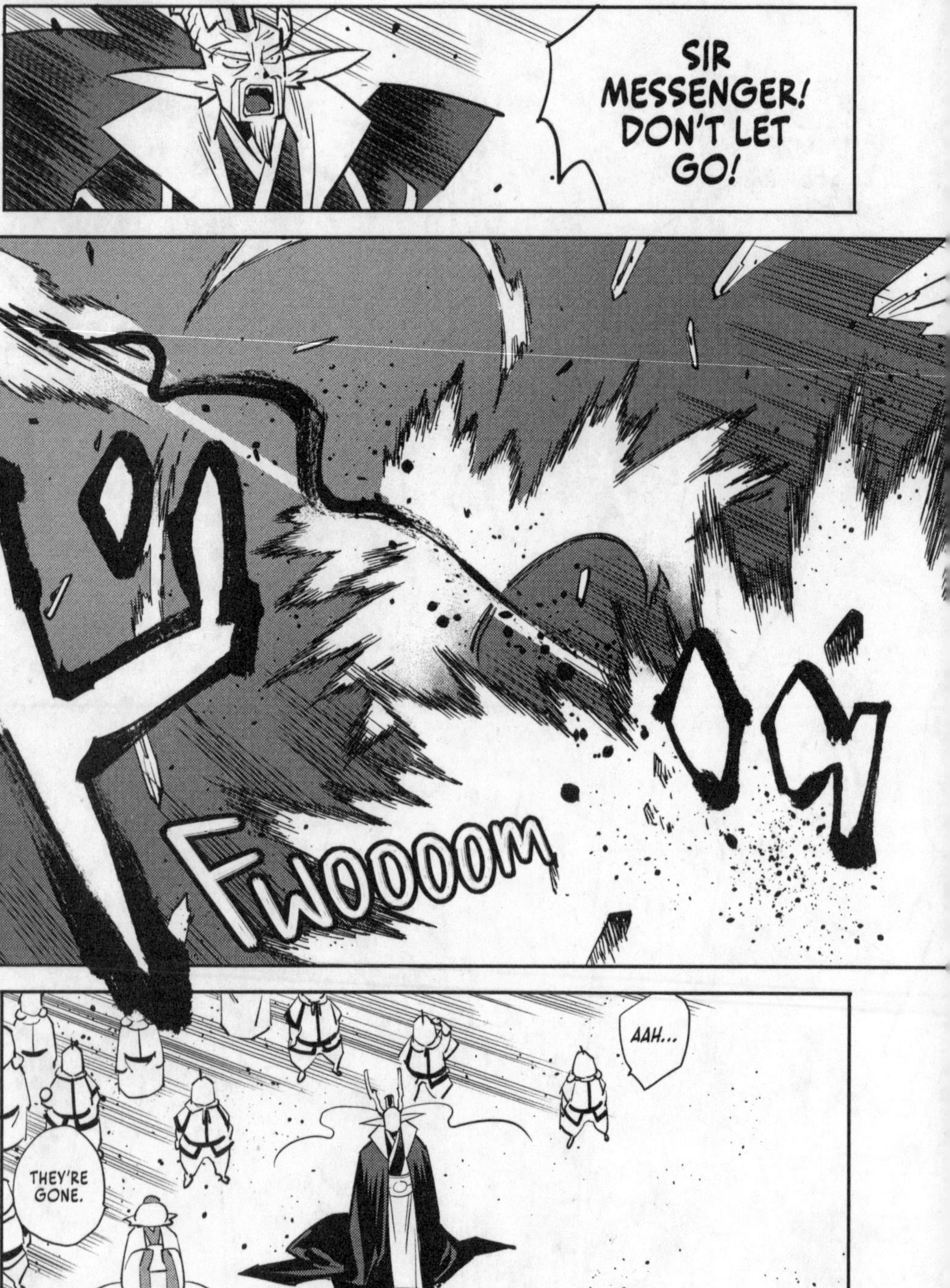
SIR MESSENGER! DON'T LET GO!
FWOOOOM
AAH...
THEY'RE GONE.

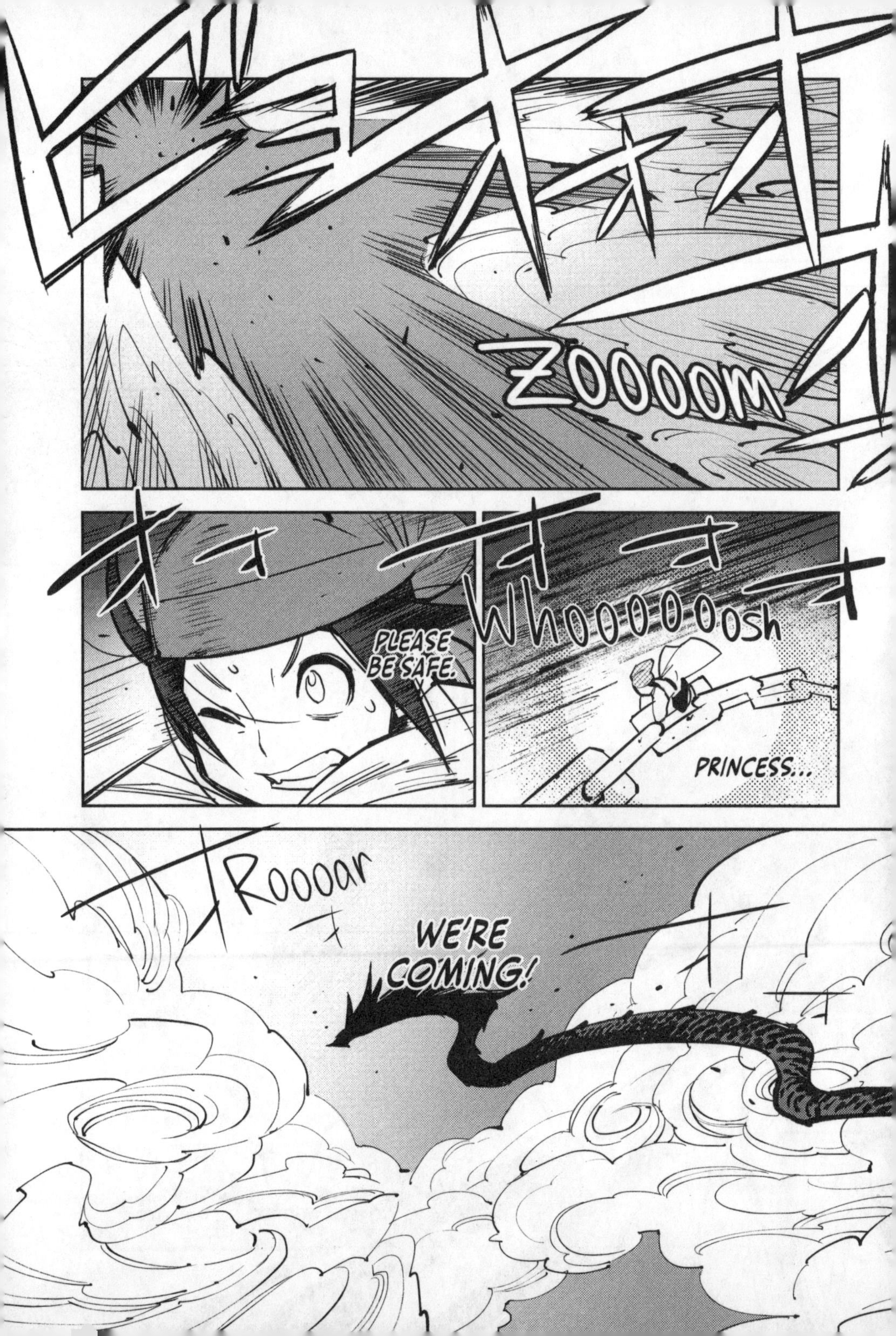
ZOOOOM
Whoooooosh
PRINCESS...
PLEASE BE SAFE.
Roooar
WE'RE COMING!

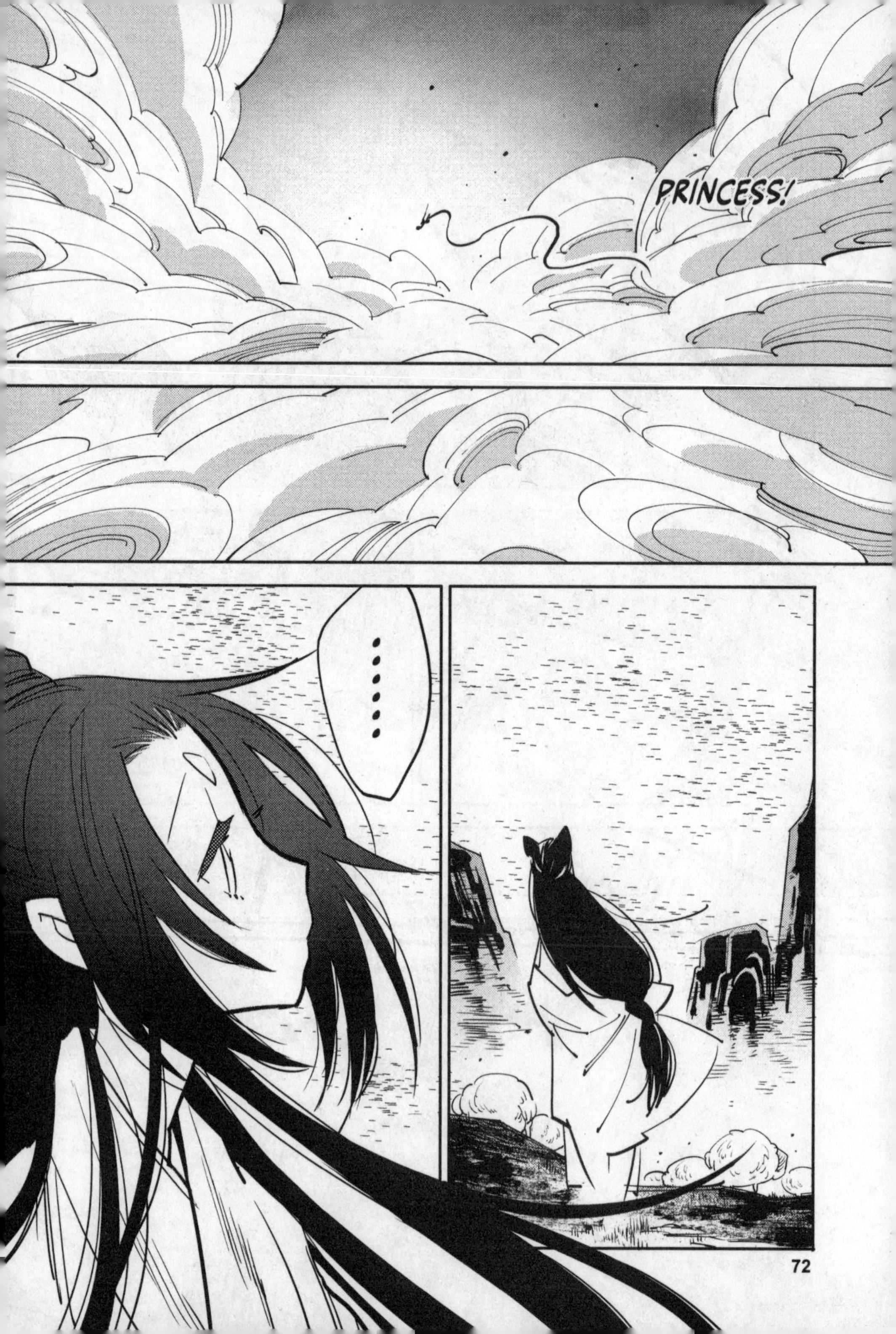
PRINCESS!
......

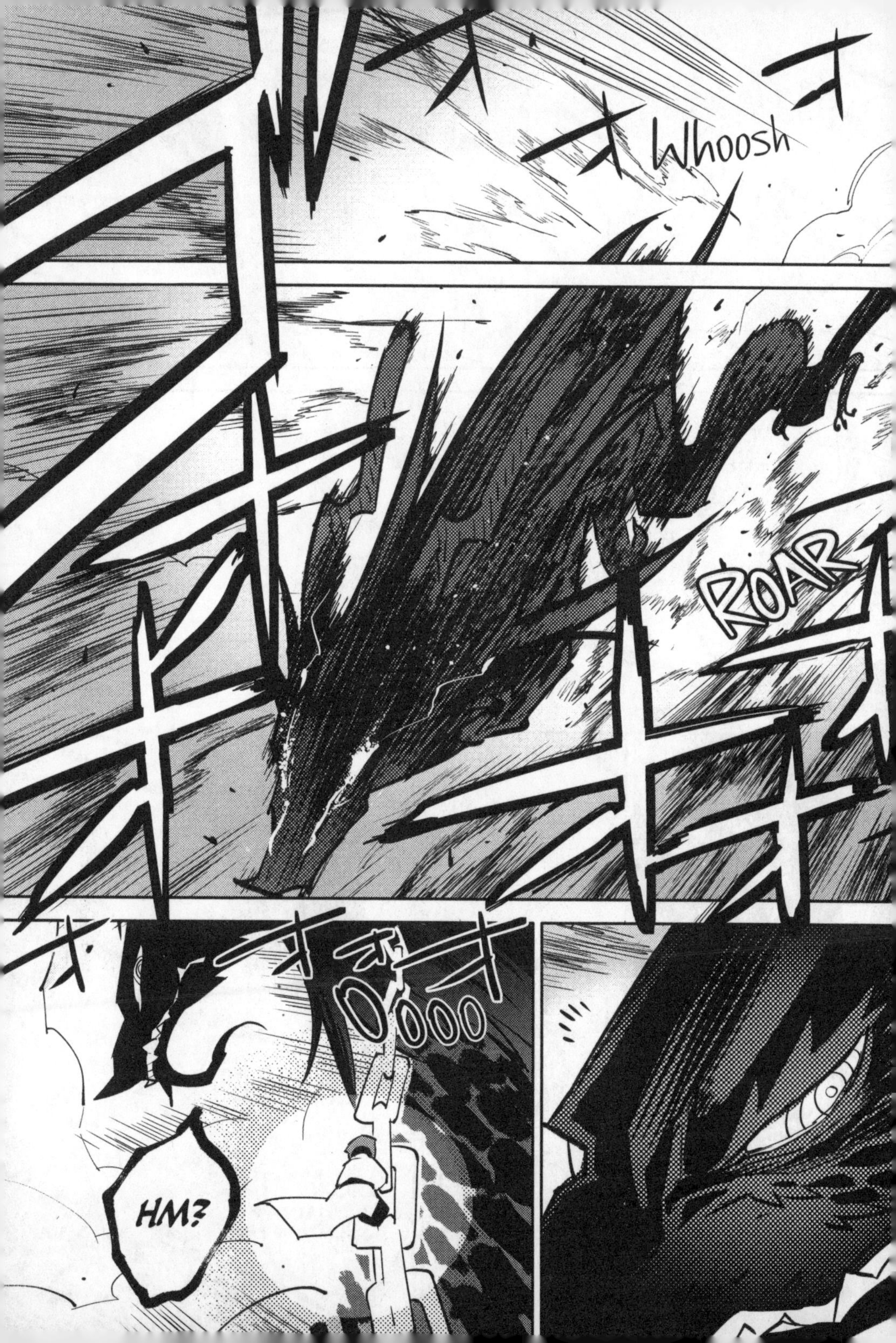
Whoosh
ROAR
OOOO
HM?

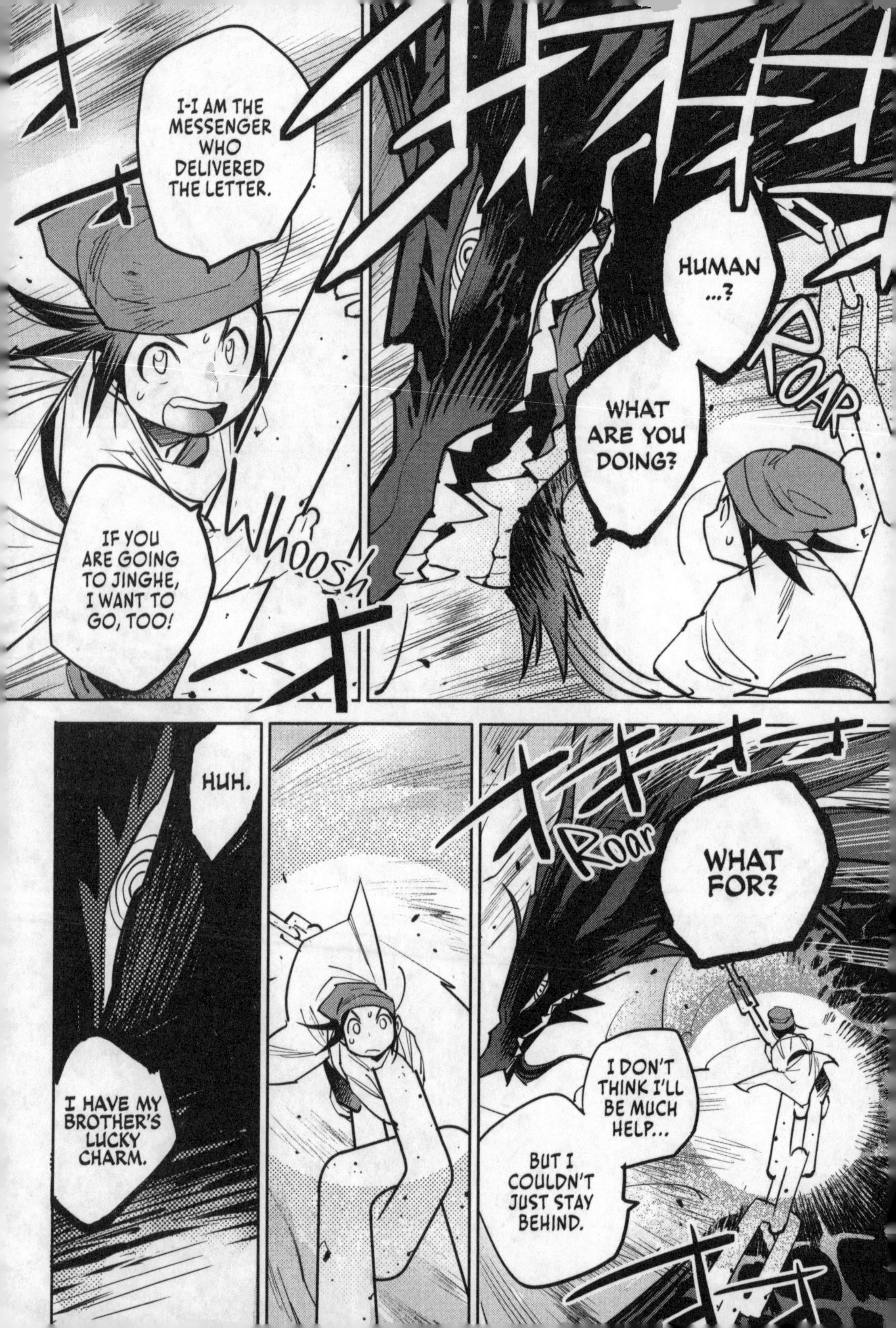
HUMAN ...?
WHAT ARE YOU DOING?
ROAR
I-I AM THE MESSENGER WHO DELIVERED THE LETTER.
IF YOU ARE GOING TO JINGHE, I WANT TO GO, TOO!
Whoosh
WHAT FOR?
Roar
I DON'T THINK I'LL BE MUCH HELP...
BUT I COULDN'T JUST STAY BEHIND.
HUH.
I HAVE MY BROTHER'S LUCKY CHARM.

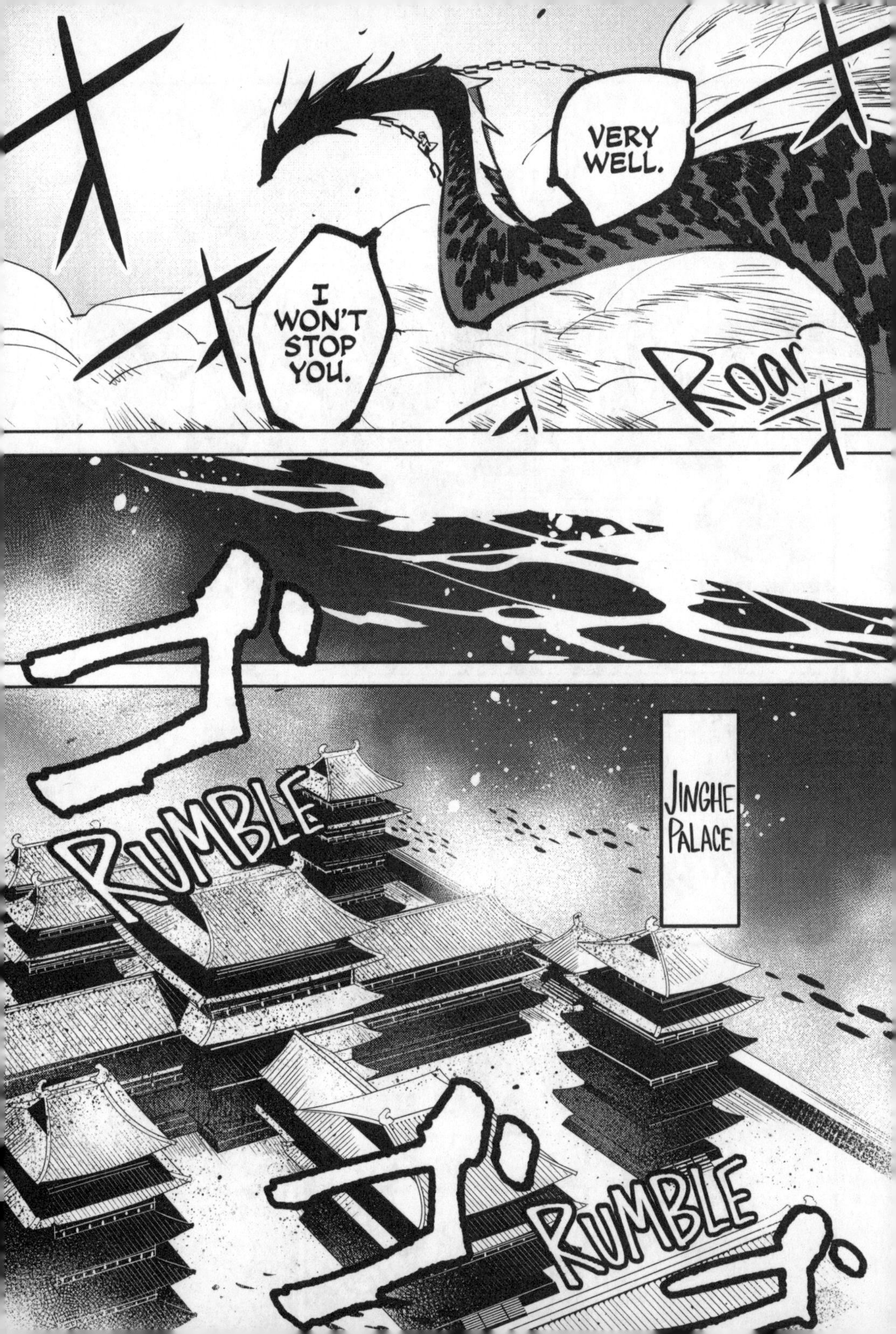
VERY WELL.
I WON'T STOP YOU.
Roar
JINGHE PALACE
RUMBLE
RUMBLE

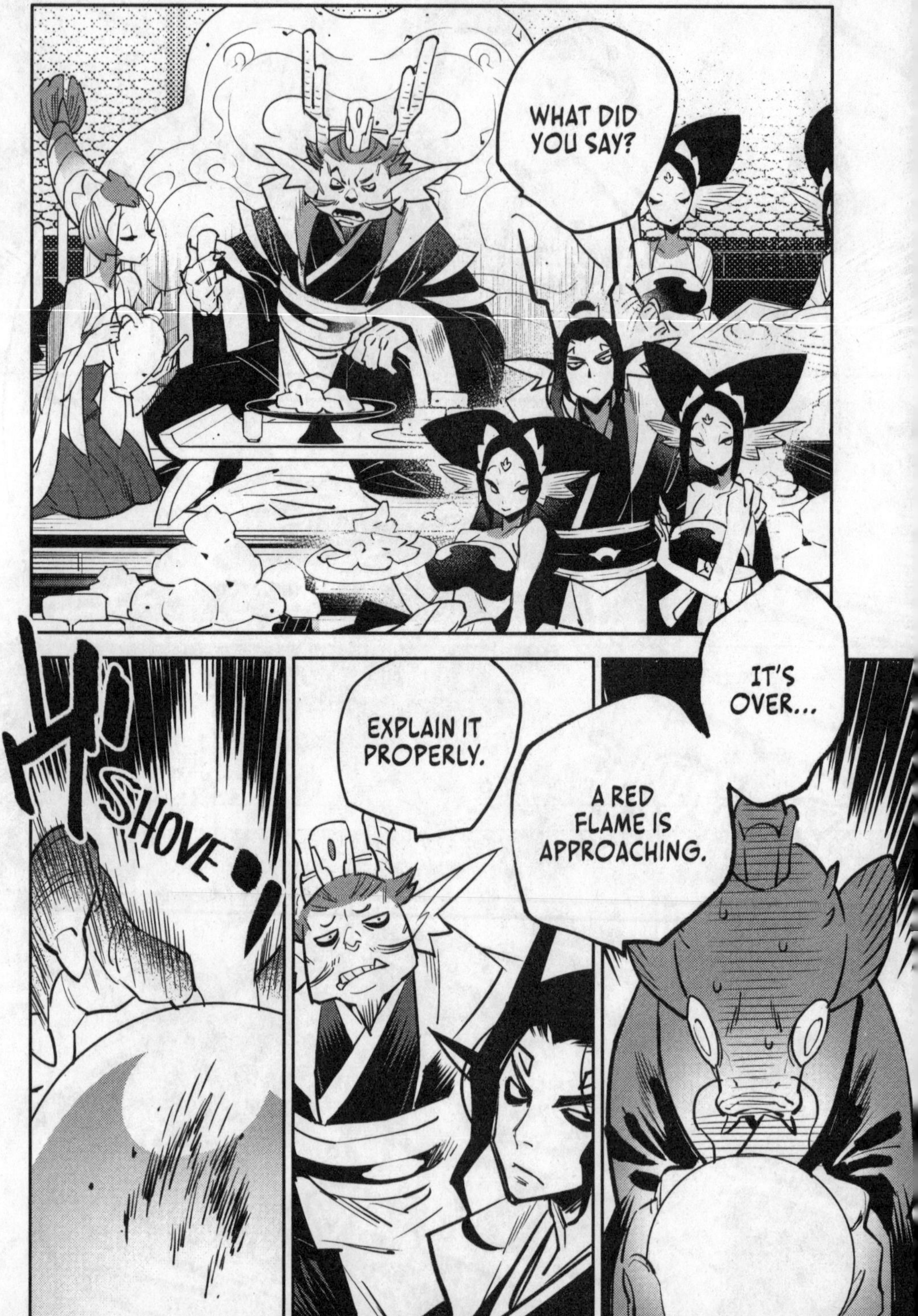
WHAT DID YOU SAY?
IT'S OVER...
A RED FLAME IS APPROACHING.
EXPLAIN IT PROPERLY.
SHOVE

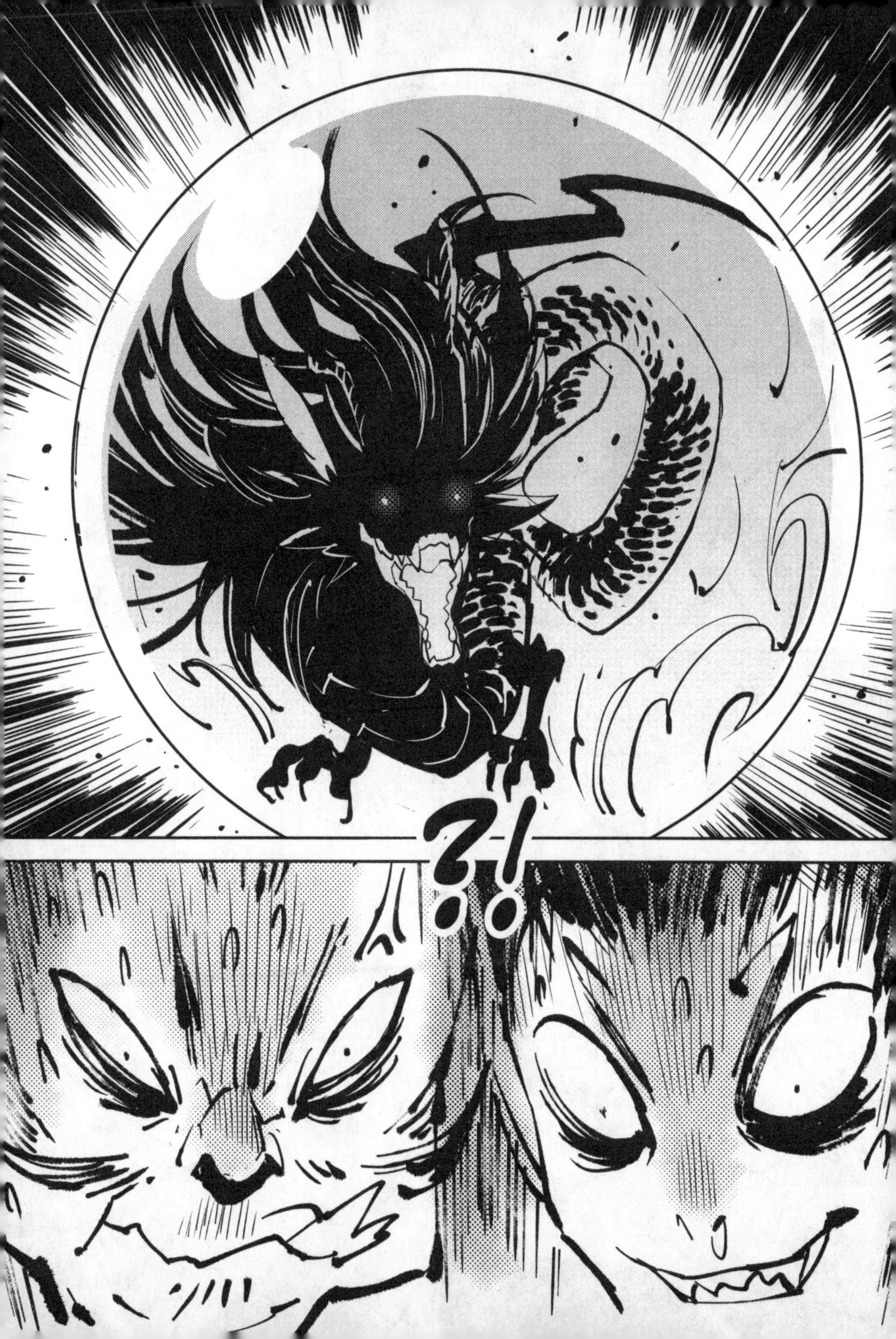
?!

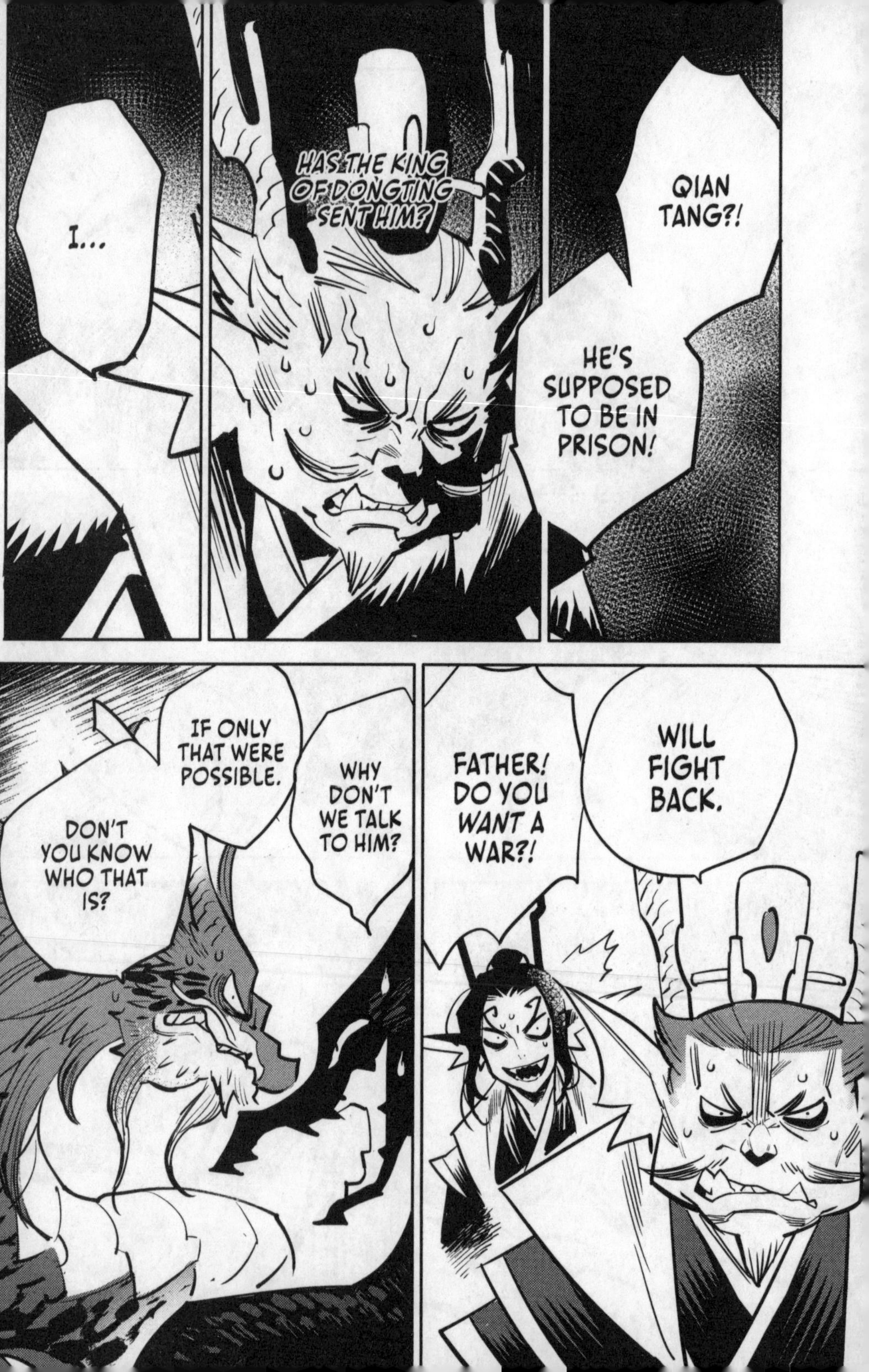
I...
HAS THE KING OF DONGTING SENT HIM?
QIAN TANG?!
HE'S SUPPOSED TO BE IN PRISON!
WHY DON'T WE TALK TO HIM?
IF ONLY THAT WERE POSSIBLE.
DON'T YOU KNOW WHO THAT IS?
FATHER! DO YOU WANT A WAR?!
WILL FIGHT BACK.

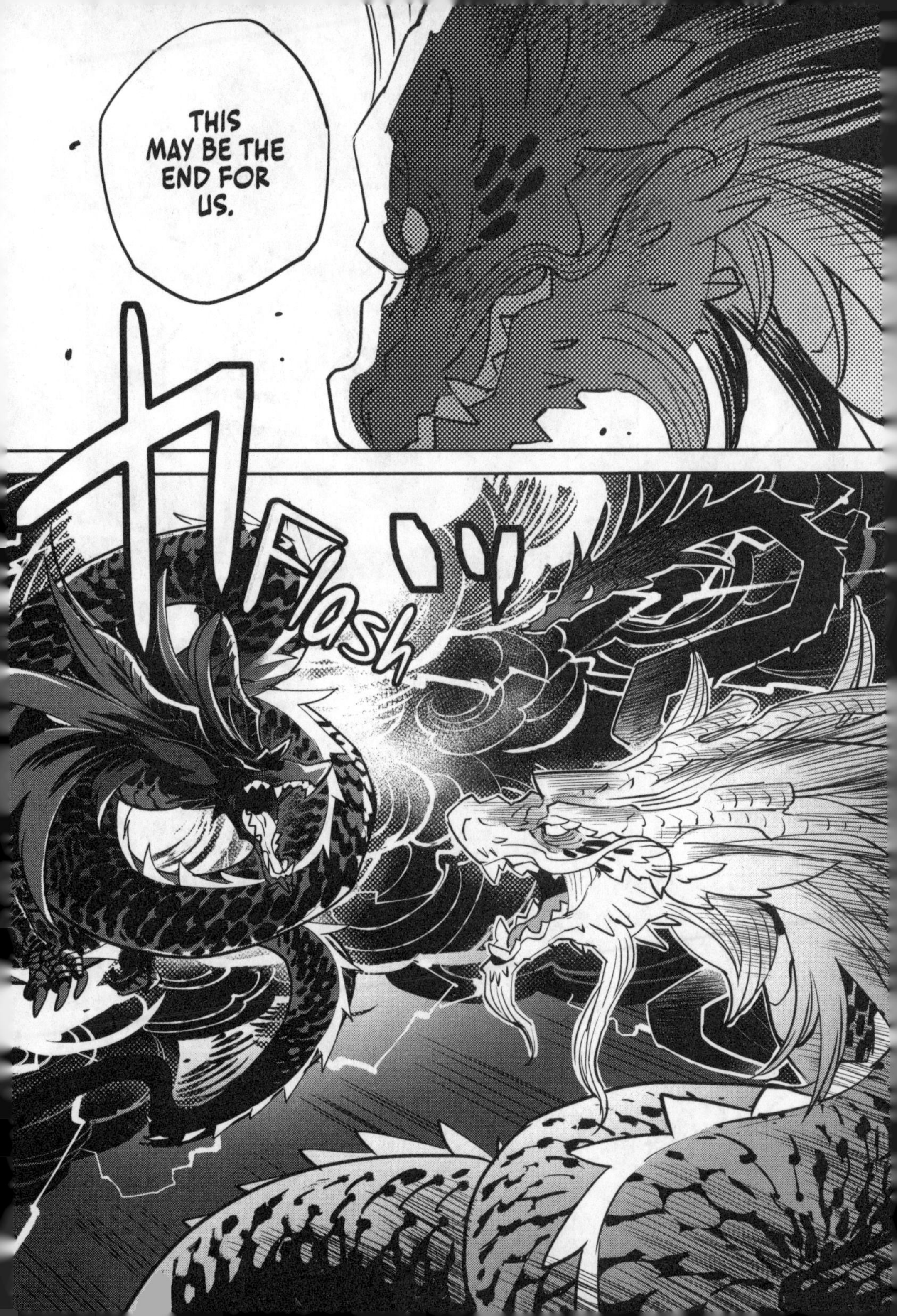
THIS MAY BE THE END FOR US.
Flash

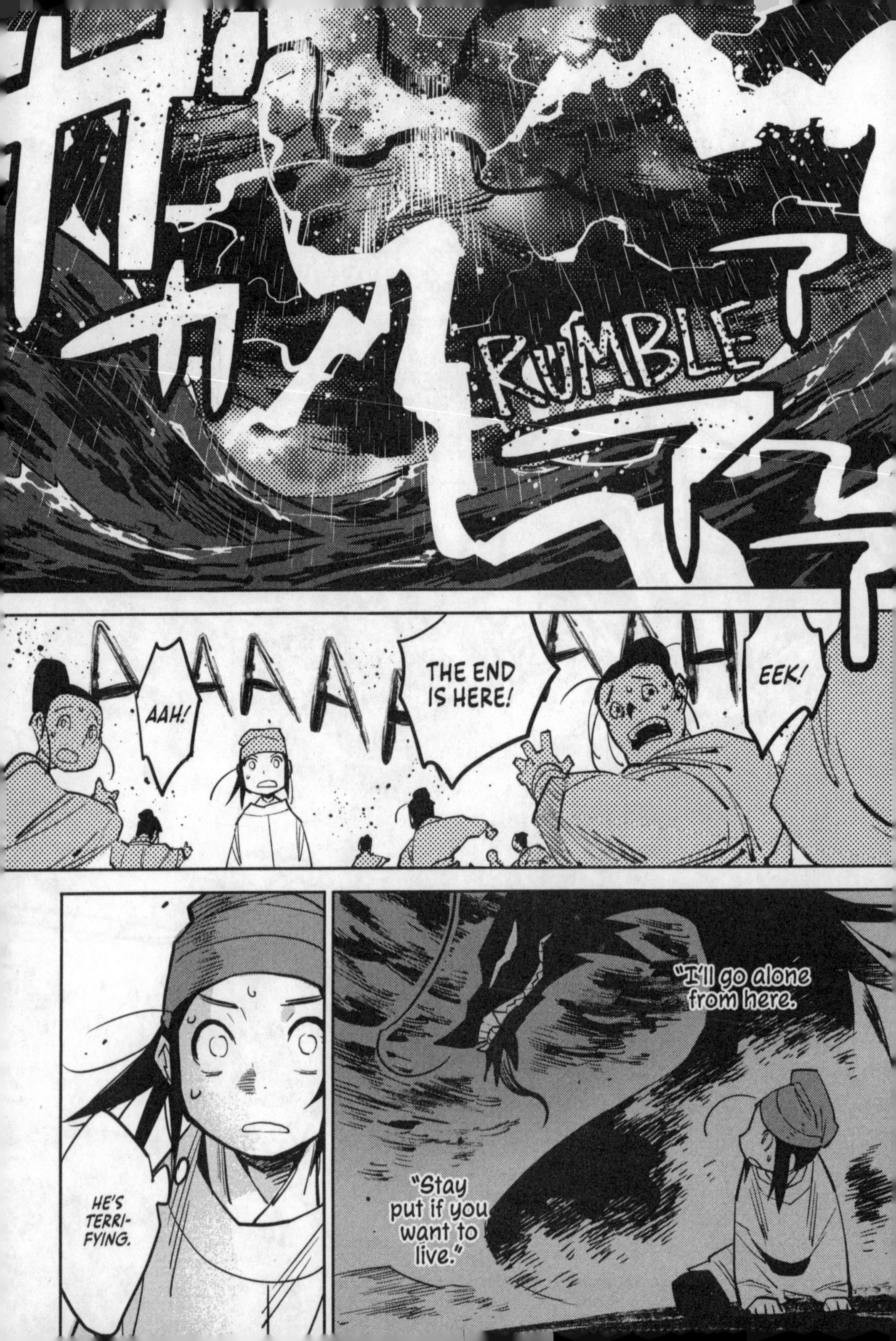

RUMBLE
AAAAAAAH
EEK!
THE END IS HERE!
AAH!
"I'll go alone from here.
"Stay put if you want to live."
HE'S TERRI-FYING.

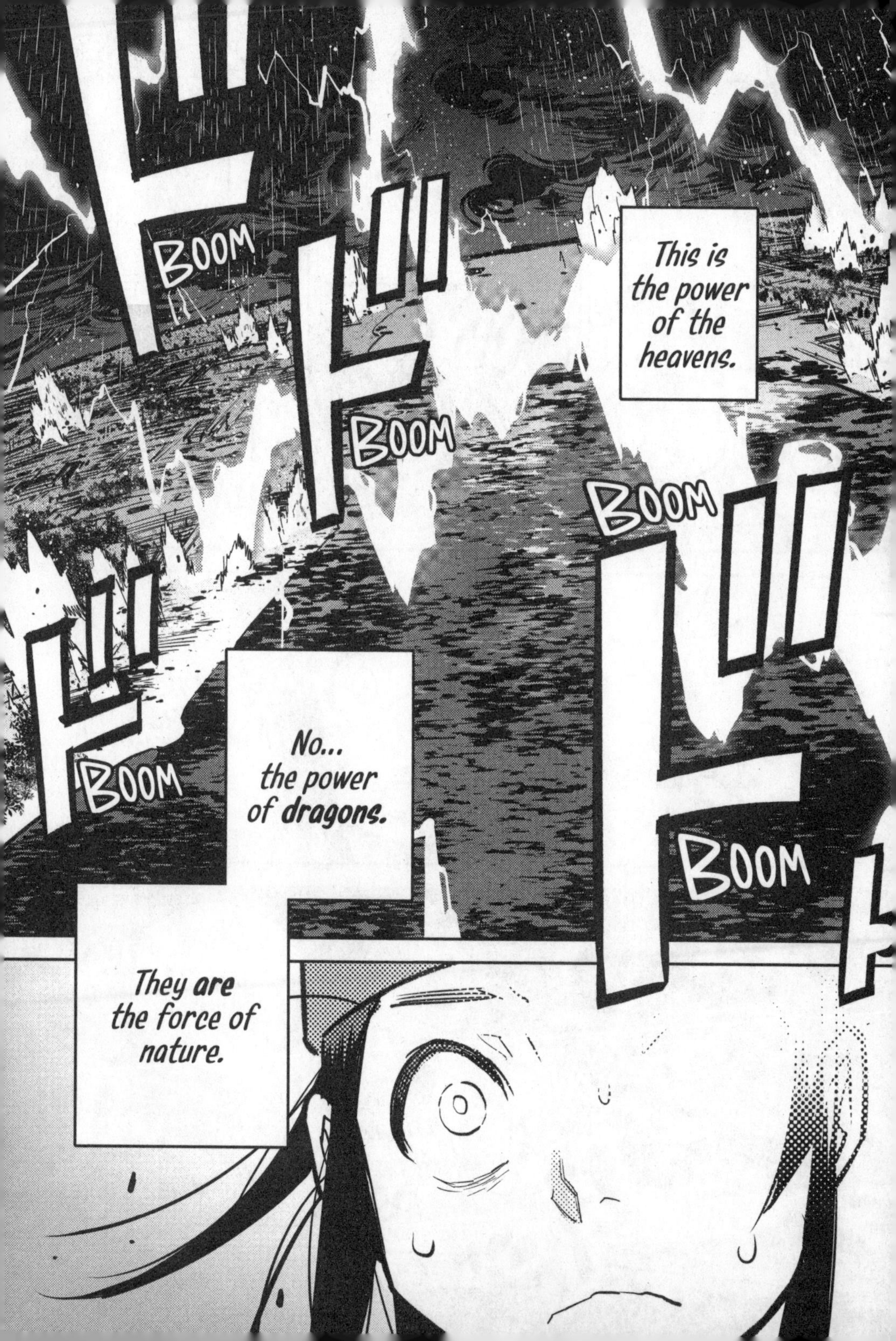
This is the power of the heavens.
BOOM
BOOM
BOOM
BOOM
BOOM
No... the power of **dragons.**
They **are** the force of nature.

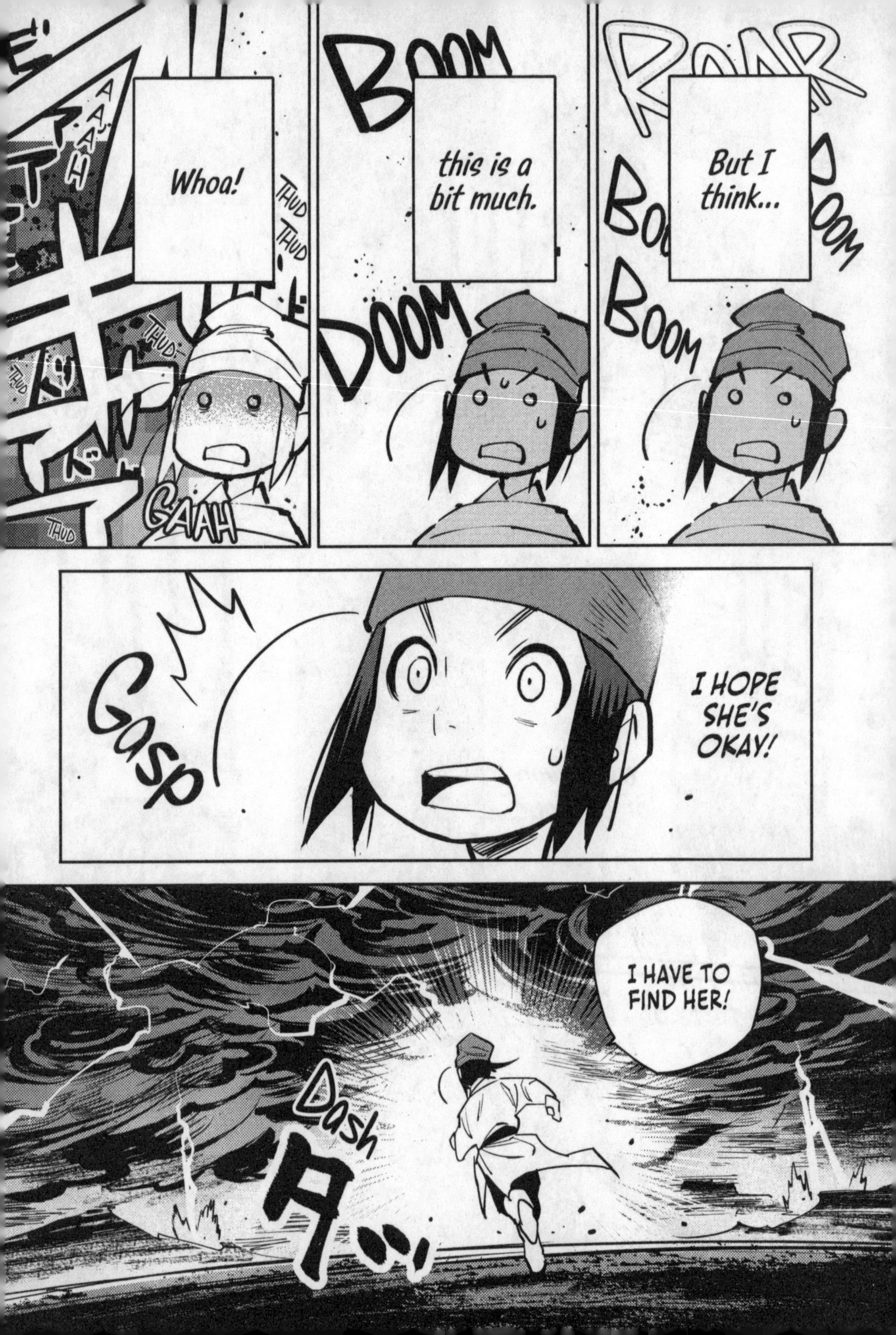
ROAR
BOOM
BOOM
BOOM
But I think...
BOOM
DOOM
this is a bit much.
AAAAH
THUD THUD
THUD
THUD
GAAH
THUD
Whoa!
Gasp
I HOPE SHE'S OKAY!
I HAVE TO FIND HER!
Dash

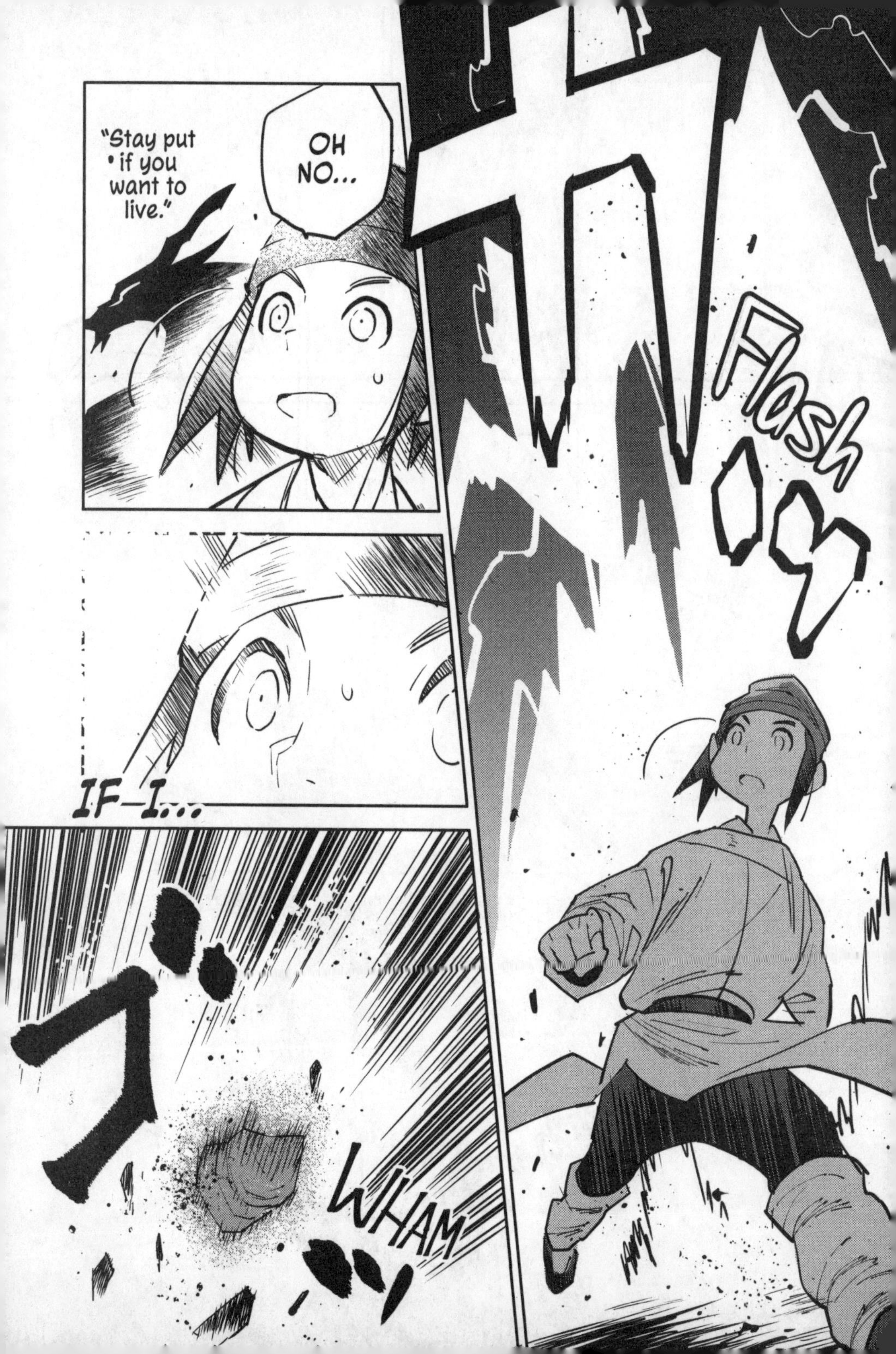
OH NO...
"Stay put if you want to live."
Flash
IF I...
WHAM

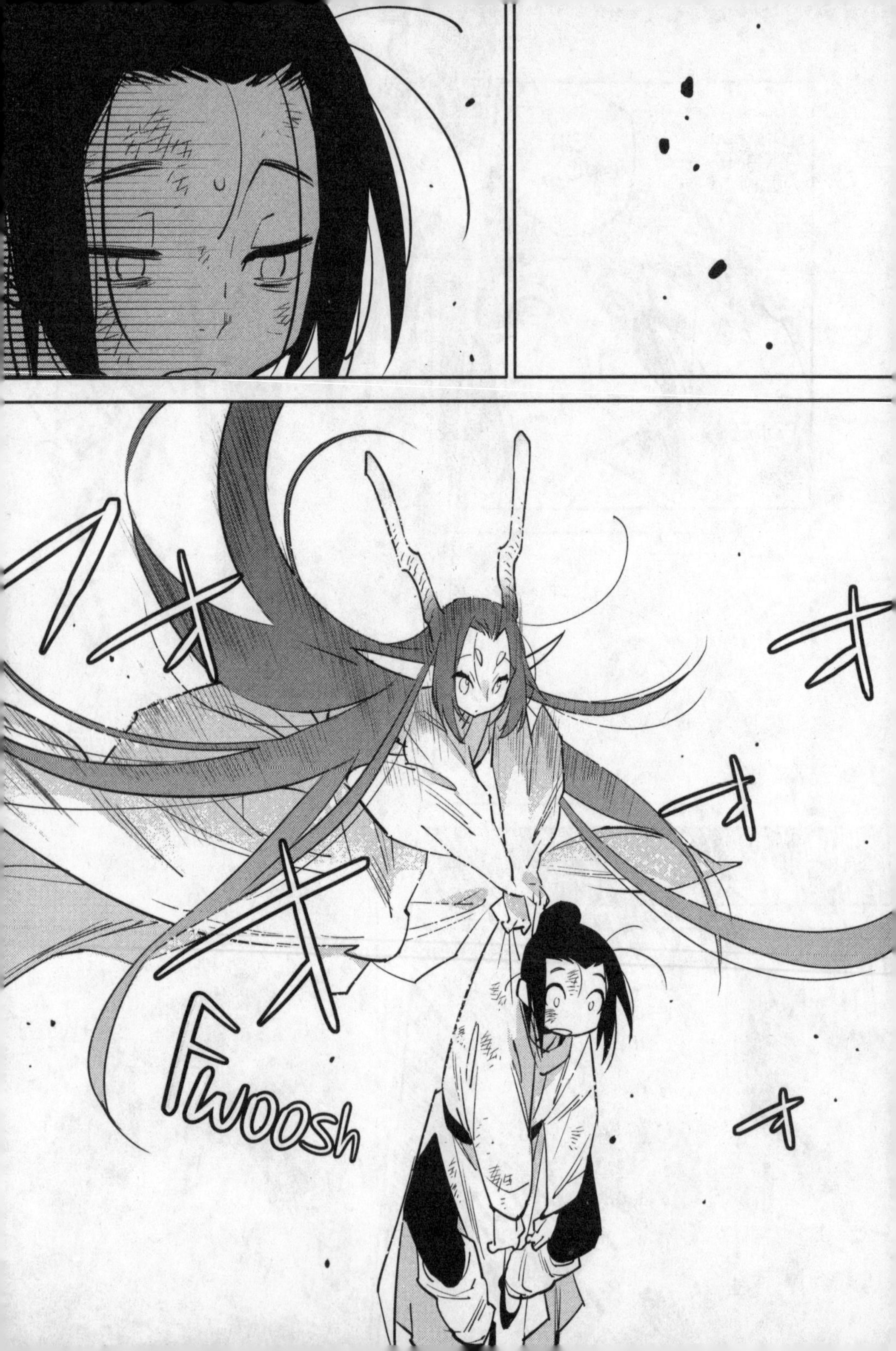
Fwoosh

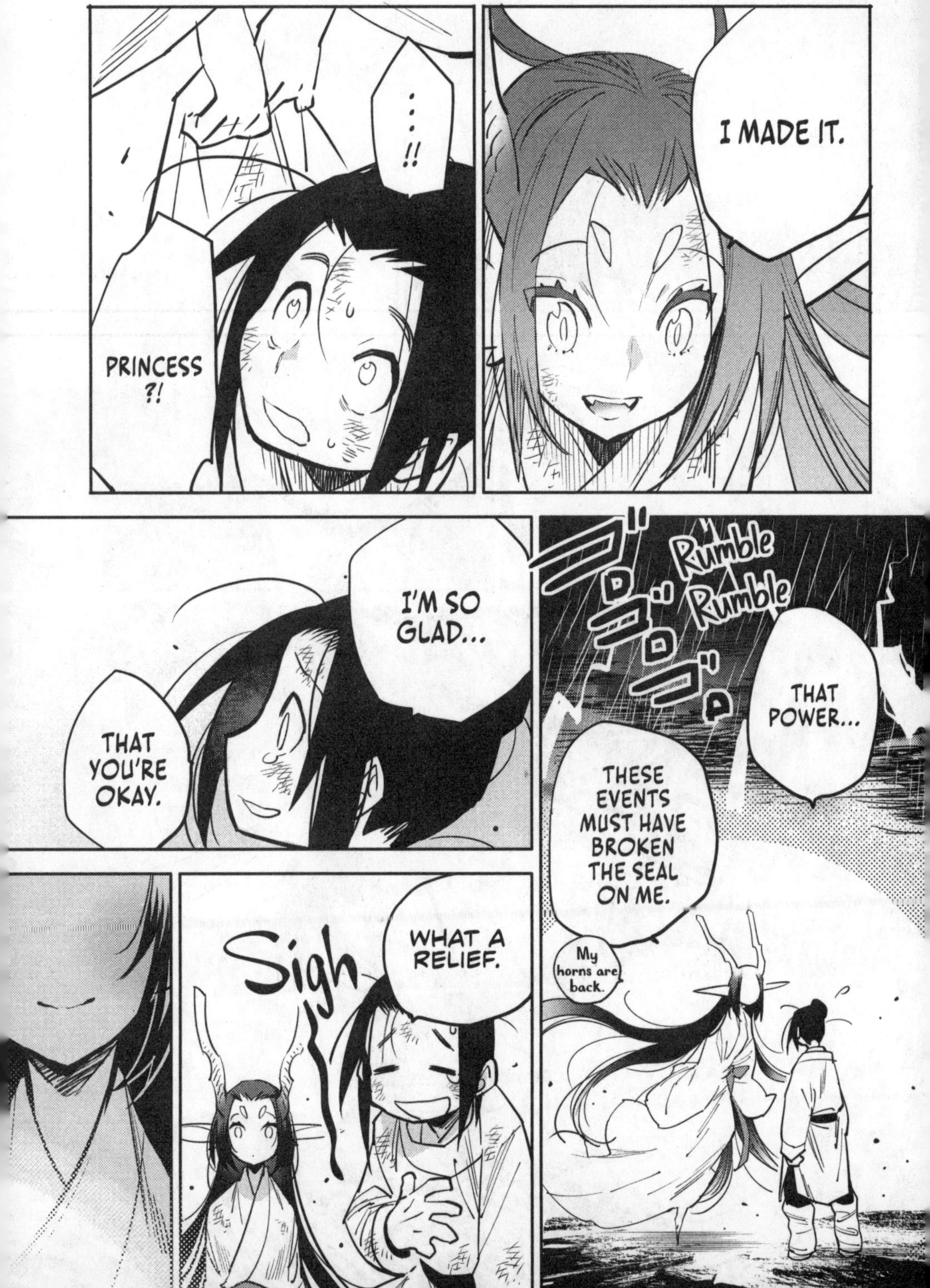
I MADE IT.
...!!
PRINCESS ?!
Rumble Rumble
THAT POWER...
THESE EVENTS MUST HAVE BROKEN THE SEAL ON ME.
My horns are back.
I'M SO GLAD...
THAT YOU'RE OKAY.
Sigh
WHAT A RELIEF.

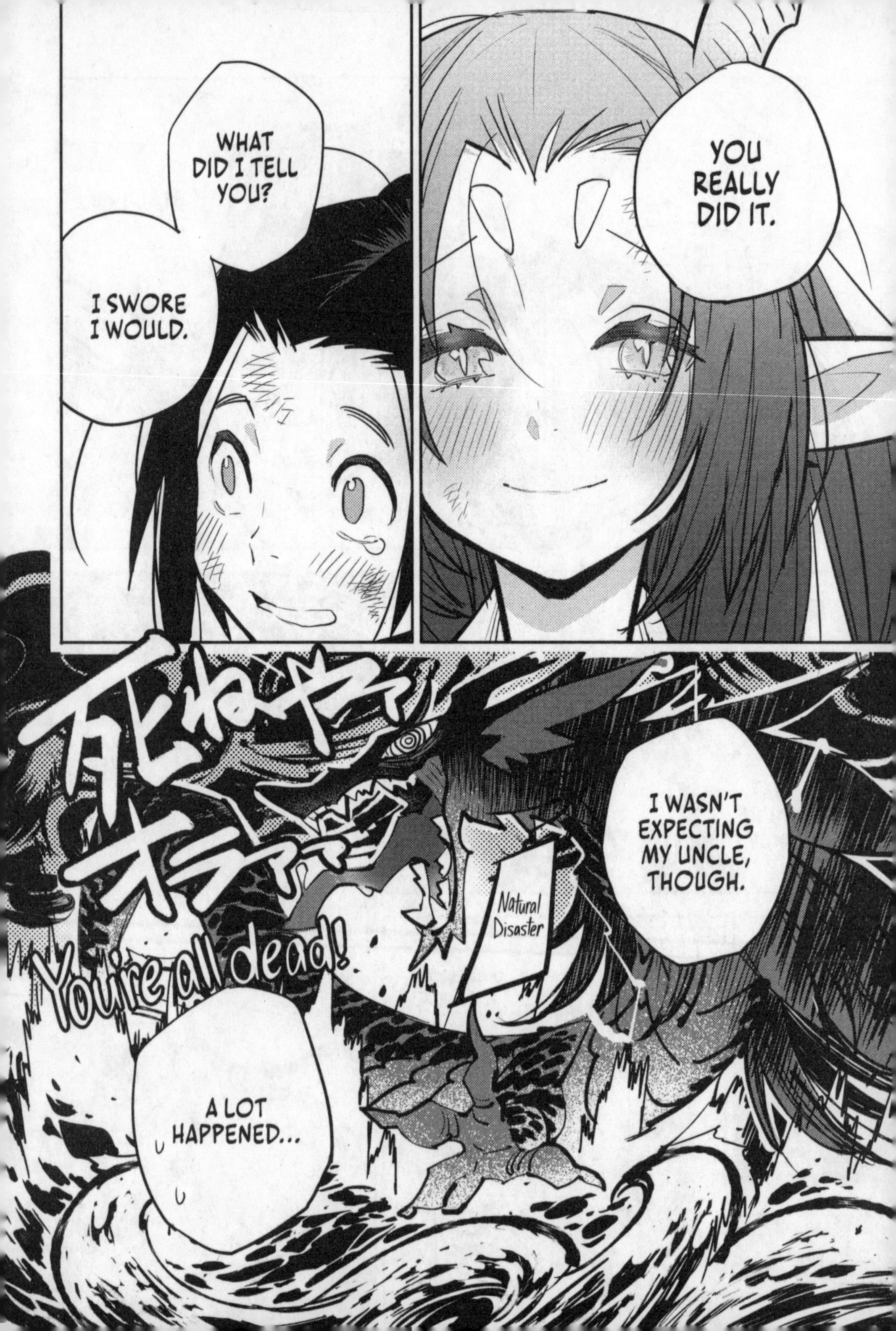
YOU REALLY DID IT.
WHAT DID I TELL YOU?
I SWORE I WOULD.
You're all dead!
I WASN'T EXPECTING MY UNCLE, THOUGH.
Natural Disaster
A LOT HAPPENED...

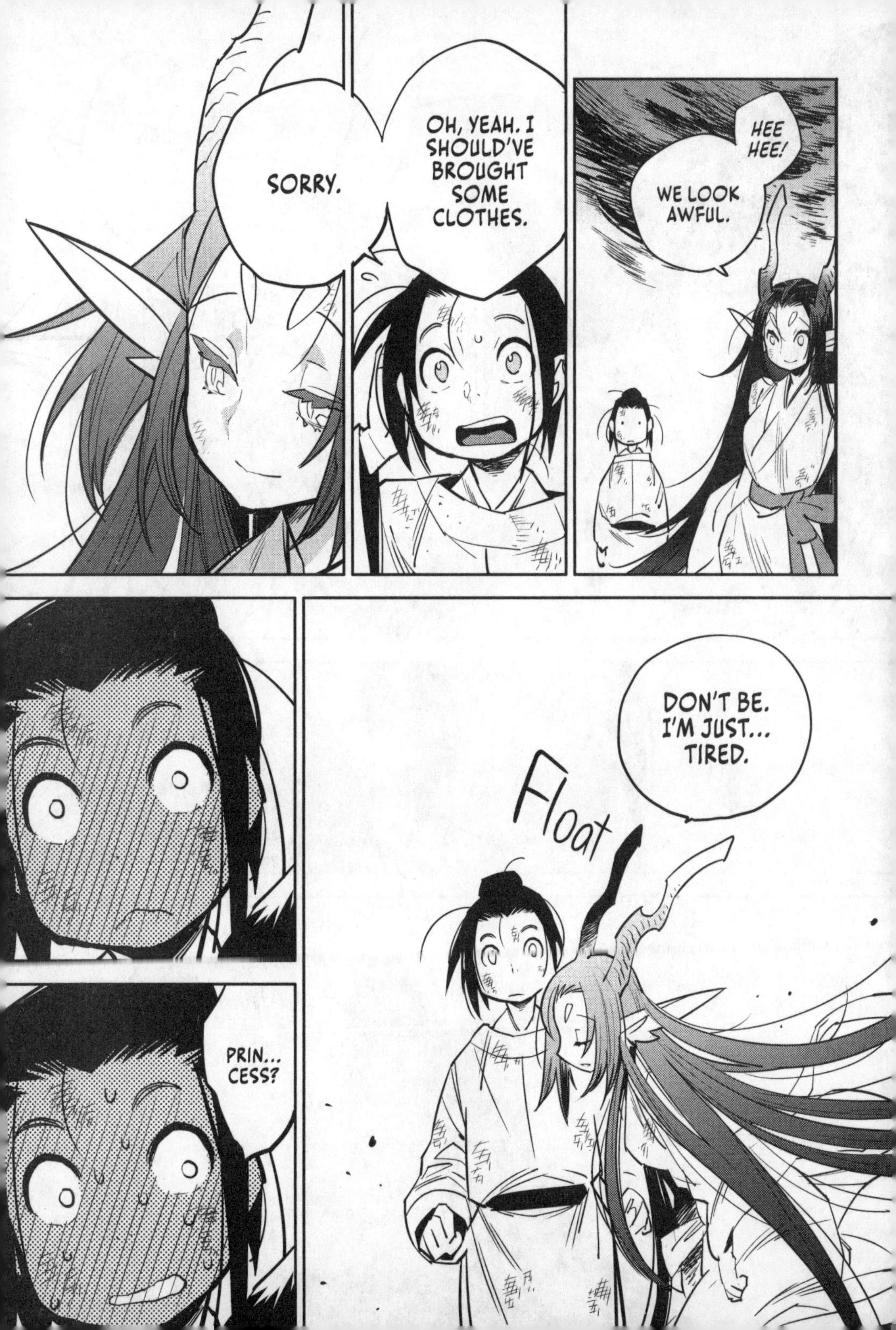
HEE HEE!
WE LOOK AWFUL.
OH, YEAH. I SHOULD'VE BROUGHT SOME CLOTHES.
SORRY.
DON'T BE. I'M JUST... TIRED.
Float
PRIN... CESS?

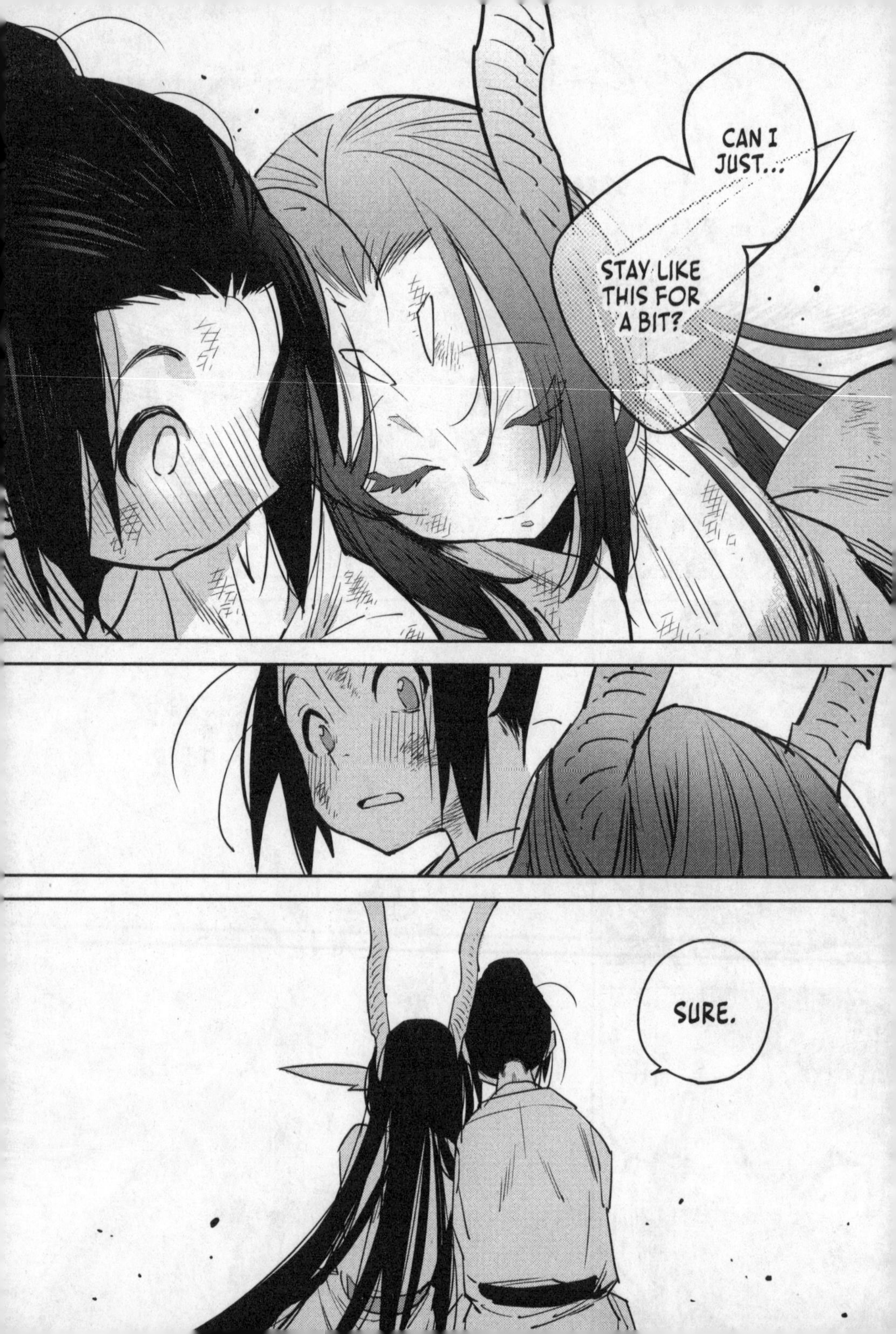
CAN I JUST...
STAY LIKE THIS FOR A BIT?
SURE.

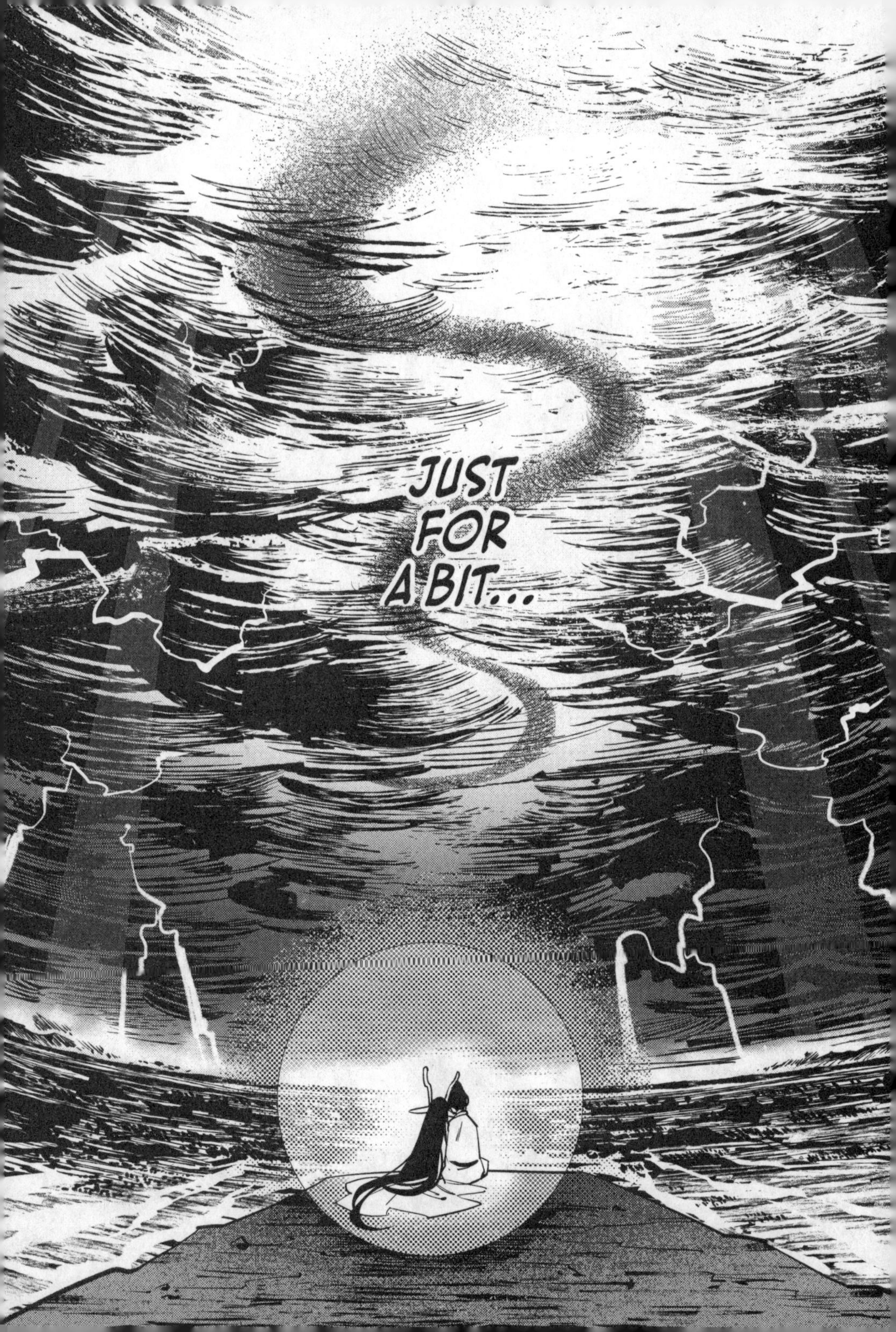
JUST FOR A BIT...

A Chinese Fantasy

The Dragon King's Daughter

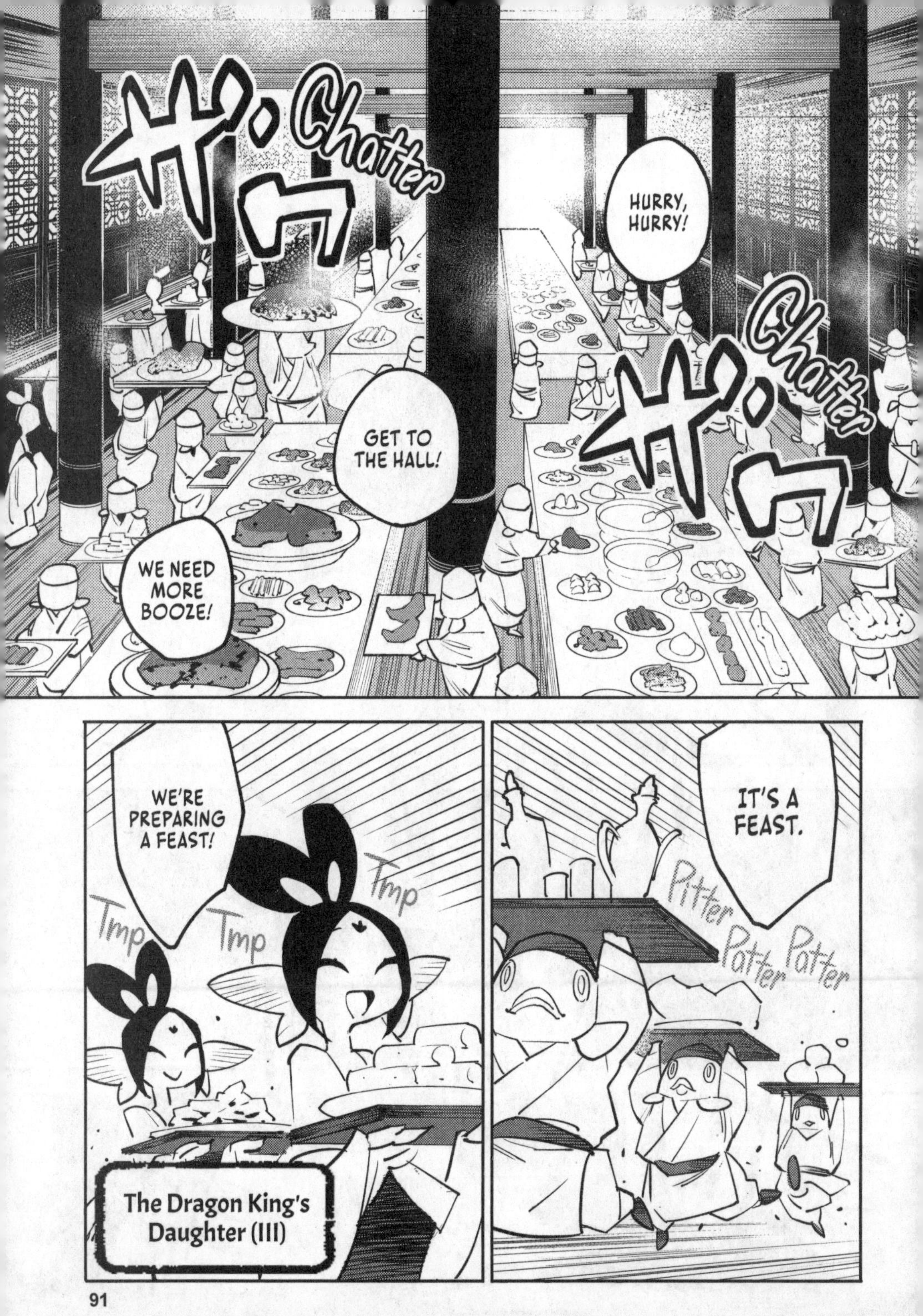

Chatter
Chatter
HURRY, HURRY!
GET TO THE HALL!
WE NEED MORE BOOZE!
IT'S A FEAST.
Pitter Patter Patter Patter
WE'RE PREPARING A FEAST!
Tmp Tmp Tmp
The Dragon King's Daughter (III)

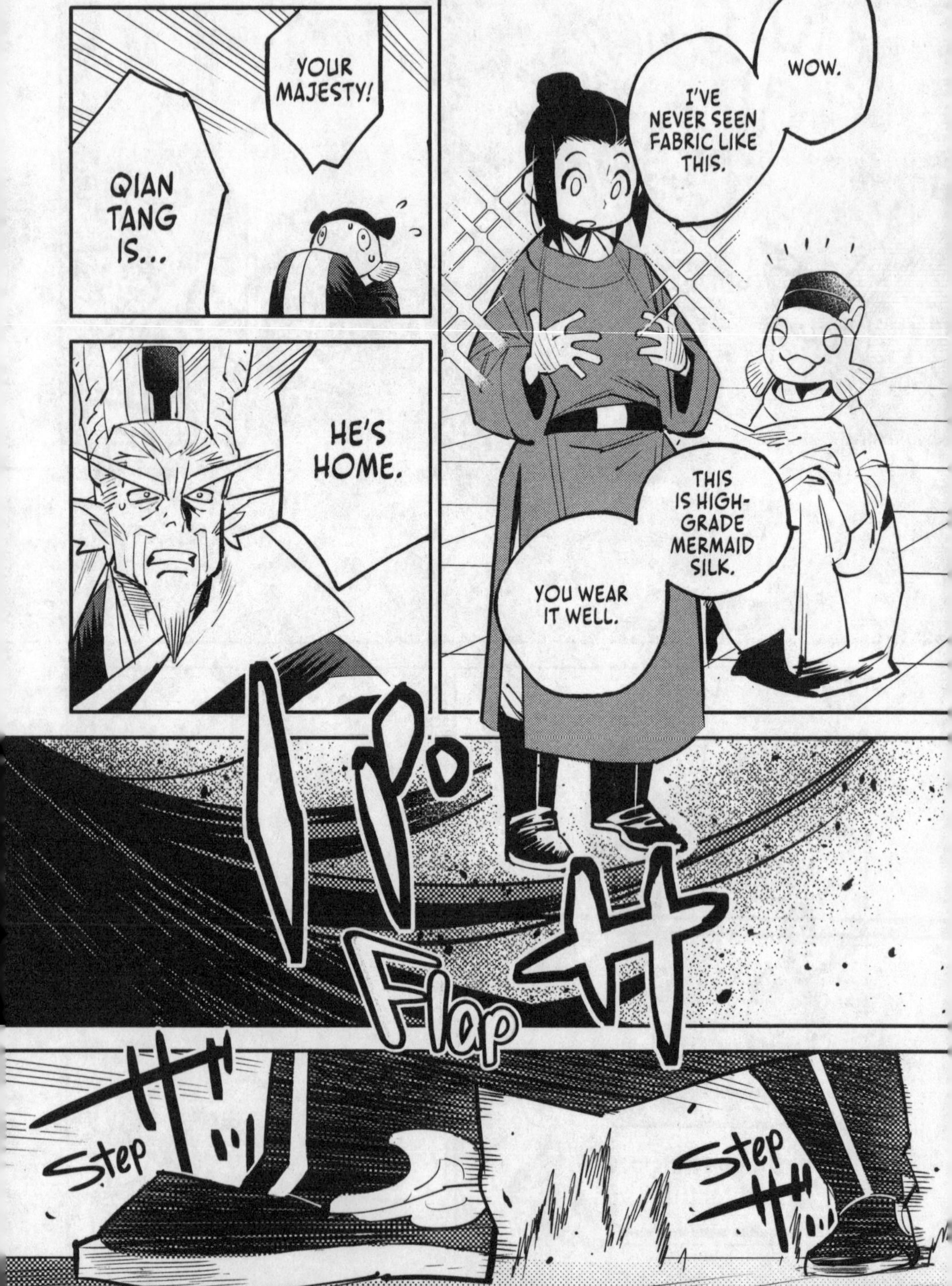
WOW.
I'VE NEVER SEEN FABRIC LIKE THIS.
THIS IS HIGH-GRADE MERMAID SILK.
YOU WEAR IT WELL.
YOUR MAJESTY!
QIAN TANG IS...
HE'S HOME.
Flap
Step
Step

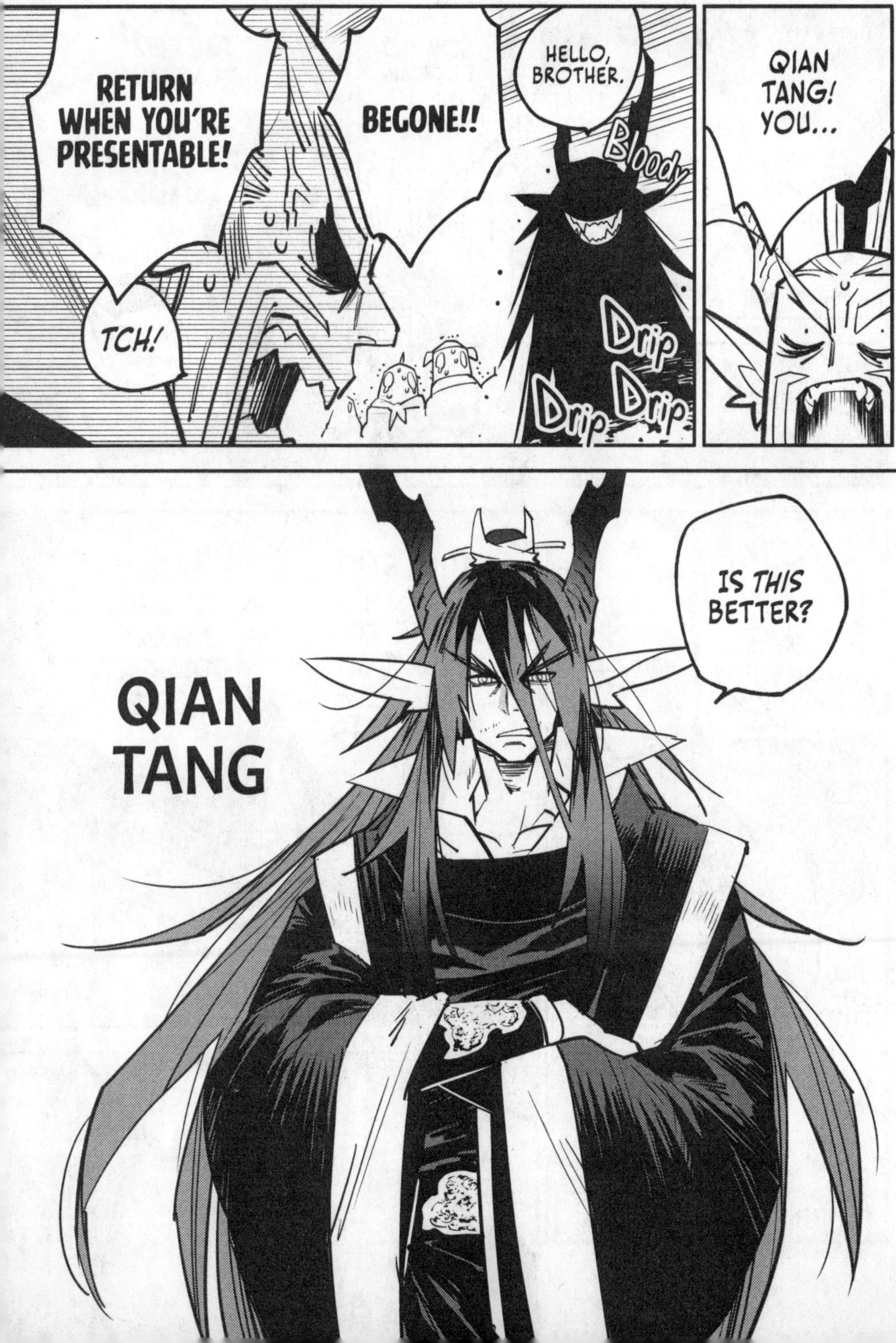
RETURN WHEN YOU'RE PRESENTABLE!
BEGONE!!
TCH!
HELLO, BROTHER.
Bloody
Drip
Drip
Drip
QIAN TANG! YOU...
IS THIS BETTER?
QIAN TANG

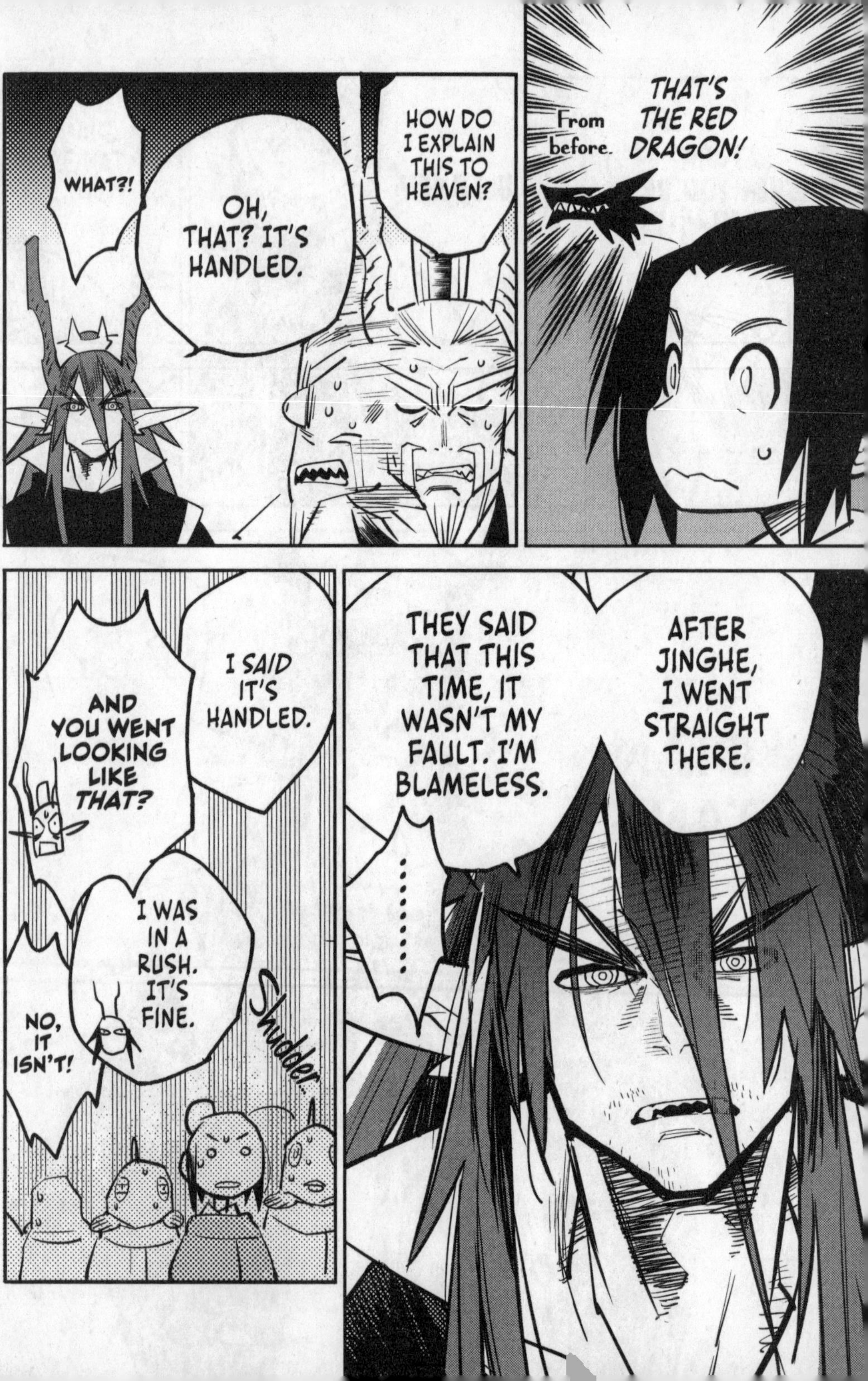
THAT'S THE RED DRAGON!
From before.
HOW DO I EXPLAIN THIS TO HEAVEN?
OH, THAT? IT'S HANDLED.
WHAT?!
AFTER JINGHE, I WENT STRAIGHT THERE.
THEY SAID THAT THIS TIME, IT WASN'T MY FAULT. I'M BLAMELESS.
......
I SAID IT'S HANDLED.
AND YOU WENT LOOKING LIKE THAT?
I WAS IN A RUSH. IT'S FINE.
NO, IT ISN'T!
Shudder...

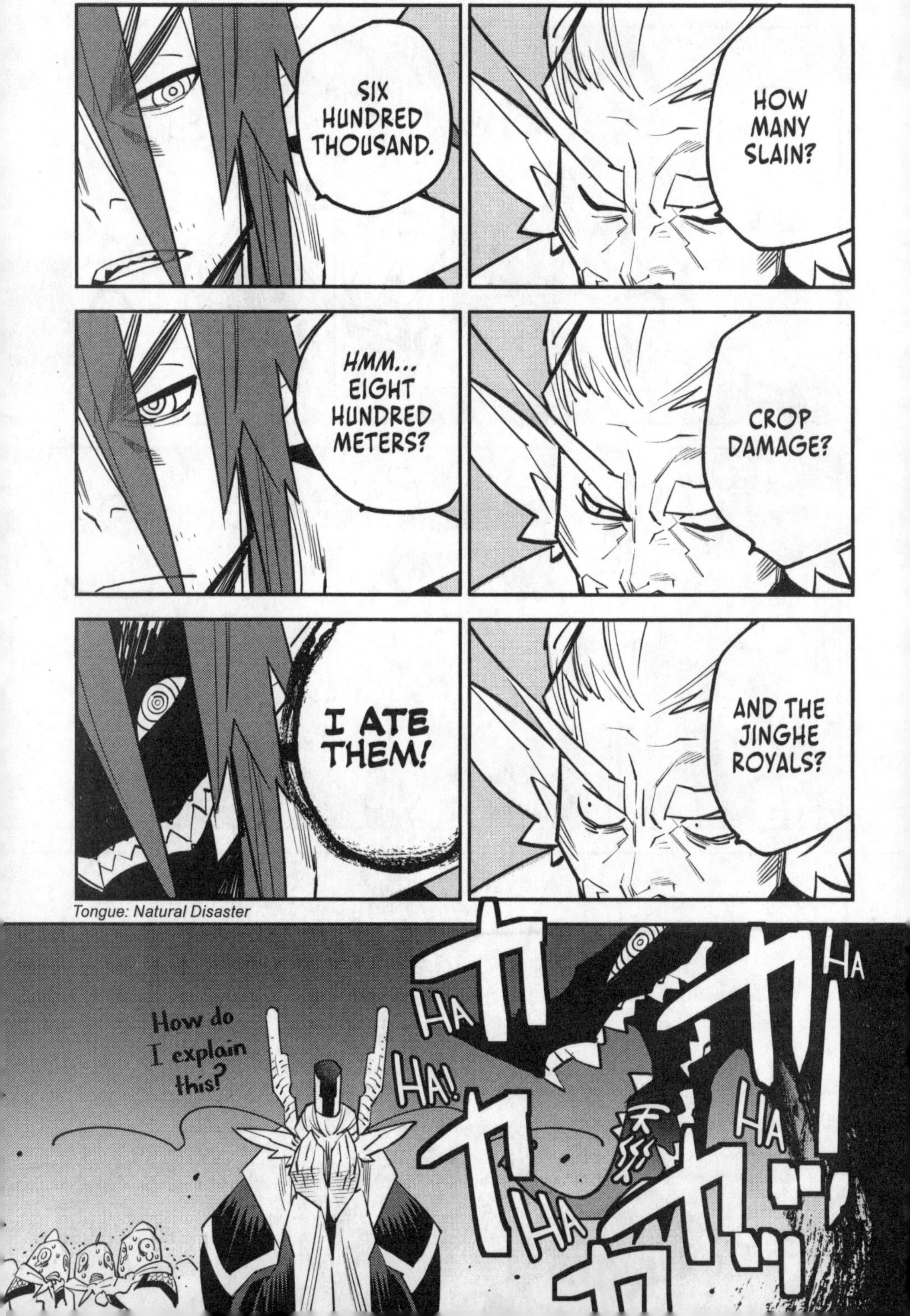
HOW MANY SLAIN?
SIX HUNDRED THOUSAND.
CROP DAMAGE?
HMM... EIGHT HUNDRED METERS?
AND THE JINGHE ROYALS?
I ATE THEM!
Tongue: Natural Disaster
HA
HA
HA!
HA
HA
HA
How do I explain this?

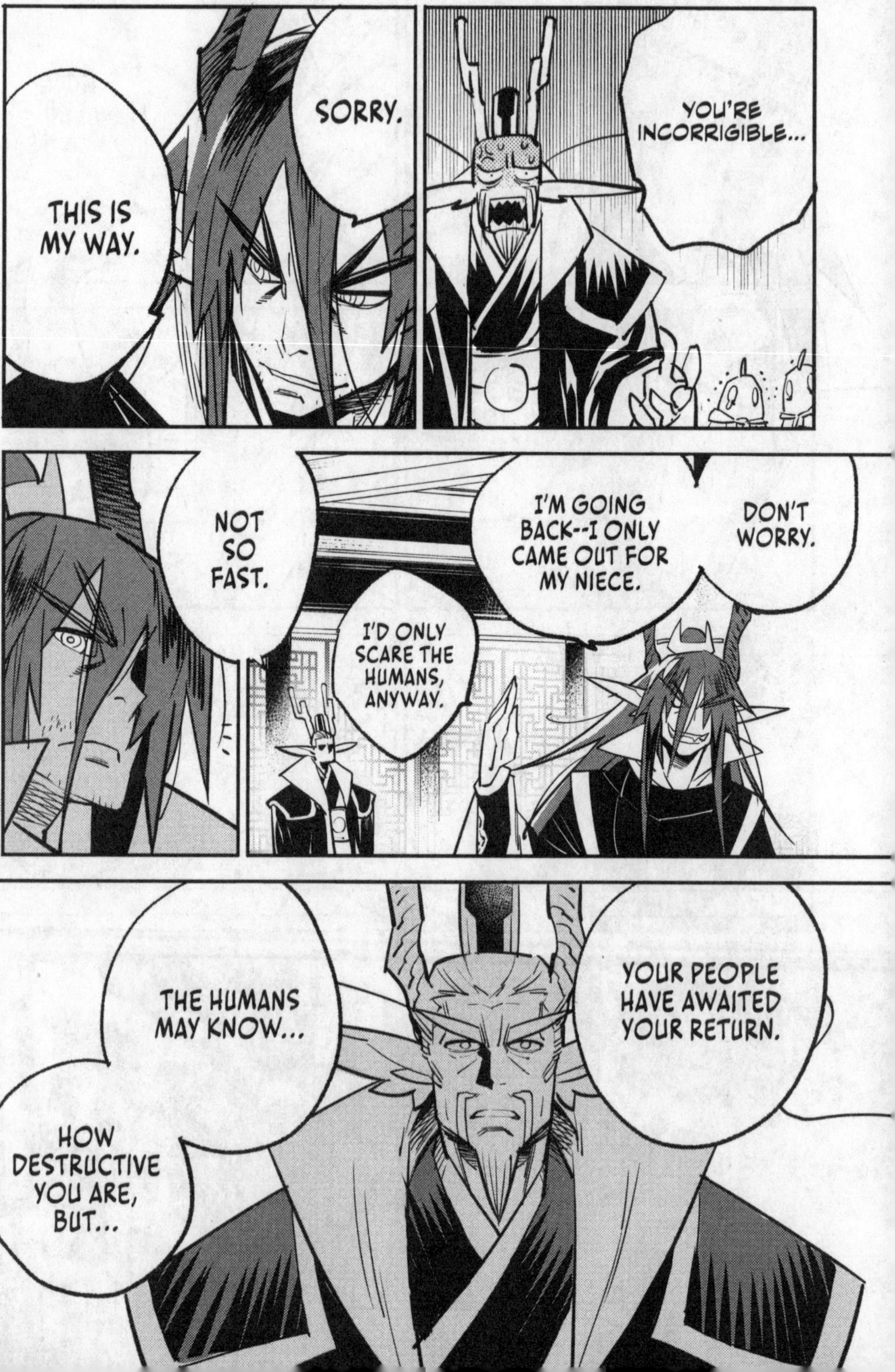
YOU'RE INCORRIGIBLE...
SORRY.
THIS IS MY WAY.
DON'T WORRY.
I'M GOING BACK--I ONLY CAME OUT FOR MY NIECE.
I'D ONLY SCARE THE HUMANS, ANYWAY.
NOT SO FAST.
YOUR PEOPLE HAVE AWAITED YOUR RETURN.
THE HUMANS MAY KNOW...
HOW DESTRUCTIVE YOU ARE, BUT...

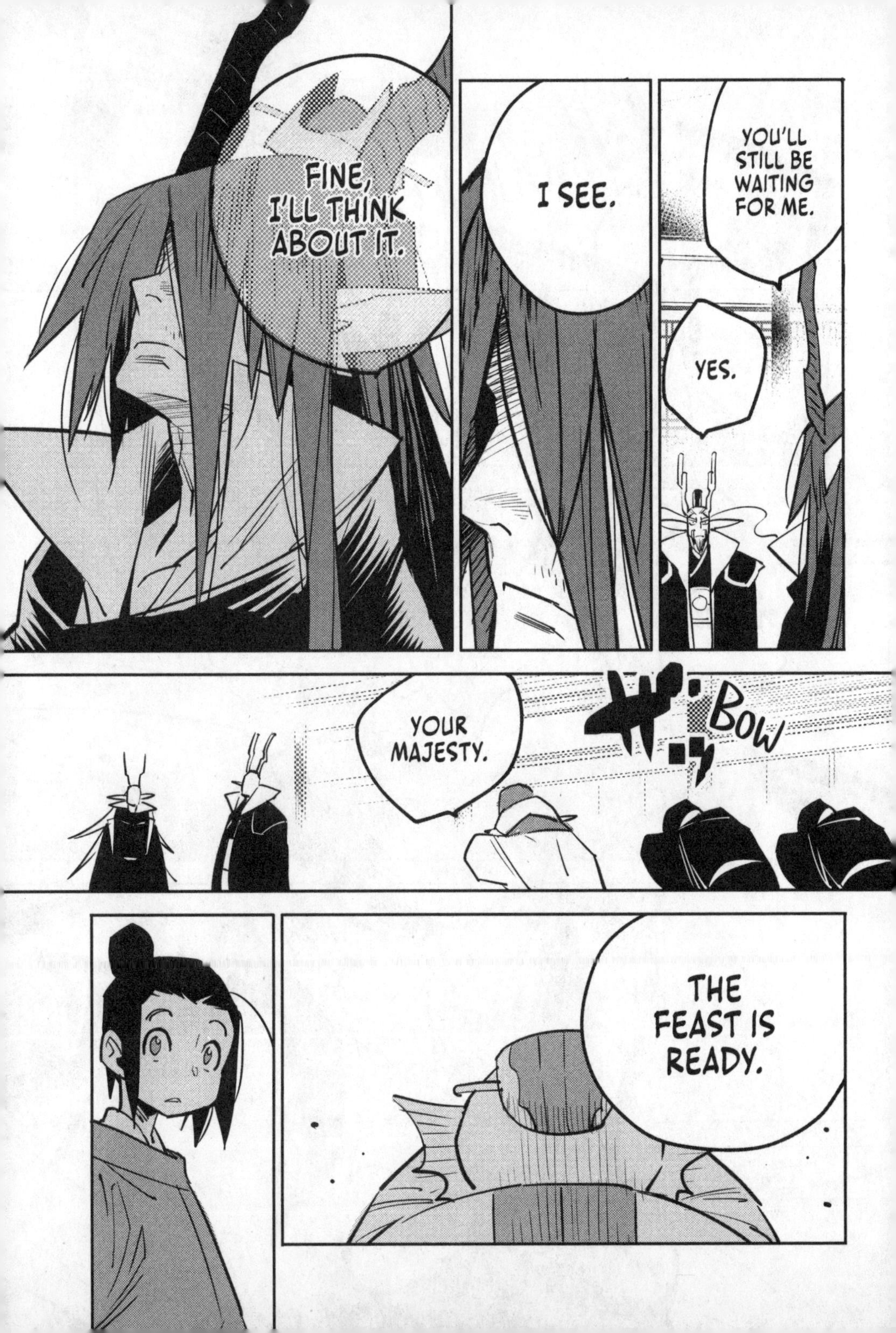
YOU'LL STILL BE WAITING FOR ME.
YES.
I SEE.
FINE, I'LL THINK ABOUT IT.
BOW
YOUR MAJESTY.
THE FEAST IS READY.

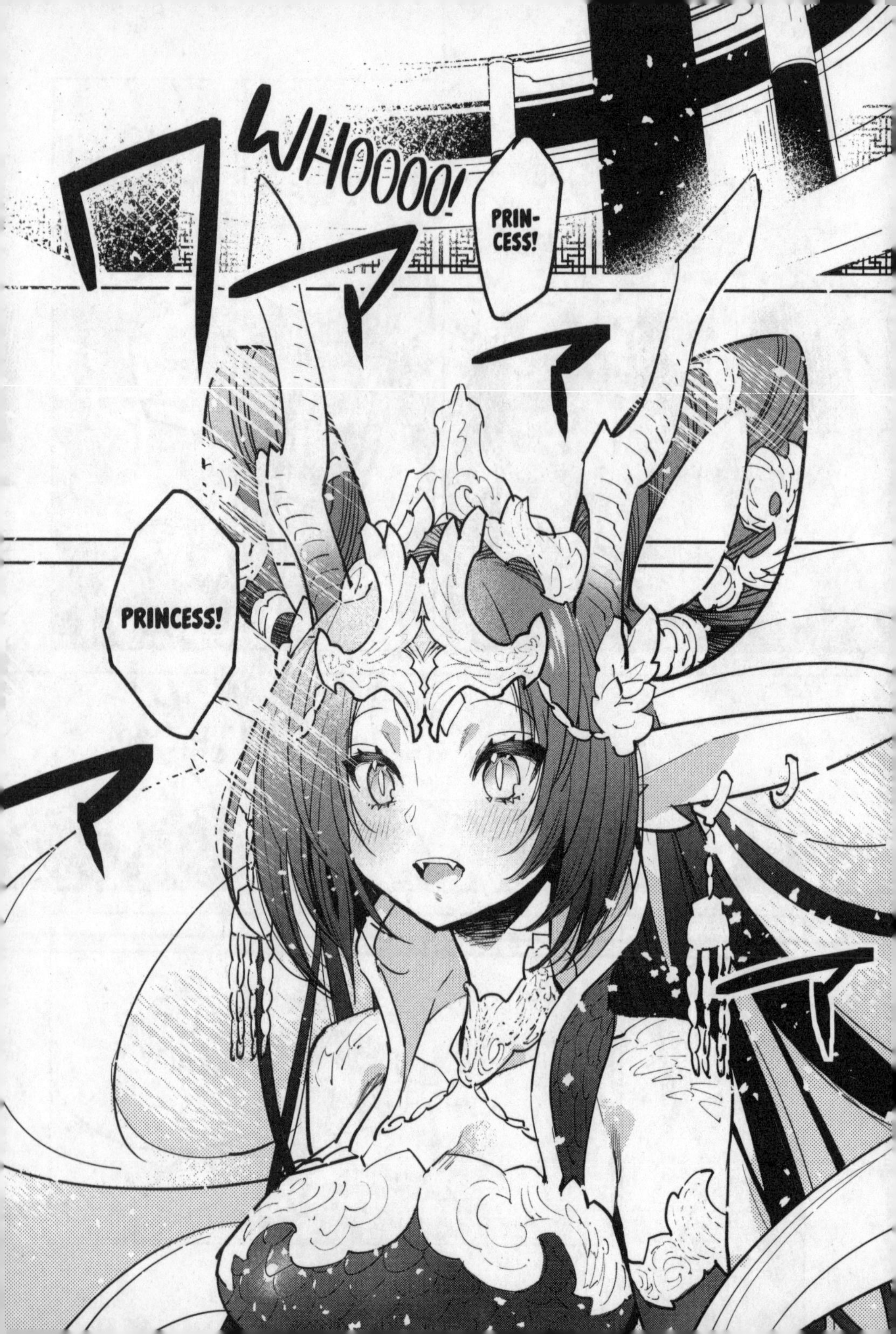

PRIN-
CESS!
WHOOOO!
PRINCESS!

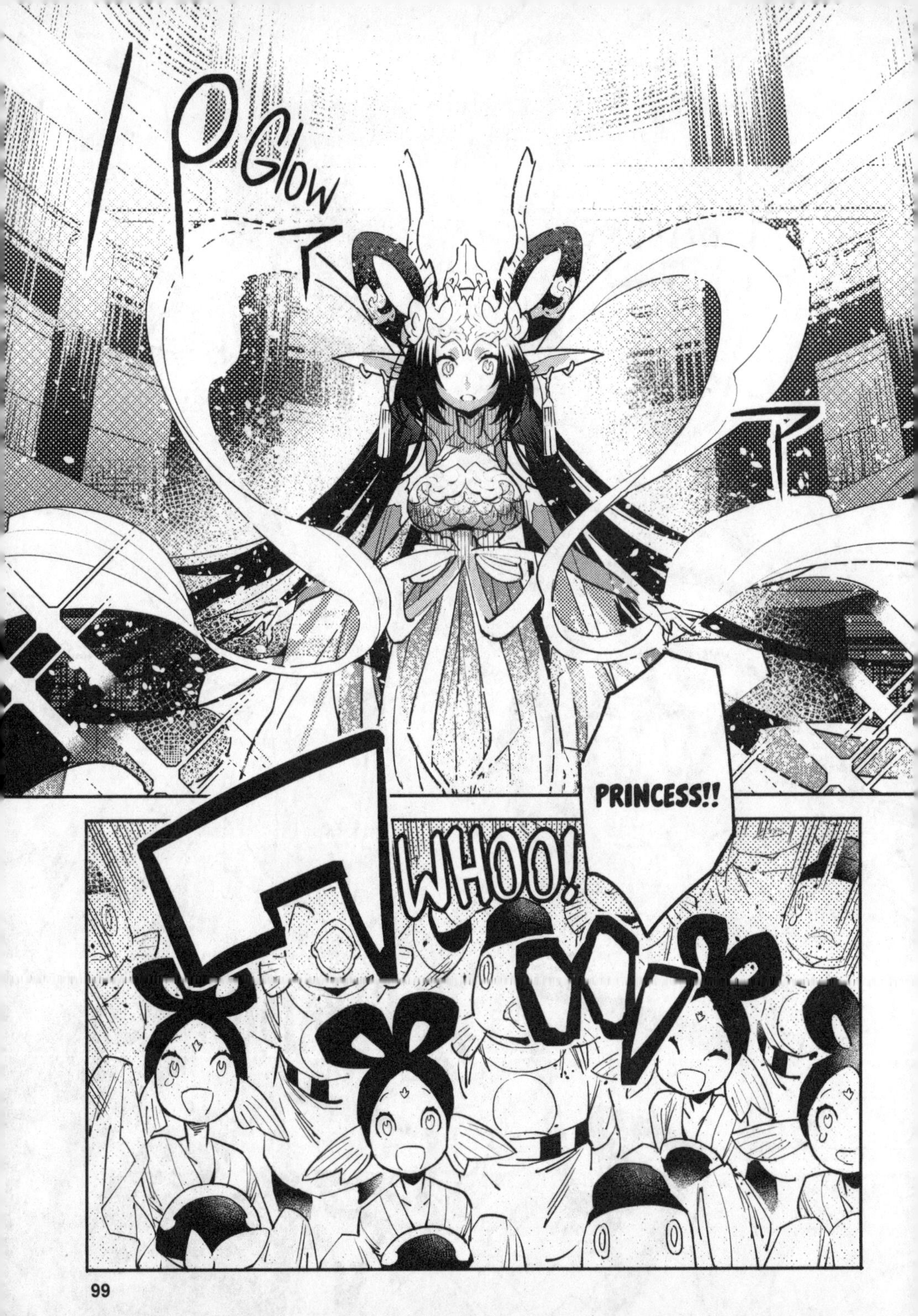
Glow
PRINCESS!!
WHOO!

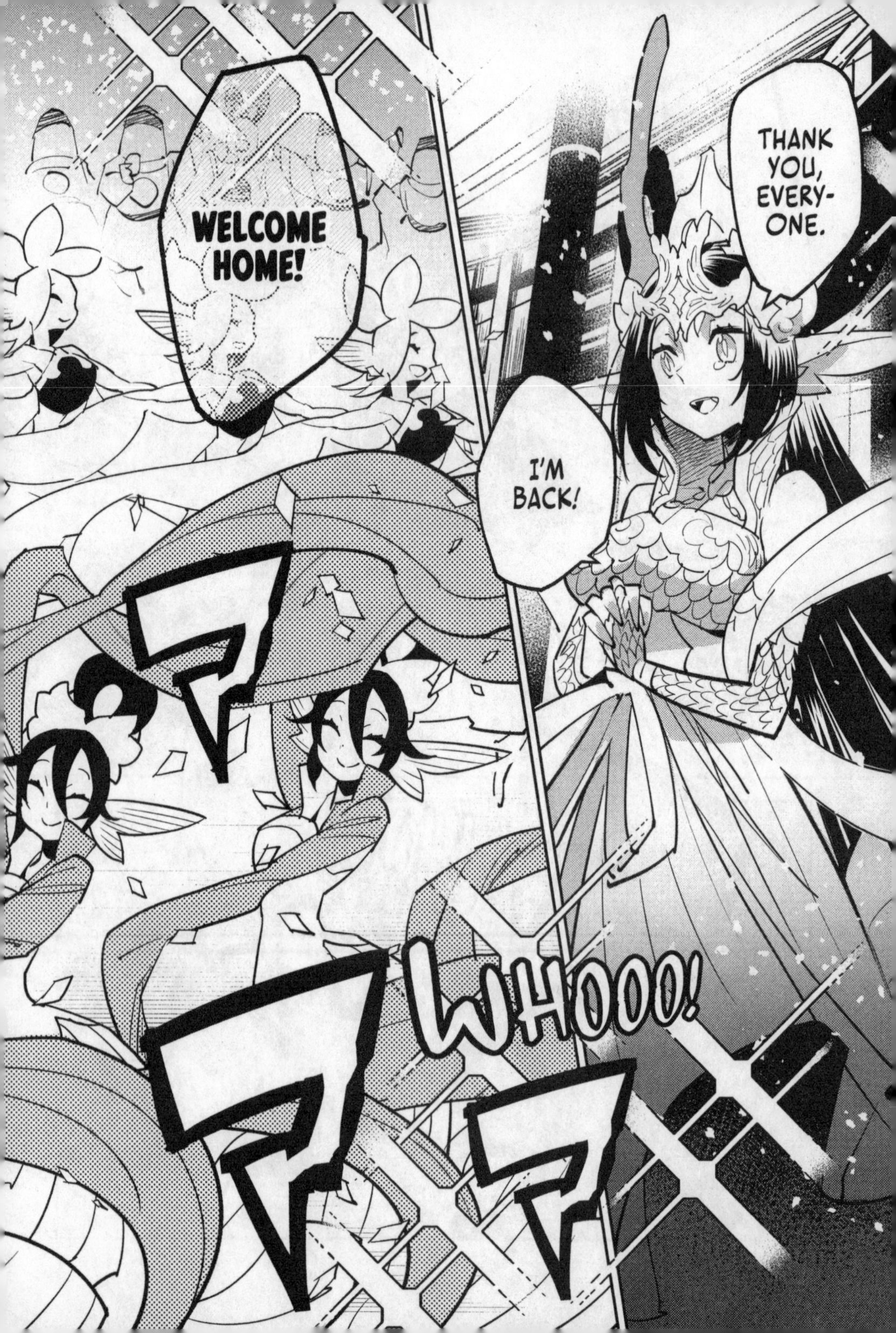
THANK YOU, EVERY-ONE.
I'M BACK!
WELCOME HOME!
WHOOO!

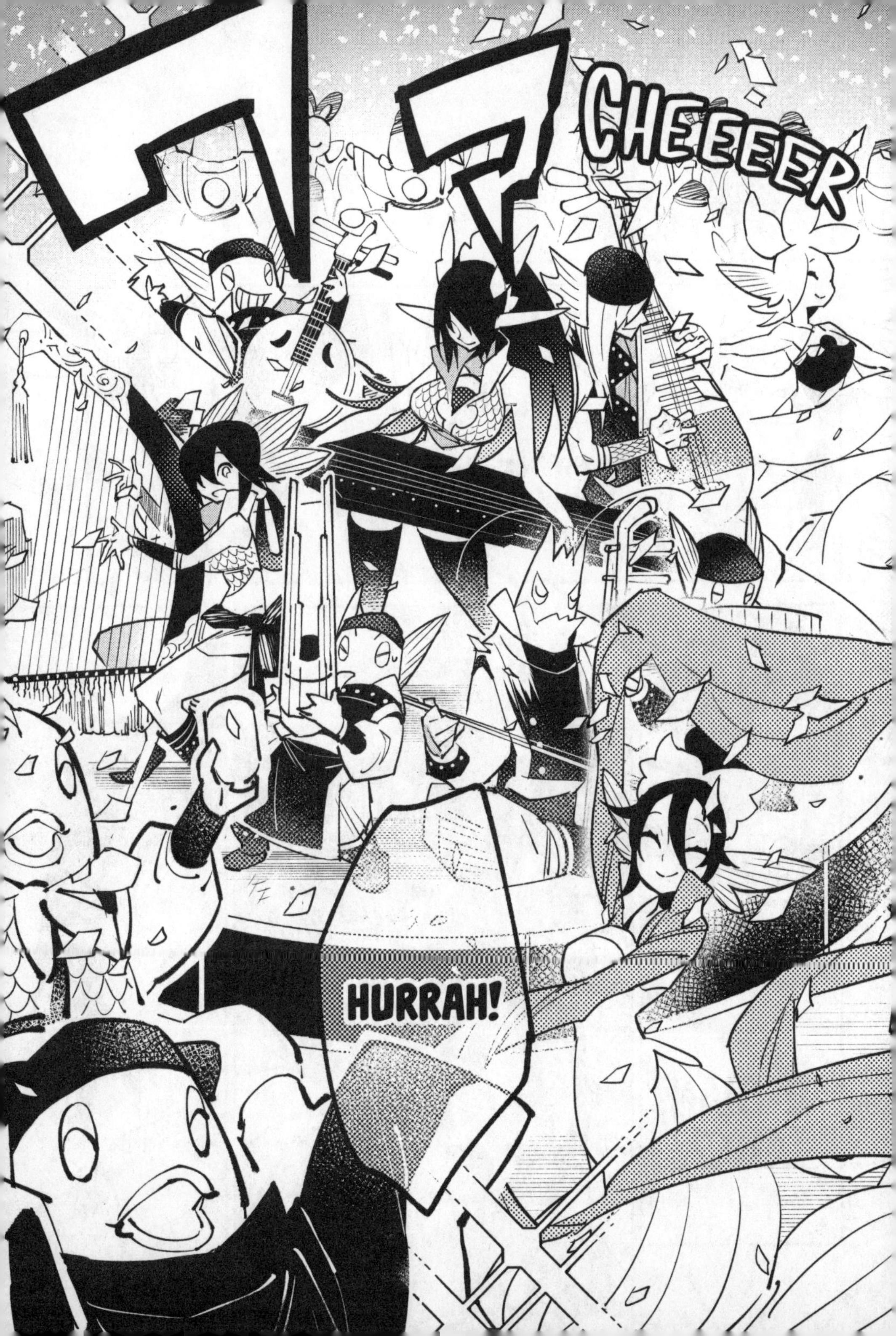
CHEEEER
HURRAH!

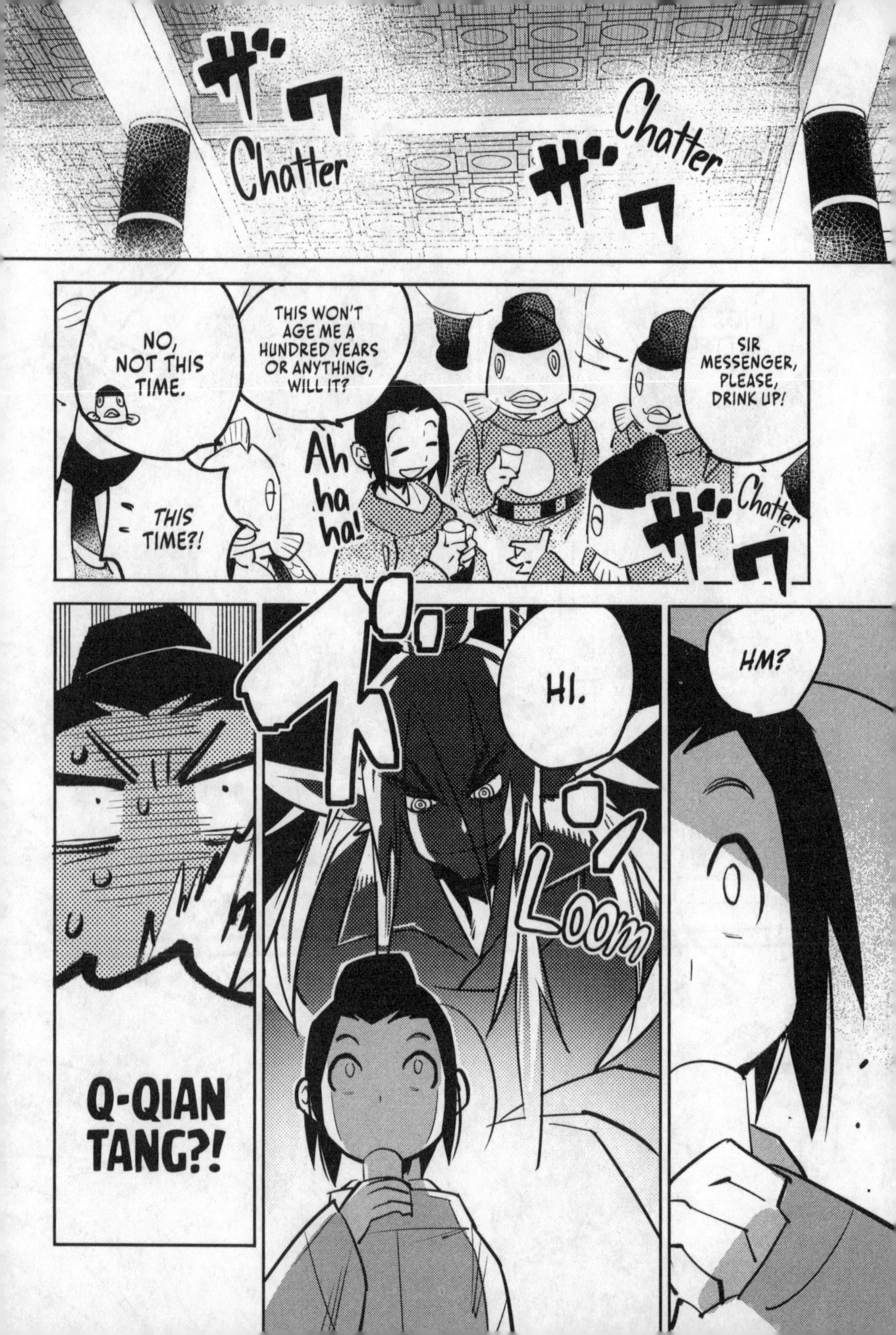
ザワ
Chatter
ザワ
Chatter
SIR MESSENGER, PLEASE, DRINK UP!
ザワ
Chatter
THIS WON'T AGE ME A HUNDRED YEARS OR ANYTHING, WILL IT?
Ah ha ha!
NO, NOT THIS TIME.
THIS TIME?!
HM?
HI.
Loom
Q-QIAN TANG?!

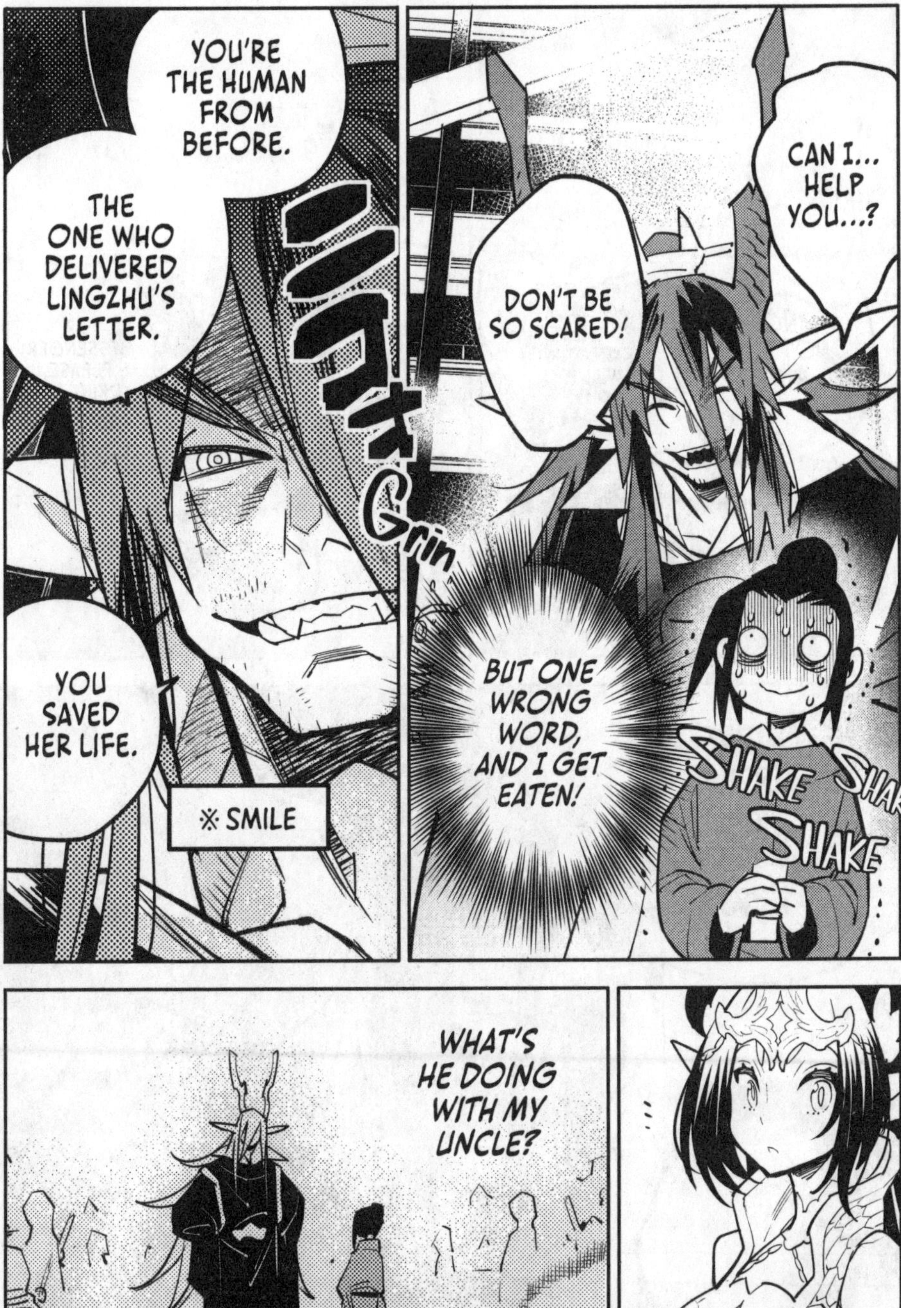
CAN I... HELP YOU...?
DON'T BE SO SCARED!
BUT ONE WRONG WORD, AND I GET EATEN!
SHAKE SHAKE SHAKE
YOU'RE THE HUMAN FROM BEFORE.
THE ONE WHO DELIVERED LINGZHU'S LETTER.
Grin
YOU SAVED HER LIFE.
※ SMILE
WHAT'S HE DOING WITH MY UNCLE?

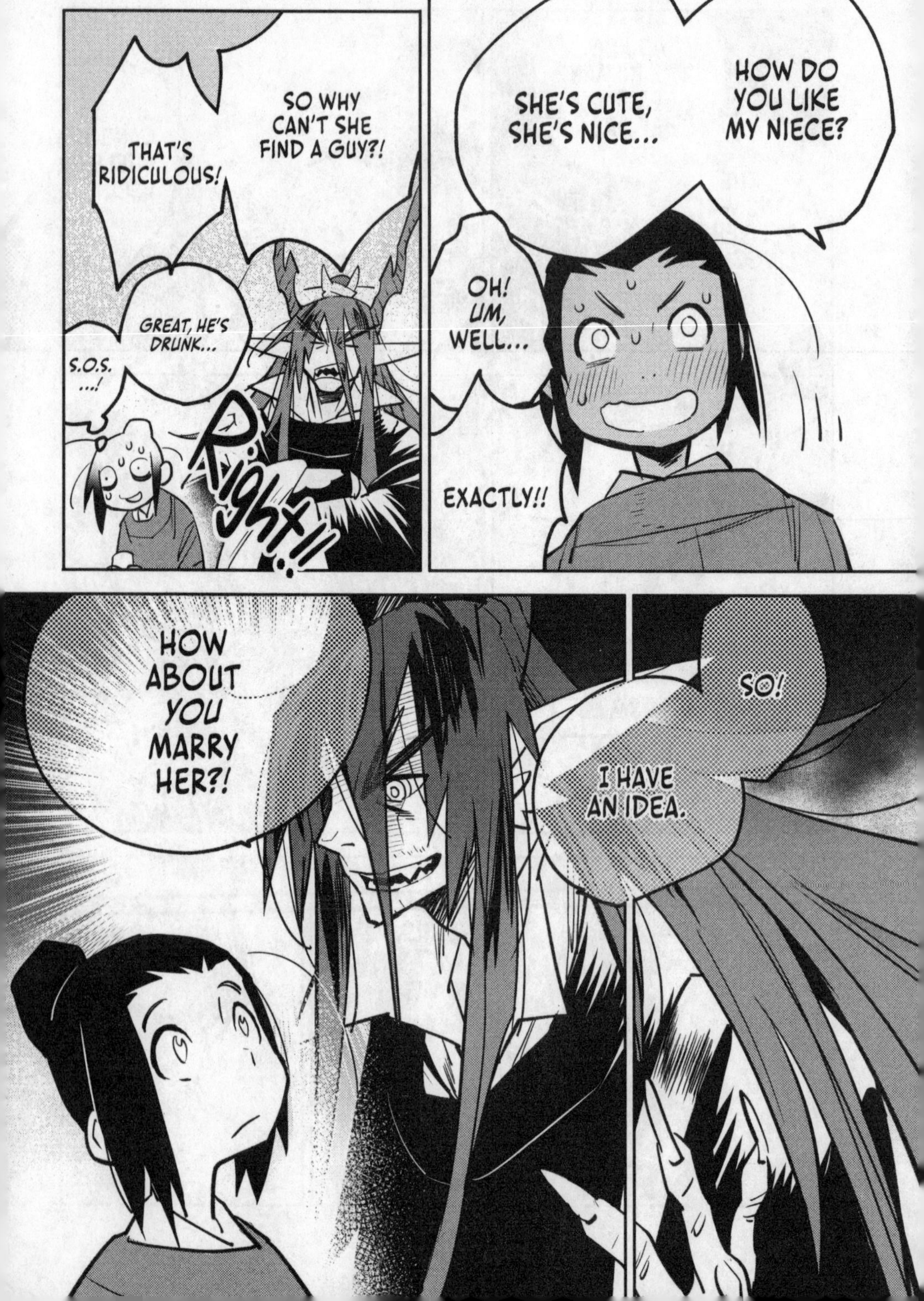
HOW DO YOU LIKE MY NIECE?
SHE'S CUTE, SHE'S NICE...
OH! UM, WELL...
EXACTLY!!
SO WHY CAN'T SHE FIND A GUY?!
THAT'S RIDICULOUS!
Right!!
GREAT, HE'S DRUNK...
S.O.S. ...!
SO!
I HAVE AN IDEA.
HOW ABOUT YOU MARRY HER?!

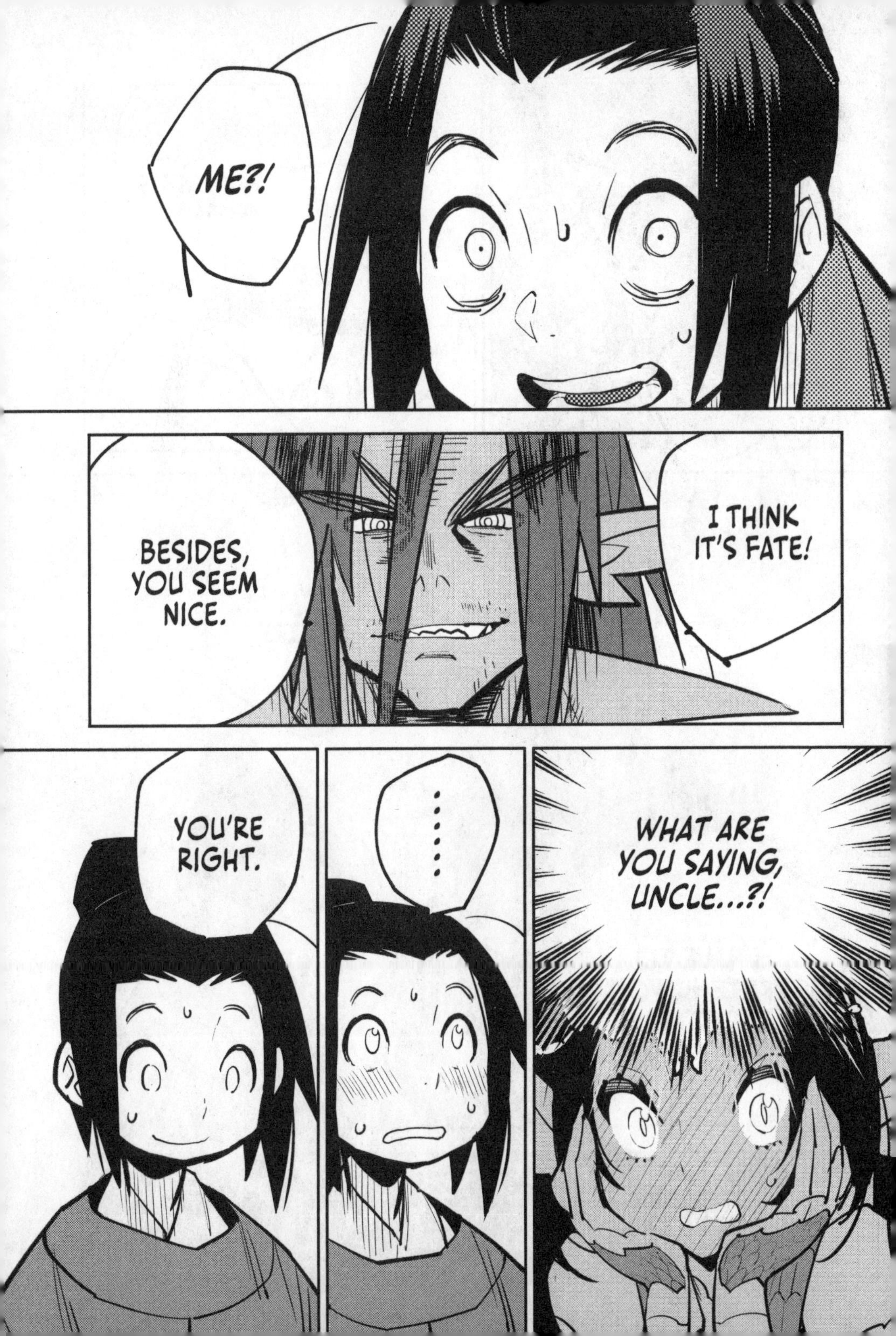
ME?!
I THINK IT'S FATE!
BESIDES, YOU SEEM NICE.
WHAT ARE YOU SAYING, UNCLE...?!
......
YOU'RE RIGHT.

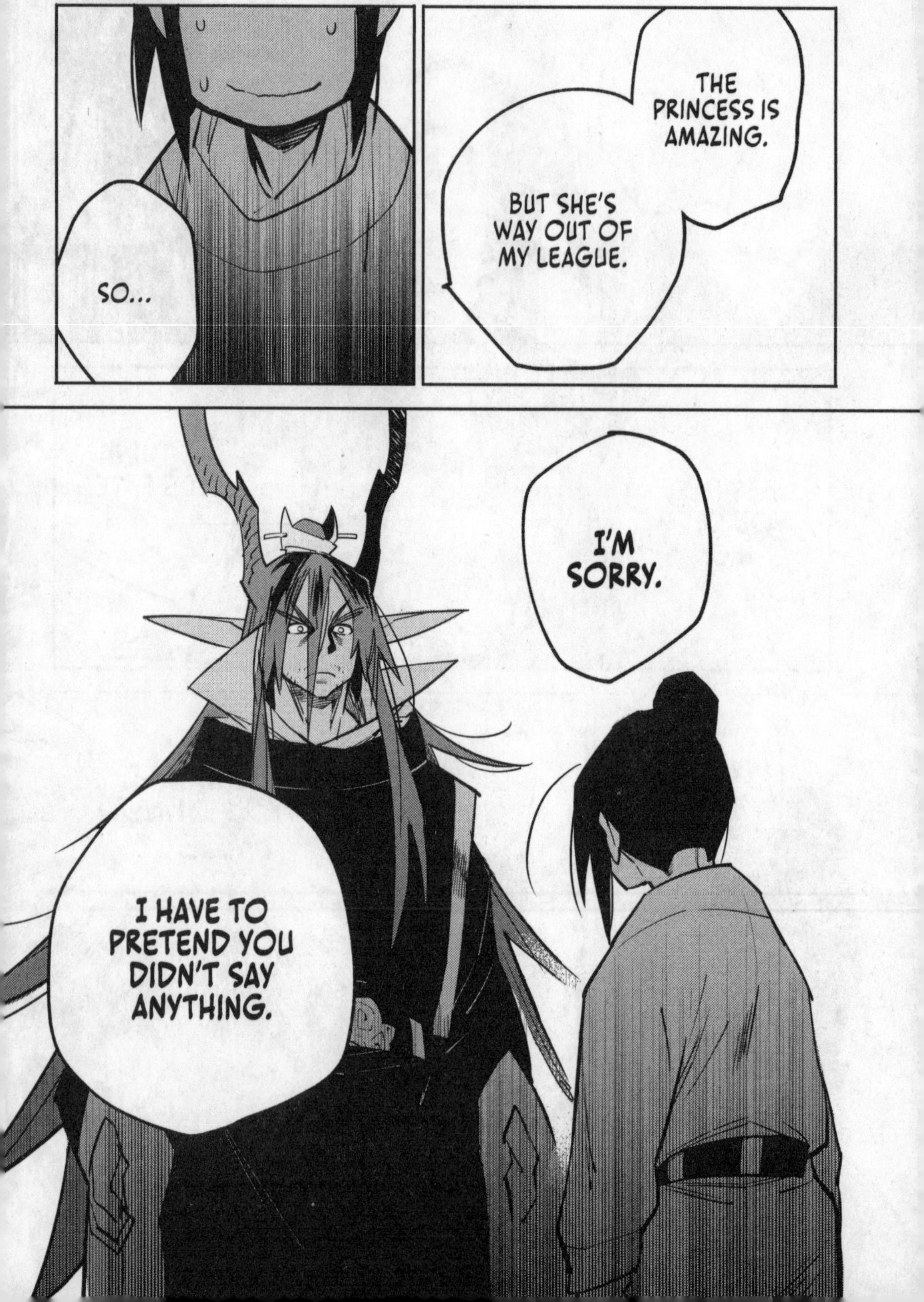
THE PRINCESS IS AMAZING.
BUT SHE'S WAY OUT OF MY LEAGUE.
SO...
I'M SORRY.
I HAVE TO PRETEND YOU DIDN'T SAY ANYTHING.

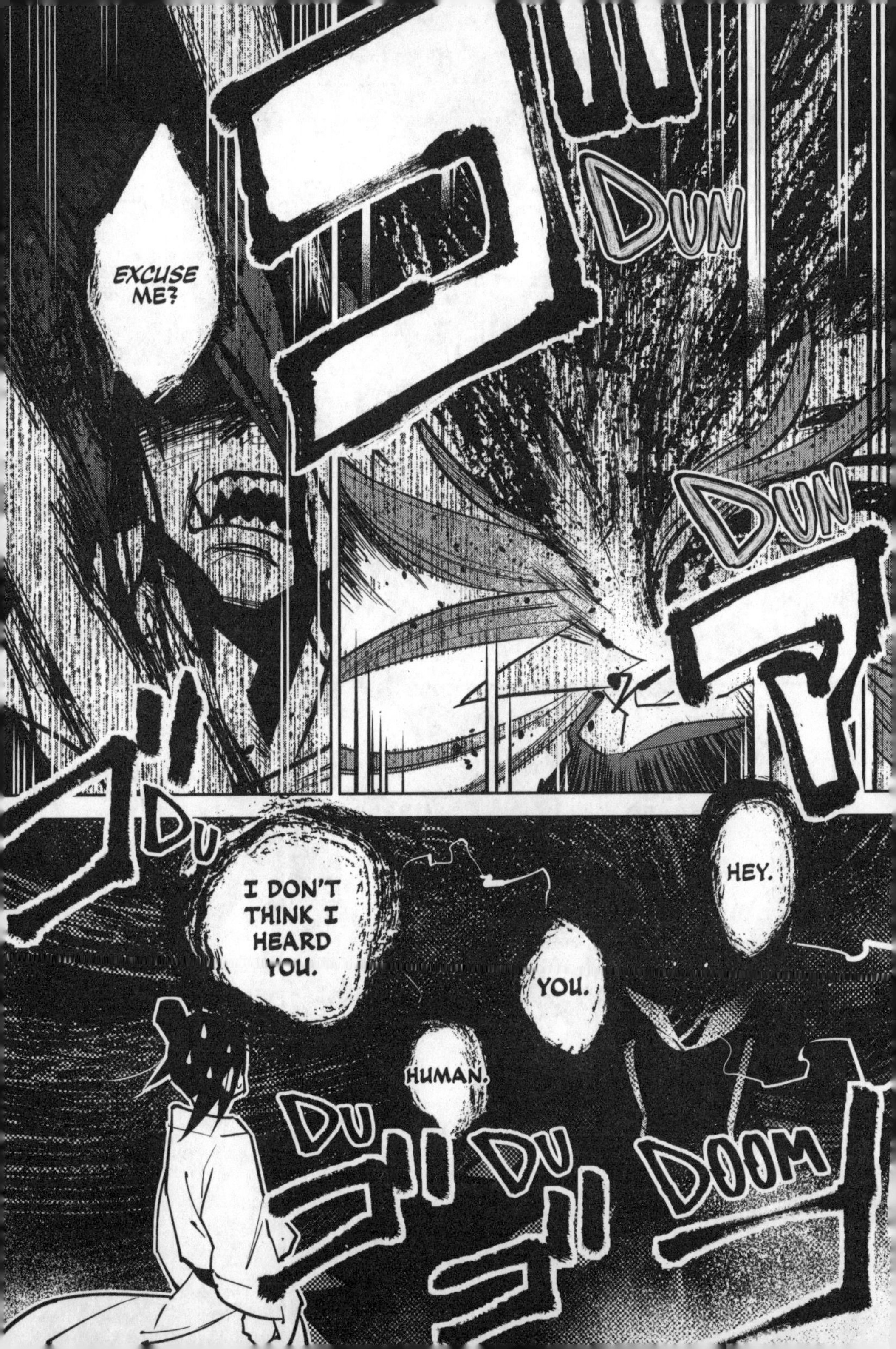
EXCUSE ME?
DUN
DUN
DU
HEY.
I DON'T THINK I HEARD YOU.
YOU.
HUMAN.
DU
DU
DOOM

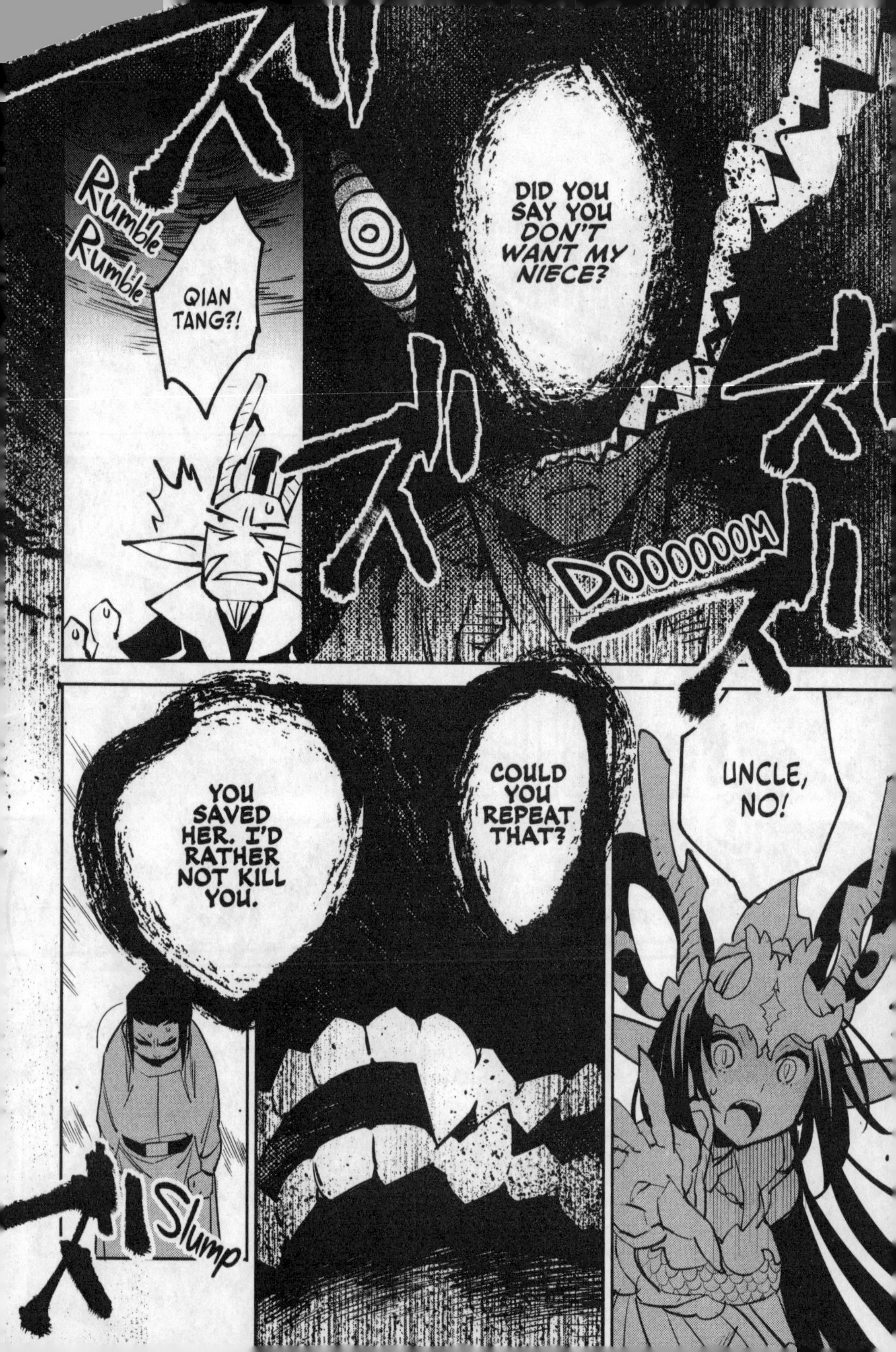
DID YOU SAY YOU DON'T WANT MY NIECE?
QIAN TANG?!
Rumble Rumble
DOOOOOOM
UNCLE, NO!
COULD YOU REPEAT THAT?
YOU SAVED HER. I'D RATHER NOT KILL YOU.
Slump

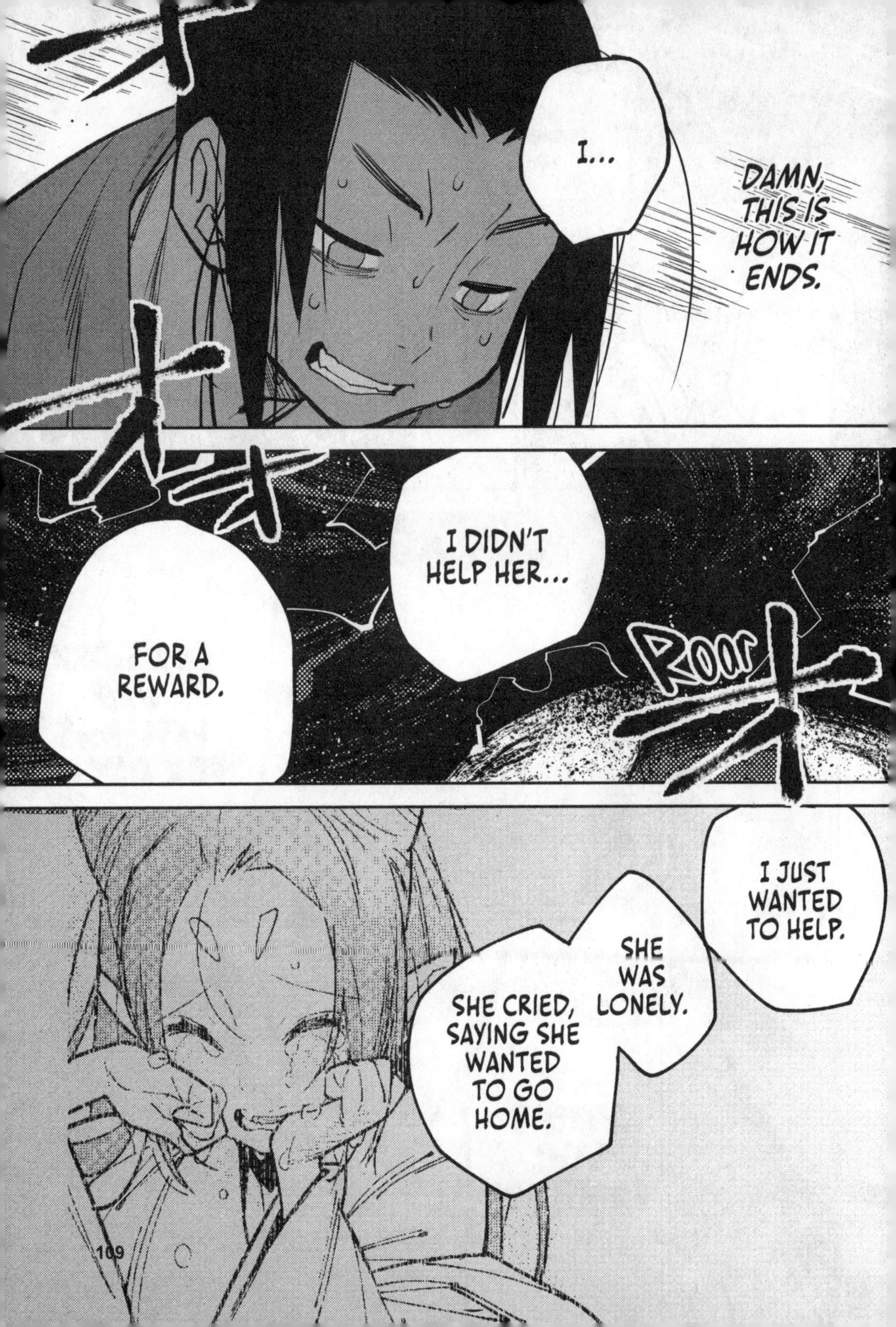
DAMN, THIS IS HOW IT ENDS.
I...
I DIDN'T HELP HER...
FOR A REWARD.
Roar
I JUST WANTED TO HELP.
SHE WAS LONELY.
SHE CRIED, SAYING SHE WANTED TO GO HOME.

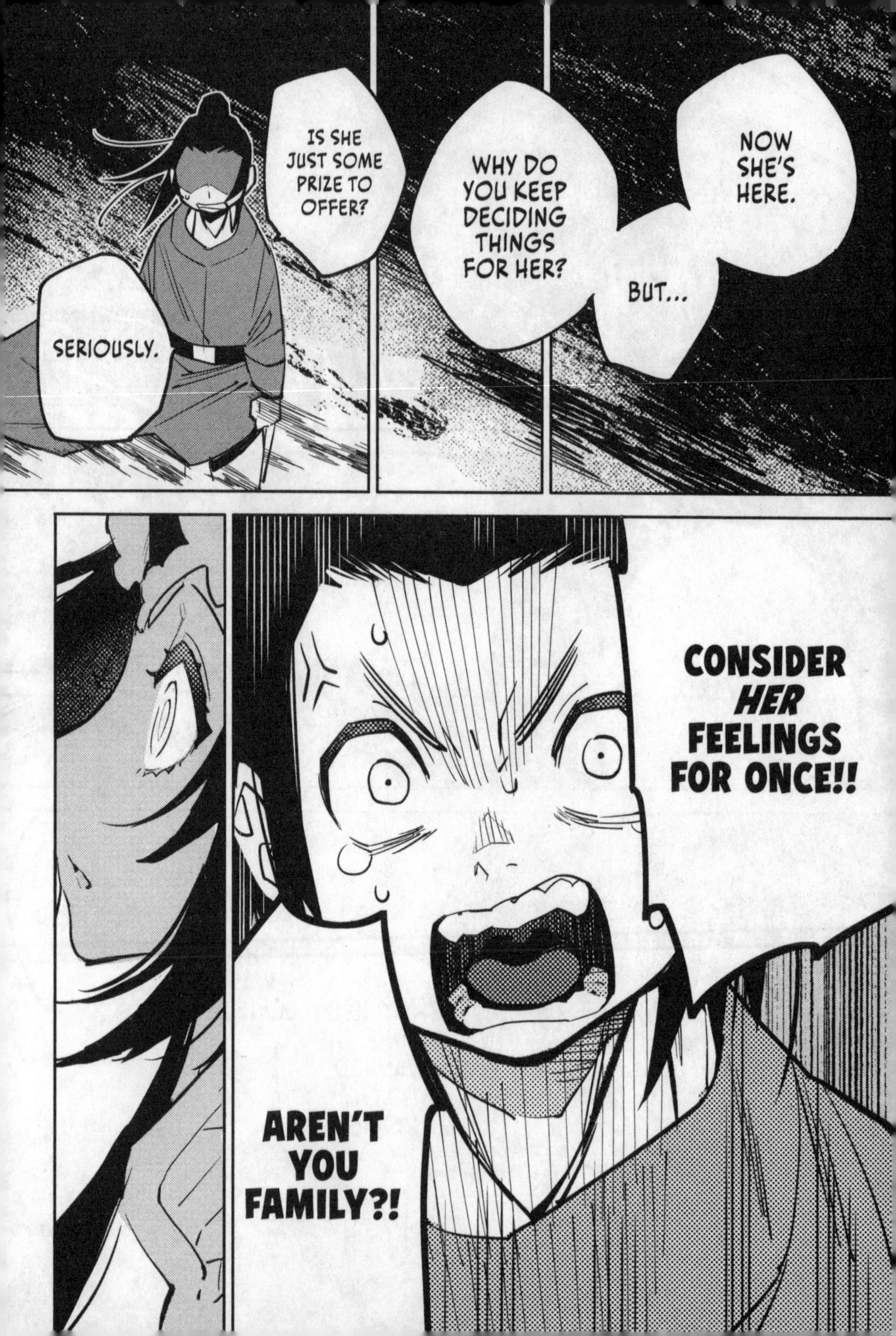
SERIOUSLY.
IS SHE JUST SOME PRIZE TO OFFER?
WHY DO YOU KEEP DECIDING THINGS FOR HER?
BUT...
NOW SHE'S HERE.
CONSIDER *HER* FEELINGS FOR ONCE!!
AREN'T YOU FAMILY?!

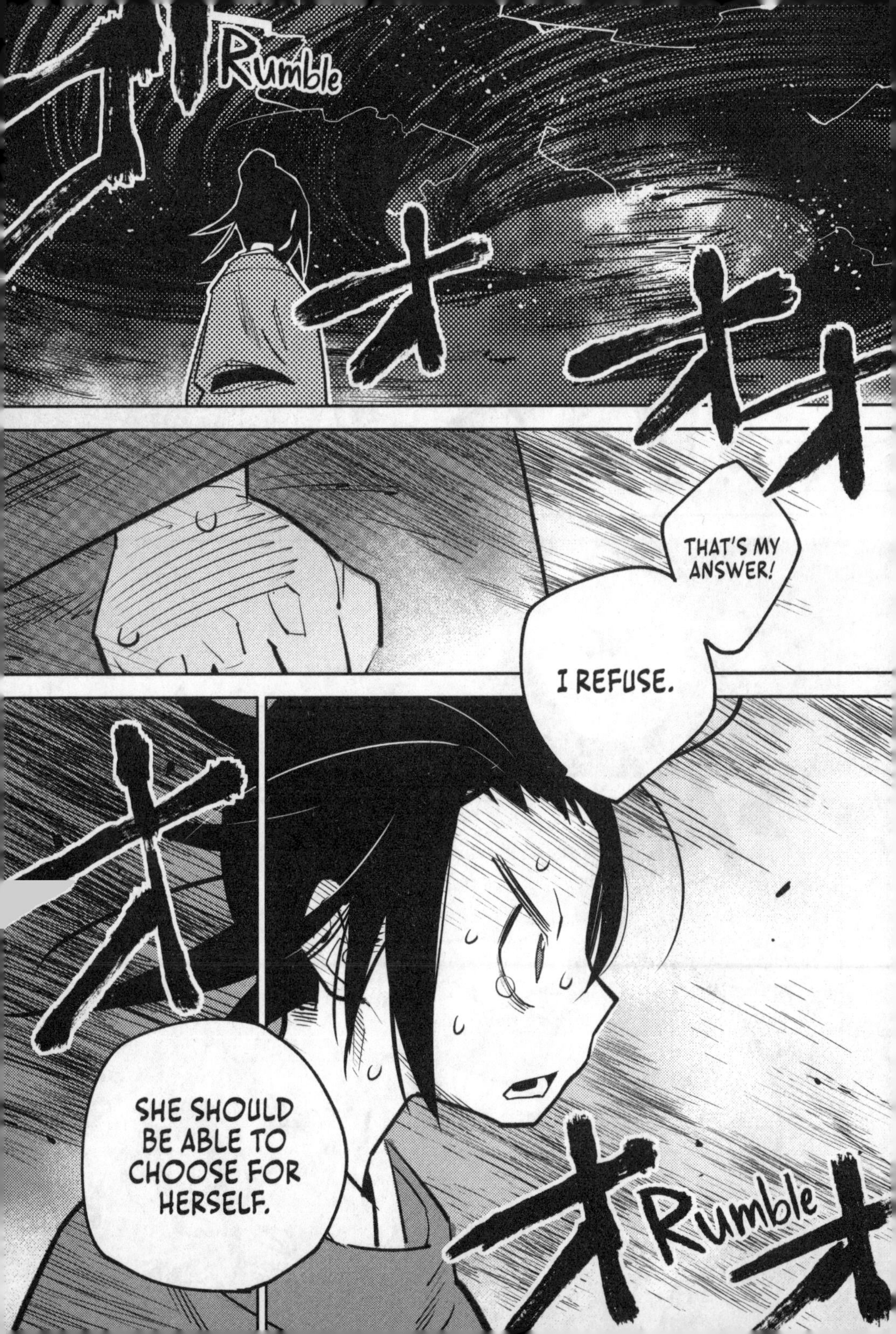
Rumble
THAT'S MY ANSWER!
I REFUSE.
SHE SHOULD BE ABLE TO CHOOSE FOR HERSELF.
Rumble

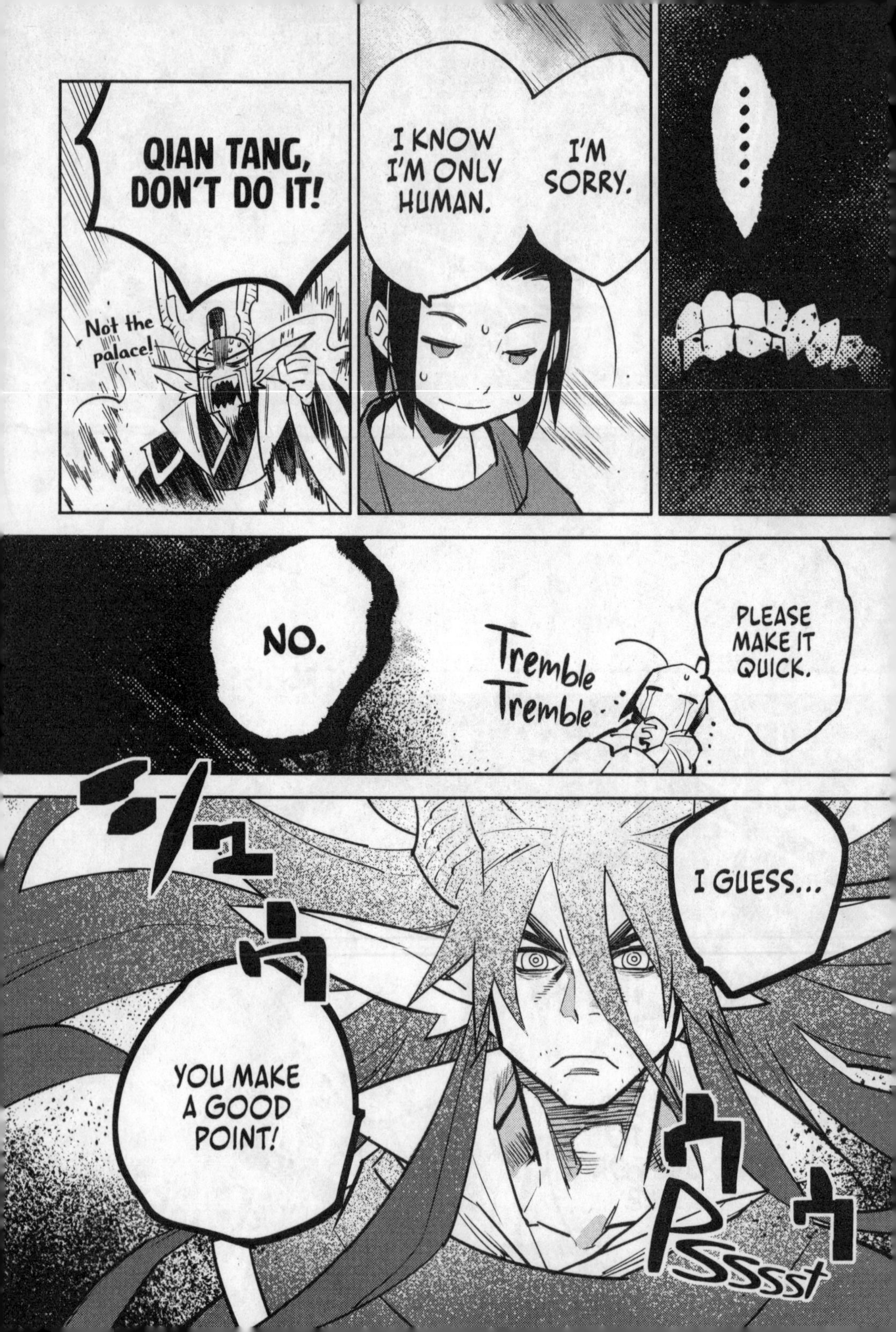
......
I'M SORRY.
I KNOW I'M ONLY HUMAN.
QIAN TANG, DON'T DO IT!
Not the palace!
PLEASE MAKE IT QUICK.
Tremble Tremble
NO.
I GUESS...
YOU MAKE A GOOD POINT!
Pssst

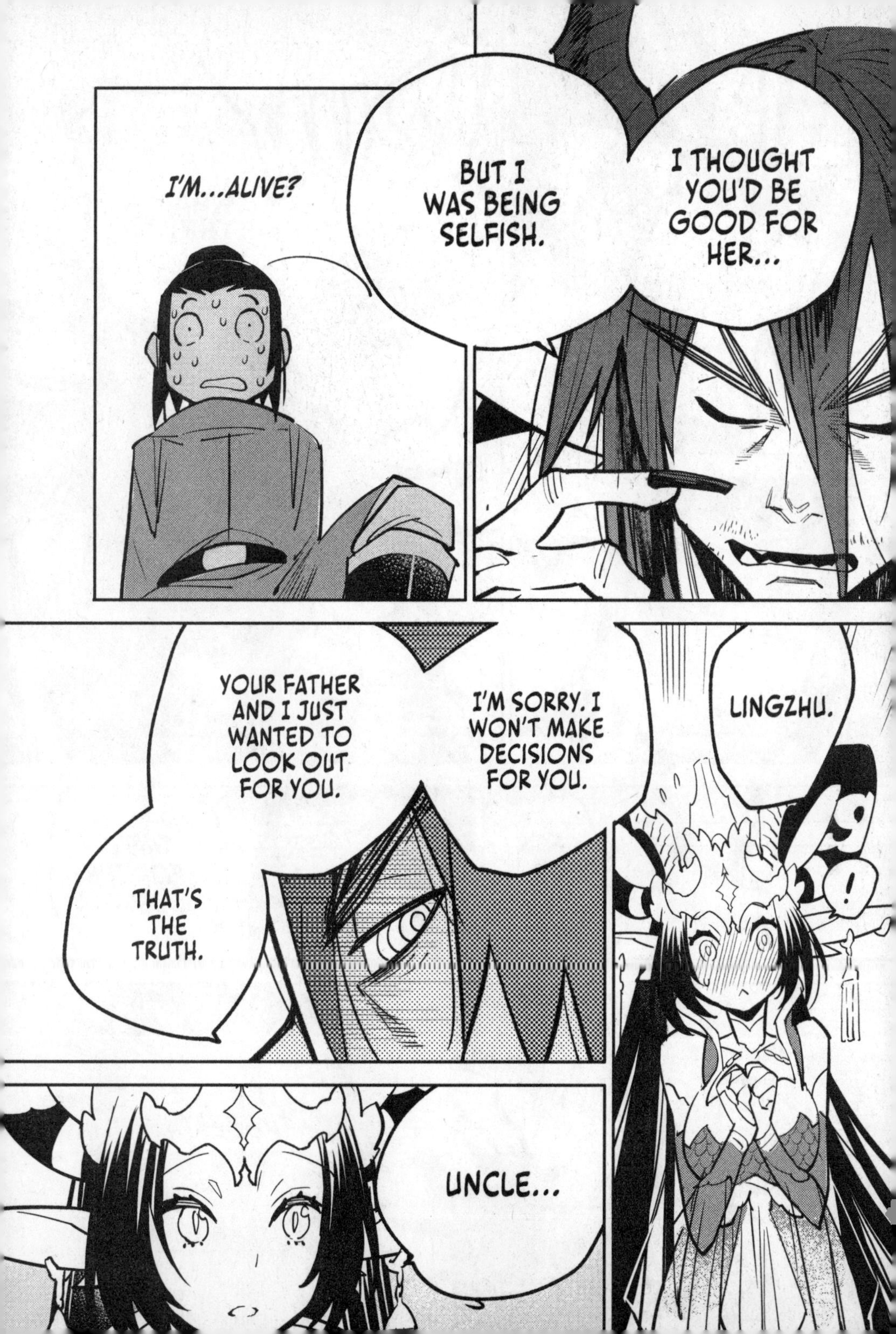
I THOUGHT YOU'D BE GOOD FOR HER...
BUT I WAS BEING SELFISH.
I'M...ALIVE?
LINGZHU.
I'M SORRY. I WON'T MAKE DECISIONS FOR YOU.
YOUR FATHER AND I JUST WANTED TO LOOK OUT FOR YOU.
THAT'S THE TRUTH.
UNCLE...

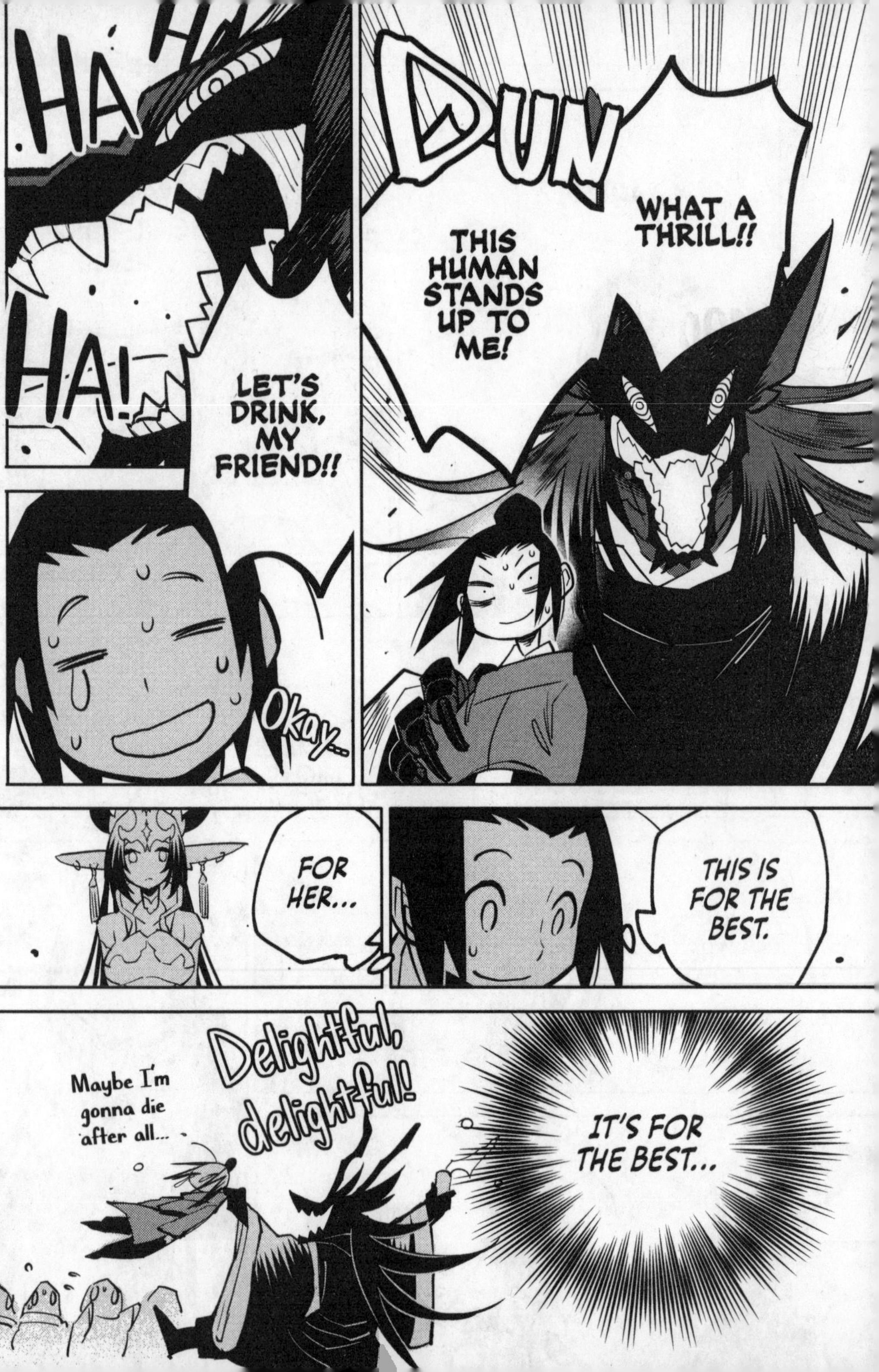

DUN
WHAT A THRILL!!
THIS HUMAN STANDS UP TO ME!
HA HA HA HA!
LET'S DRINK, MY FRIEND!!
Okay...
THIS IS FOR THE BEST.
FOR HER...
IT'S FOR THE BEST...
Delightful, delightful!
Maybe I'm gonna die after all...

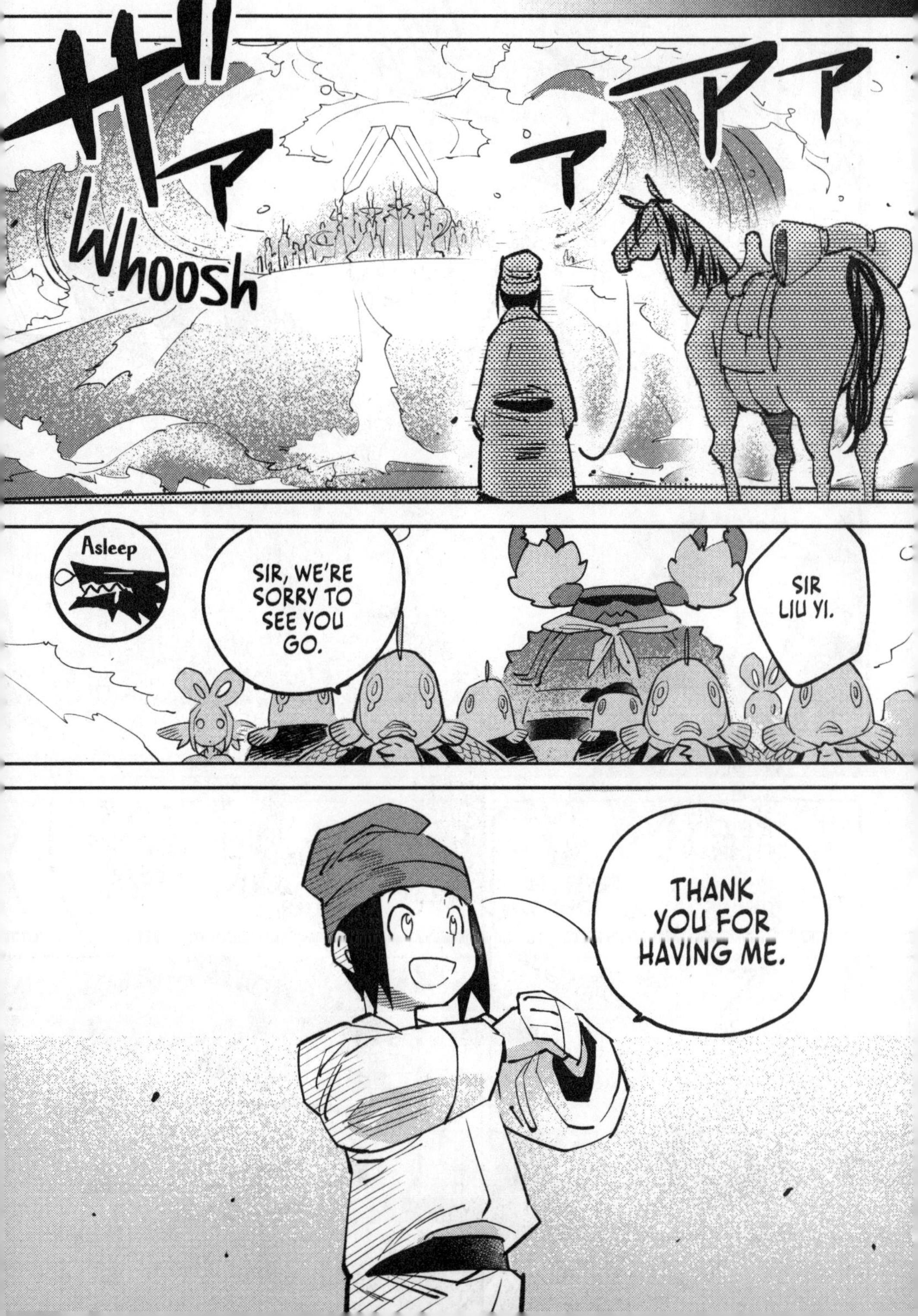
ザァァァァ
Whoosh
Asleep
SIR LIU YI.
SIR, WE'RE SORRY TO SEE YOU GO.
THANK YOU FOR HAVING ME.

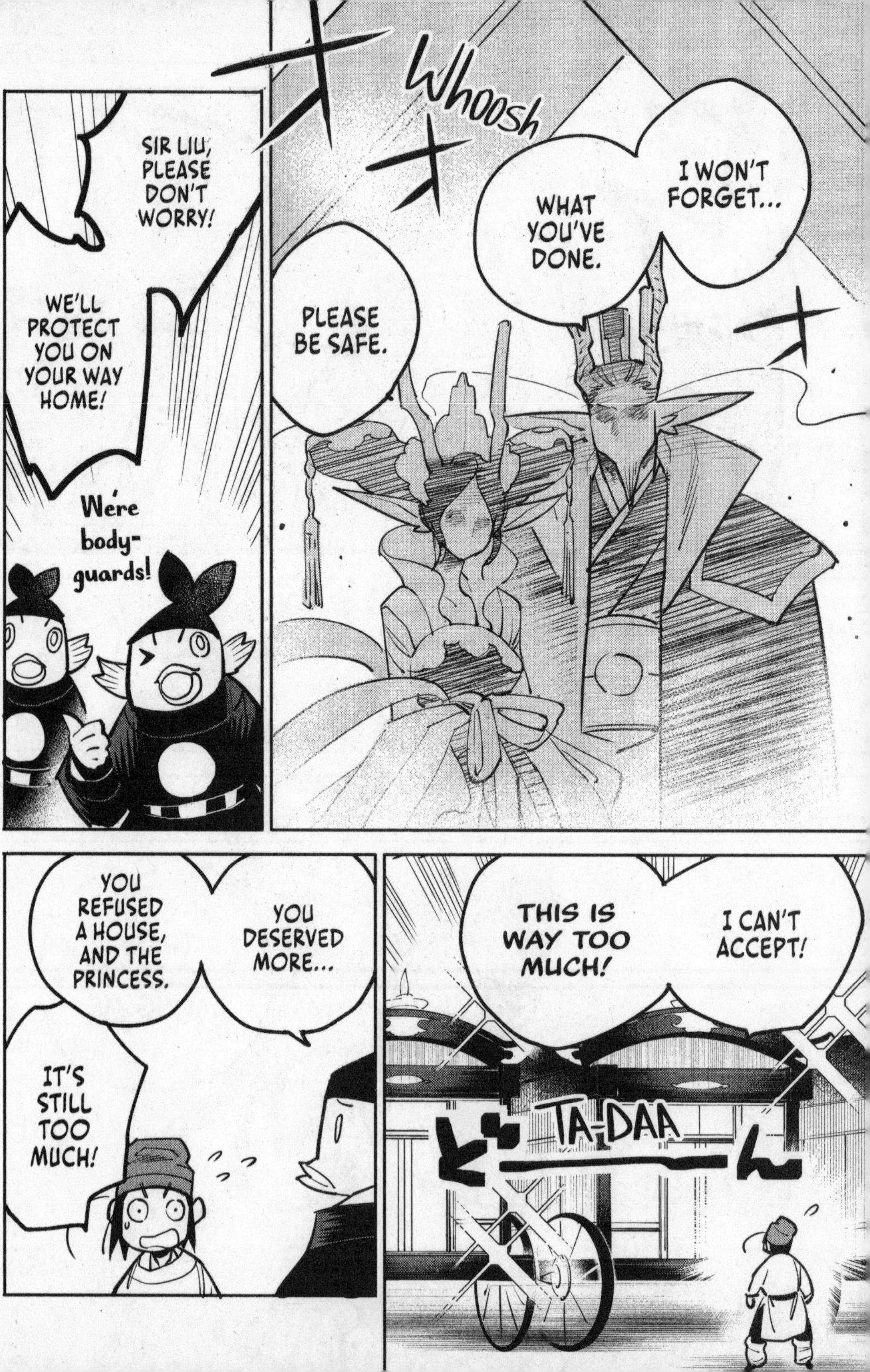
Whoosh
I WON'T FORGET...
WHAT YOU'VE DONE.
PLEASE BE SAFE.
SIR LIU, PLEASE DON'T WORRY!
WE'LL PROTECT YOU ON YOUR WAY HOME!
We're body-guards!
I CAN'T ACCEPT!
THIS IS WAY TOO MUCH!
TA-DAA
YOU DESERVED MORE...
YOU REFUSED A HOUSE, AND THE PRINCESS.
IT'S STILL TOO MUCH!

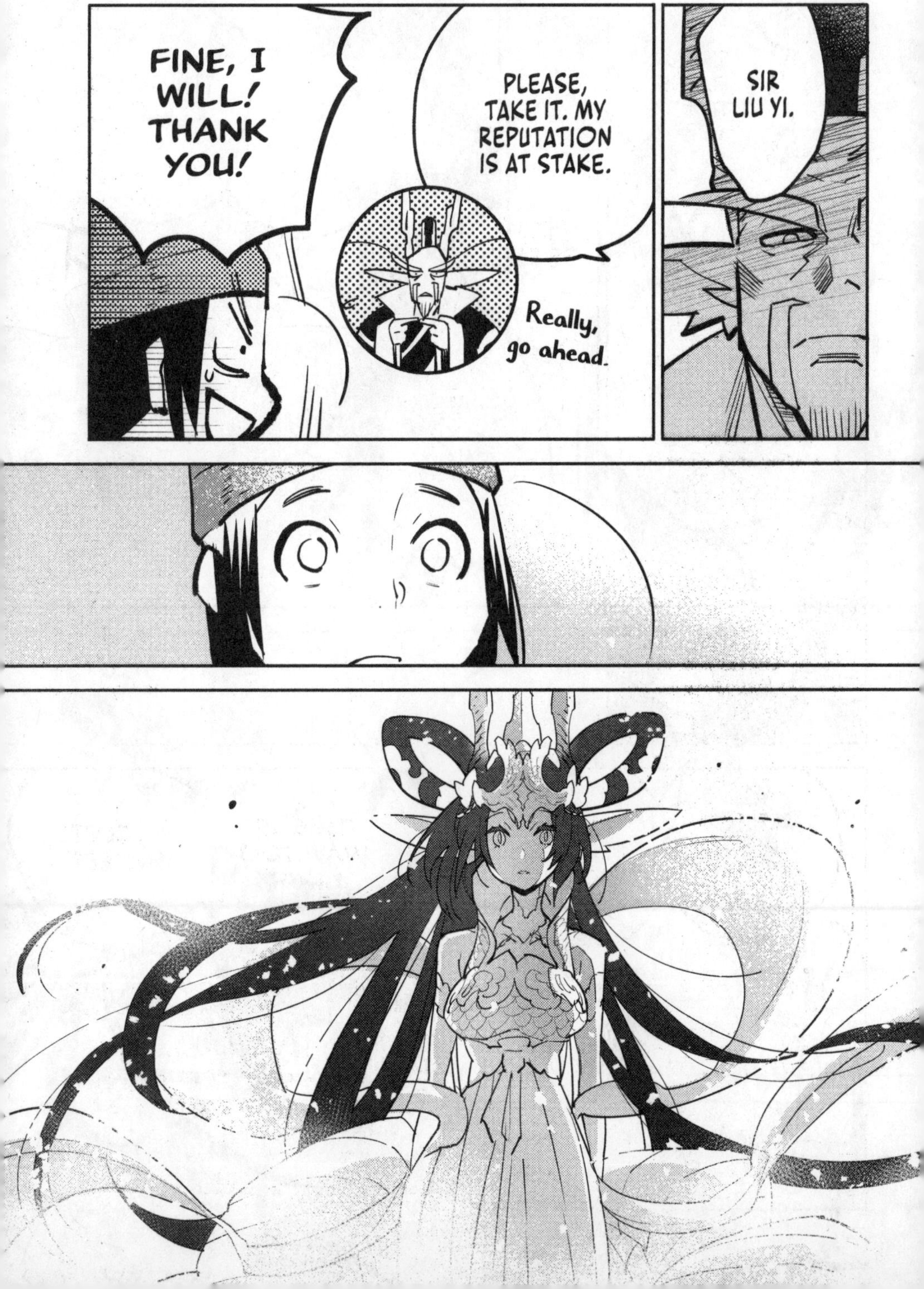
SIR LIU YI.
PLEASE, TAKE IT. MY REPUTATION IS AT STAKE.
Really, go ahead.
FINE, I WILL! THANK YOU!

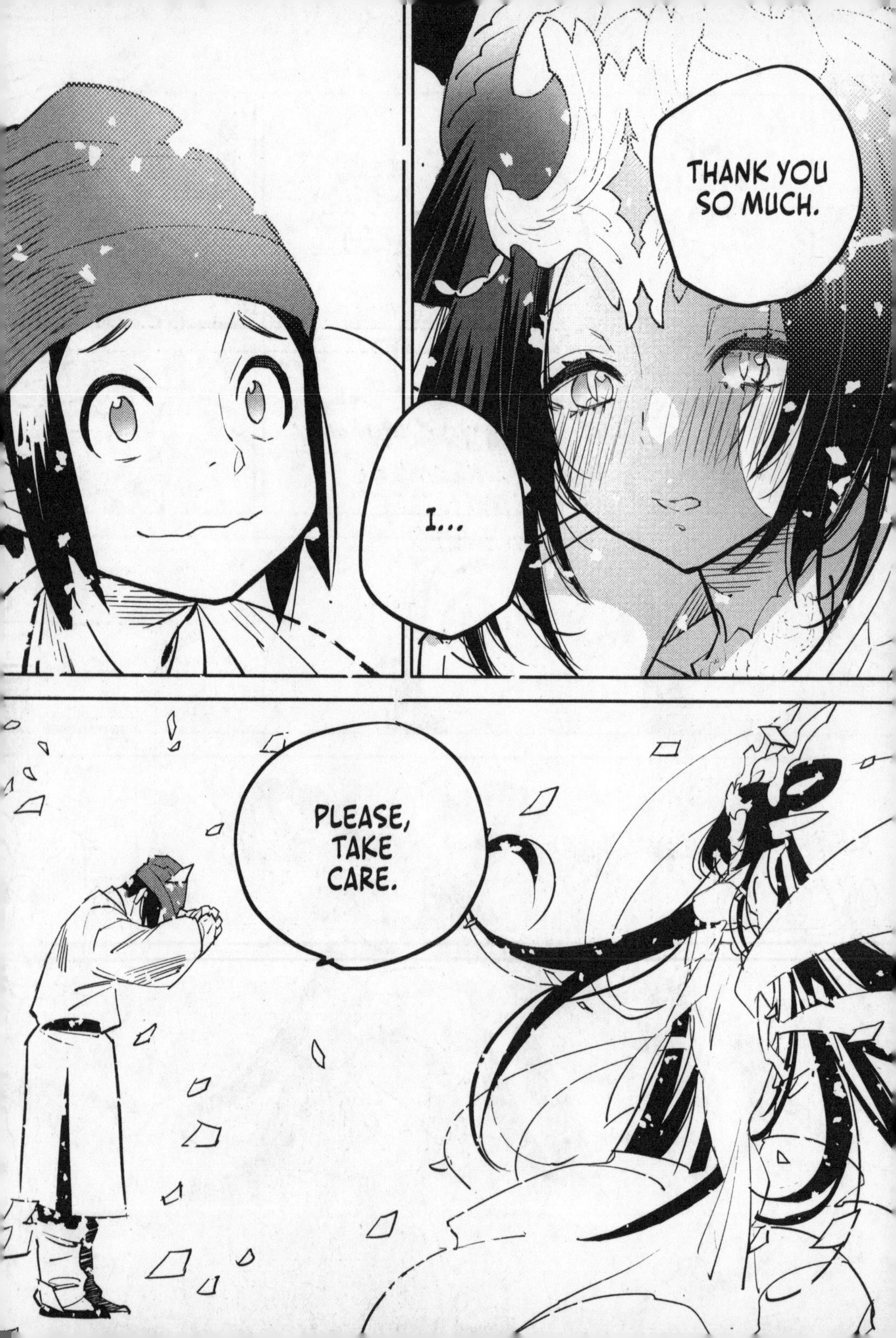
THANK YOU SO MUCH.
I...
PLEASE, TAKE CARE.

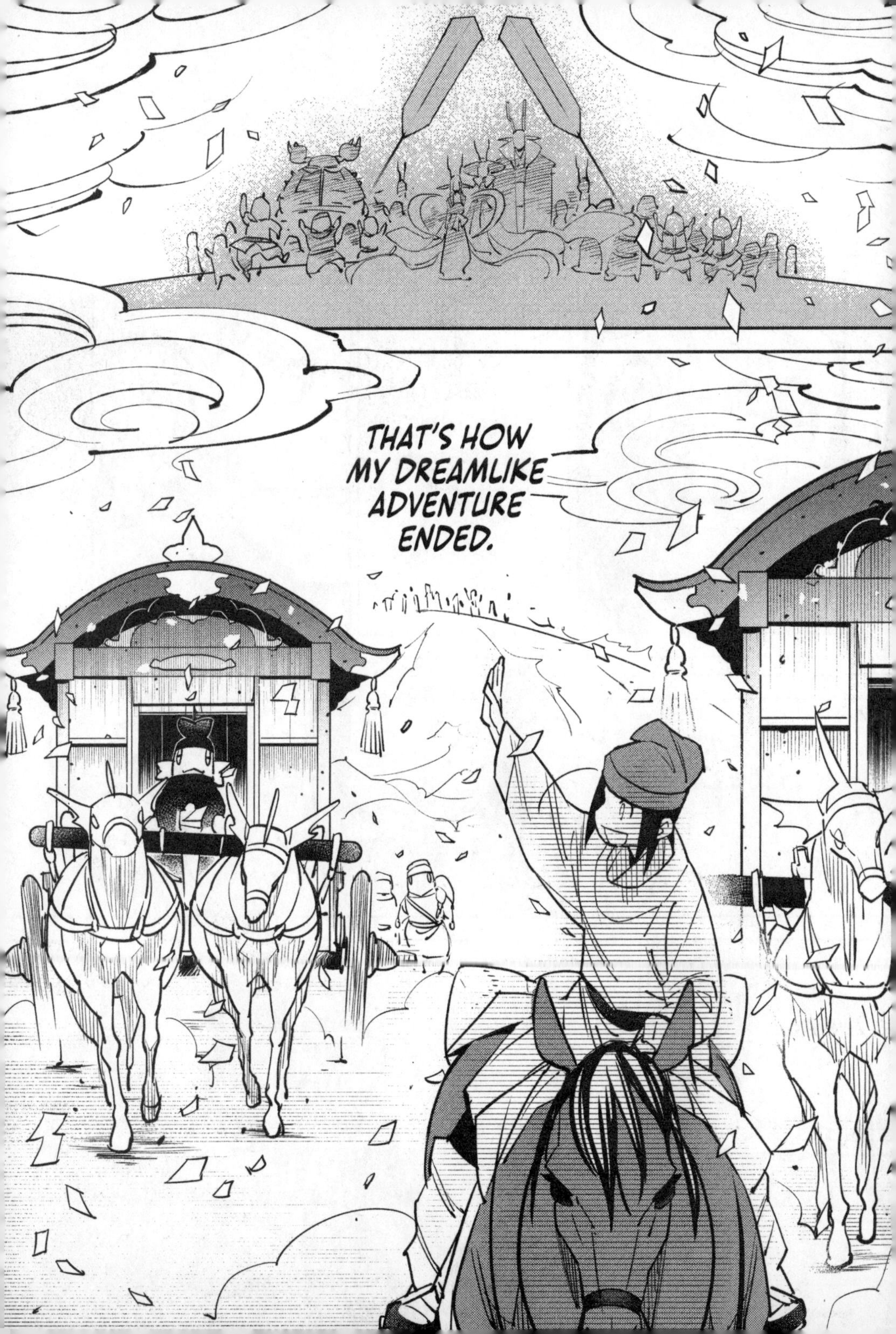
THAT'S HOW MY DREAMLIKE ADVENTURE ENDED.

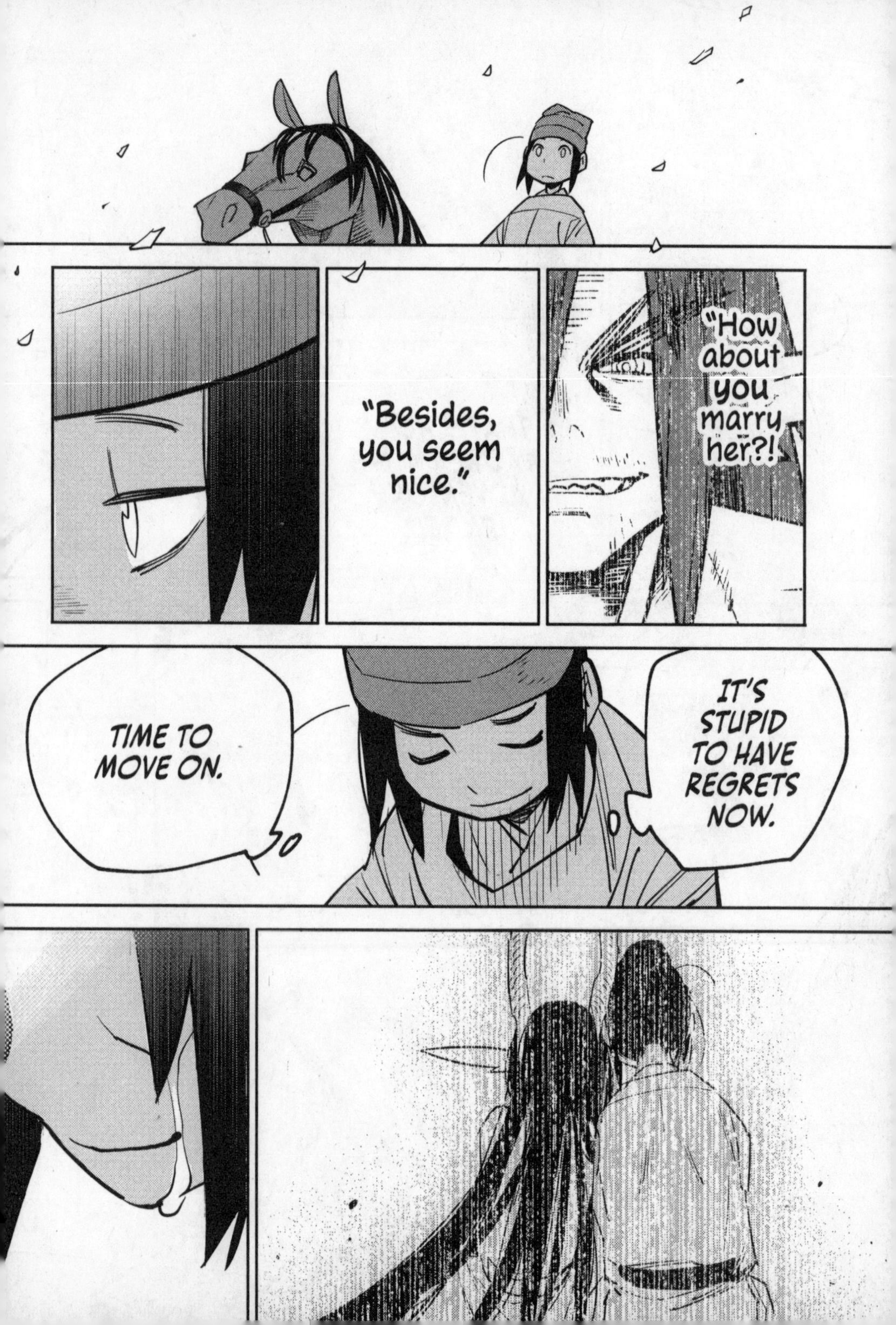
"How about you marry her?!
"Besides, you seem nice."
IT'S STUPID TO HAVE REGRETS NOW.
TIME TO MOVE ON.

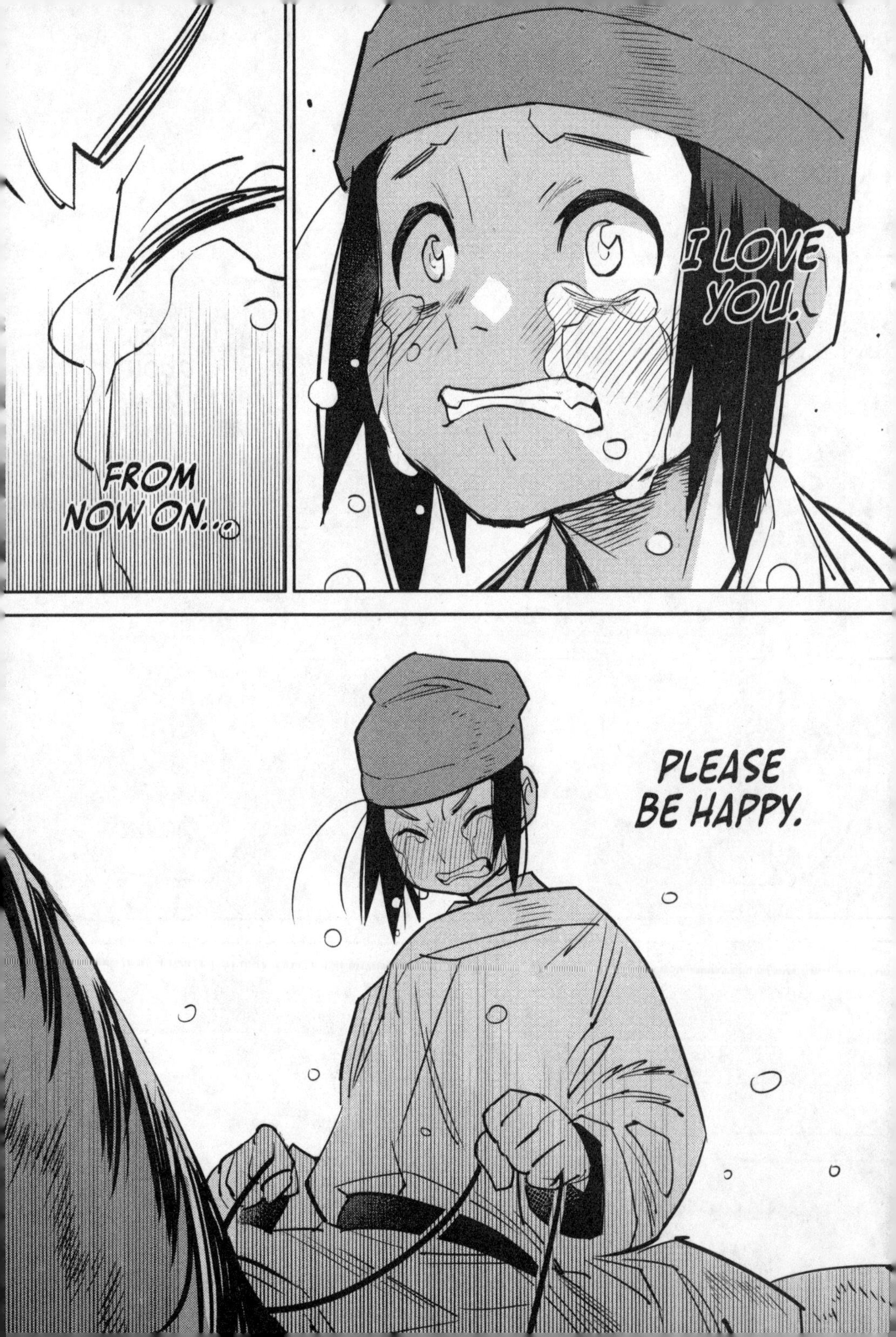
I LOVE YOU.
FROM NOW ON...
PLEASE BE HAPPY.

A Chinese Fantasy

The Dragon King's Daughter

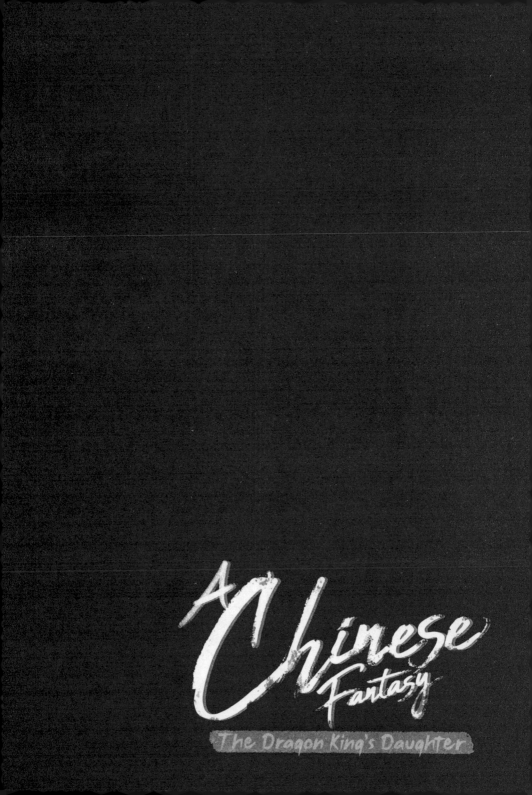

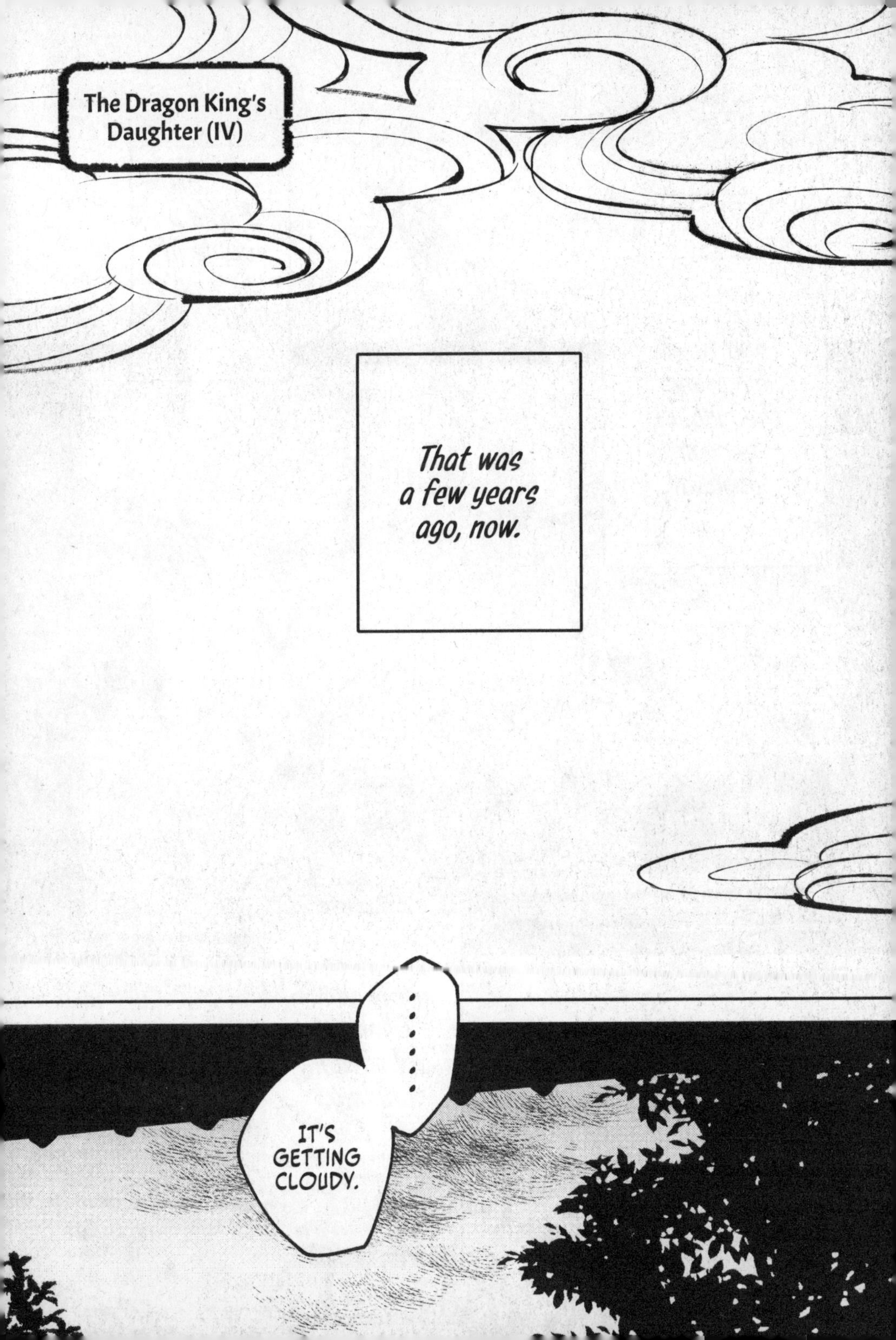
The Dragon King's Daughter (IV)
That was a few years ago, now.
......
IT'S GETTING CLOUDY.

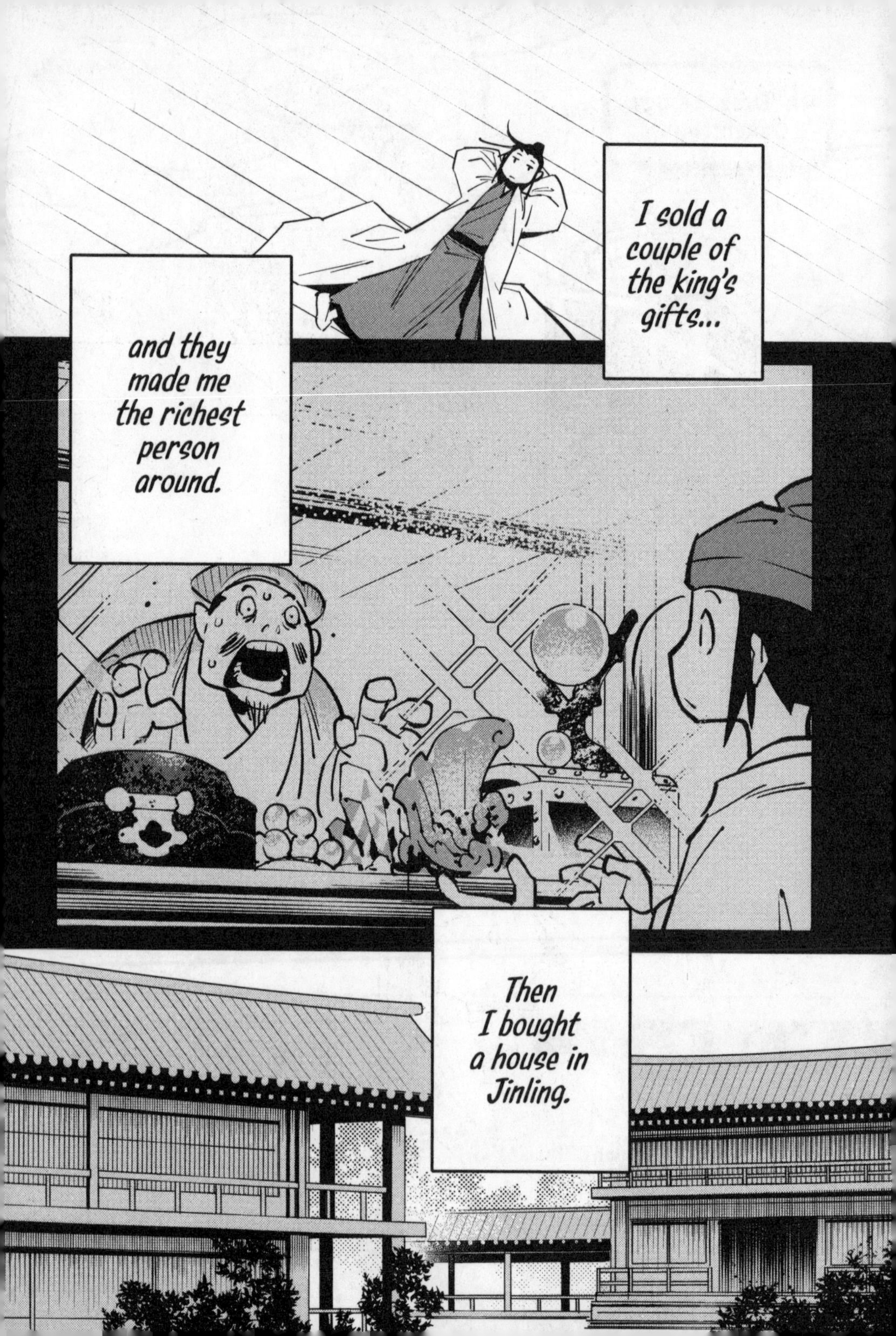
I sold a couple of the king's gifts...
and they made me the richest person around.
Then I bought a house in Jinling.

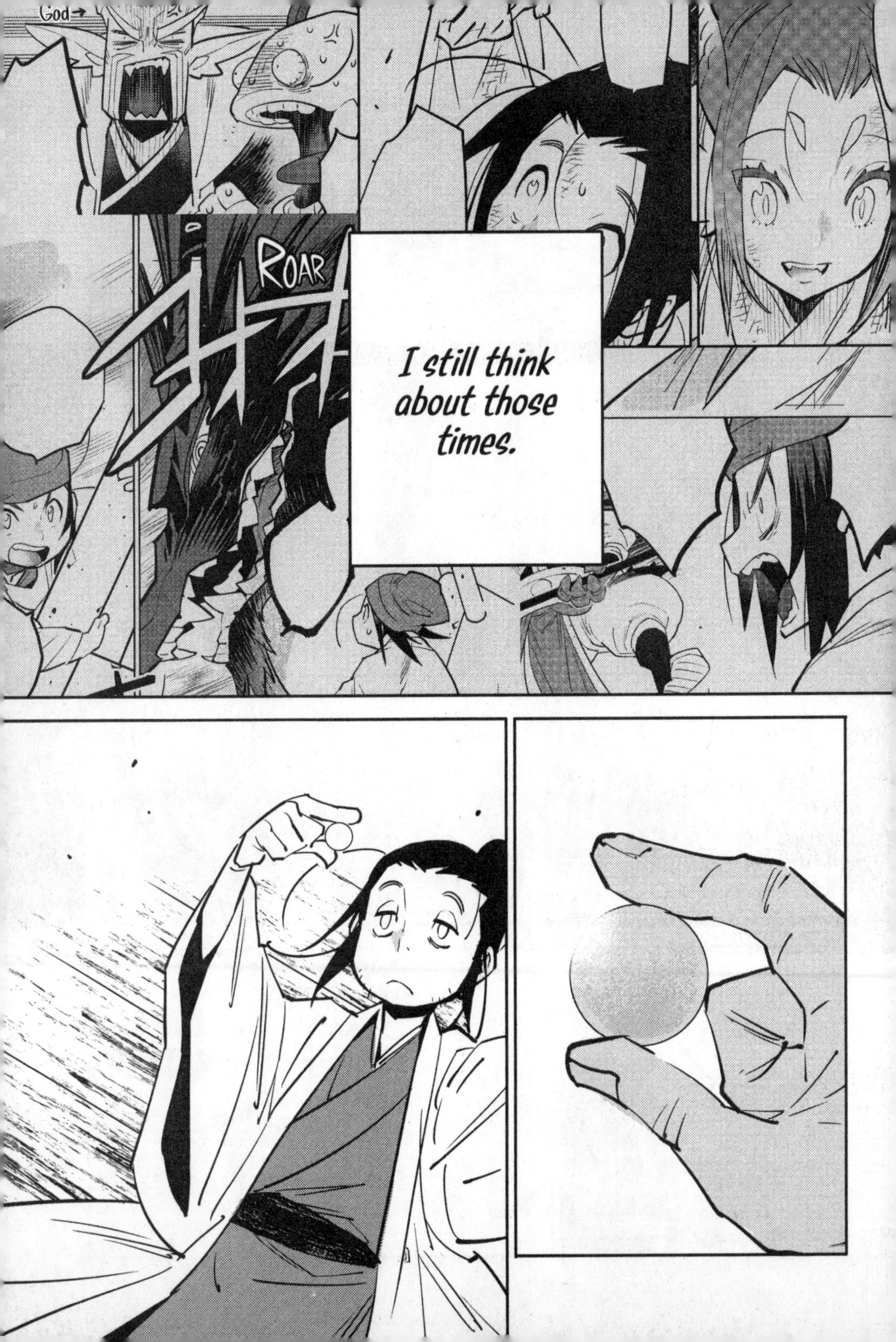
God→
ROAR
I still think about those times.

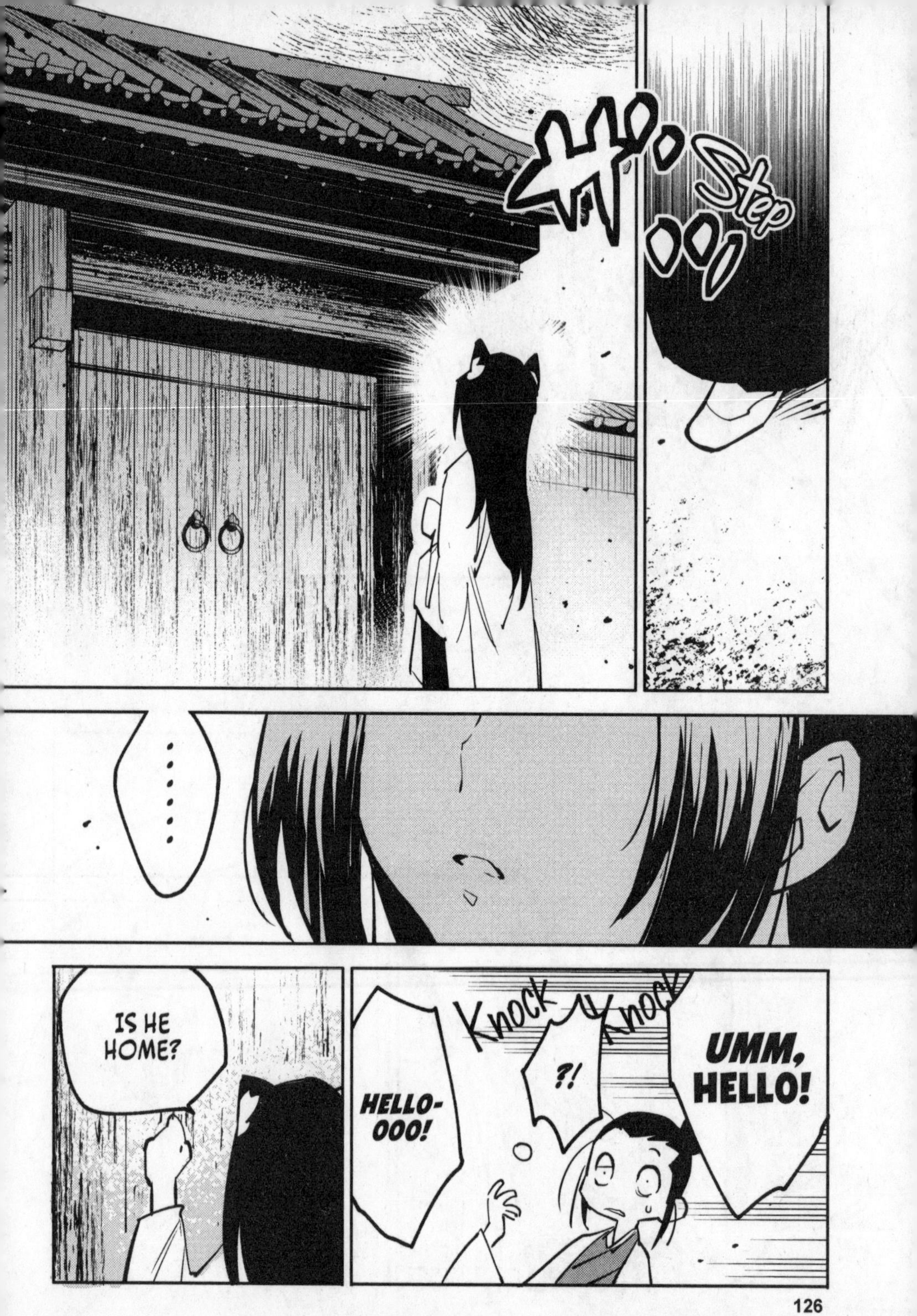
Step
......
UMM, HELLO!
?!
Knock Knock
HELLO-OOO!
IS HE HOME?

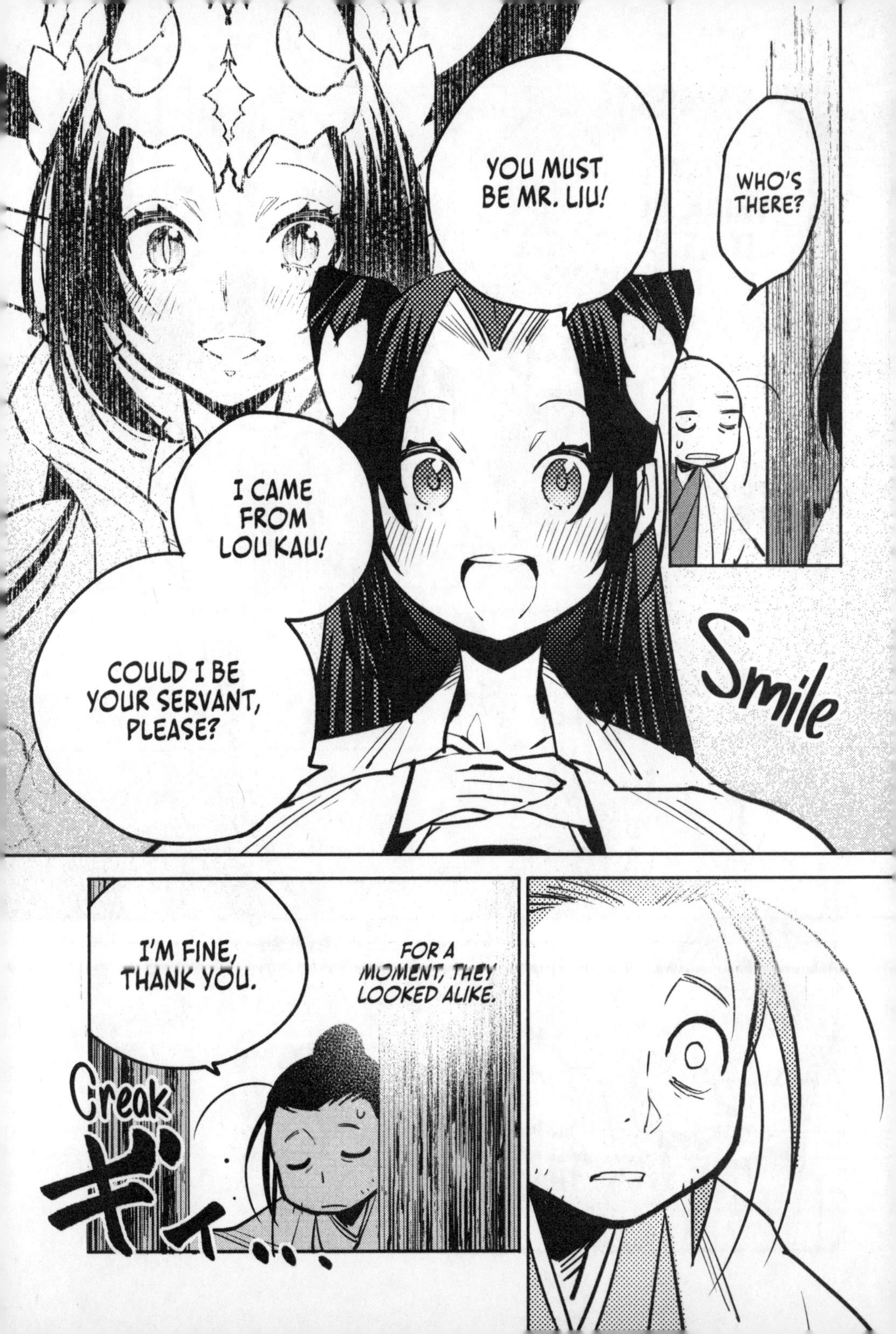
WHO'S THERE?
YOU MUST BE MR. LIU!
I CAME FROM LOU KAU!
COULD I BE YOUR SERVANT, PLEASE?
Smile
FOR A MOMENT, THEY LOOKED ALIKE.
I'M FINE, THANK YOU.
Creak
ギィ…

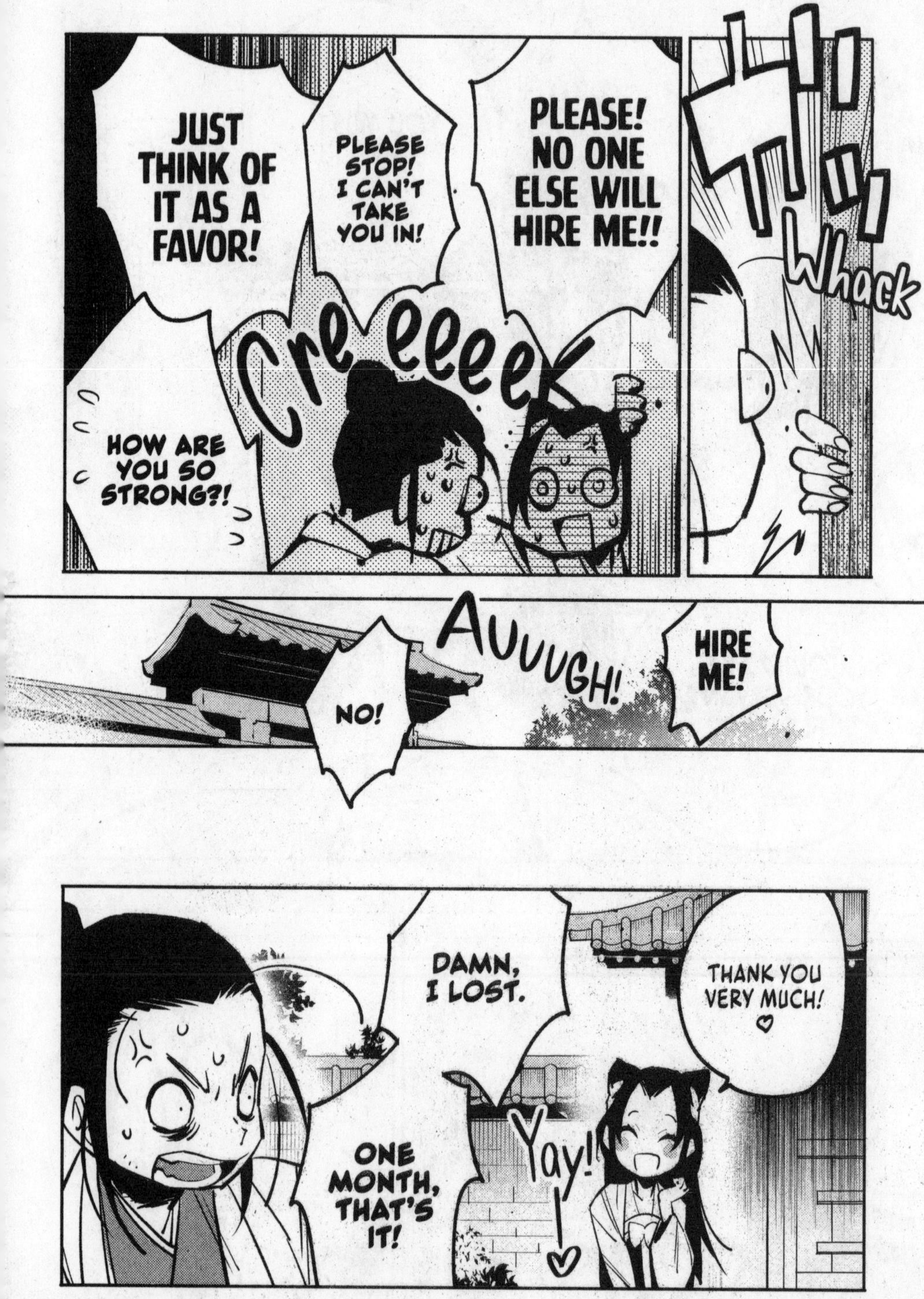
Whack
PLEASE! NO ONE ELSE WILL HIRE ME!!
PLEASE STOP! I CAN'T TAKE YOU IN!
JUST THINK OF IT AS A FAVOR!
Creeeeek
HOW ARE YOU SO STRONG?!
HIRE ME!
AUUUGH!
NO!
THANK YOU VERY MUCH! ♡
Yay! ♡
DAMN, I LOST.
ONE MONTH, THAT'S IT!

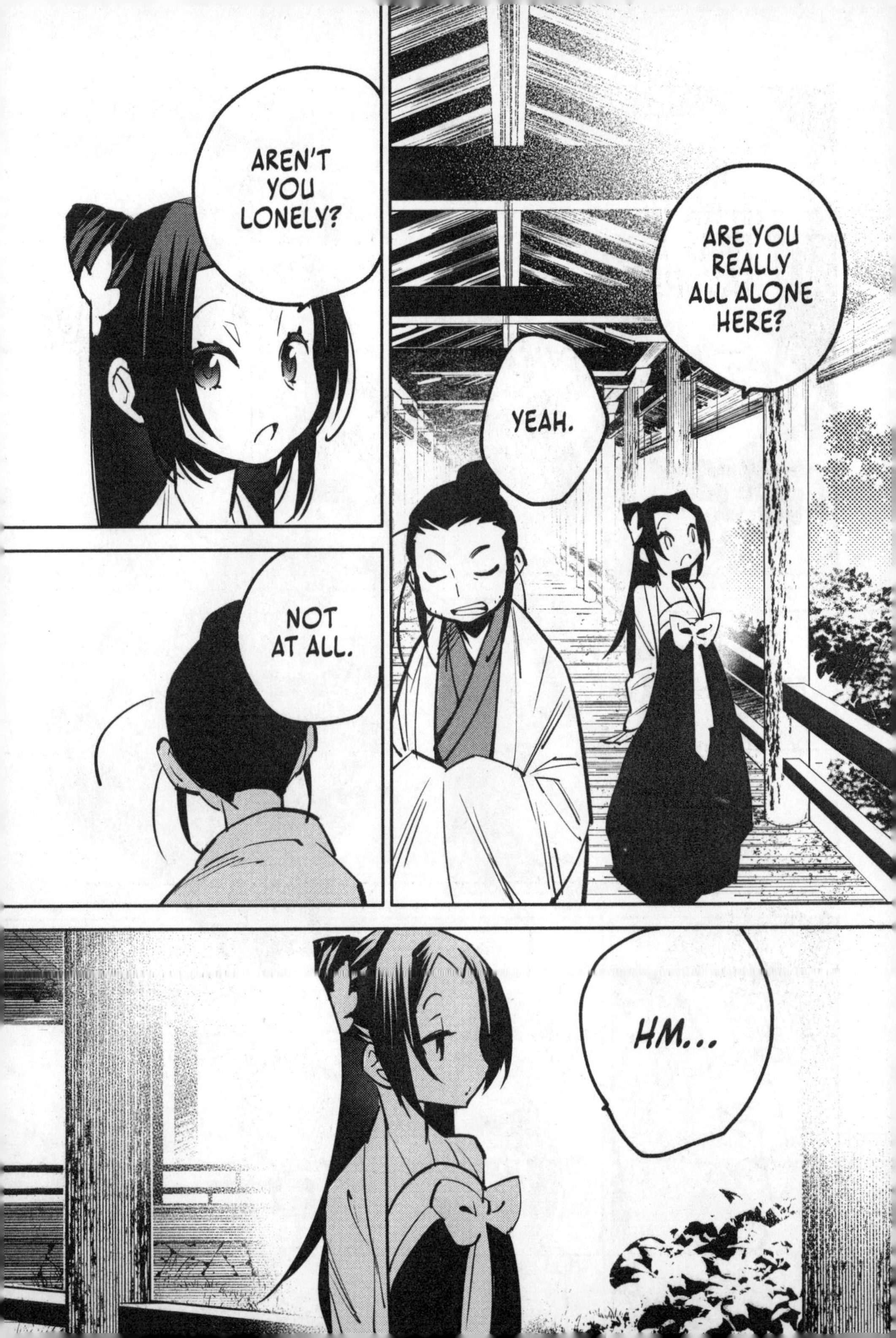
ARE YOU REALLY ALL ALONE HERE?
YEAH.
AREN'T YOU LONELY?
NOT AT ALL.
HM...

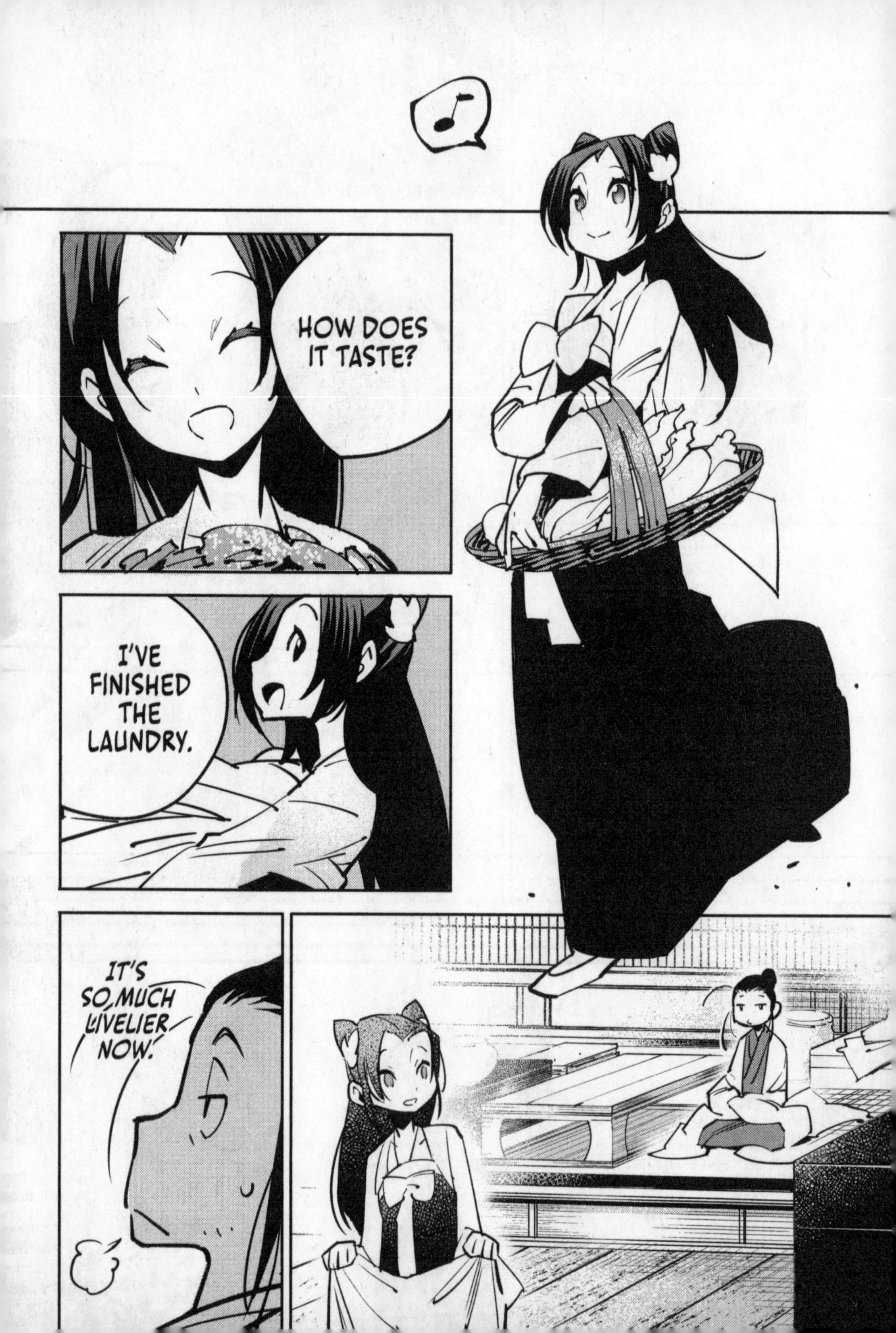
HOW DOES IT TASTE?
I'VE FINISHED THE LAUNDRY.
IT'S SO MUCH LIVELIER NOW.

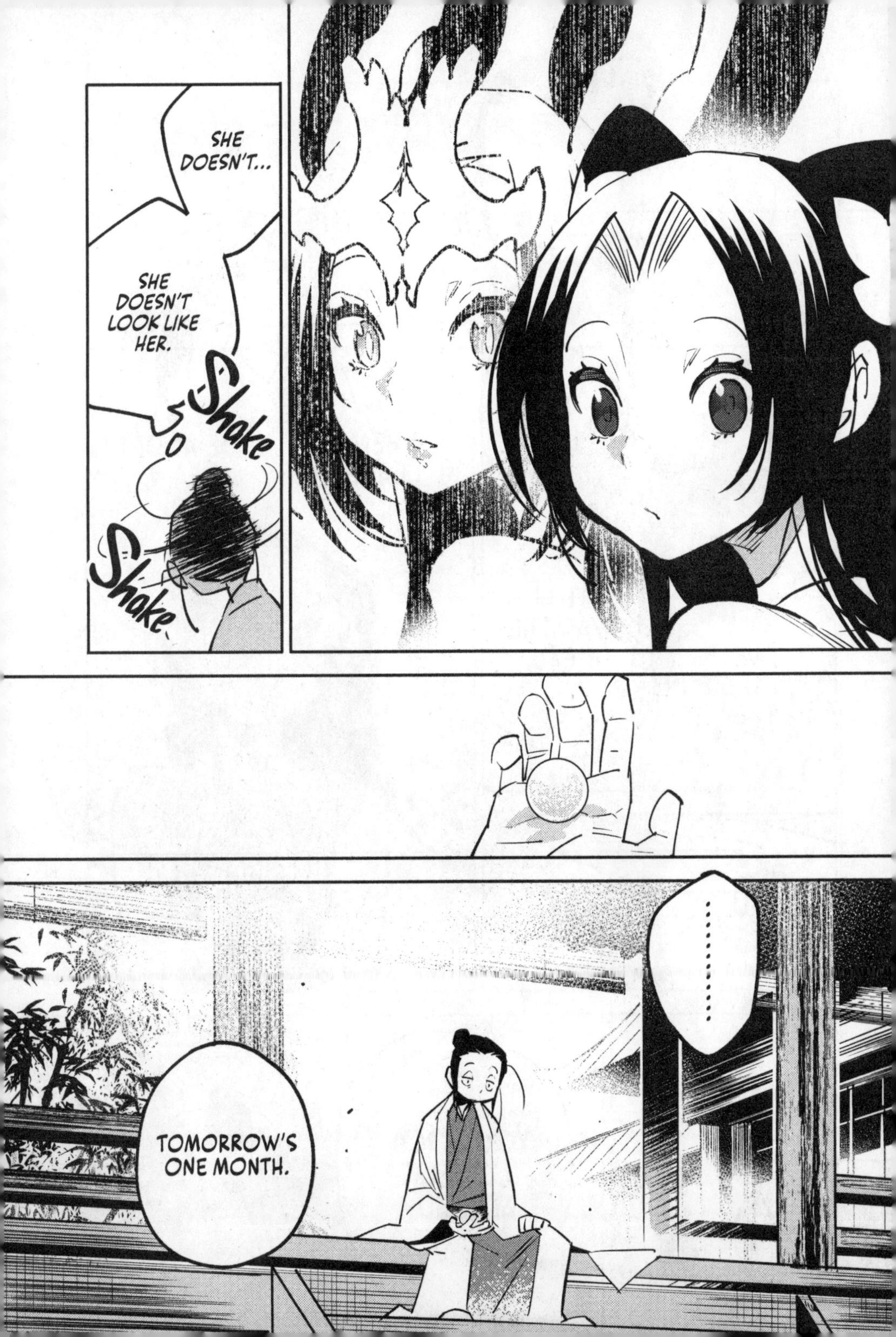
SHE DOESN'T...
SHE DOESN'T LOOK LIKE HER.
Shake
Shake
......
TOMORROW'S ONE MONTH.

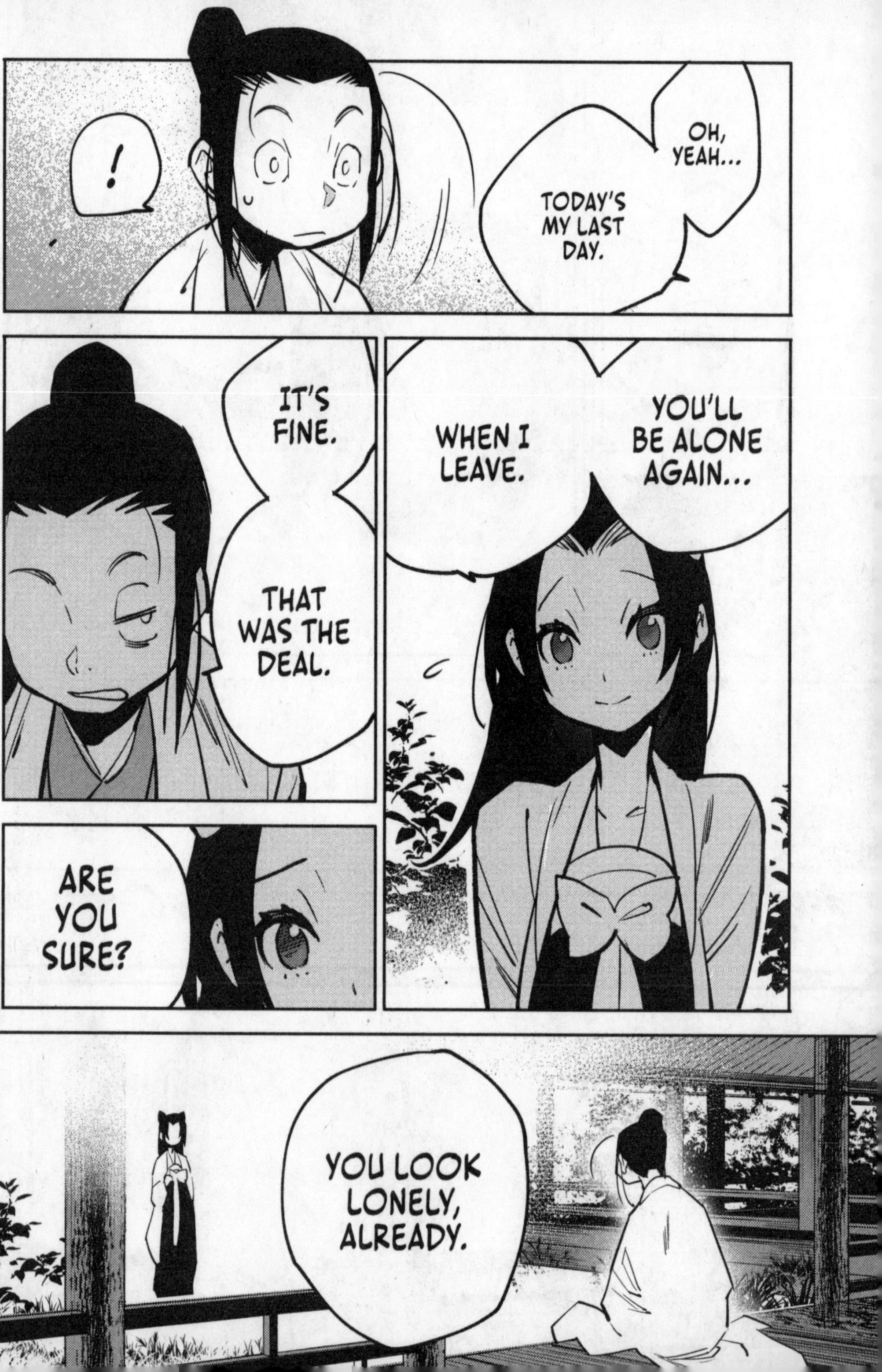
OH, YEAH...
TODAY'S MY LAST DAY.
!
YOU'LL BE ALONE AGAIN...
WHEN I LEAVE.
IT'S FINE.
THAT WAS THE DEAL.
ARE YOU SURE?
YOU LOOK LONELY, ALREADY.

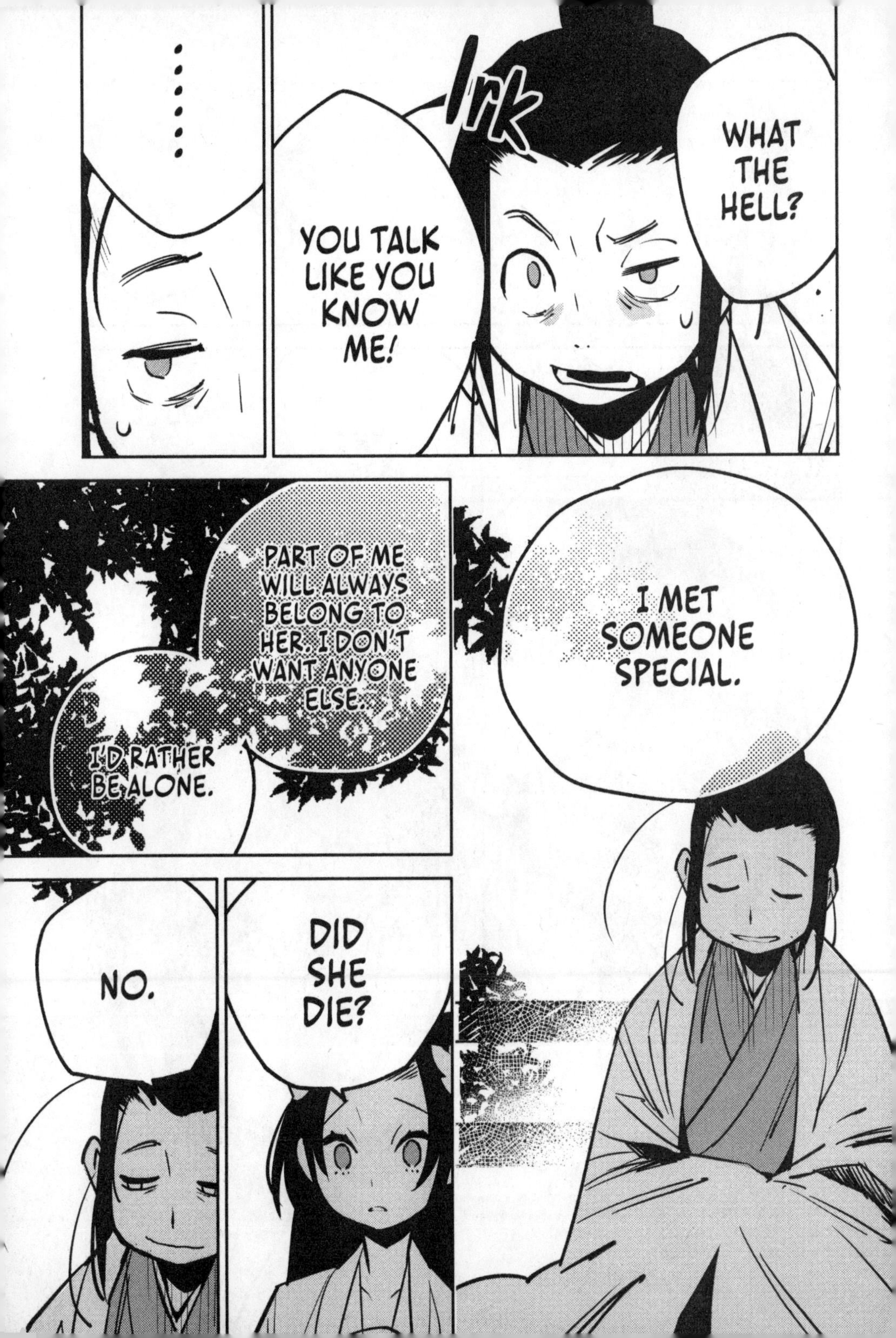
Irk
WHAT THE HELL?
YOU TALK LIKE YOU KNOW ME!
......
I MET SOMEONE SPECIAL.
PART OF ME WILL ALWAYS BELONG TO HER. I DON'T WANT ANYONE ELSE.
I'D RATHER BE ALONE.
DID SHE DIE?
NO.

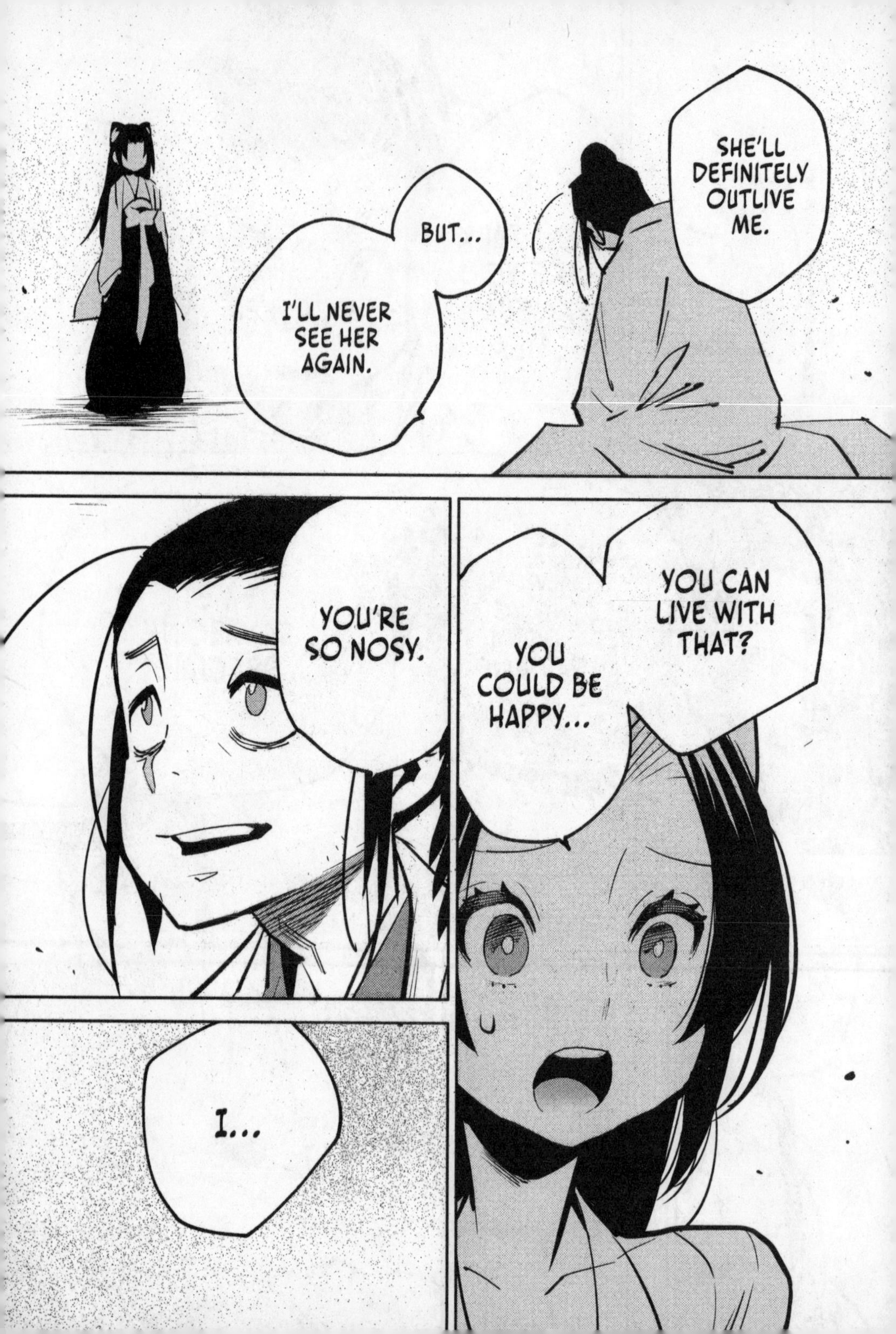
SHE'LL DEFINITELY OUTLIVE ME.
BUT...
I'LL NEVER SEE HER AGAIN.
YOU CAN LIVE WITH THAT?
YOU COULD BE HAPPY...
YOU'RE SO NOSY.
I...

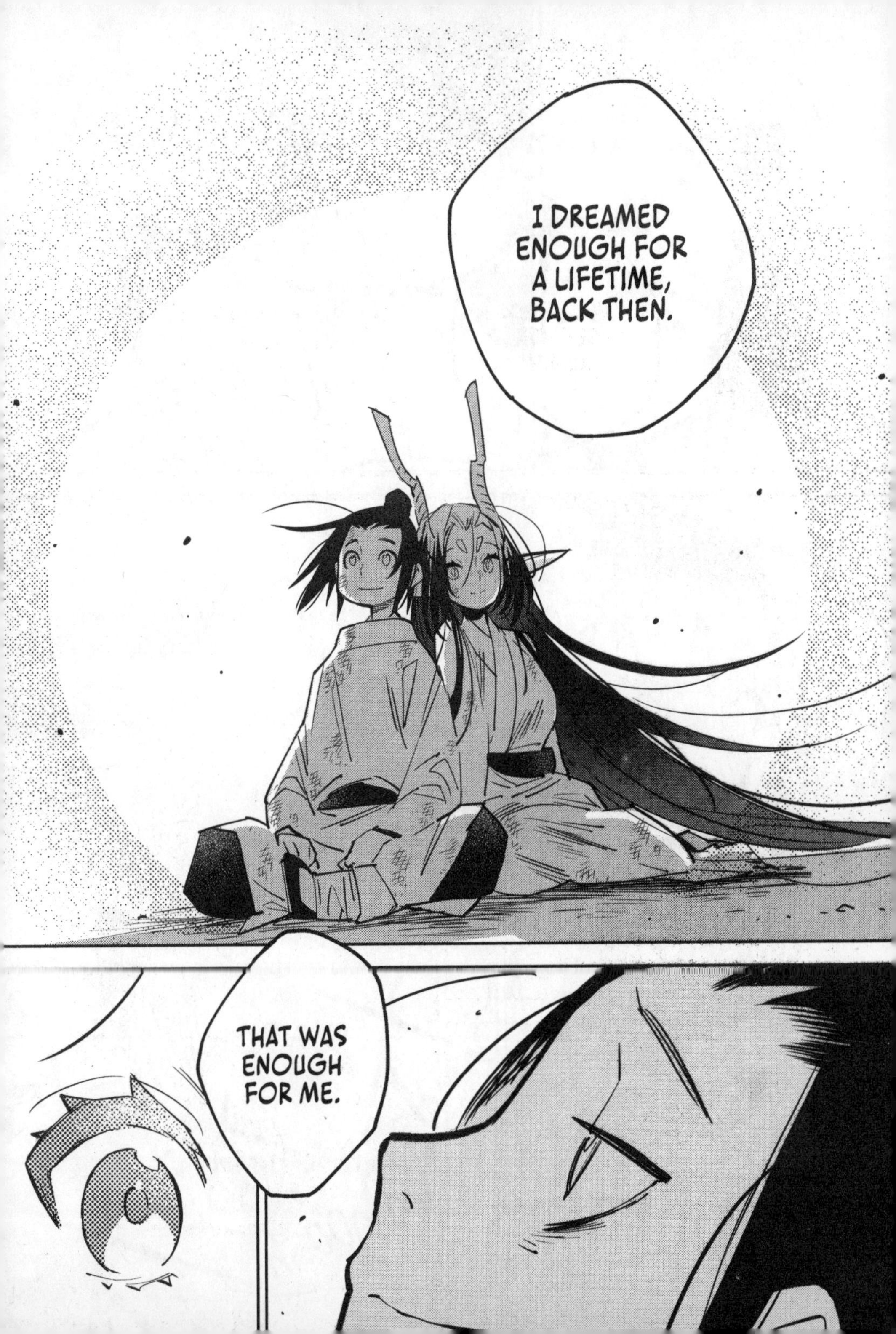
I DREAMED ENOUGH FOR A LIFETIME, BACK THEN.
THAT WAS ENOUGH FOR ME.

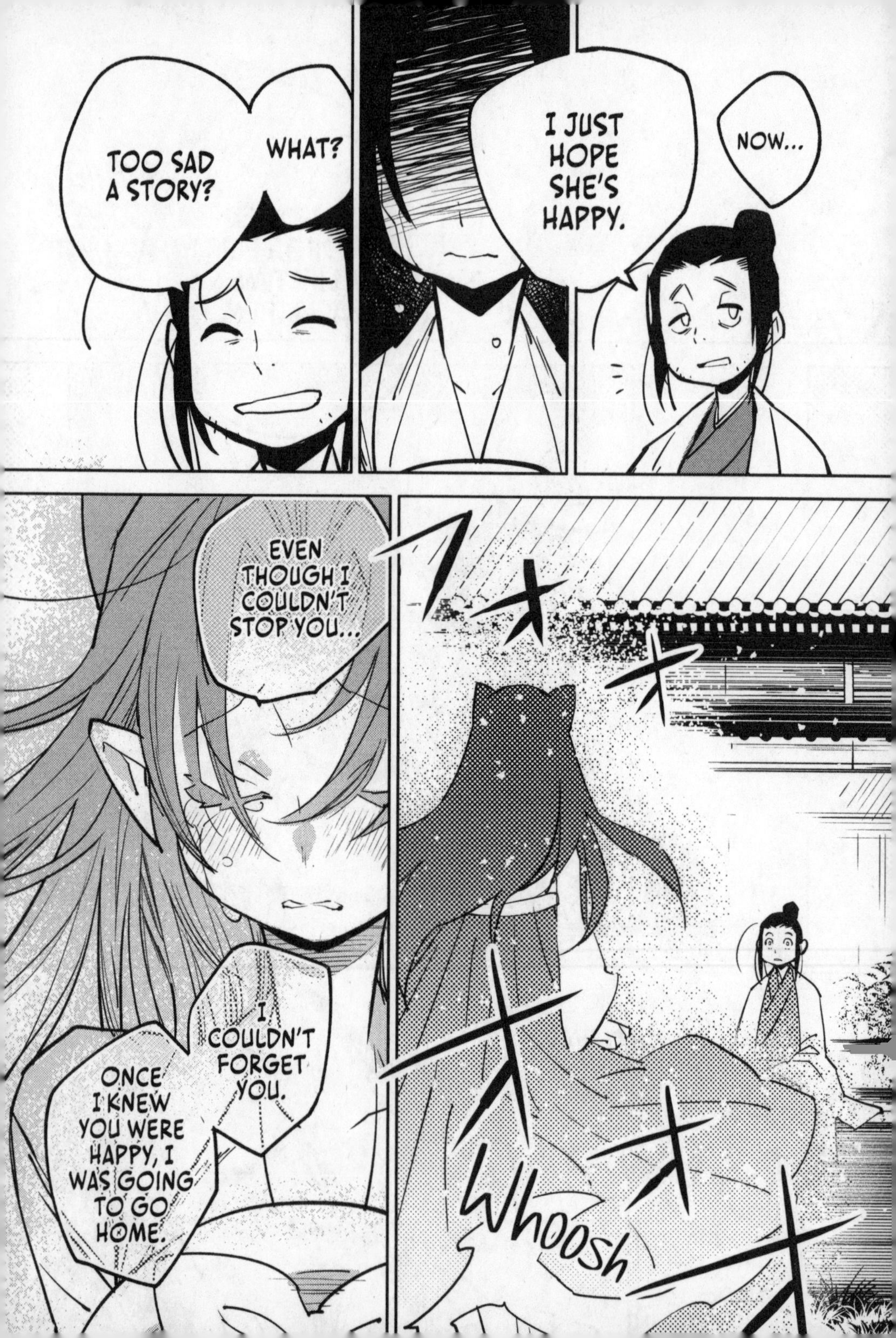
NOW...
I JUST HOPE SHE'S HAPPY.
WHAT?
TOO SAD A STORY?
Whoosh
EVEN THOUGH I COULDN'T STOP YOU...
I COULDN'T FORGET YOU.
ONCE I KNEW YOU WERE HAPPY, I WAS GOING TO GO HOME.

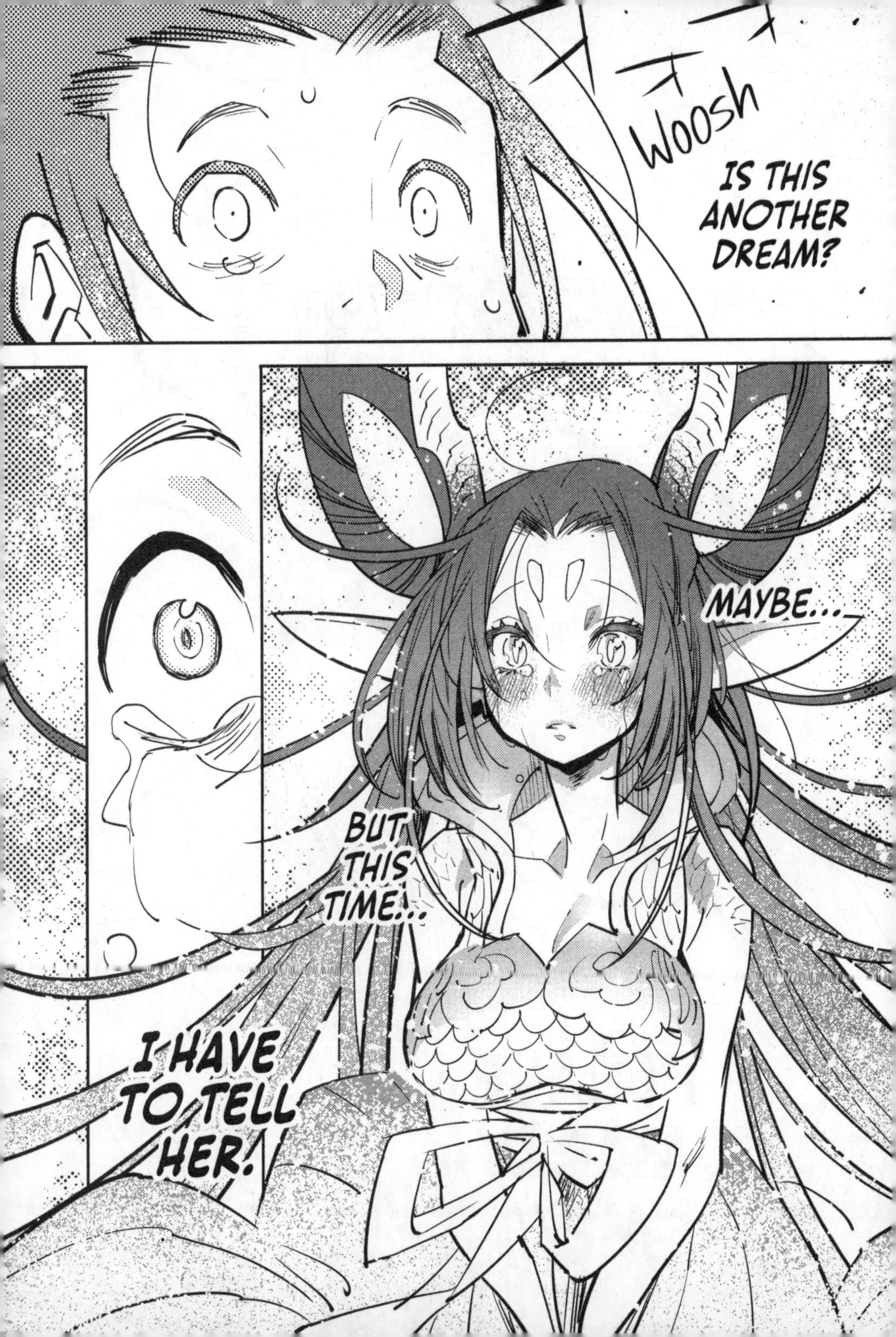
Woosh
IS THIS ANOTHER DREAM?
MAYBE...
BUT THIS TIME...
I HAVE TO TELL HER!

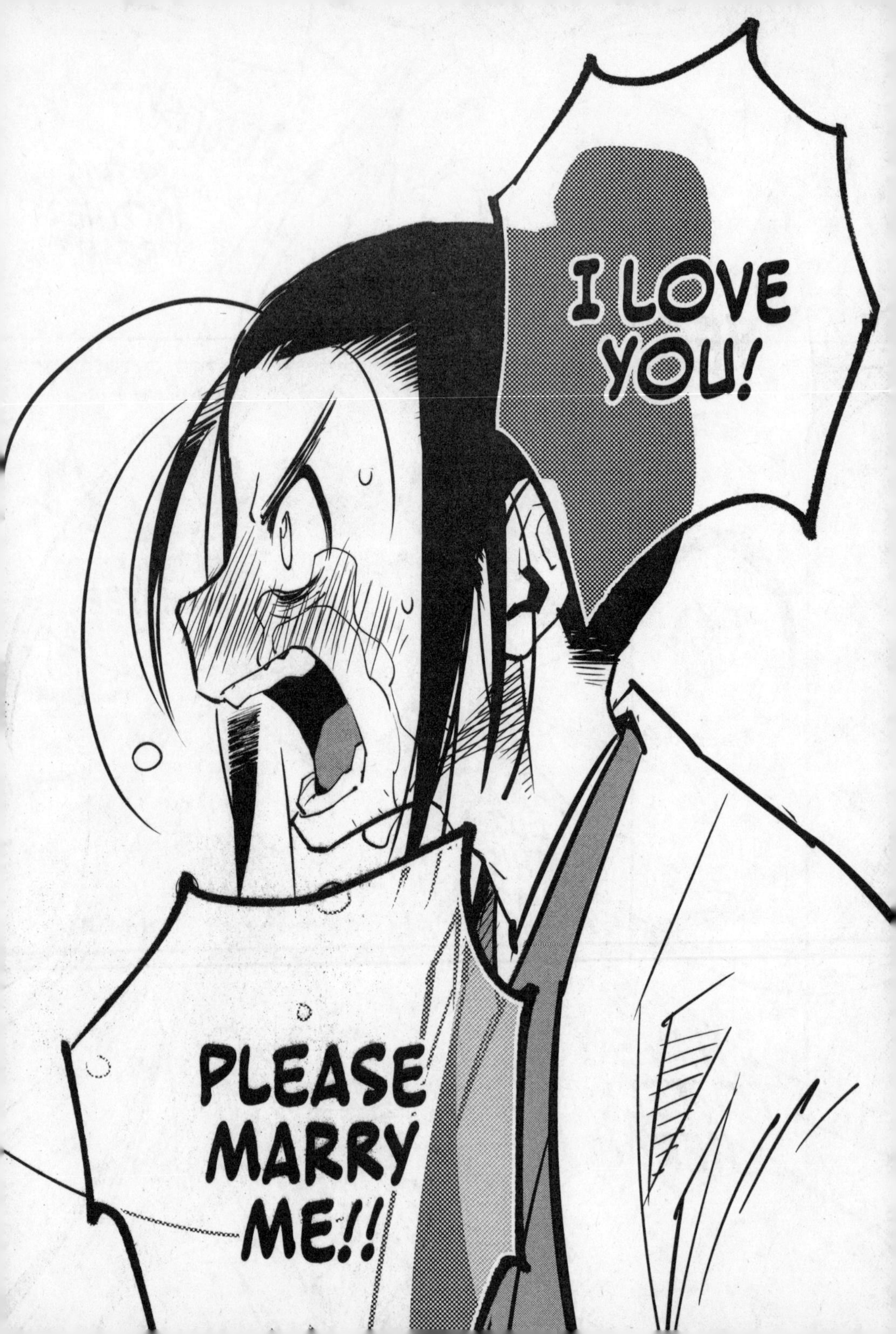
I LOVE YOU!
PLEASE MARRY ME!!

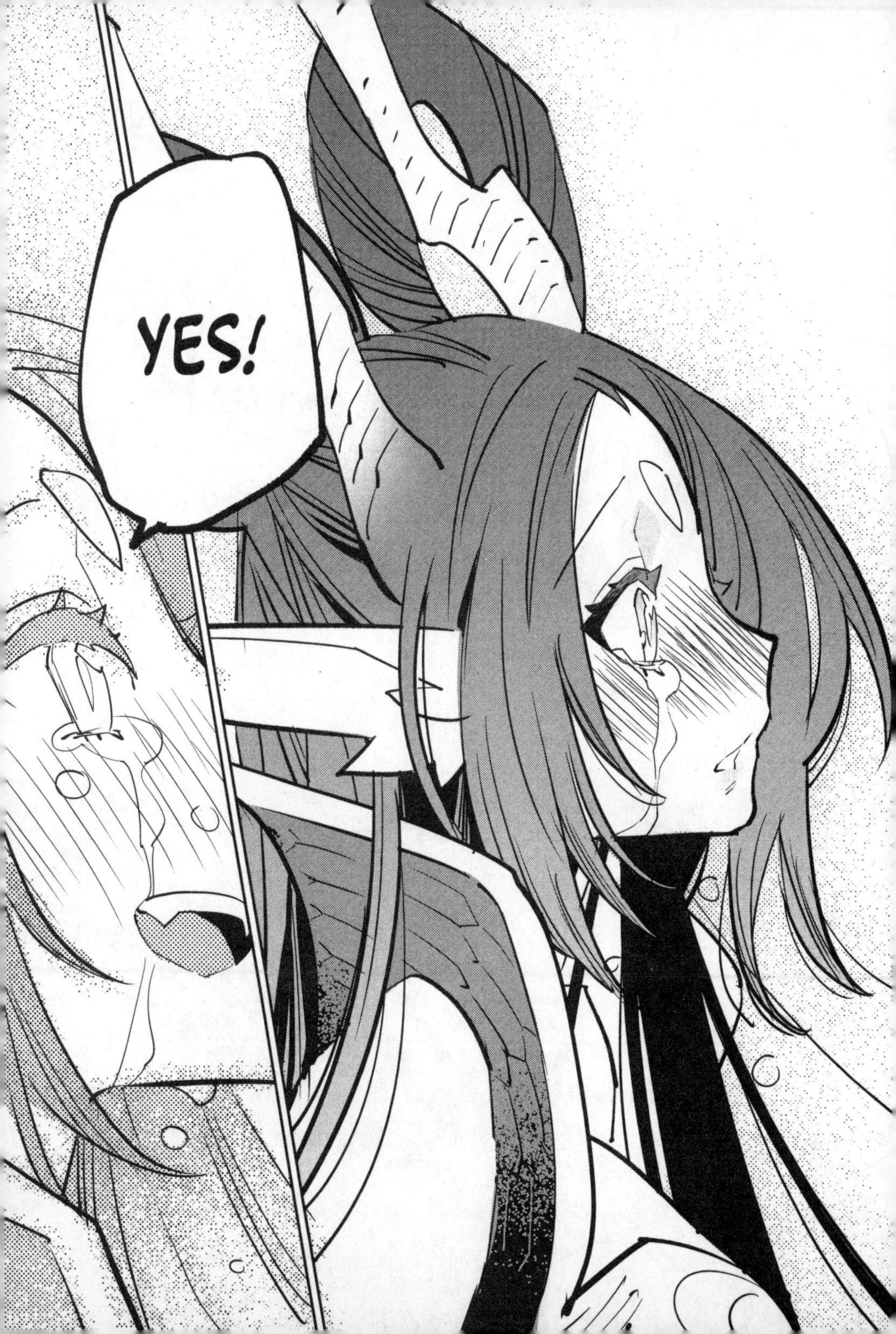
YES!

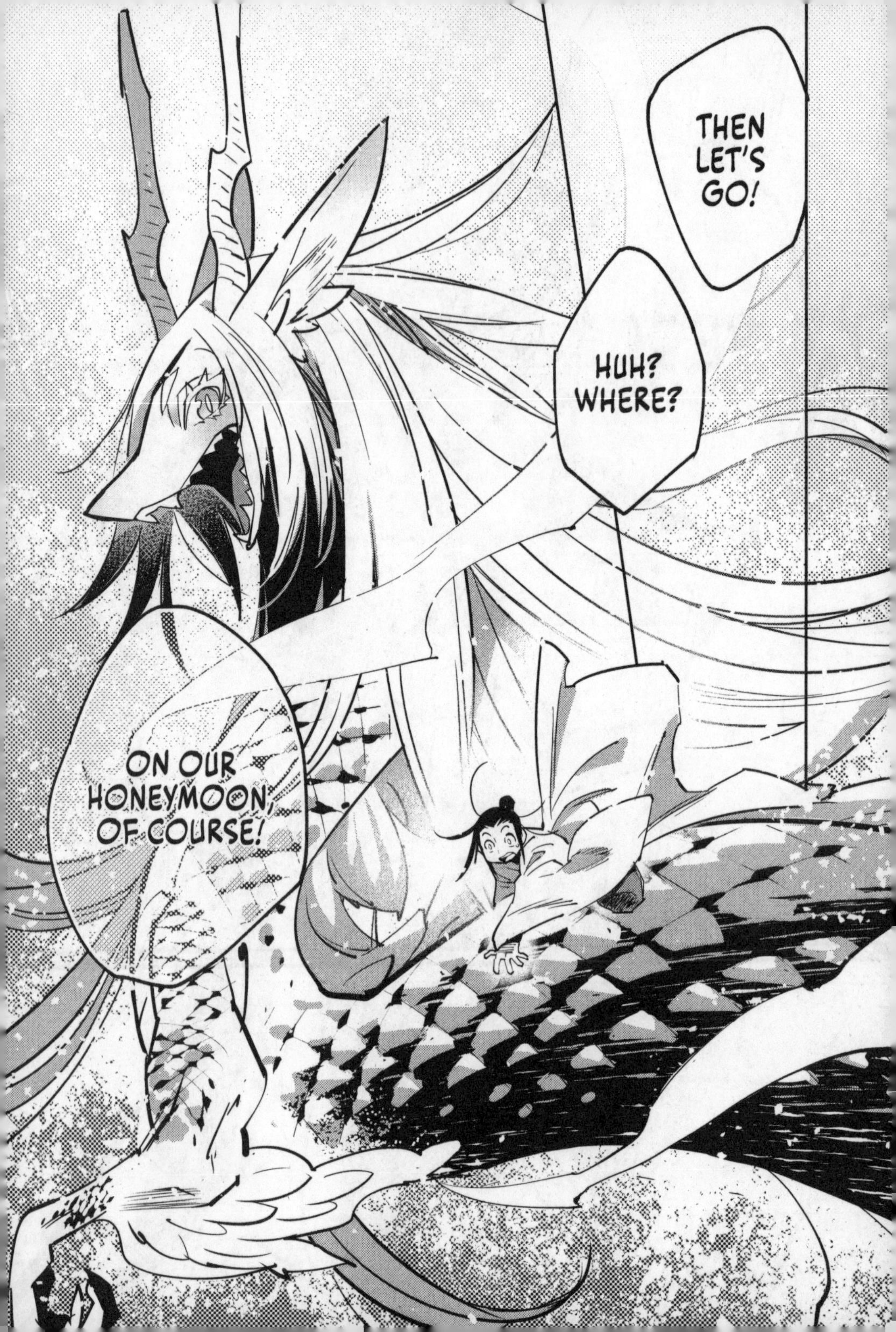
THEN LET'S GO!
HUH? WHERE?
ON OUR HONEYMOON, OF COURSE!

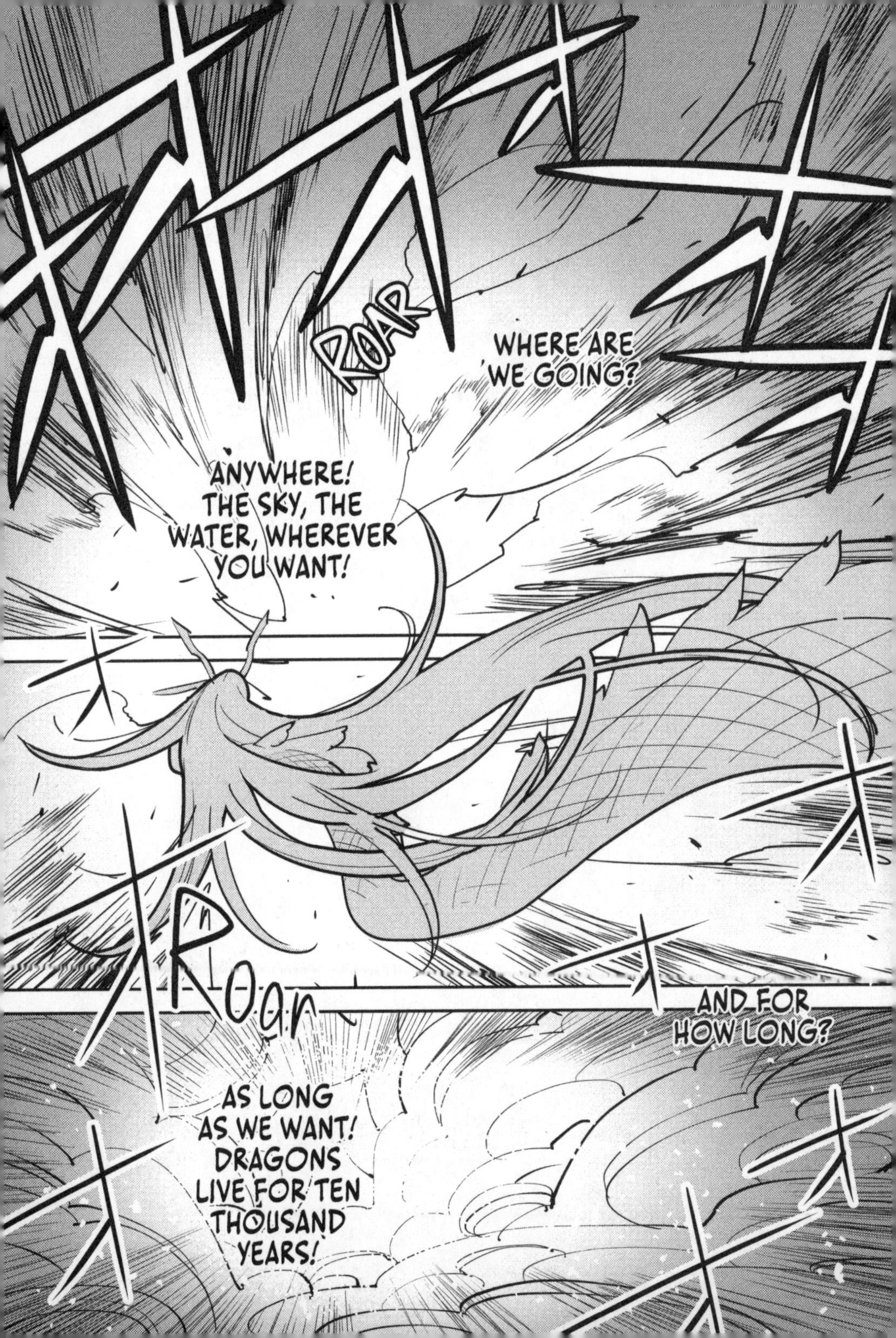
ROAR
WHERE ARE WE GOING?
ANYWHERE! THE SKY, THE WATER, WHEREVER YOU WANT!
ROAR
AND FOR HOW LONG?
AS LONG AS WE WANT! DRAGONS LIVE FOR TEN THOUSAND YEARS!

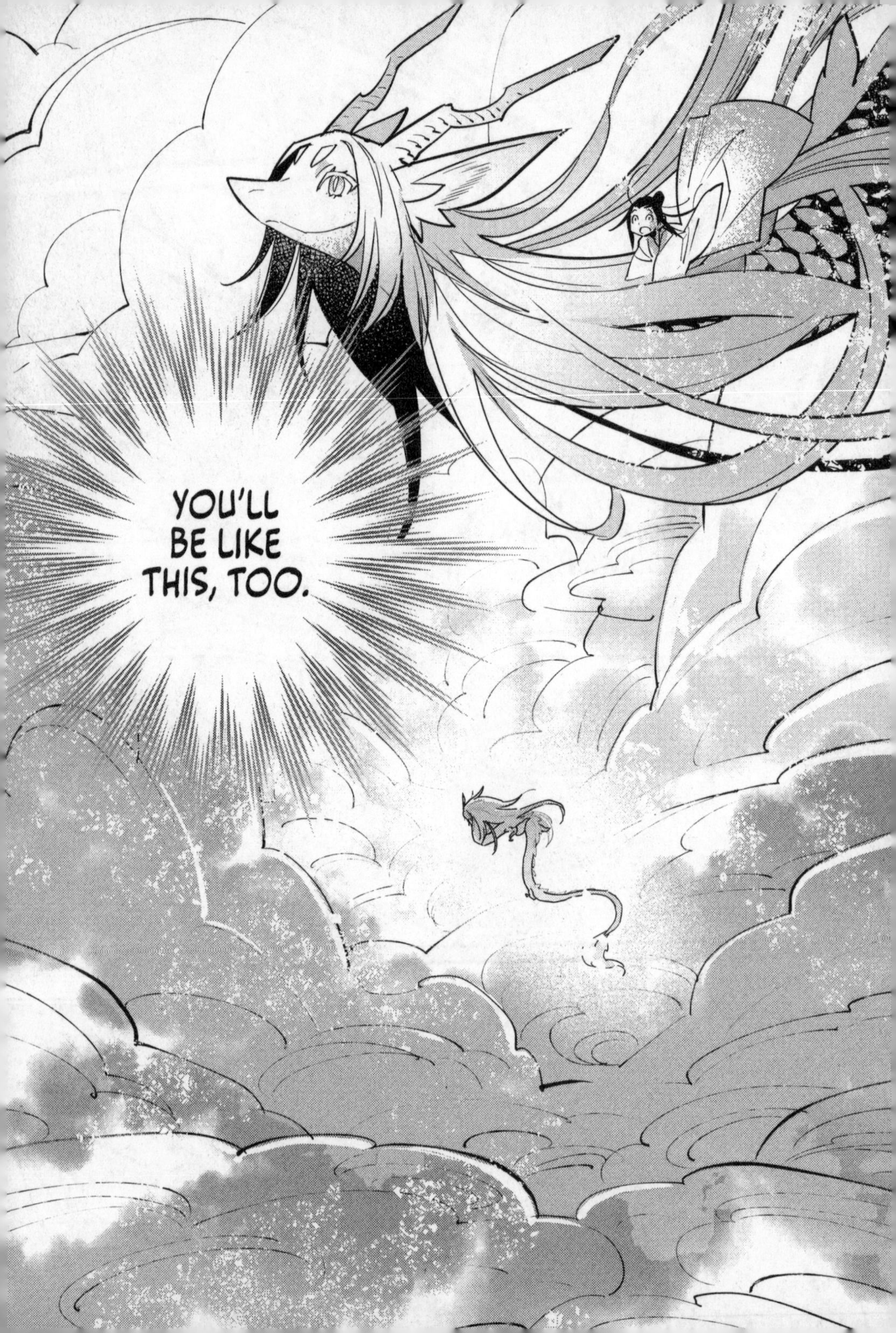
YOU'LL BE LIKE THIS, TOO.

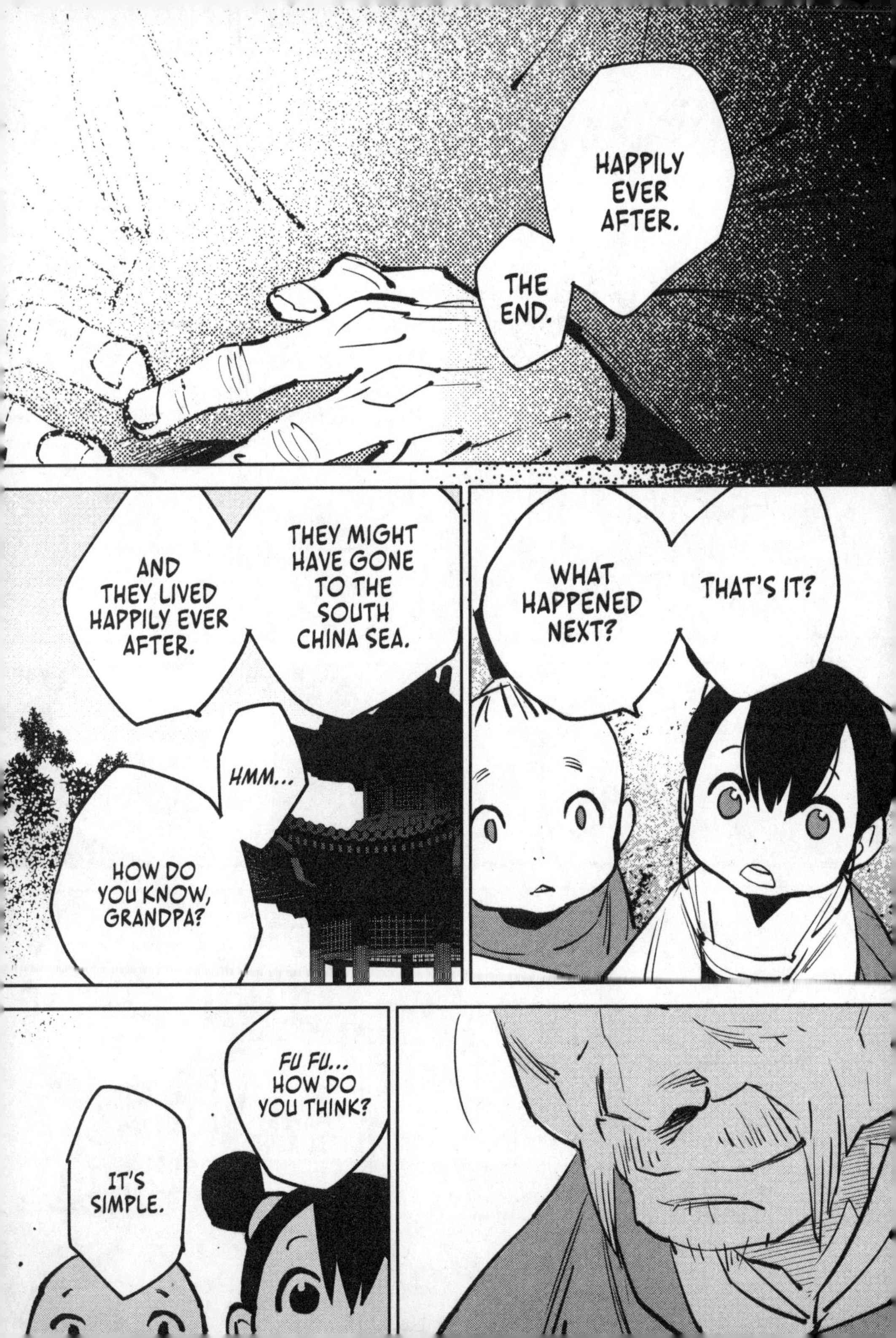
HAPPILY EVER AFTER.
THE END.
THAT'S IT?
WHAT HAPPENED NEXT?
THEY MIGHT HAVE GONE TO THE SOUTH CHINA SEA.
AND THEY LIVED HAPPILY EVER AFTER.
HMM...
HOW DO YOU KNOW, GRANDPA?
FU FU... HOW DO YOU THINK?
IT'S SIMPLE.

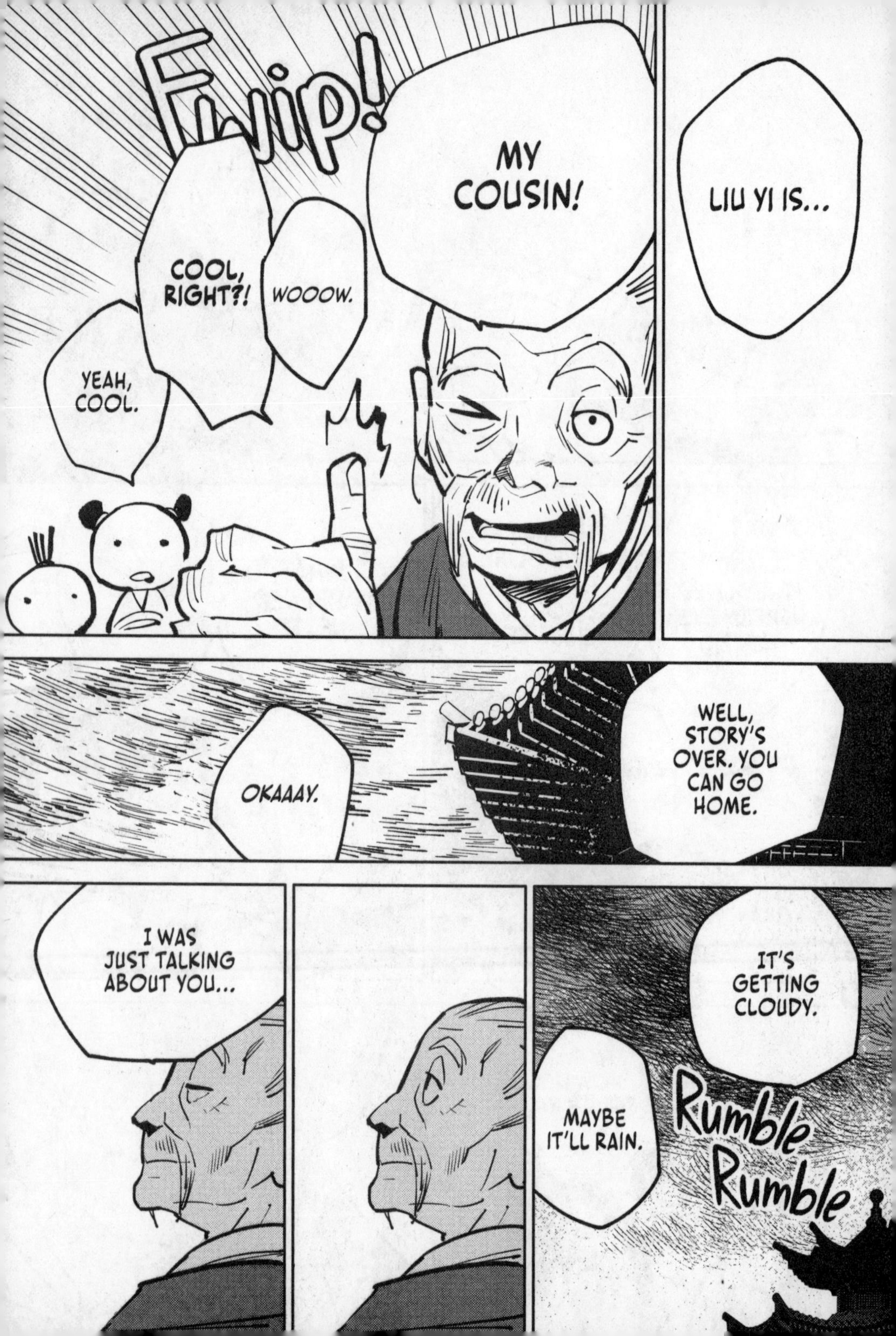
LIU YI IS...
MY COUSIN!
Fwip!
WOOOW.
COOL, RIGHT?!
YEAH, COOL.
WELL, STORY'S OVER. YOU CAN GO HOME.
OKAAAY.
IT'S GETTING CLOUDY.
MAYBE IT'LL RAIN.
Rumble Rumble
I WAS JUST TALKING ABOUT YOU...

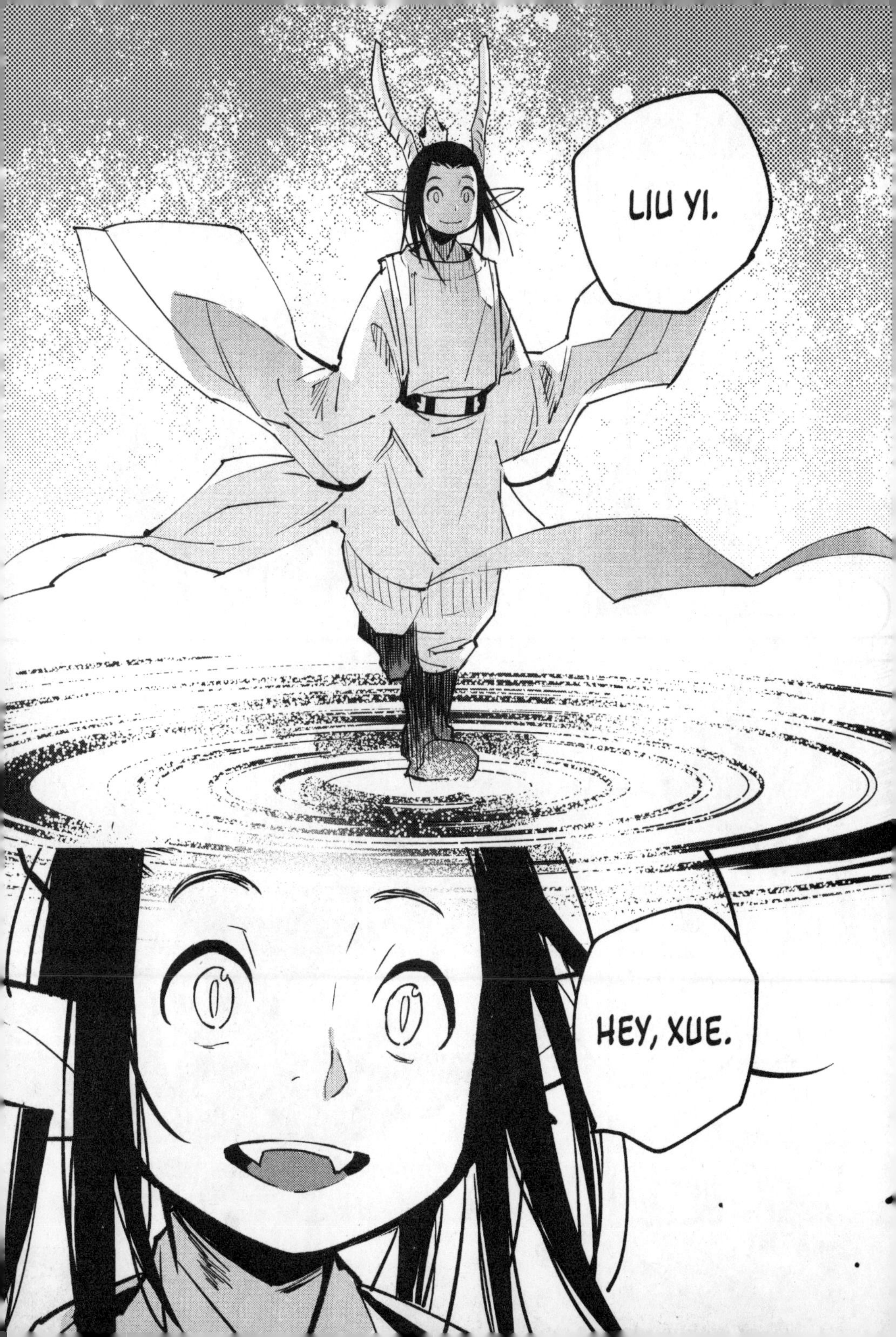
LIU YI.
HEY, XUE.

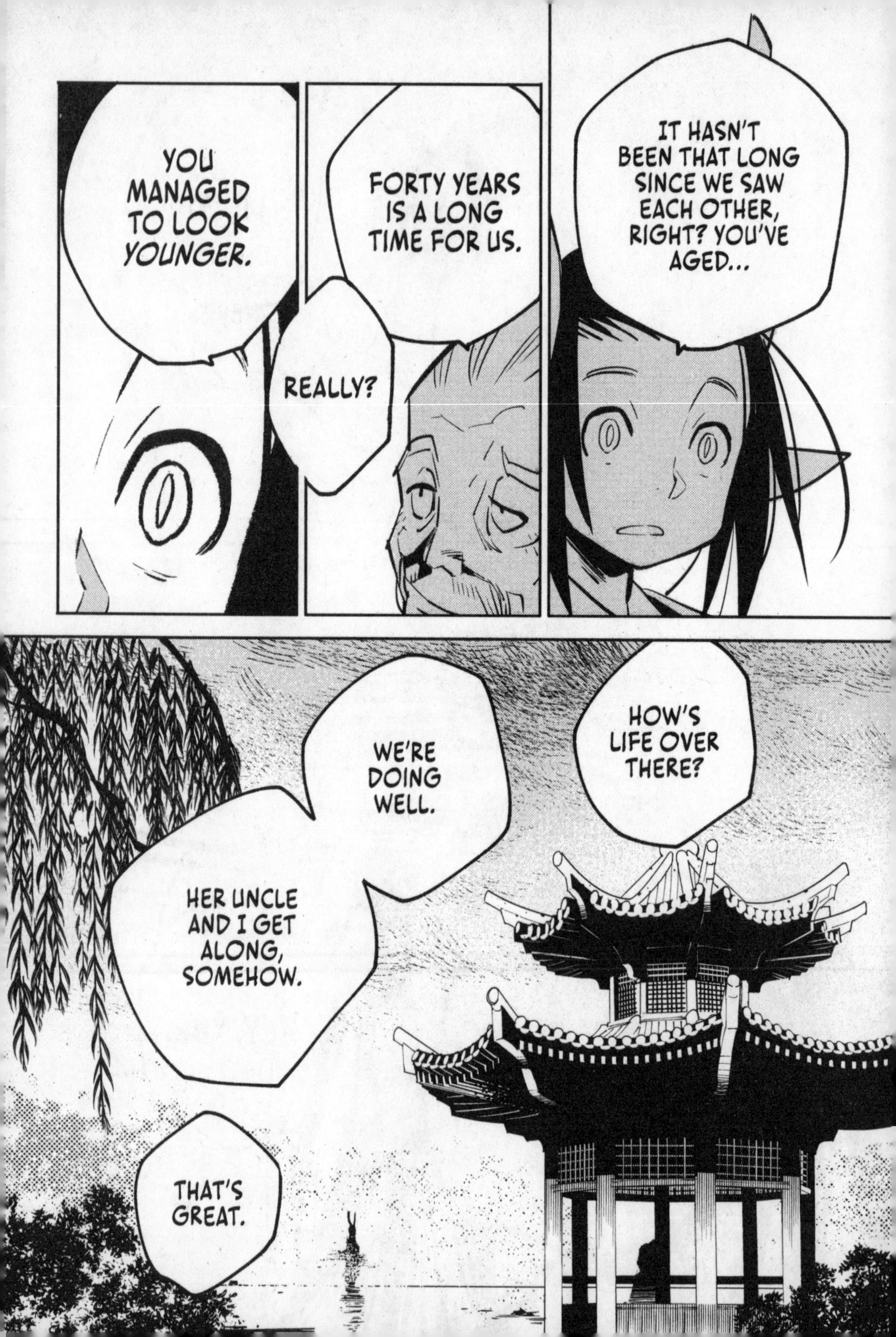
IT HASN'T BEEN THAT LONG SINCE WE SAW EACH OTHER, RIGHT? YOU'VE AGED...
FORTY YEARS IS A LONG TIME FOR US.
YOU MANAGED TO LOOK *YOUNGER.*
REALLY?
HOW'S LIFE OVER THERE?
WE'RE DOING WELL.
HER UNCLE AND I GET ALONG, SOMEHOW.
THAT'S GREAT.

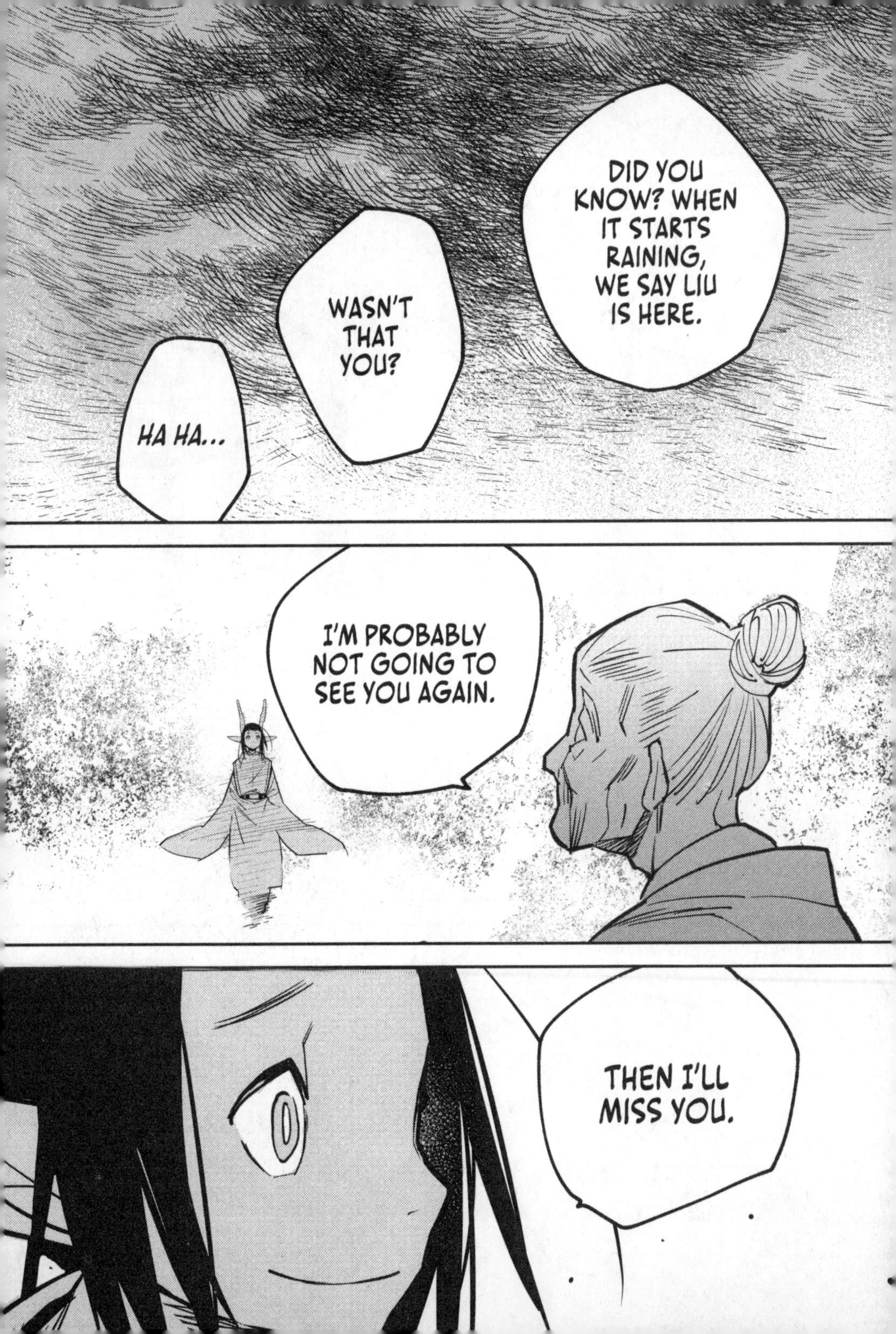
DID YOU KNOW? WHEN IT STARTS RAINING, WE SAY LIU IS HERE.
WASN'T THAT YOU?
HA HA...
I'M PROBABLY NOT GOING TO SEE YOU AGAIN.
THEN I'LL MISS YOU.

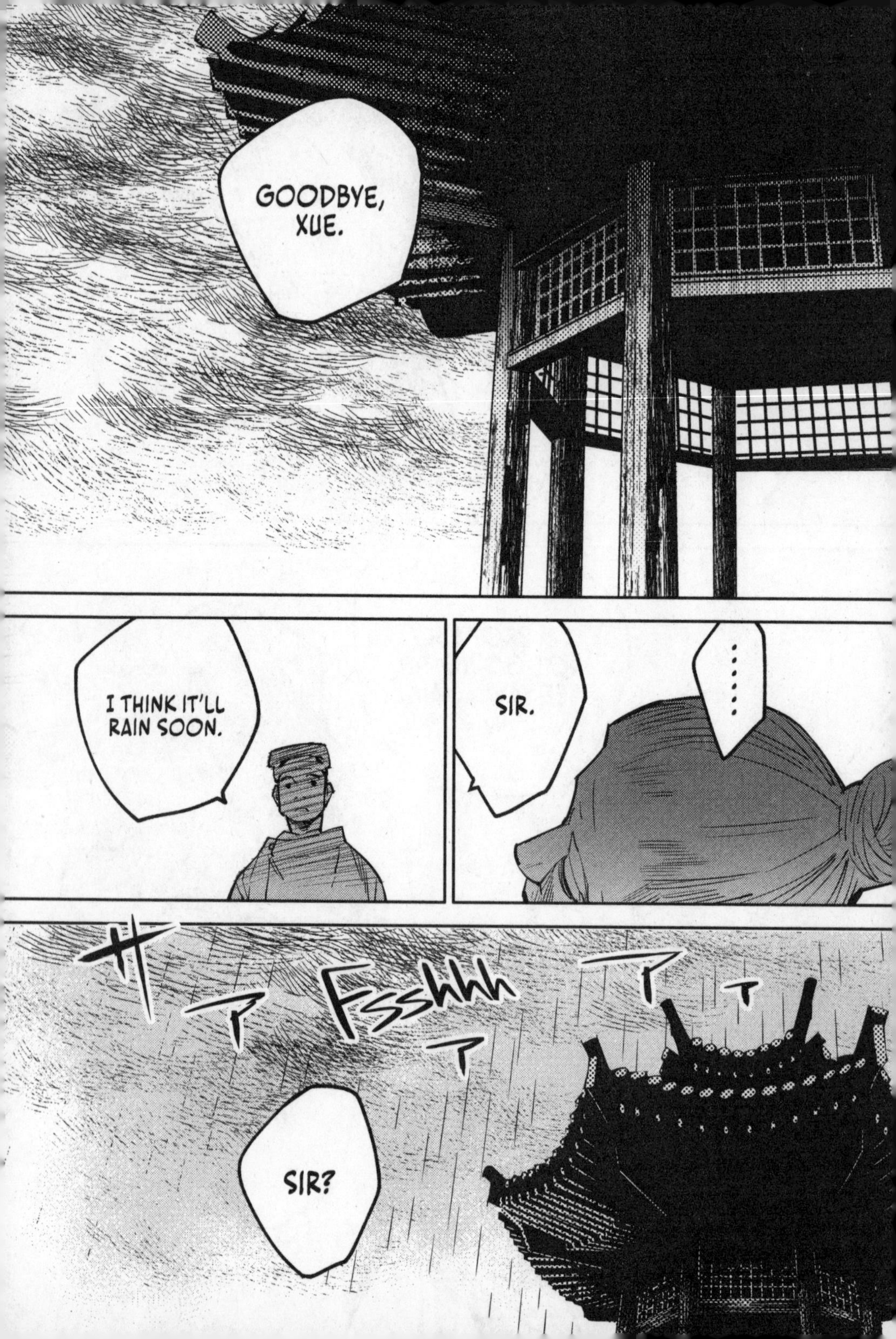
GOODBYE, XUE.
......
SIR.
I THINK IT'LL RAIN SOON.
Fsshhh
SIR?

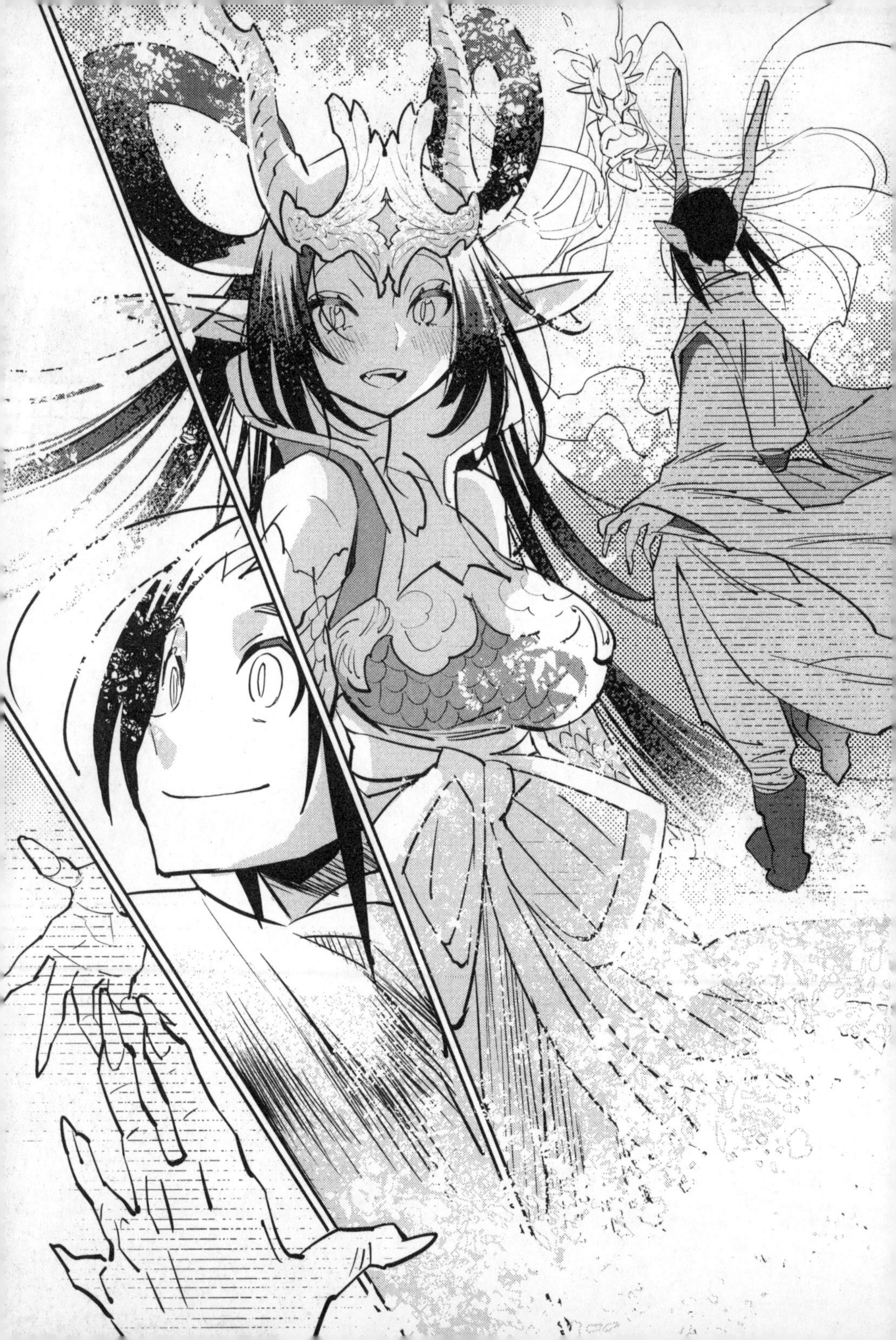

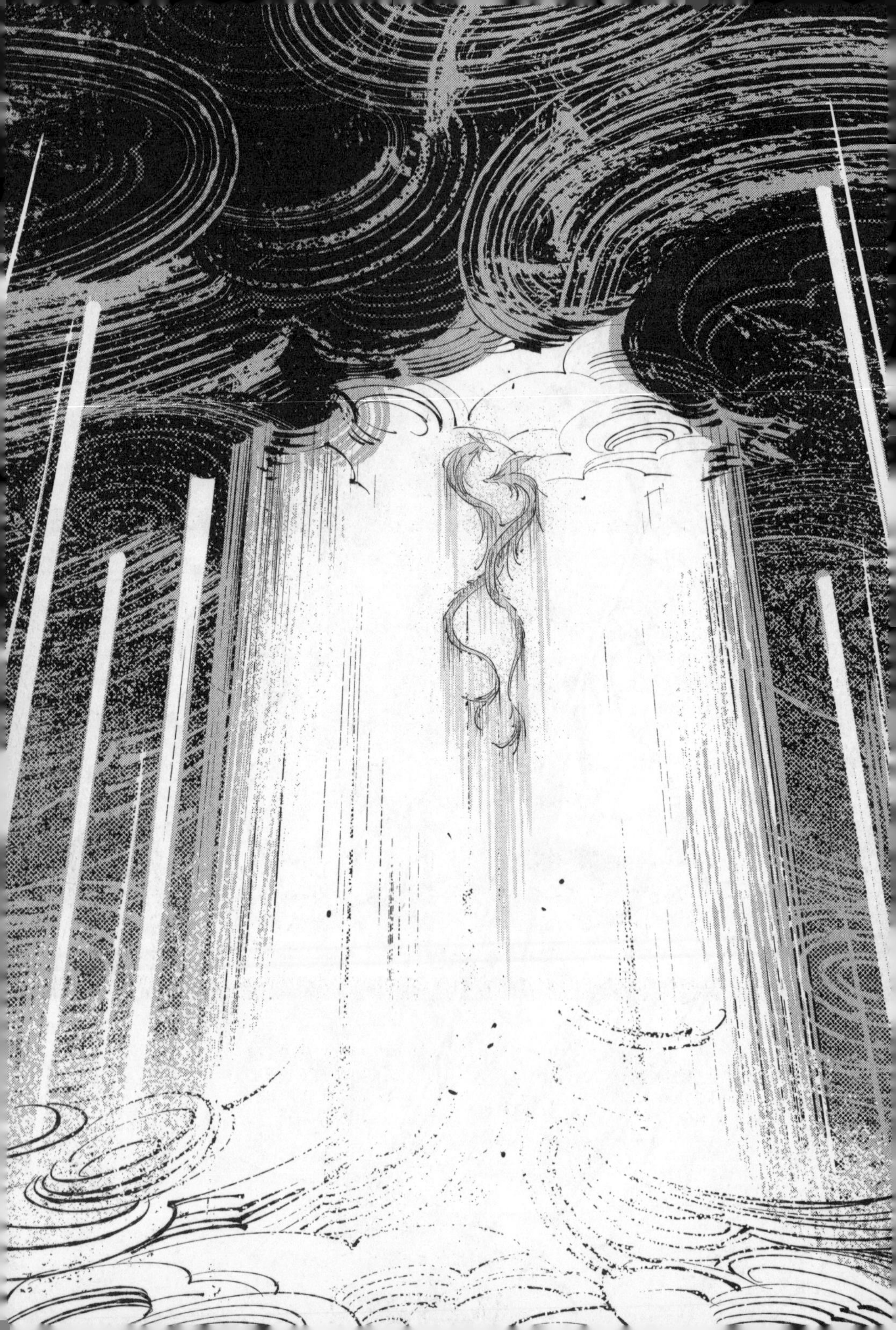

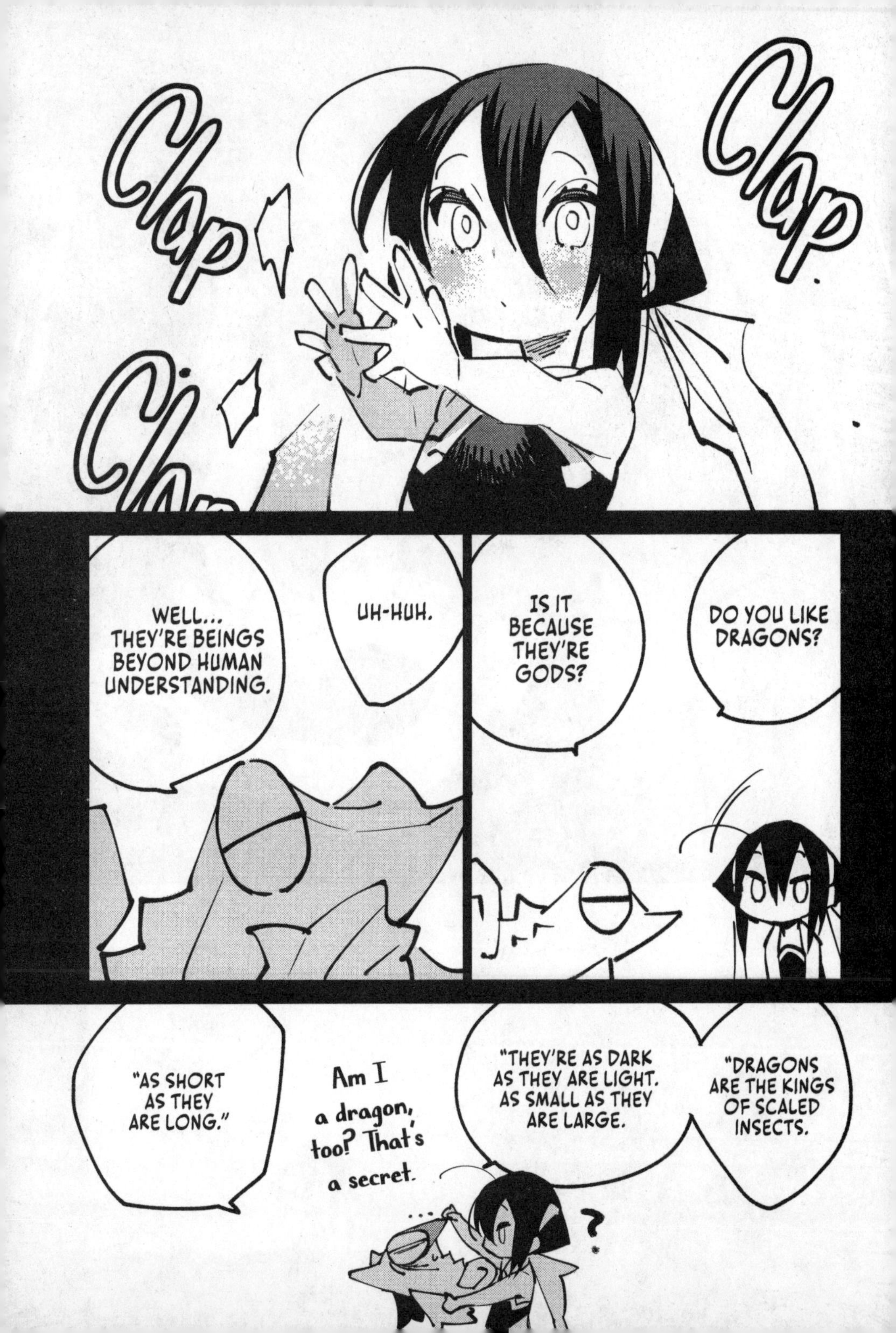
Clap
Clap
Clap
DO YOU LIKE DRAGONS?
IS IT BECAUSE THEY'RE GODS?
UH-HUH.
WELL... THEY'RE BEINGS BEYOND HUMAN UNDERSTANDING.
"DRAGONS ARE THE KINGS OF SCALED INSECTS.
"THEY'RE AS DARK AS THEY ARE LIGHT. AS SMALL AS THEY ARE LARGE.
"AS SHORT AS THEY ARE LONG."
Am I a dragon, too? That's a secret.
...
?

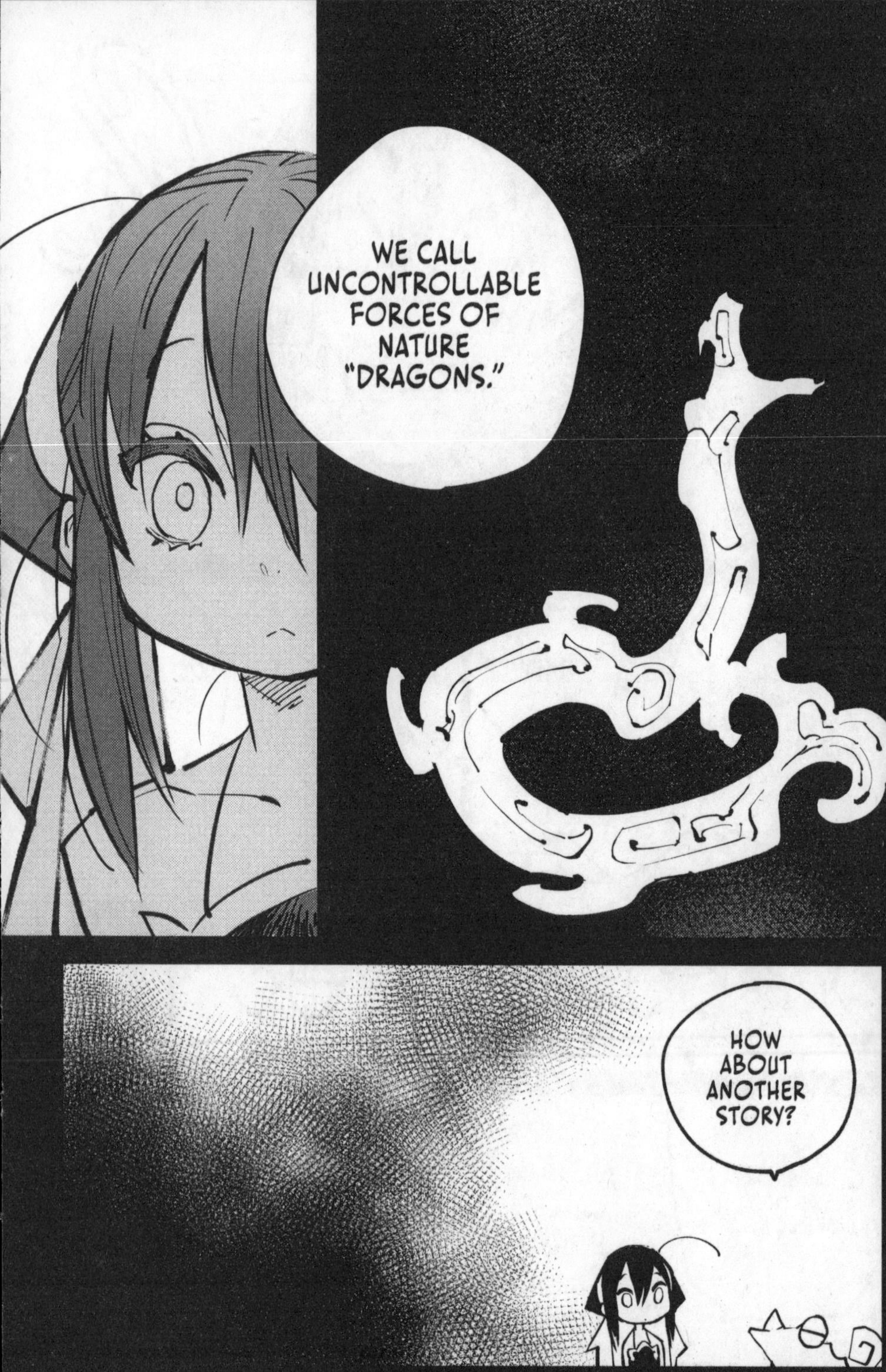
WE CALL UNCONTROLLABLE FORCES OF NATURE "DRAGONS."
HOW ABOUT ANOTHER STORY?

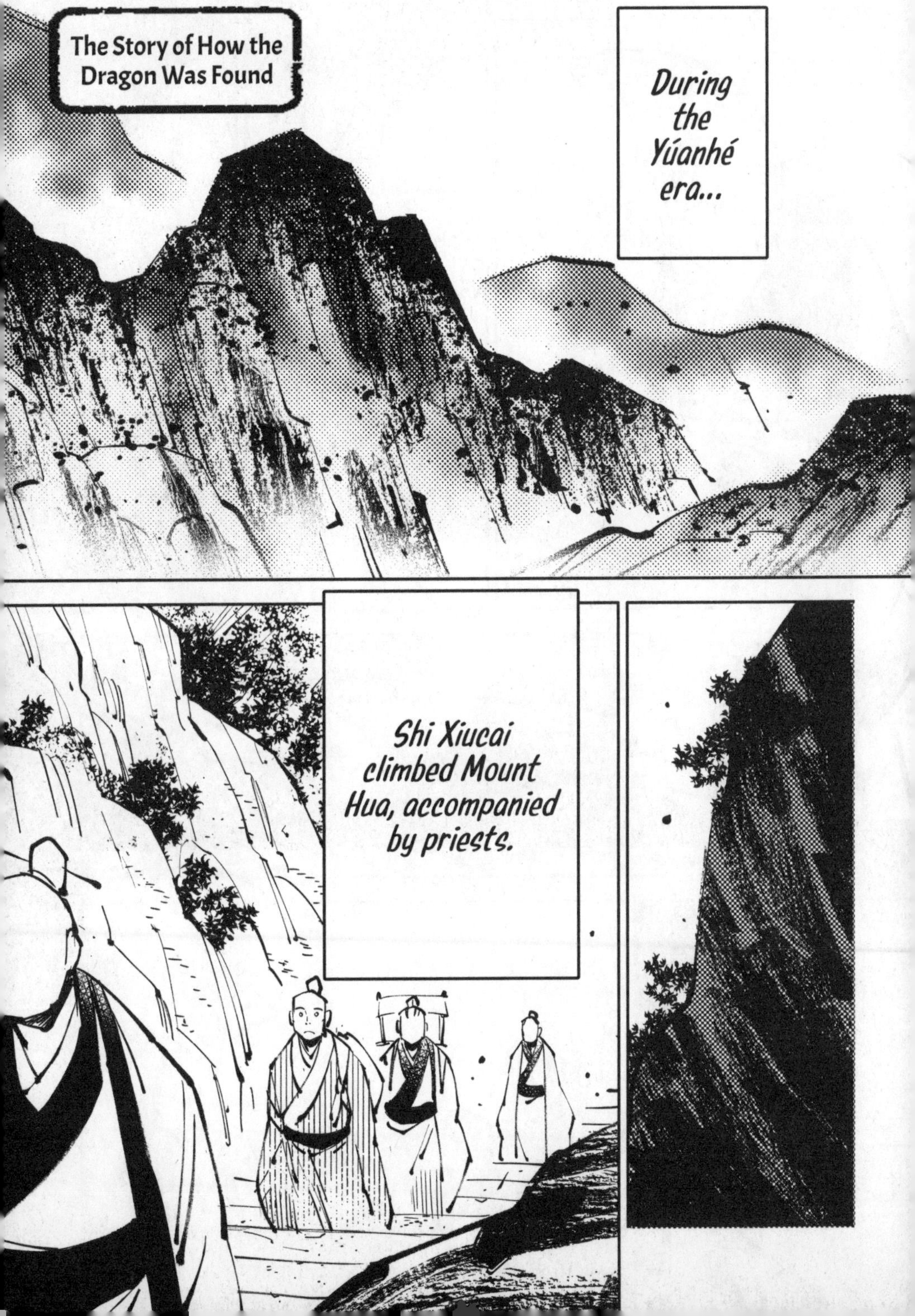
The Story of How the Dragon Was Found
During the Yúanhé era...
Shi Xiucai climbed Mount Hua, accompanied by priests.

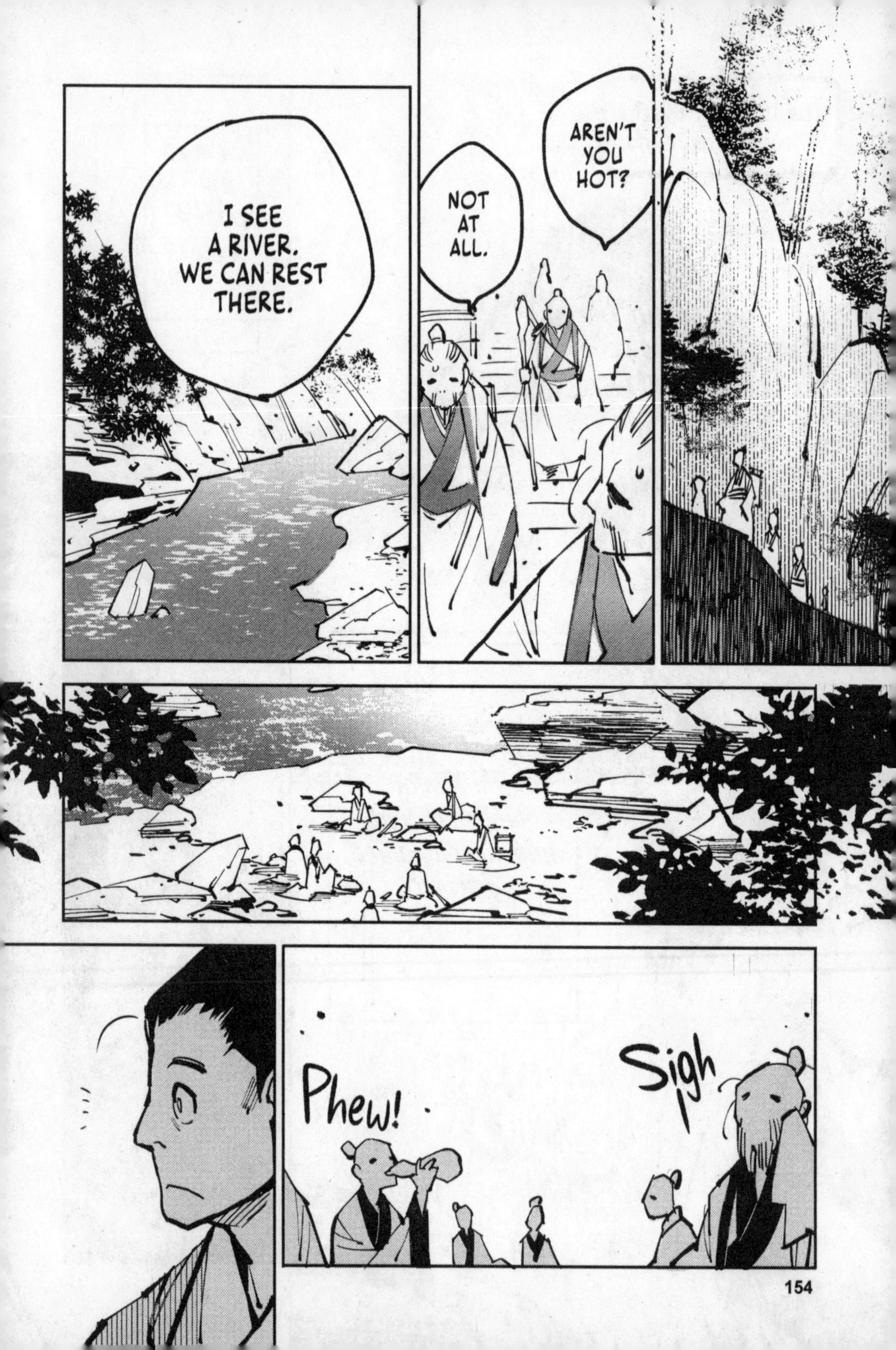
AREN'T YOU HOT?
NOT AT ALL.
I SEE A RIVER. WE CAN REST THERE.
Sigh
Phew!

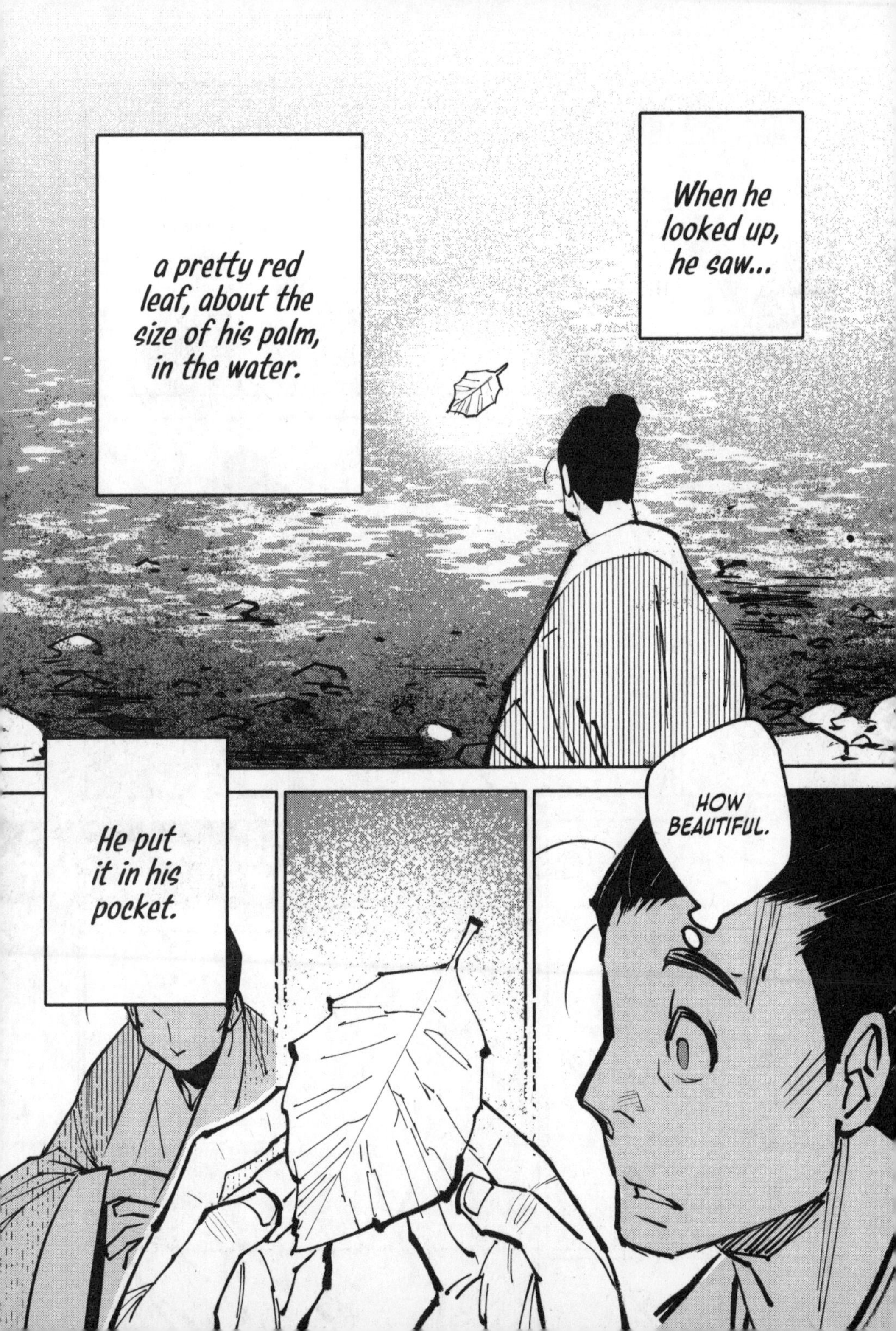
When he looked up, he saw...
a pretty red leaf, about the size of his palm, in the water.
HOW BEAUTIFUL.
He put it in his pocket.

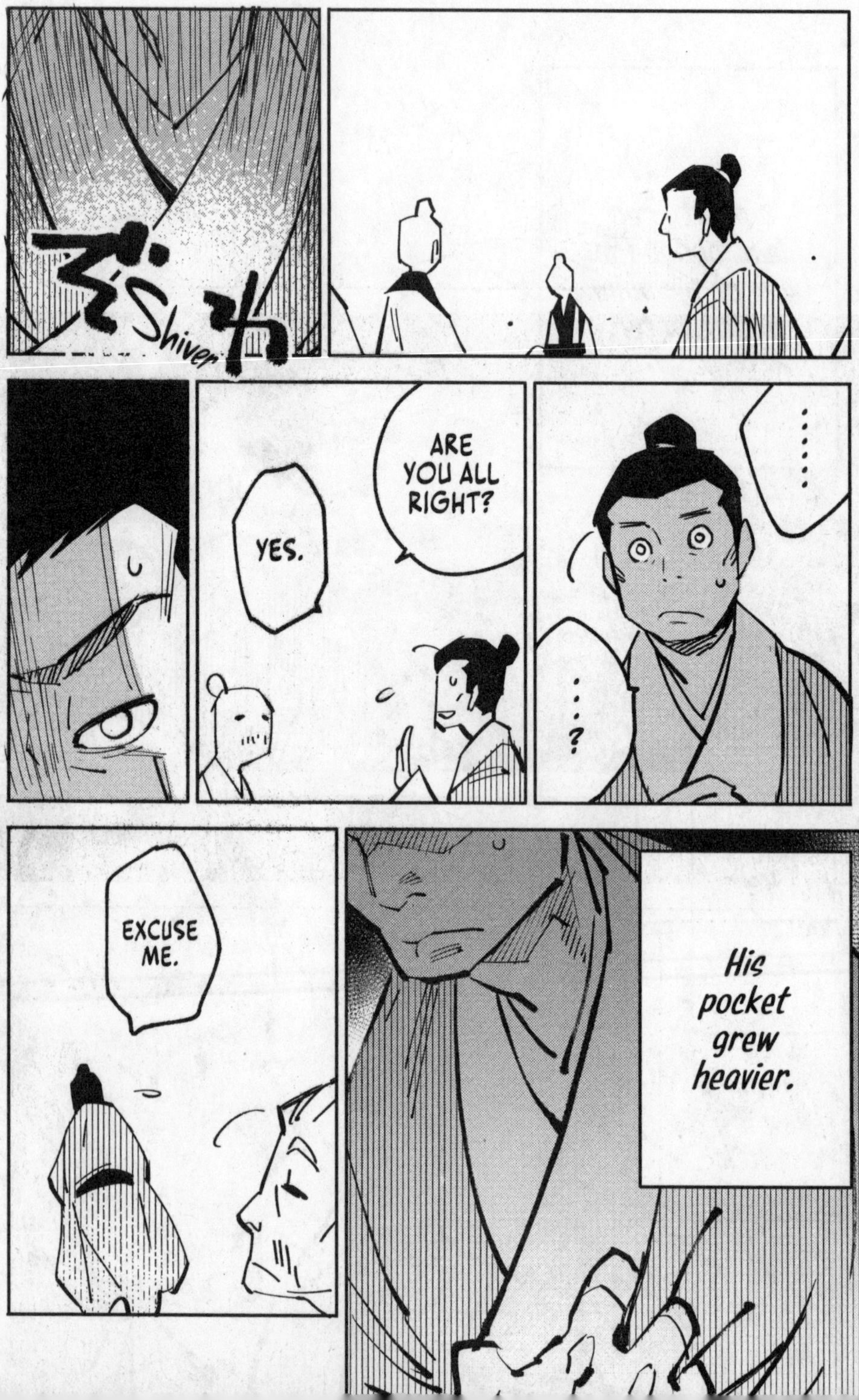
Shiver
......
...?
ARE YOU ALL RIGHT?
YES.
His pocket grew heavier.
EXCUSE ME.

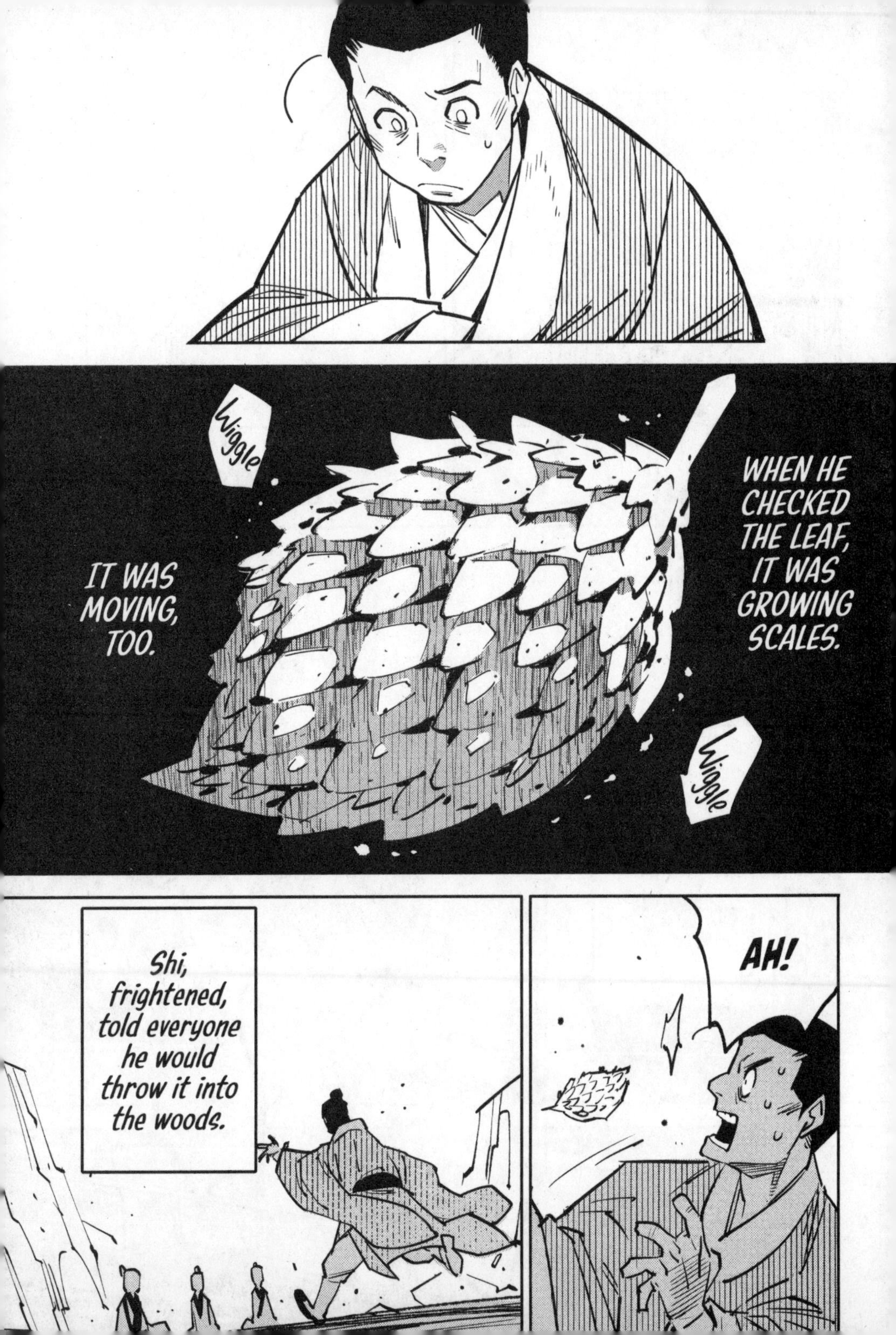

WHEN HE CHECKED THE LEAF, IT WAS GROWING SCALES.
Wiggle
Wiggle
IT WAS MOVING, TOO.
AH!
Shi, frightened, told everyone he would throw it into the woods.

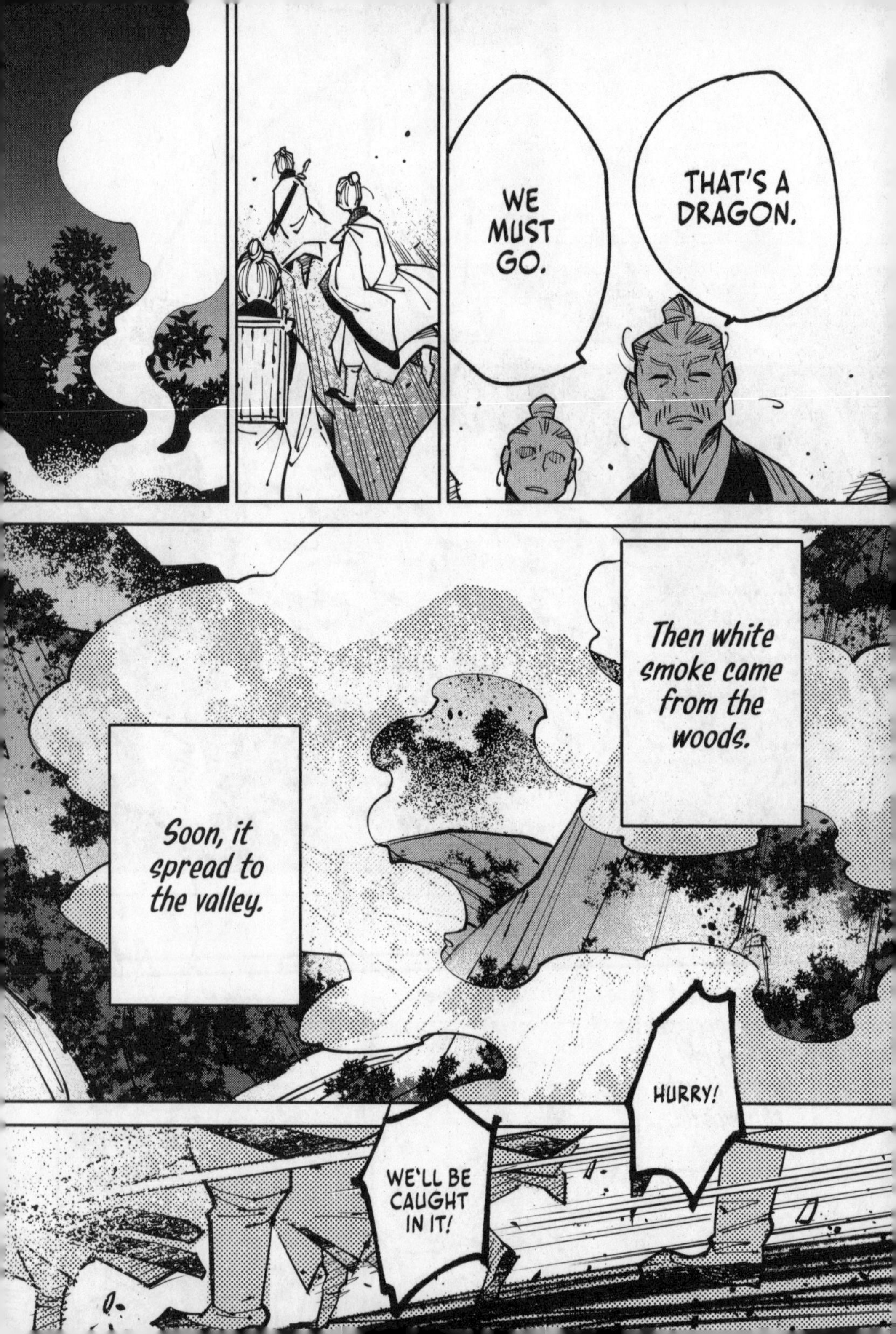
THAT'S A DRAGON.
WE MUST GO.
Then white smoke came from the woods.
Soon, it spread to the valley.
HURRY!
WE'LL BE CAUGHT IN IT!

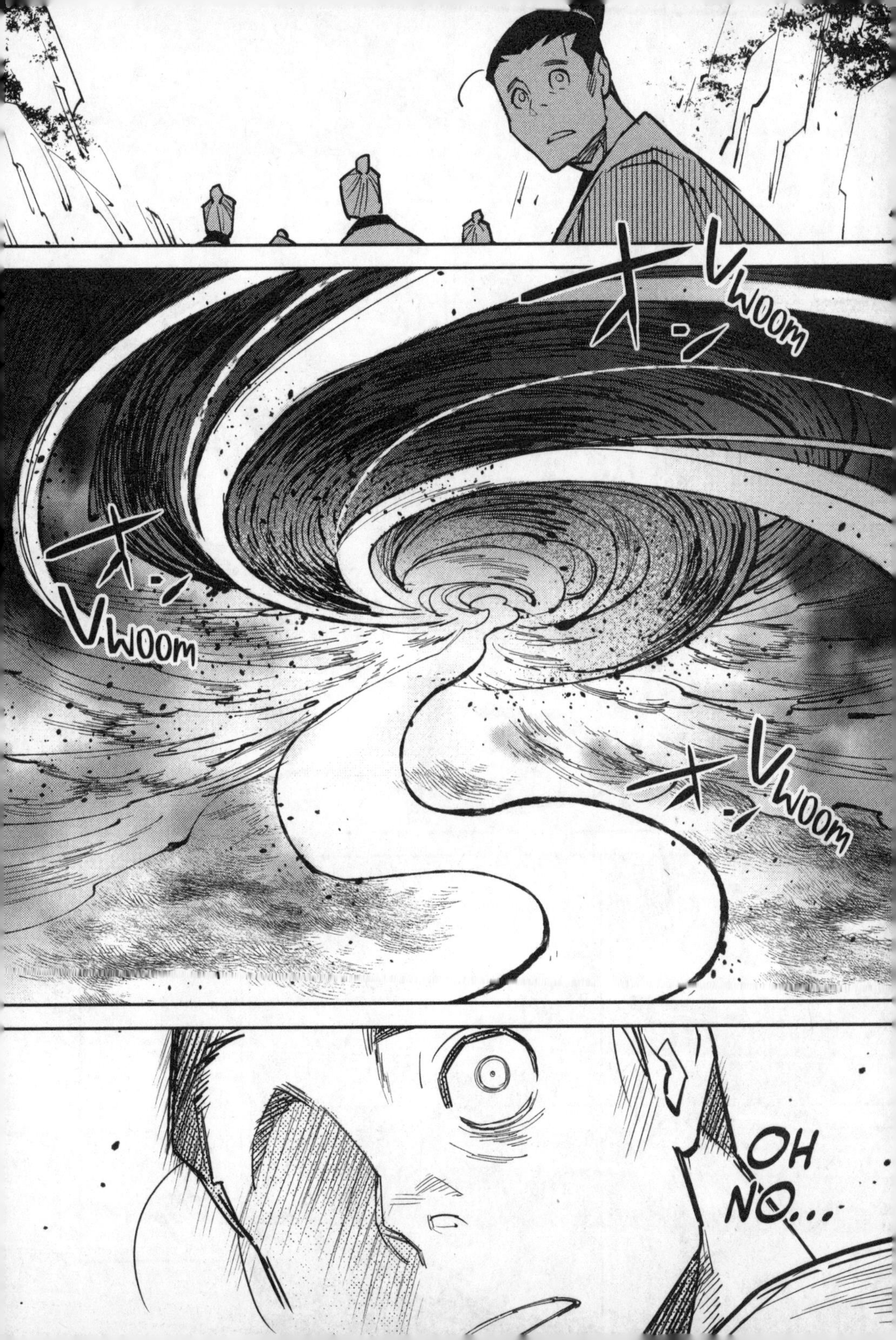
VWOOM
VWOOM
VWOOM
OH NO...

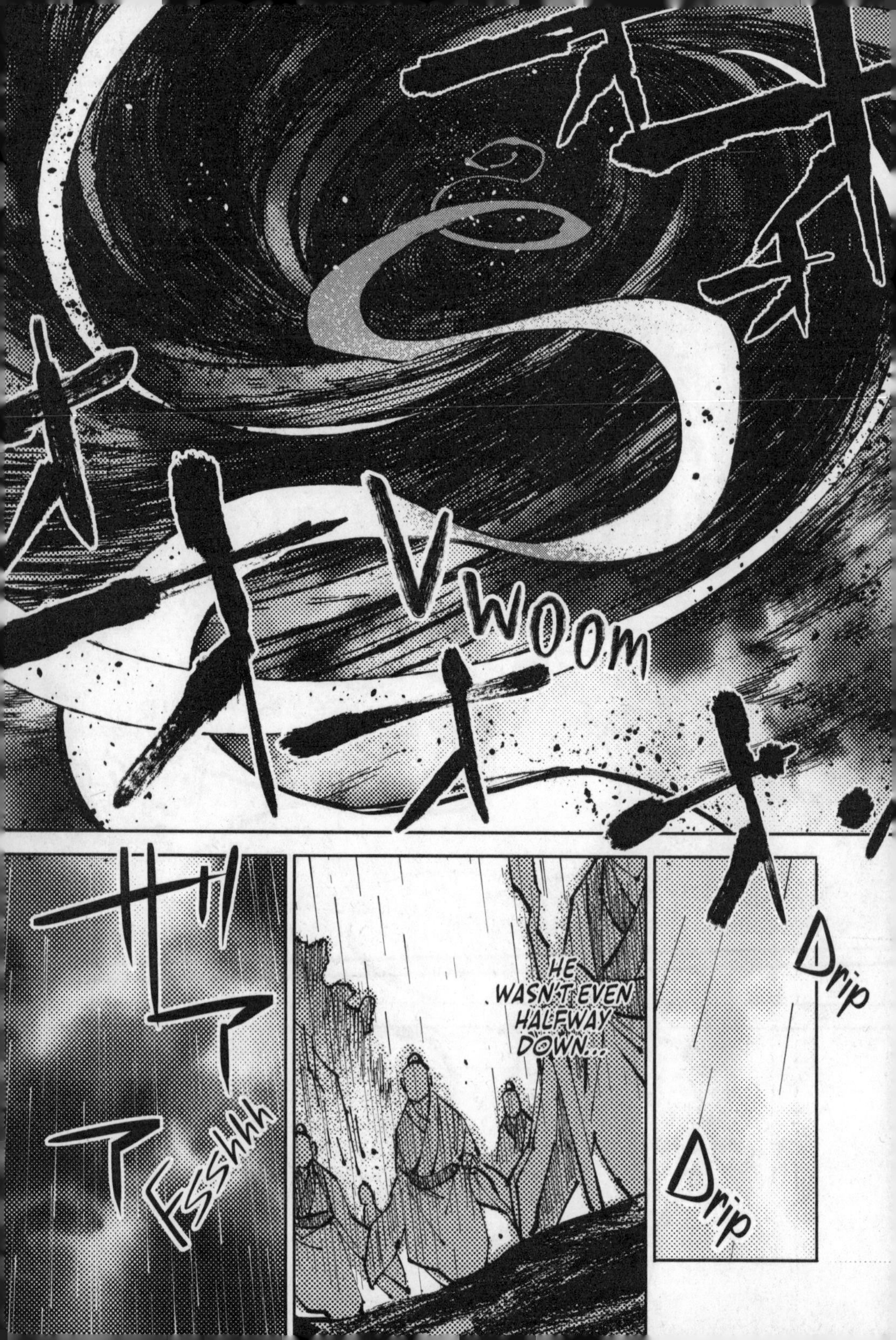
VWOOM
Drip
Drip
HE WASN'T EVEN HALFWAY DOWN...
Fsshhh

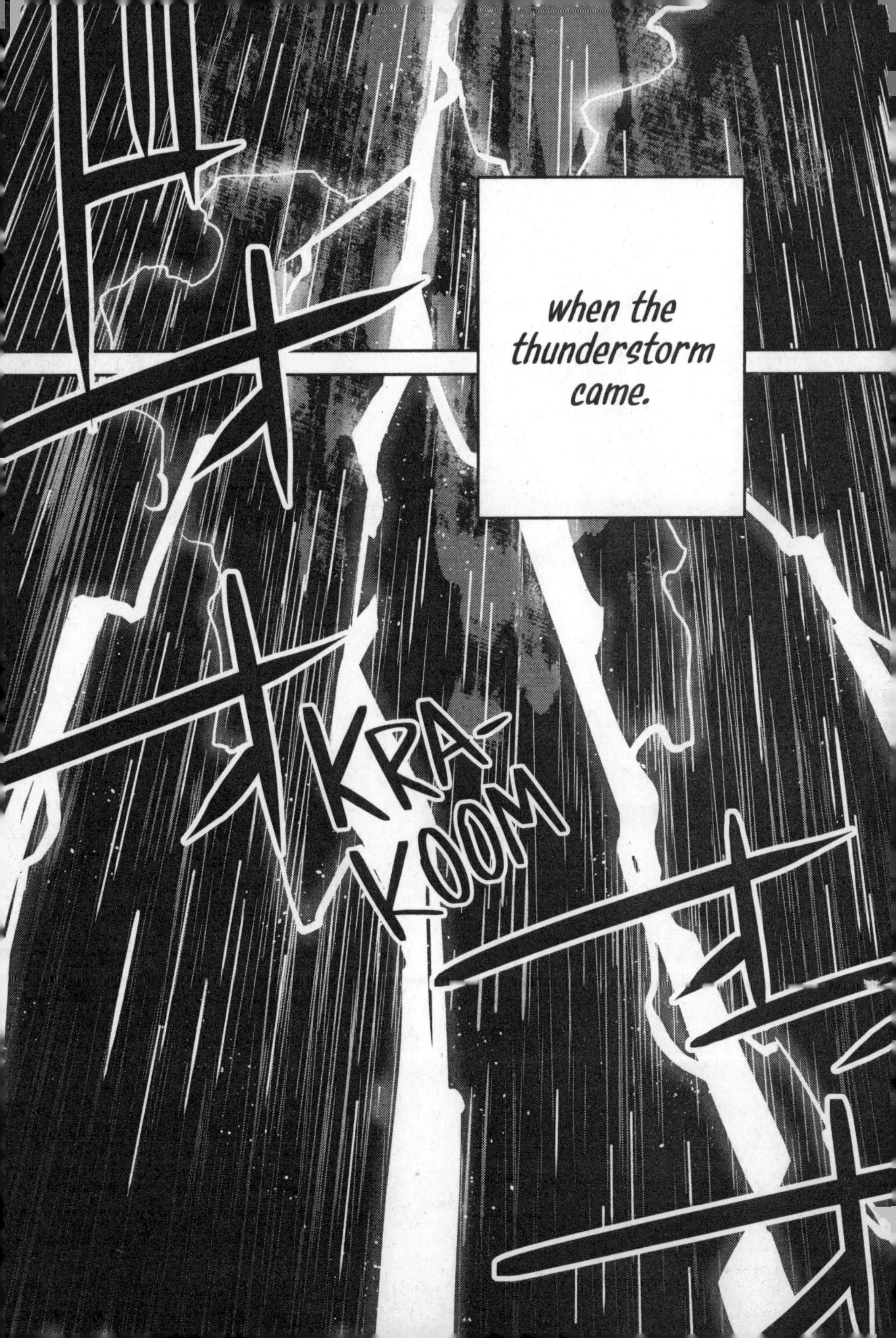
when the thunderstorm came.
KRA-KOOM

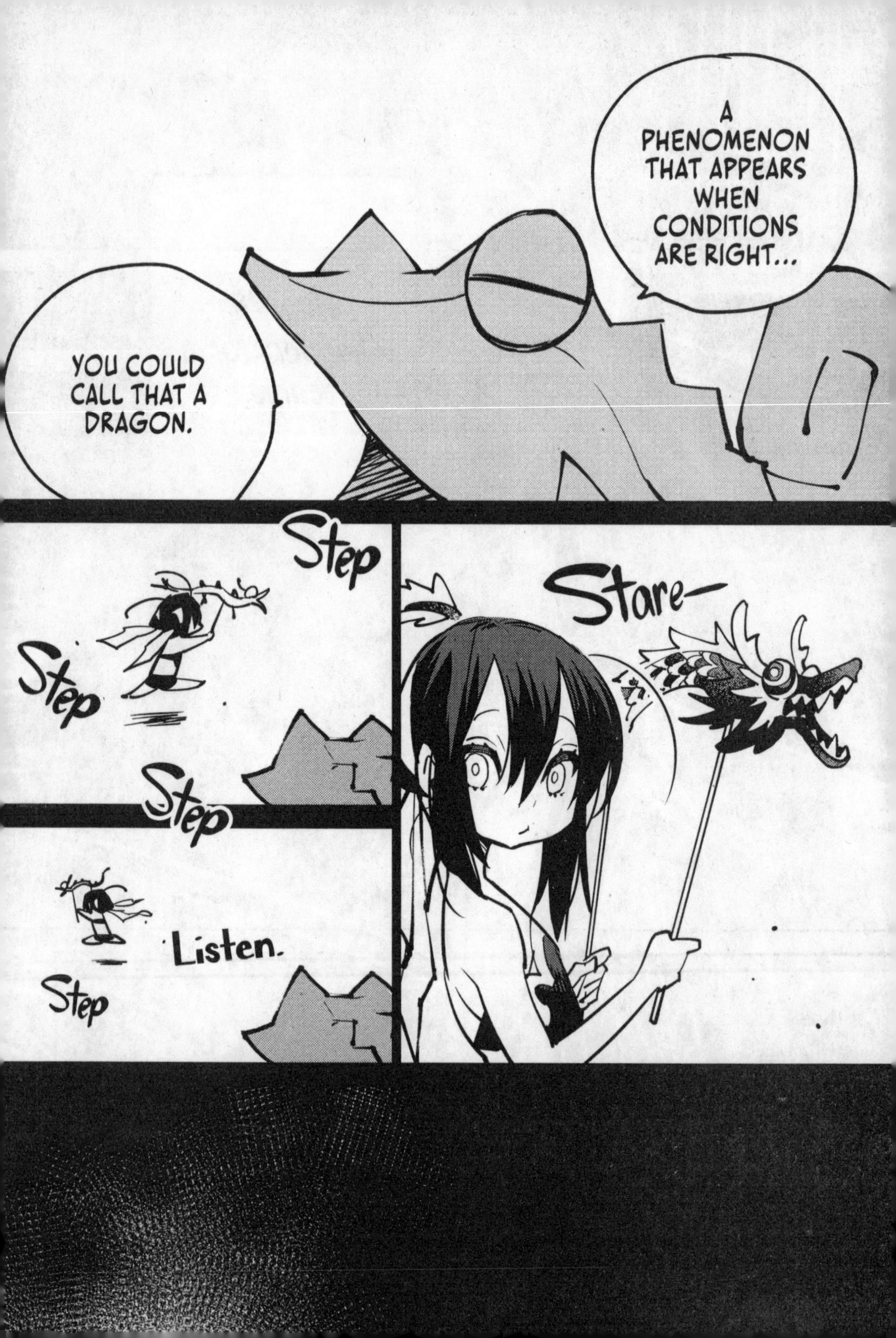
A PHENOMENON THAT APPEARS WHEN CONDITIONS ARE RIGHT...
YOU COULD CALL THAT A DRAGON.
Stare-
Step
Step
Step
Listen.
Step

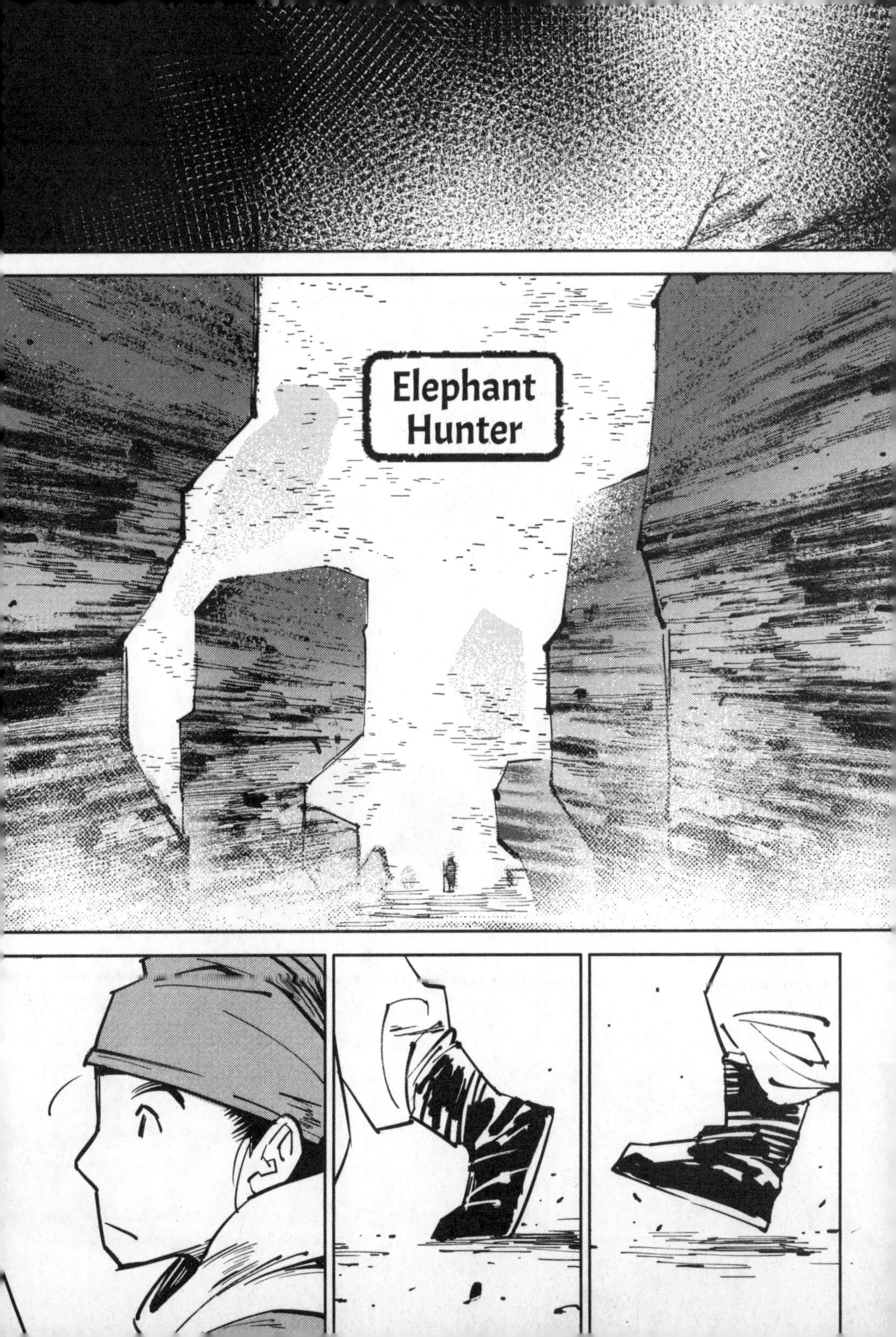
Elephant
Hunter

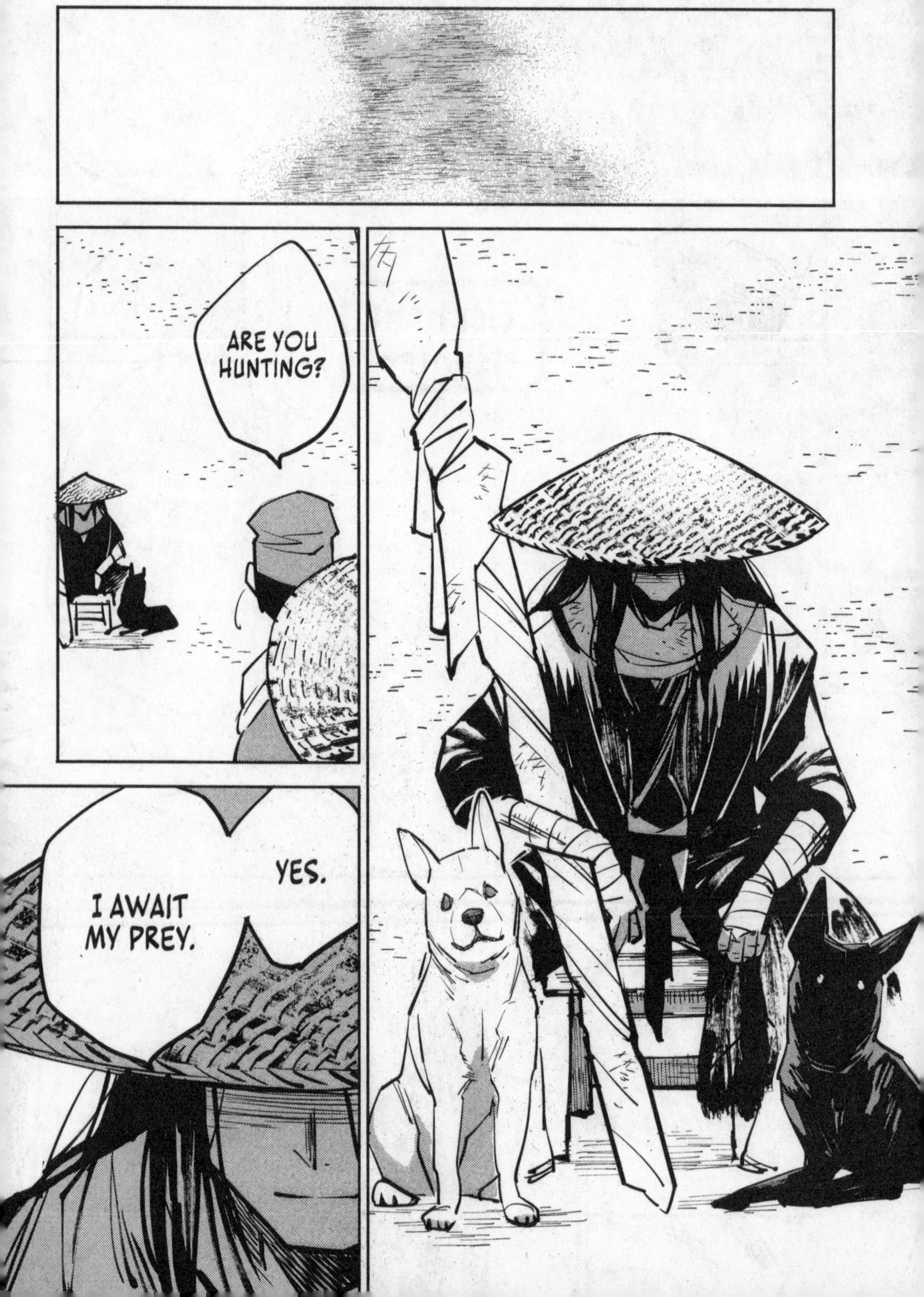
ARE YOU HUNTING?
YES.
I AWAIT MY PREY.

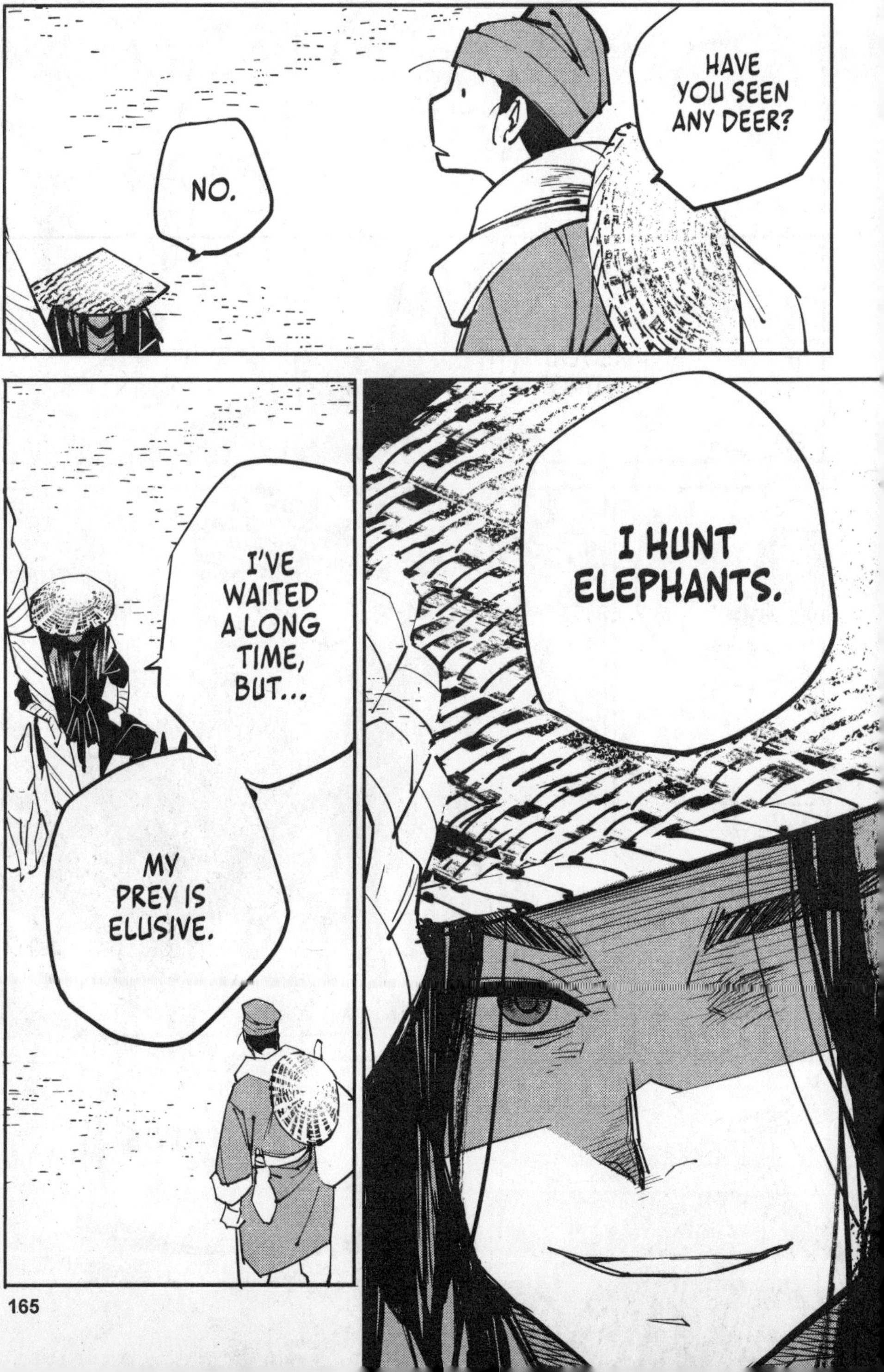
HAVE YOU SEEN ANY DEER?
NO.
I HUNT ELEPHANTS.
I'VE WAITED A LONG TIME, BUT...
MY PREY IS ELUSIVE.

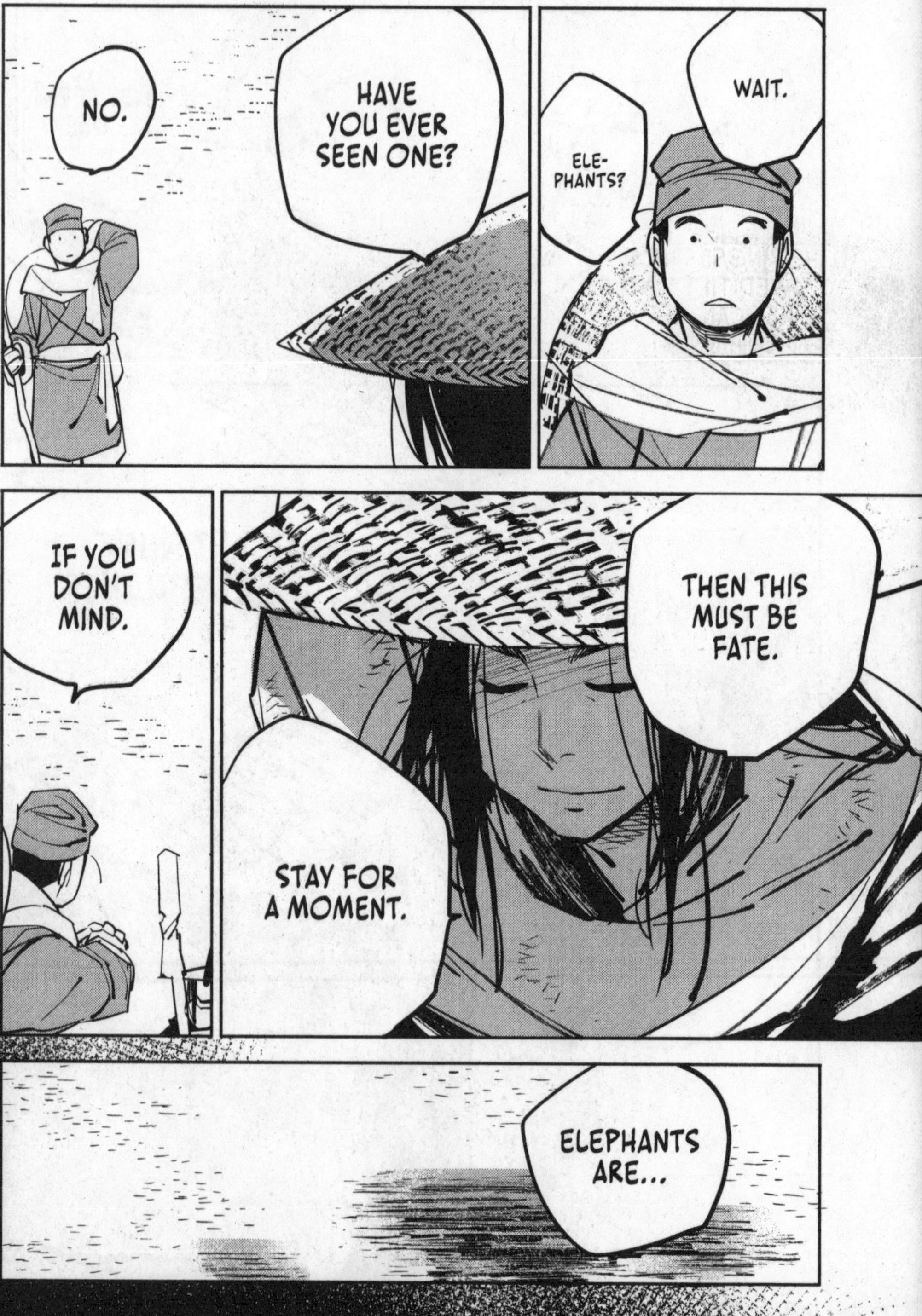
WAIT.
ELE-PHANTS?
HAVE YOU EVER SEEN ONE?
NO.
THEN THIS MUST BE FATE.
STAY FOR A MOMENT.
IF YOU DON'T MIND.
ELEPHANTS ARE...

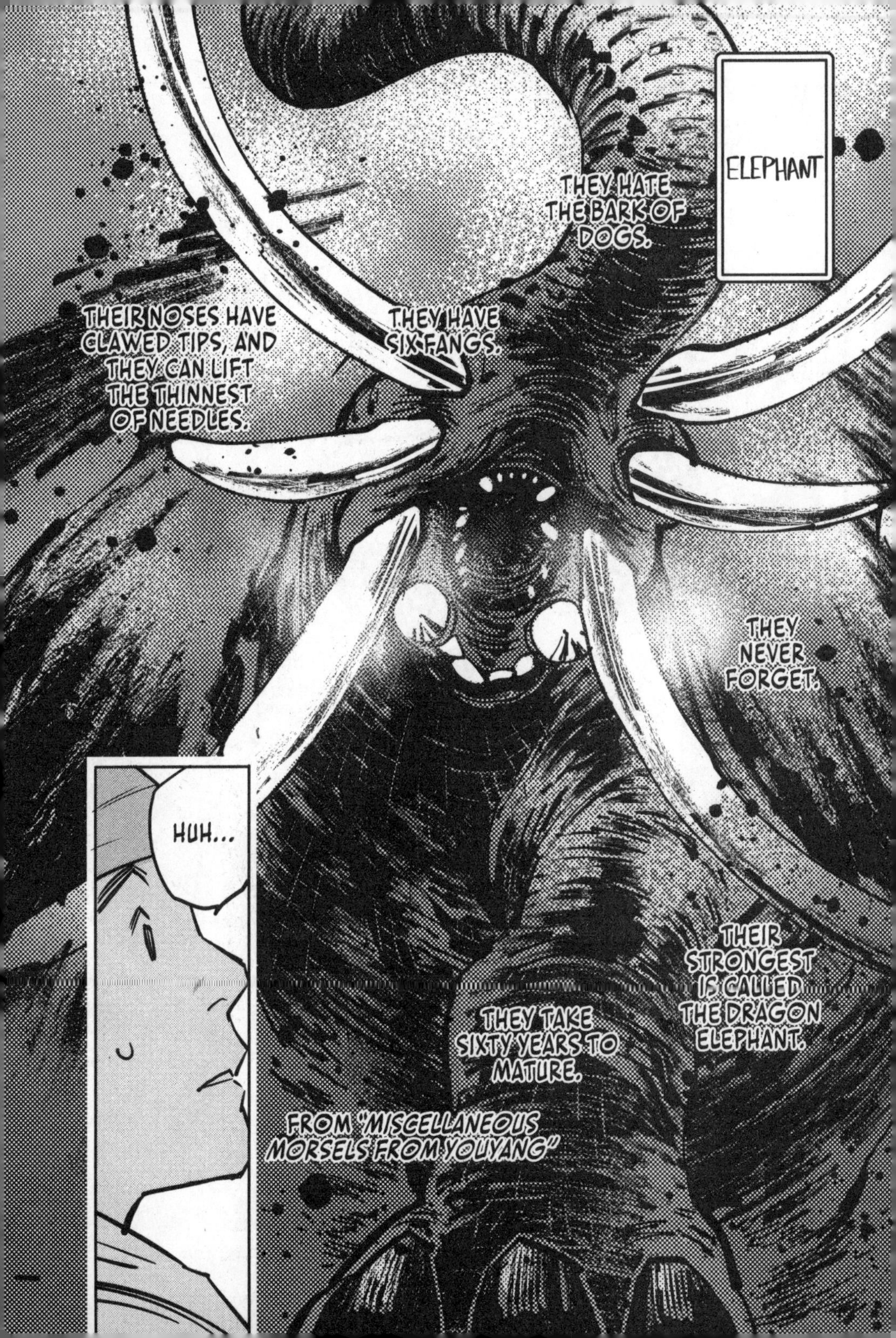
ELEPHANT
THEY HATE THE BARK OF DOGS.
THEY HAVE SIX FANGS.
THEIR NOSES HAVE CLAWED TIPS, AND THEY CAN LIFT THE THINNEST OF NEEDLES.
THEY NEVER FORGET.
THEIR STRONGEST IS CALLED THE DRAGON ELEPHANT.
THEY TAKE SIXTY YEARS TO MATURE.
FROM "MISCELLANEOUS MORSELS FROM YOUYANG"
HUH...

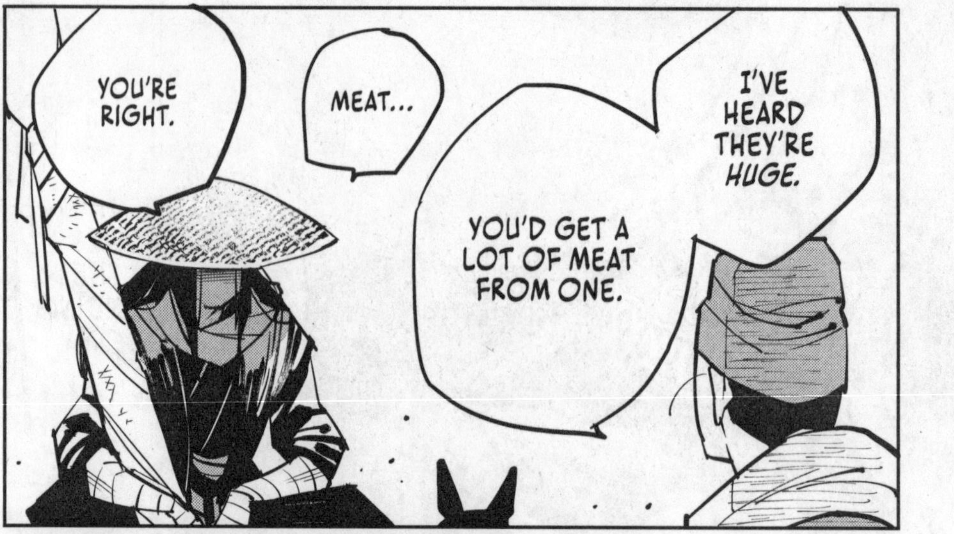
I'VE HEARD THEY'RE *HUGE.*
YOU'D GET A LOT OF MEAT FROM ONE.
MEAT...
YOU'RE RIGHT.

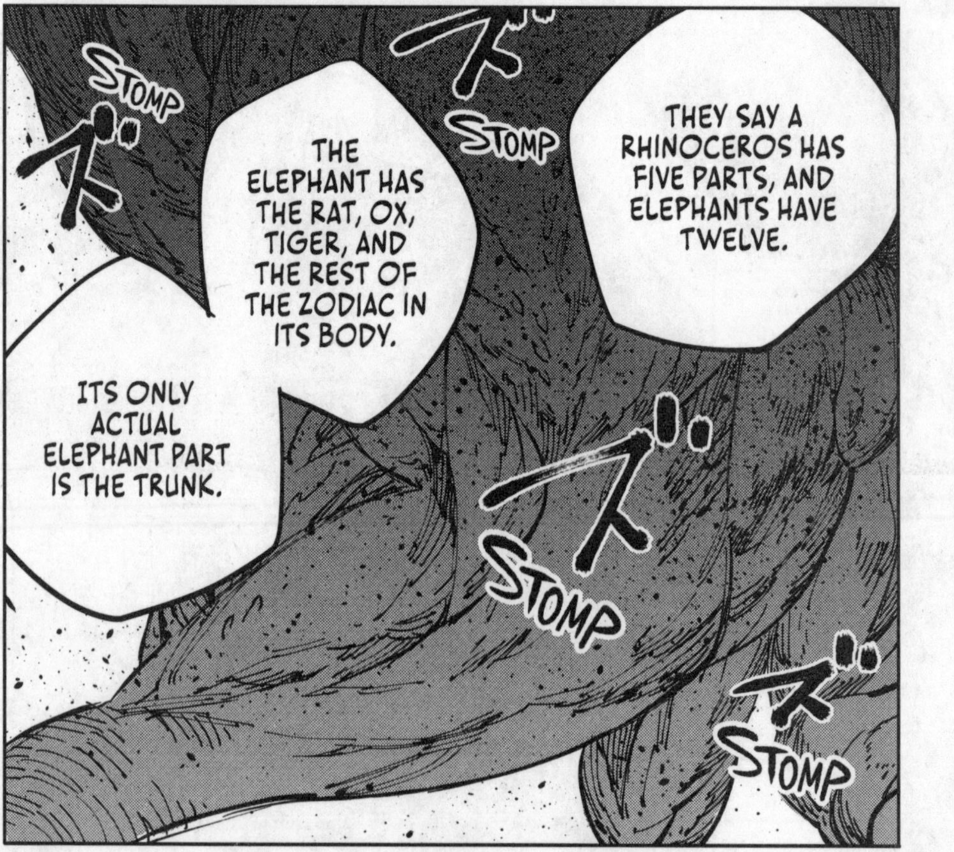
STOMP
THEY SAY A RHINOCEROS HAS FIVE PARTS, AND ELEPHANTS HAVE TWELVE.
STOMP
THE ELEPHANT HAS THE RAT, OX, TIGER, AND THE REST OF THE ZODIAC IN ITS BODY.
ITS ONLY ACTUAL ELEPHANT PART IS THE TRUNK.
STOMP
STOMP

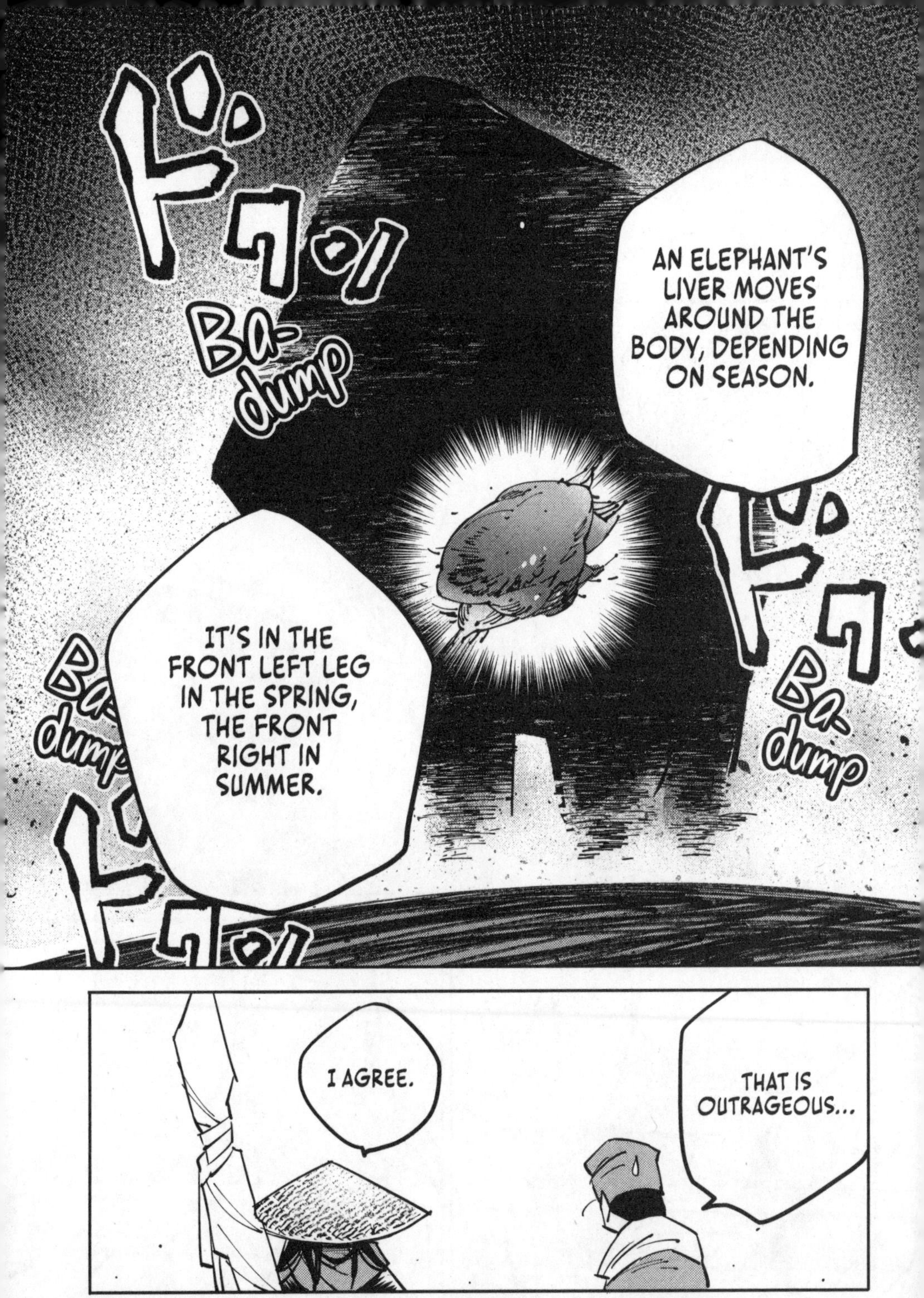
AN ELEPHANT'S LIVER MOVES AROUND THE BODY, DEPENDING ON SEASON.
BA-DUMP
BA-DUMP
IT'S IN THE FRONT LEFT LEG IN THE SPRING, THE FRONT RIGHT IN SUMMER.
THAT IS OUTRAGEOUS...
I AGREE.

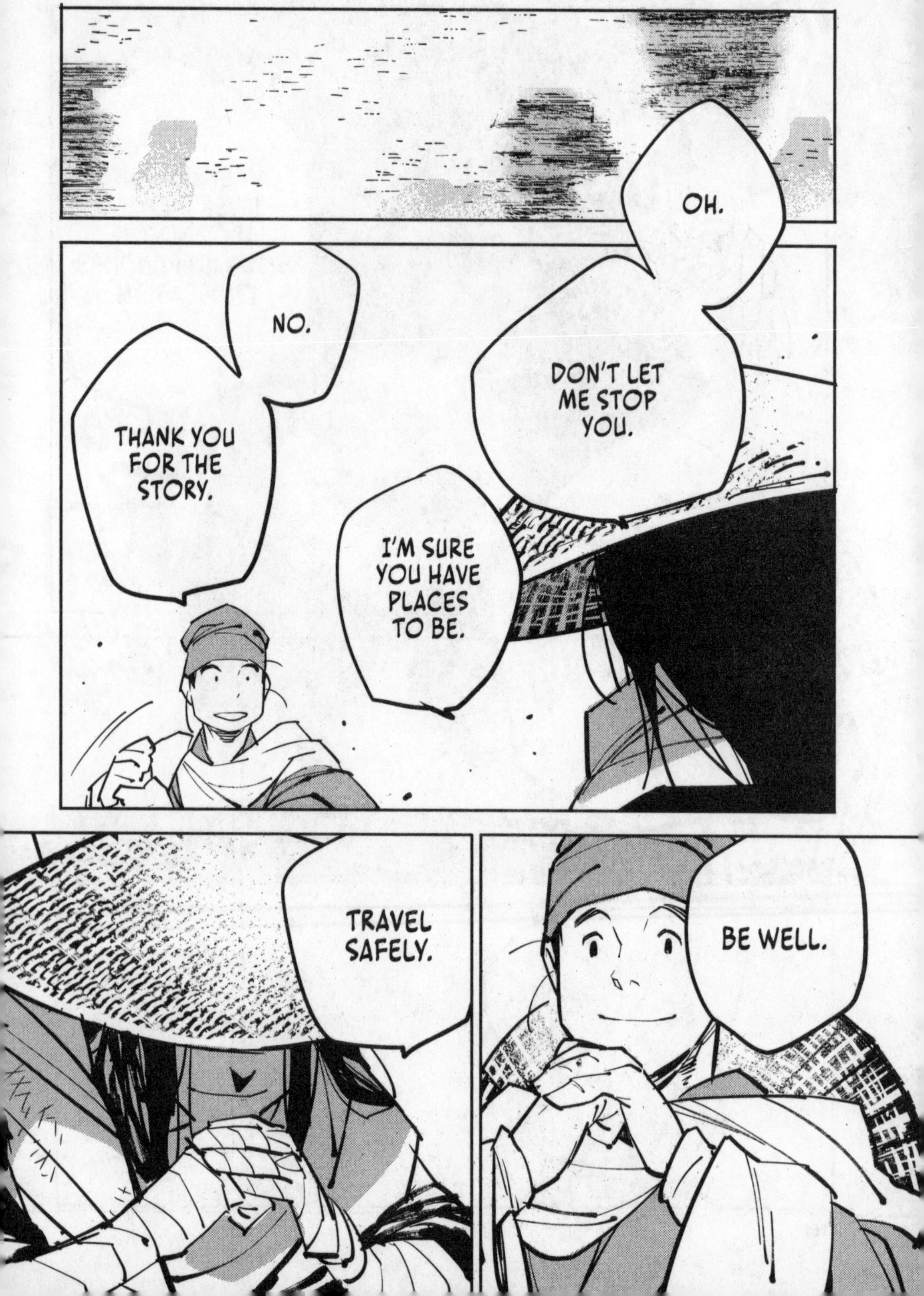
OH.
DON'T LET ME STOP YOU.
I'M SURE YOU HAVE PLACES TO BE.
NO.
THANK YOU FOR THE STORY.
BE WELL.
TRAVEL SAFELY.

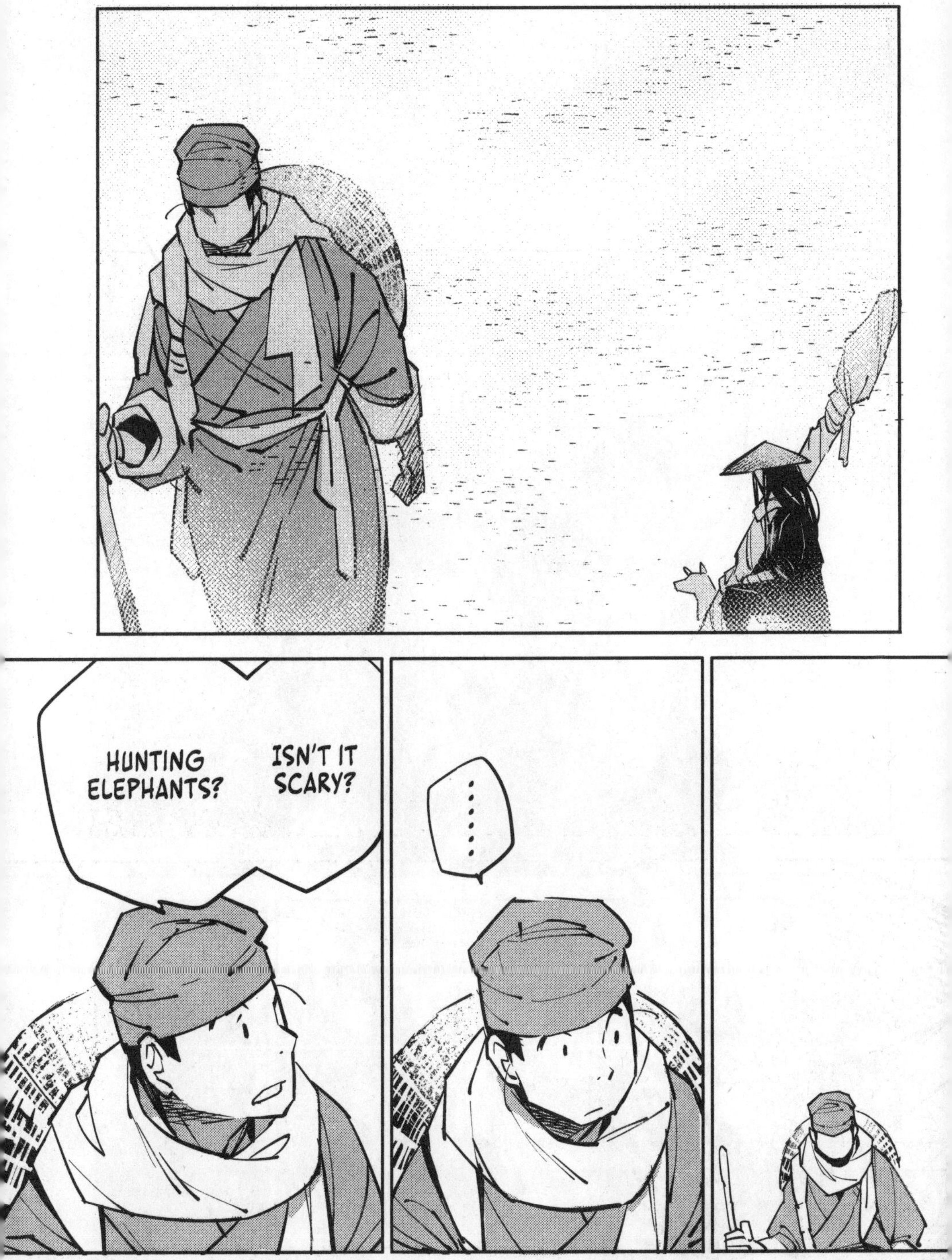
HUNTING ELEPHANTS?
ISN'T IT SCARY?
......

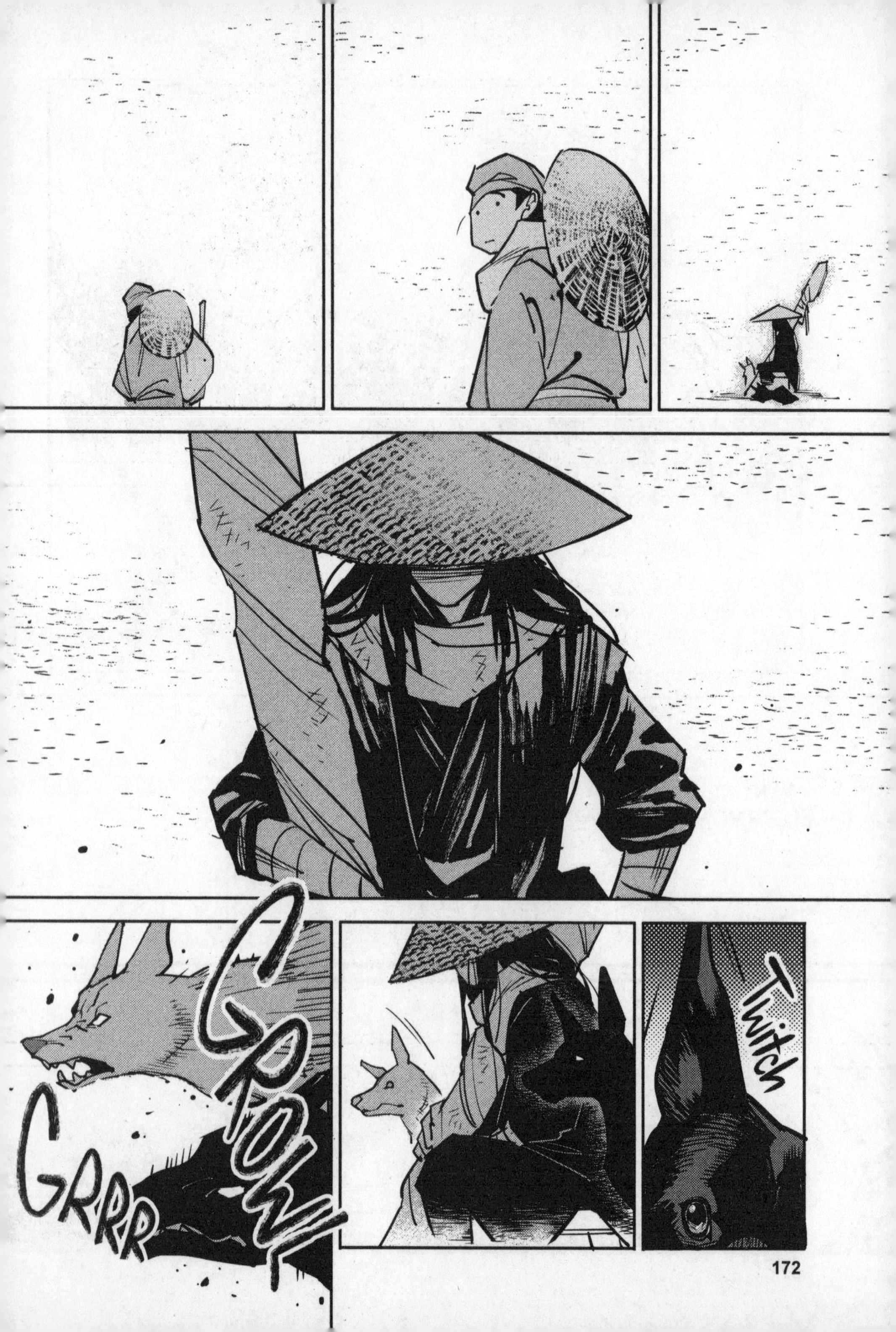
GROWL
GRRR
Twitch

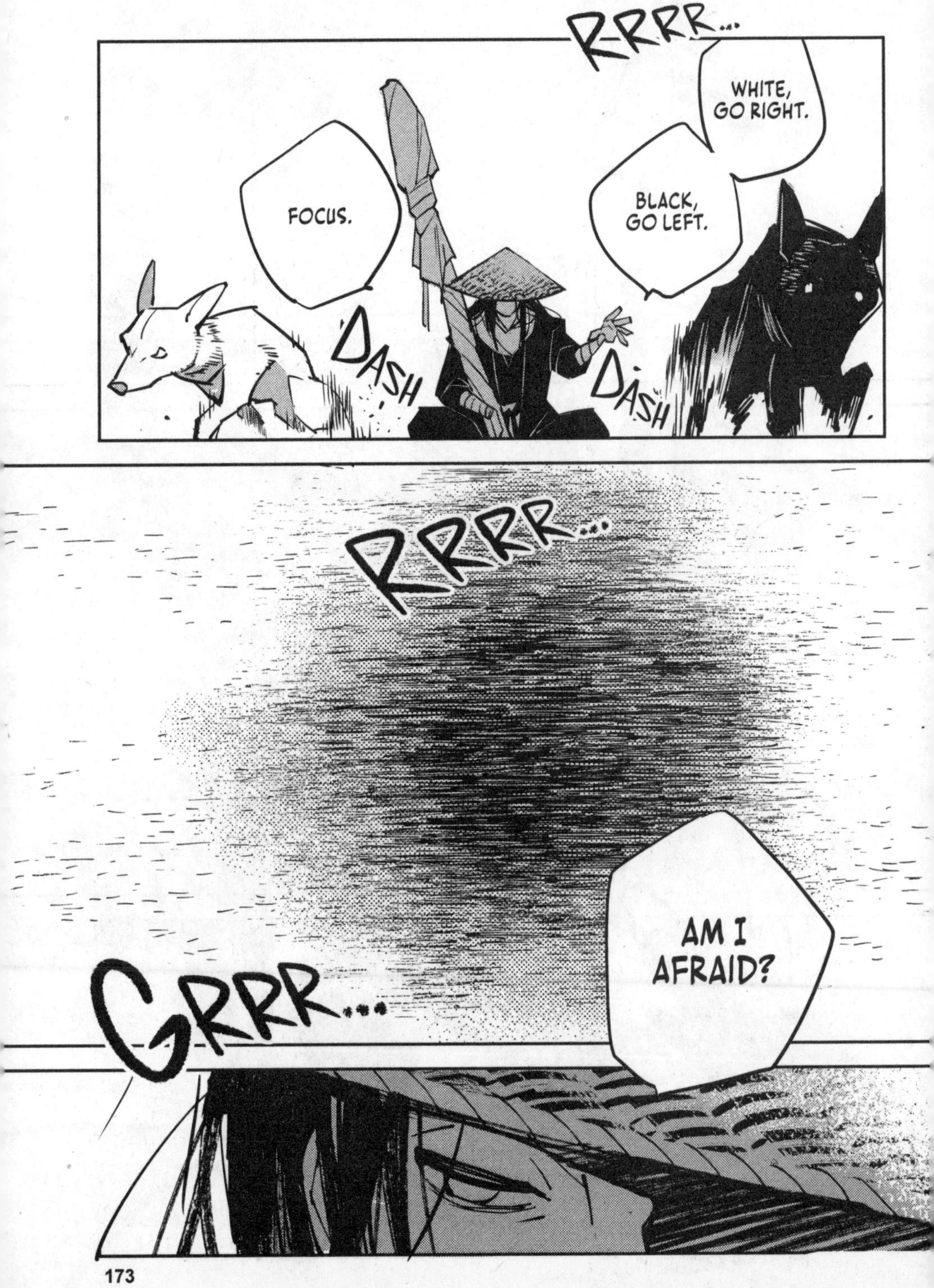
R-R-R-R...
FOCUS.
WHITE, GO RIGHT.
BLACK, GO LEFT.
DASH
DASH
RRRR...
AM I AFRAID?
GRRR...

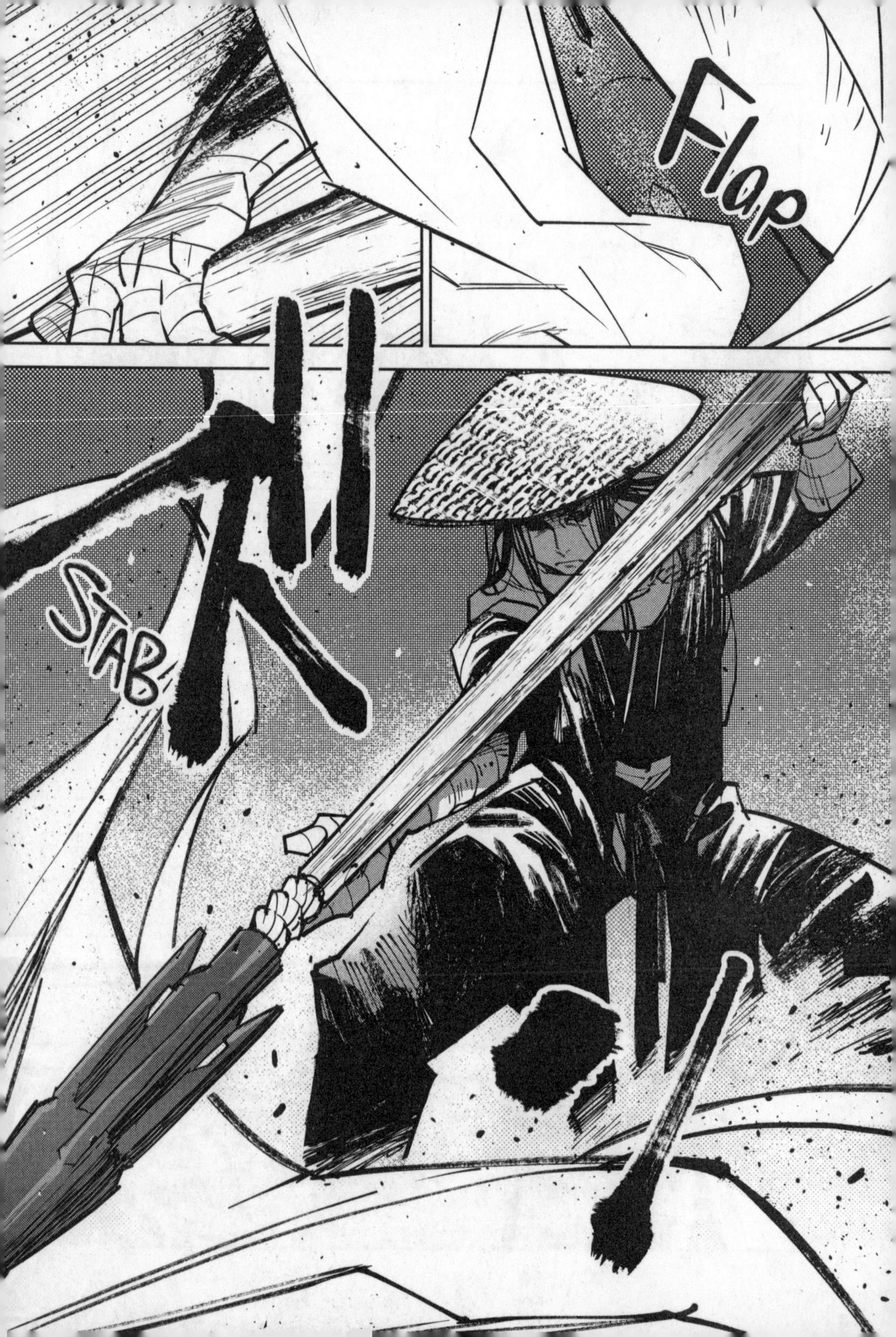
Flap
STAB

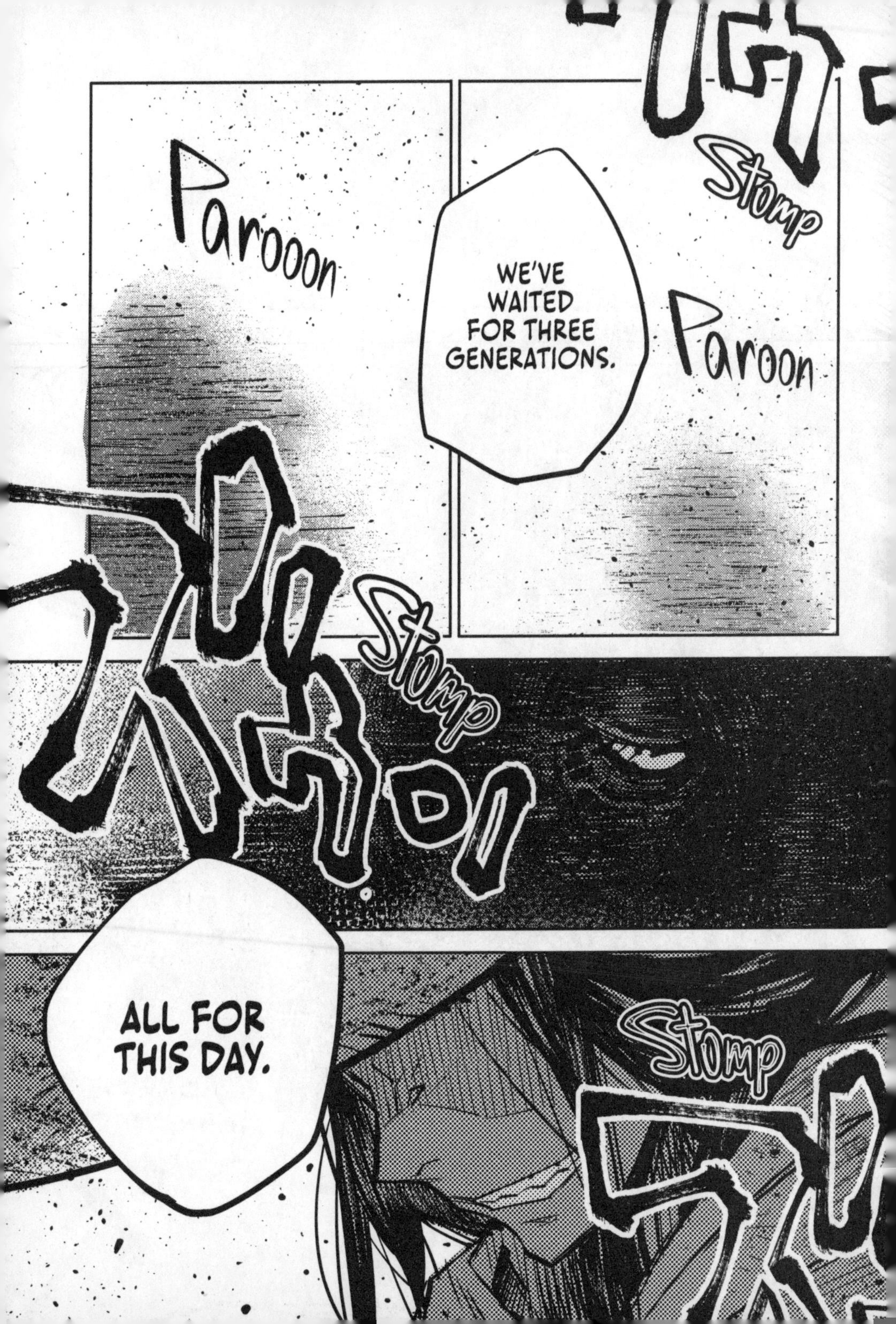
Stomp
Paroon
WE'VE WAITED FOR THREE GENERATIONS.
Parooon
Stomp
ALL FOR THIS DAY.
Stomp

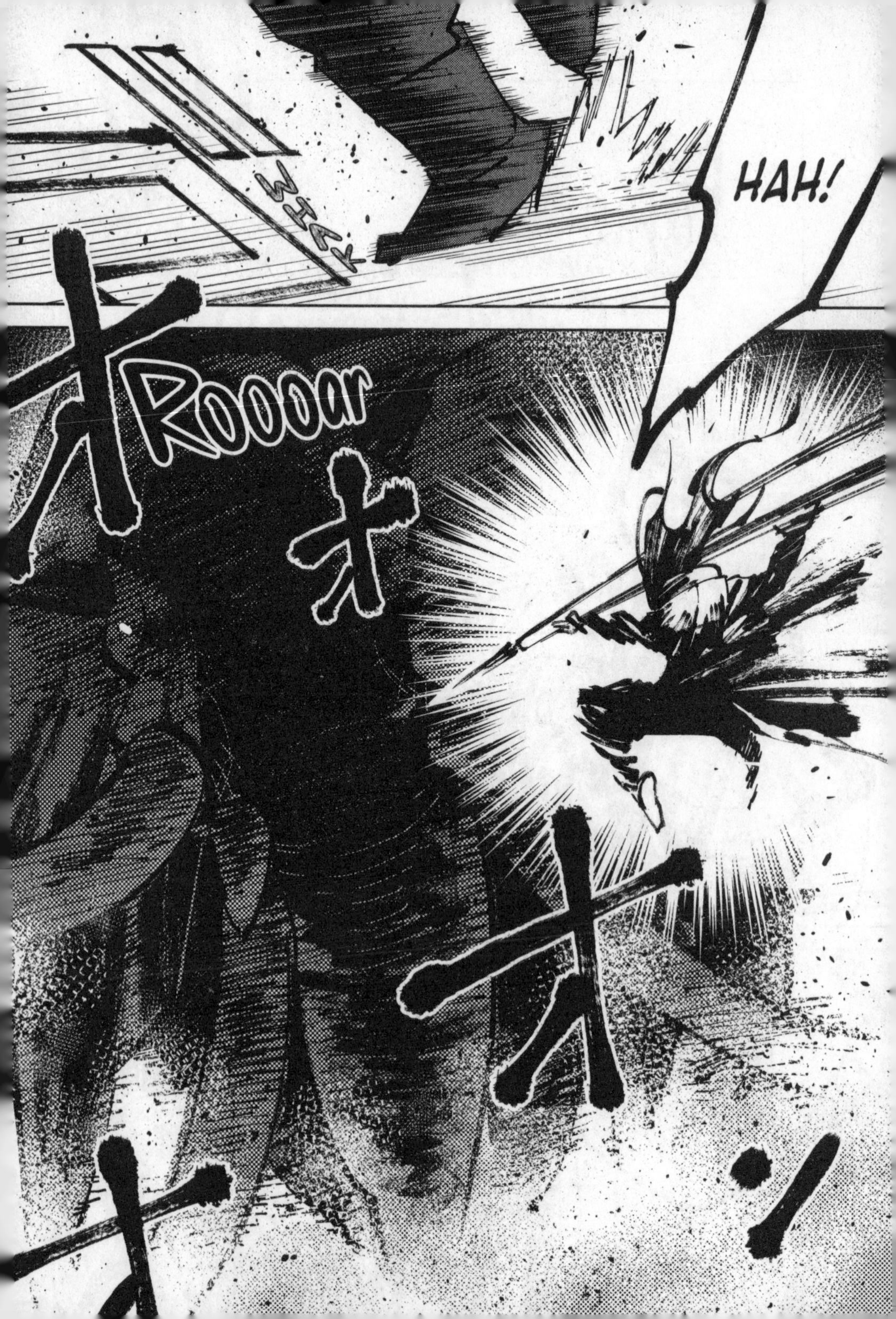

HAH!
WHACK
Roooar

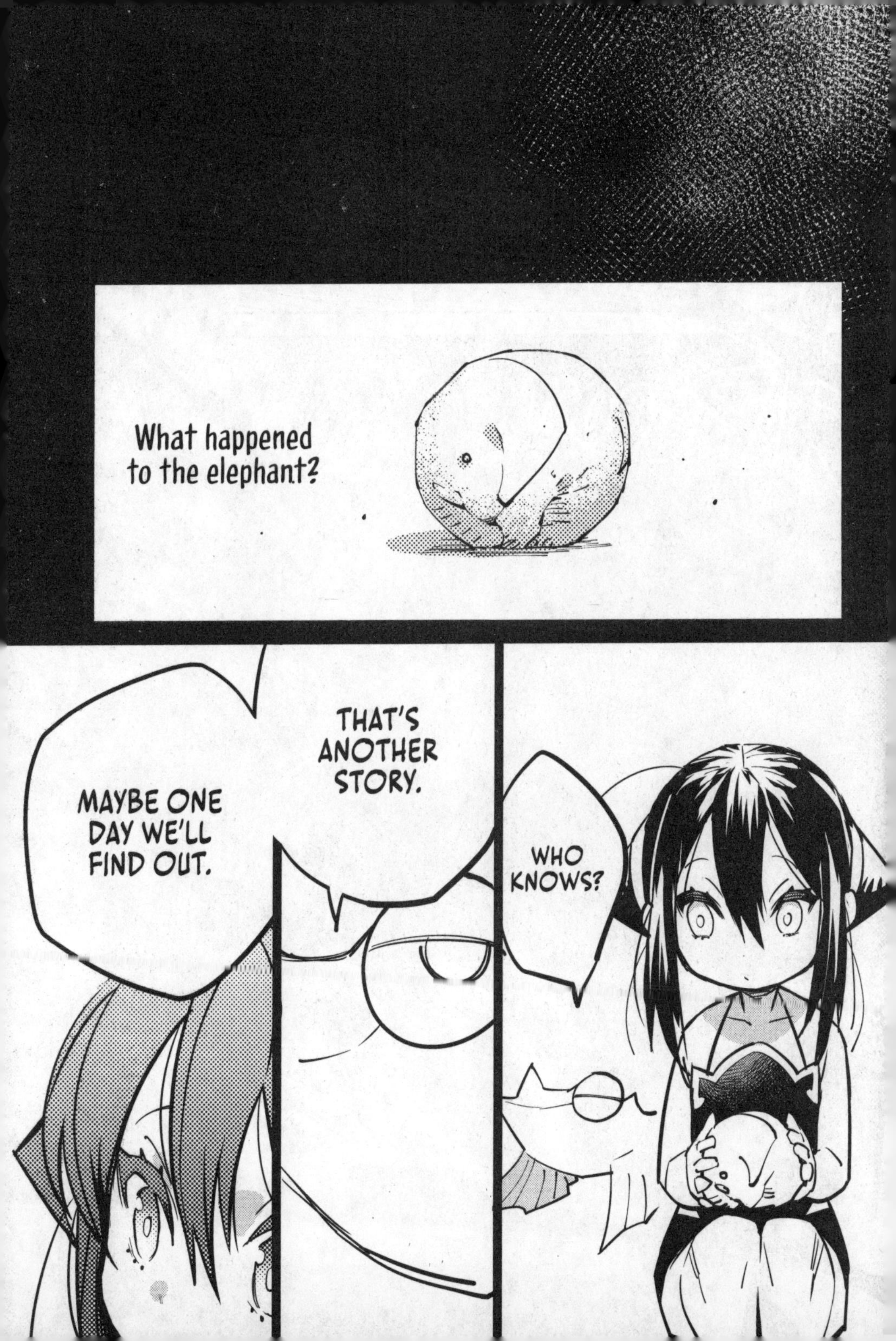
What happened to the elephant?
WHO KNOWS?
THAT'S ANOTHER STORY.
MAYBE ONE DAY WE'LL FIND OUT.

A Chinese Fantasy

The Dragon King's Daughter

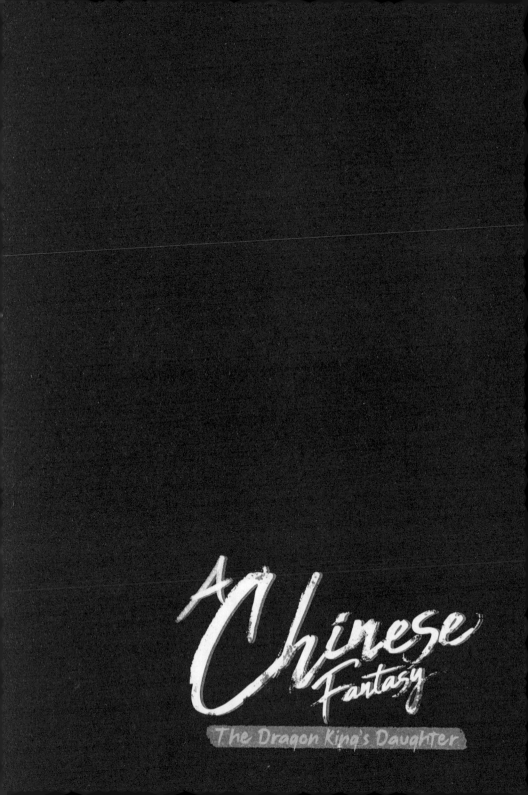

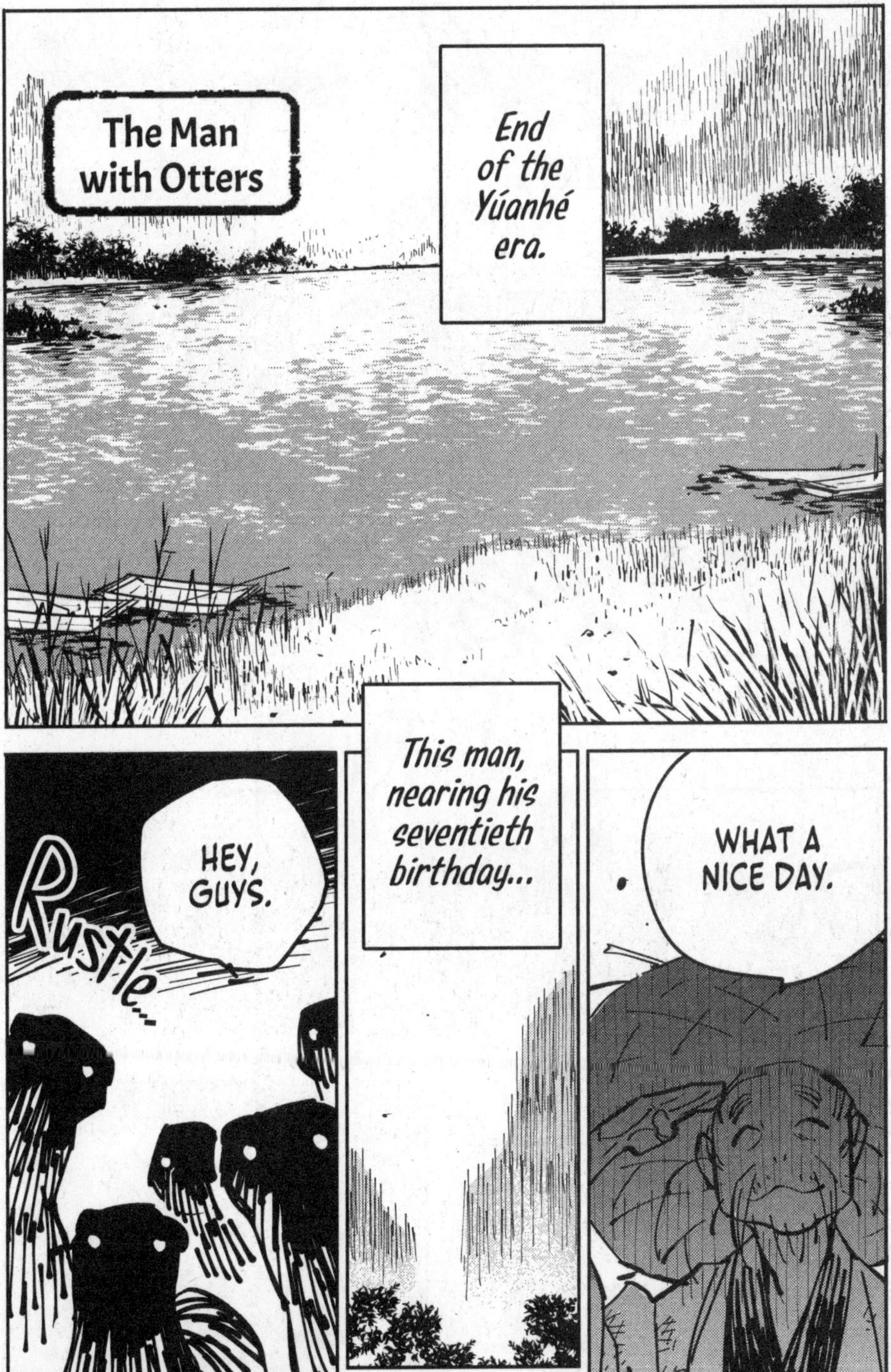
The Man with Otters
End of the Yúanhé era.
This man, nearing his seventieth birthday...
WHAT A NICE DAY.
HEY, GUYS.
Rustle...

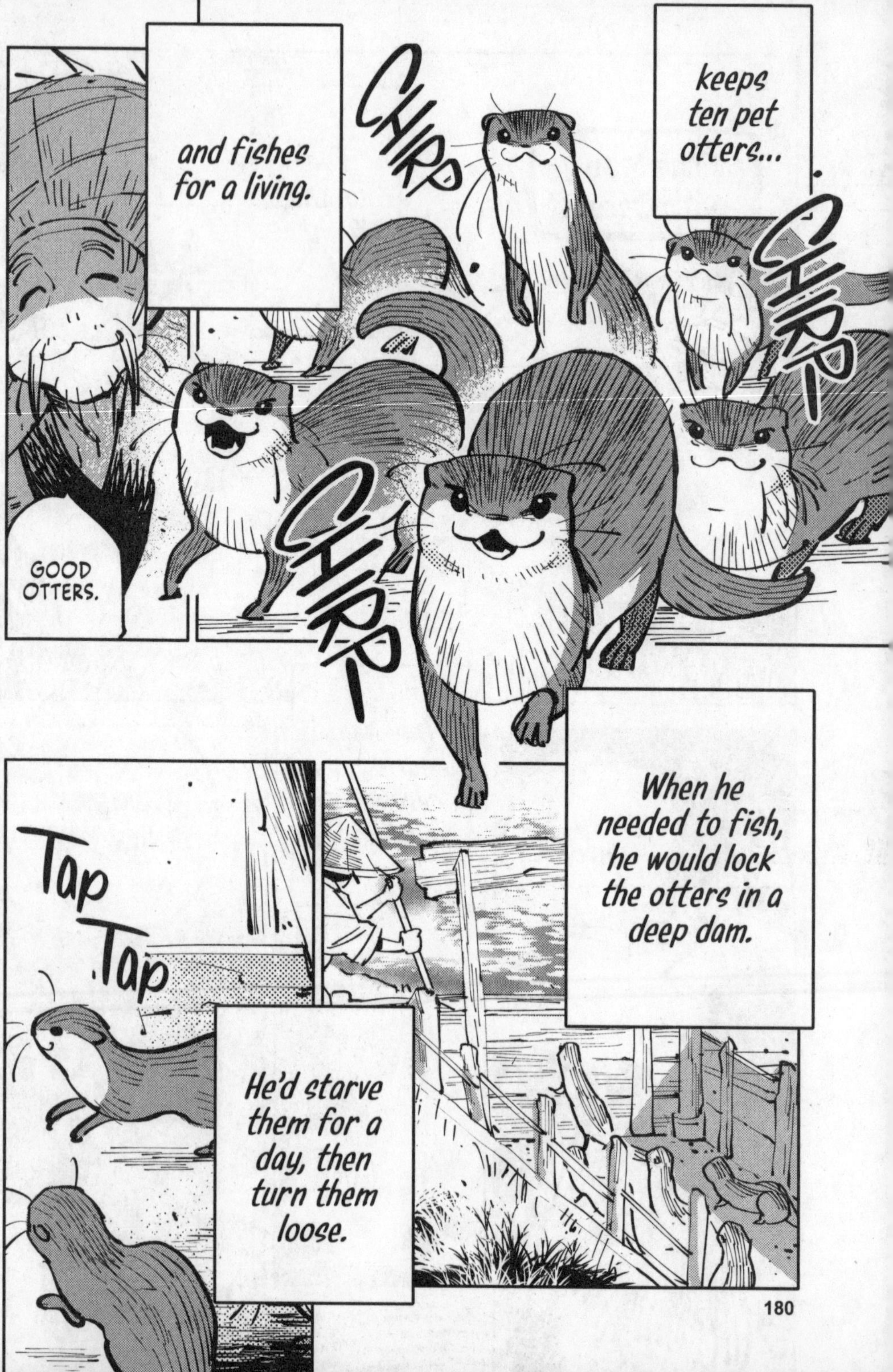
keeps ten pet otters...
CHIRP
CHIRP
and fishes for a living.
CHIRP
CHIRP
GOOD OTTERS.
When he needed to fish, he would lock the otters in a deep dam.
He'd starve them for a day, then turn them loose.
Tap
Tap

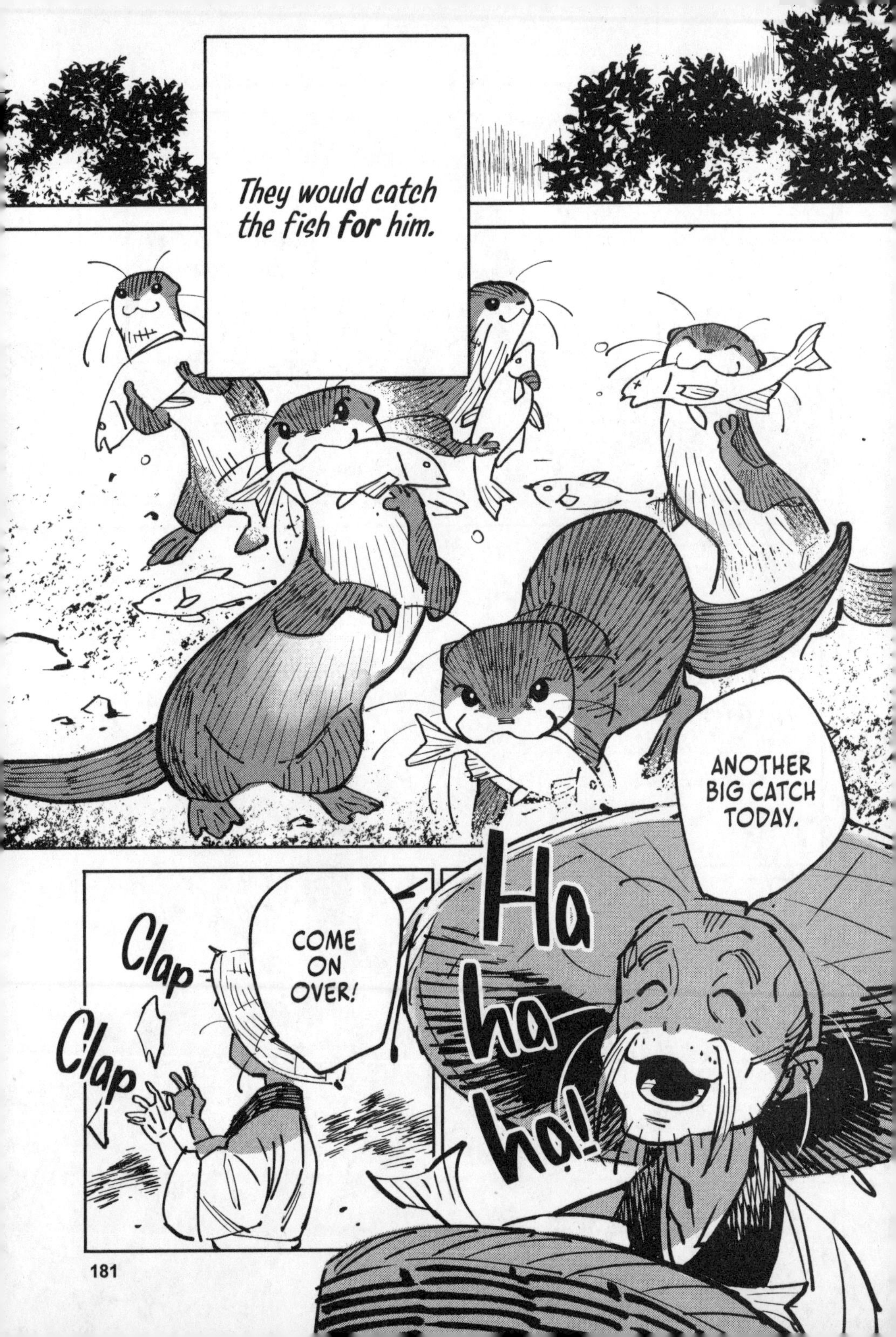
They would catch the fish **for** him.
ANOTHER BIG CATCH TODAY.
Ha ha ha!
Clap
Clap
COME ON OVER!

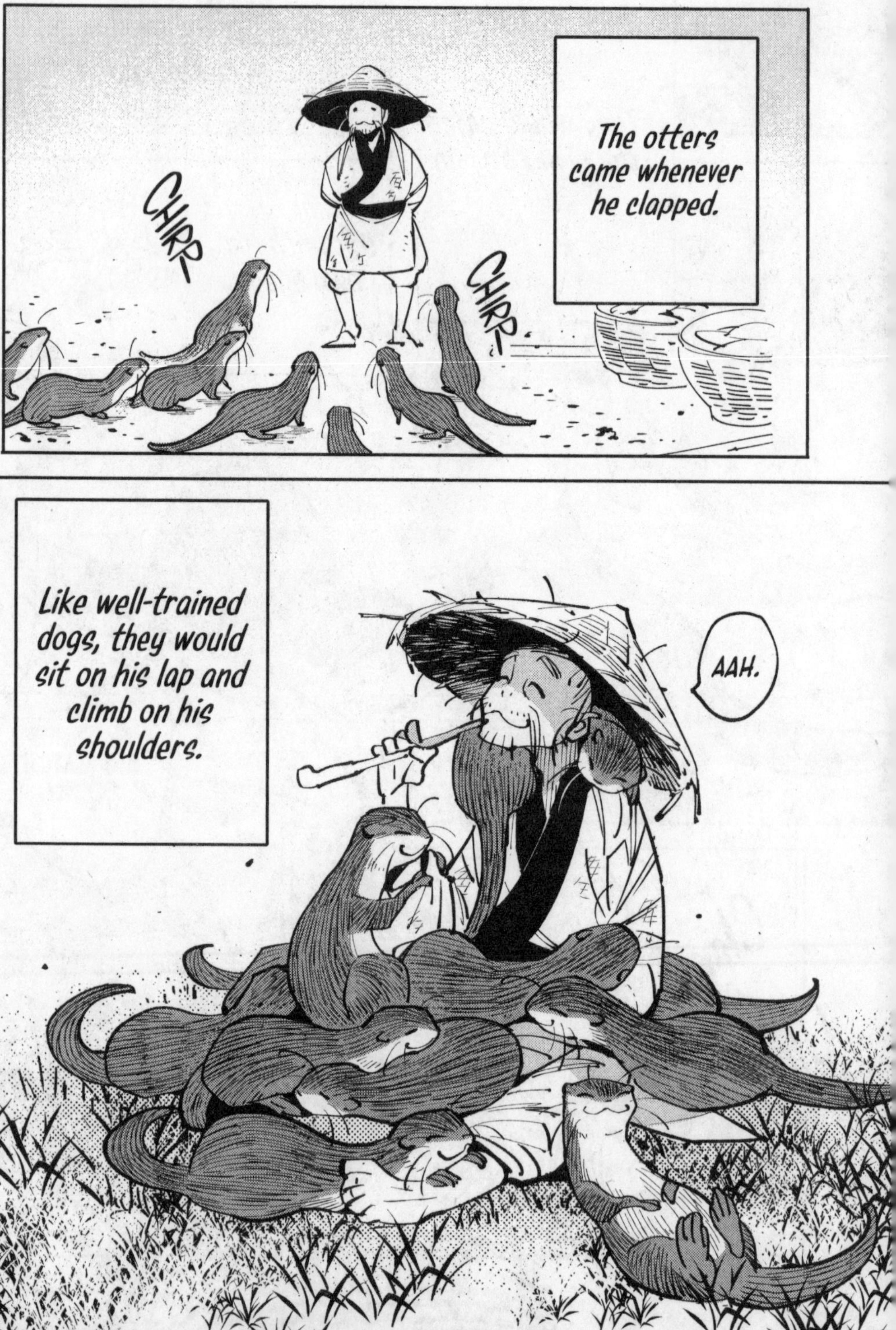
The otters came whenever he clapped.
CHIRP
CHIRP
Like well-trained dogs, they would sit on his lap and climb on his shoulders.
AAH.

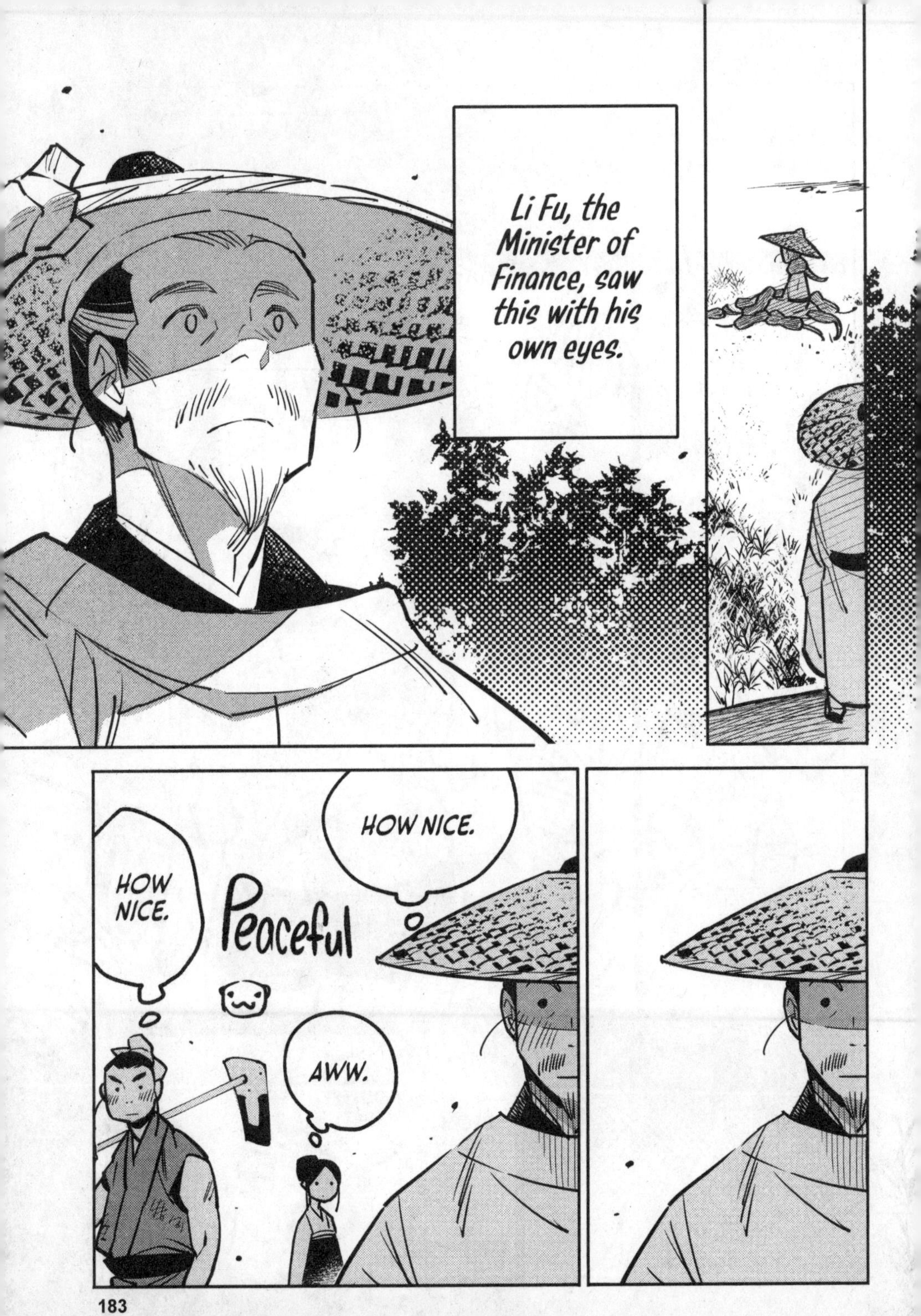
Li Fu, the Minister of Finance, saw this with his own eyes.
HOW NICE.
HOW NICE.
Peaceful
AWW.

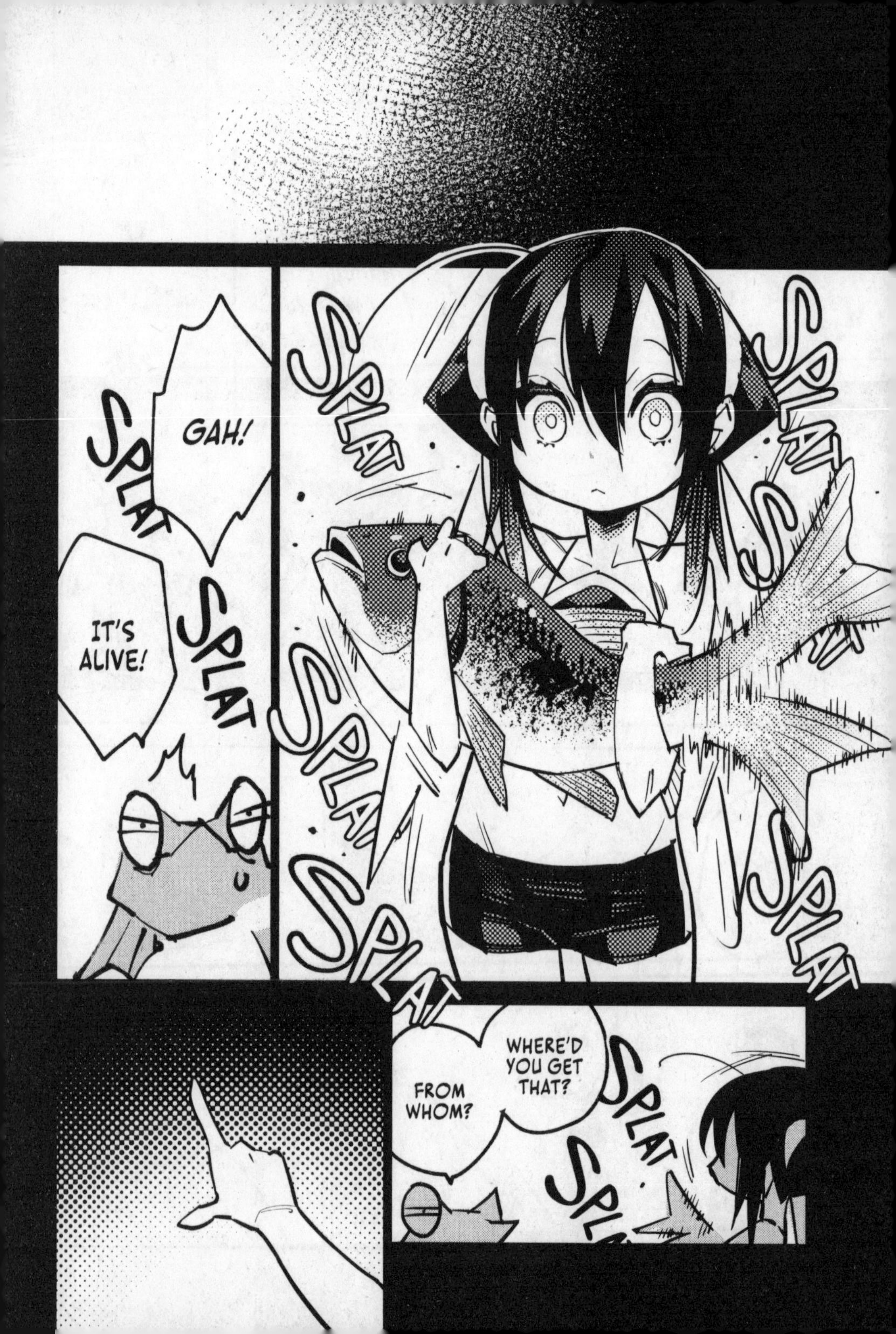
SPLAT
SPLAT
SPLAT
SPLAT
SPLAT
SPLAT
GAH!
IT'S ALIVE!
SPLAT
SPLAT
WHERE'D YOU GET THAT?
FROM WHOM?
SPLAT.

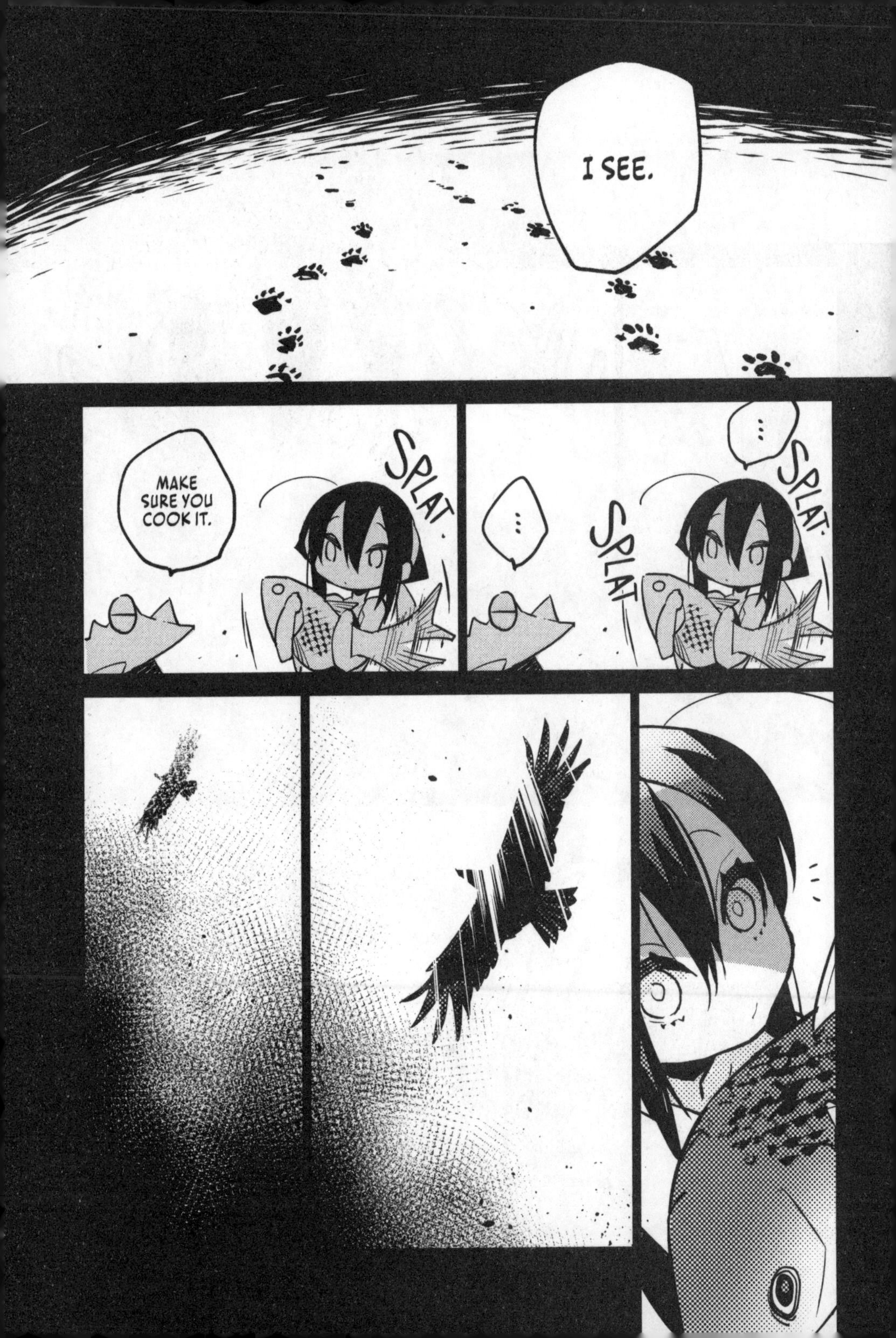
I SEE.
SPLAT
MAKE SURE YOU COOK IT.
...
SPLAT
SPLAT
...

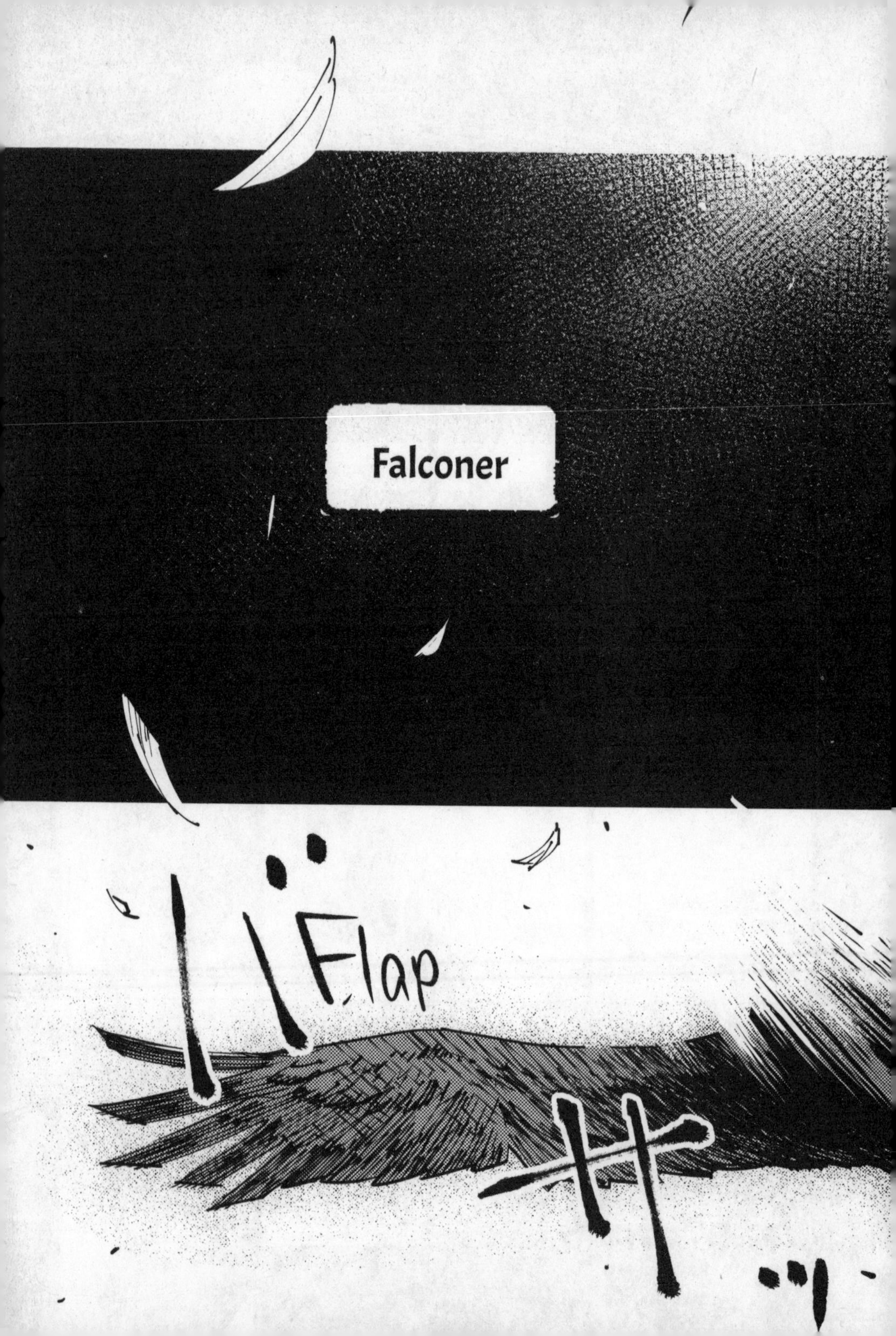
Falconer
Flap

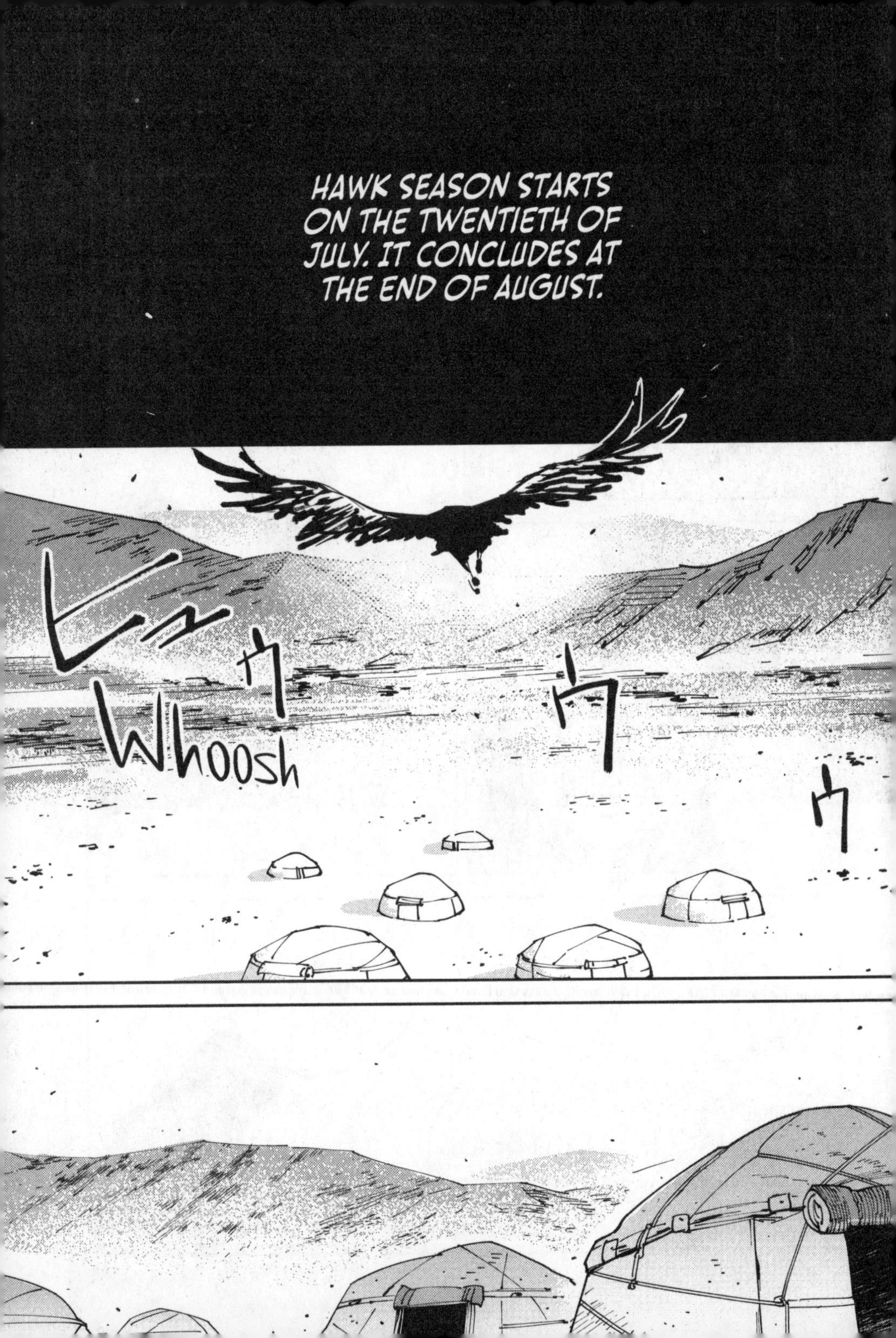

HAWK SEASON STARTS ON THE TWENTIETH OF JULY. IT CONCLUDES AT THE END OF AUGUST.
Whoosh

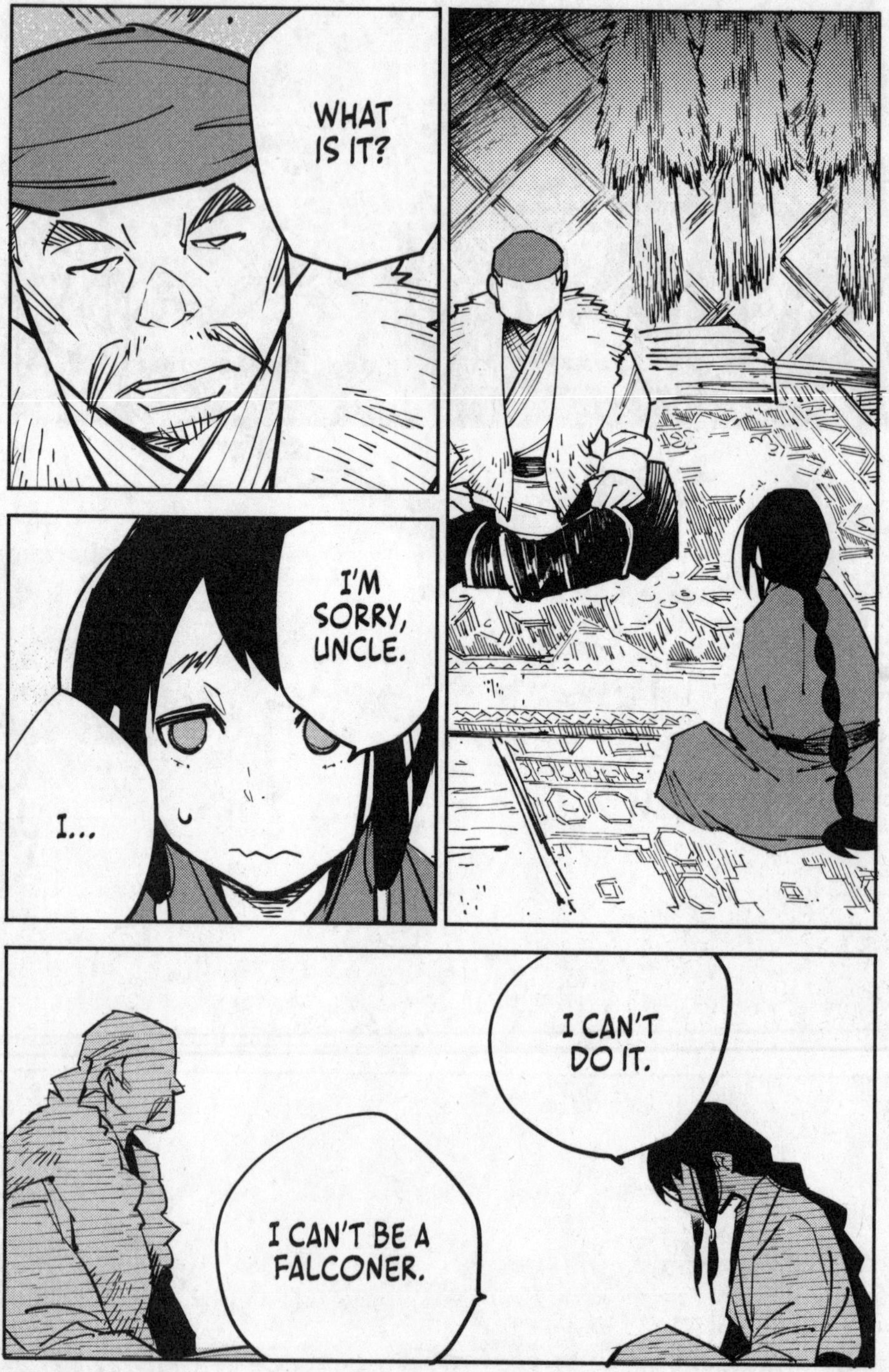
WHAT IS IT?
I'M SORRY, UNCLE.
I...
I CAN'T DO IT.
I CAN'T BE A FALCONER.

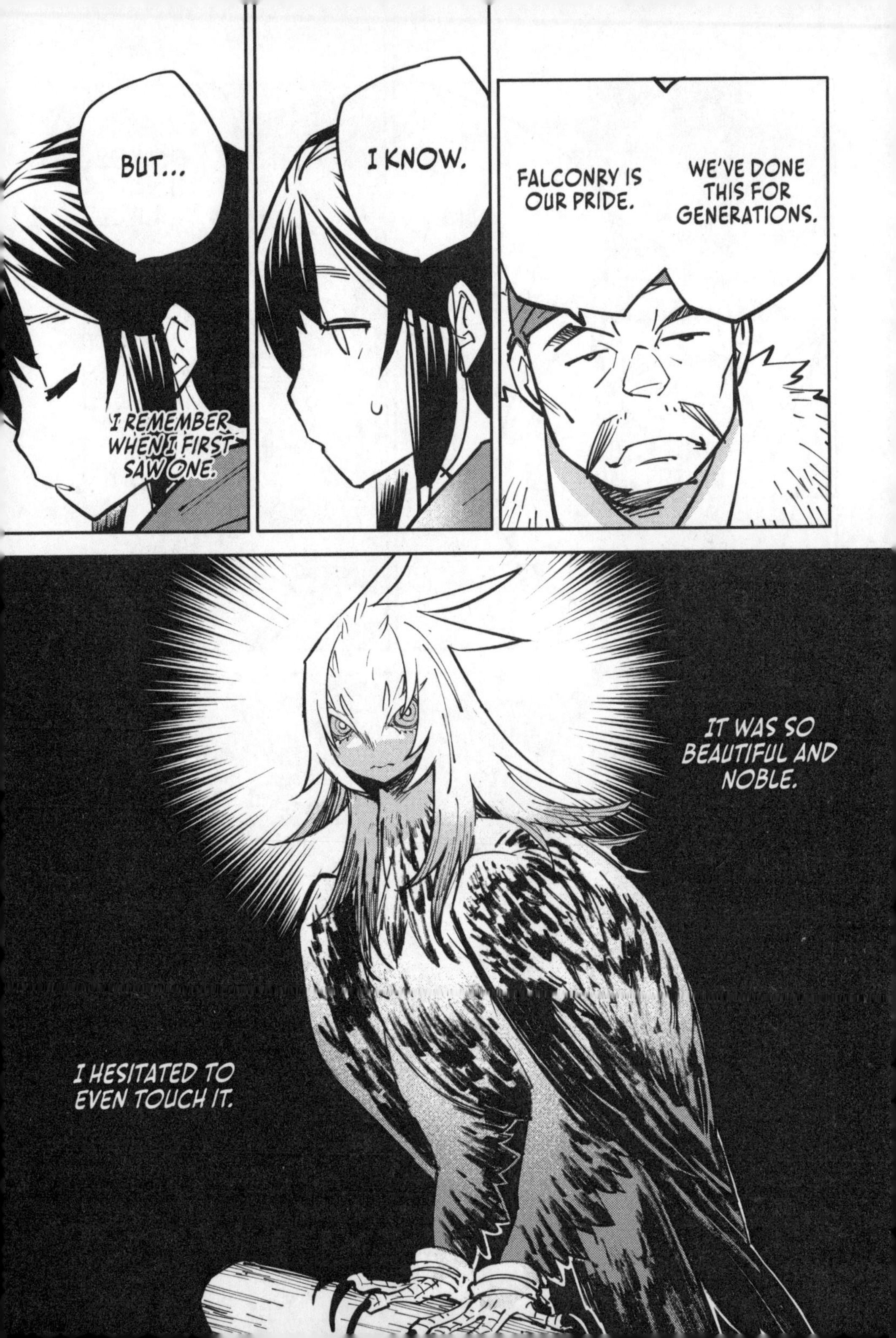
FALCONRY IS OUR PRIDE.
WE'VE DONE THIS FOR GENERATIONS.
I KNOW.
BUT...
I REMEMBER WHEN I FIRST SAW ONE.
IT WAS SO BEAUTIFUL AND NOBLE.
I HESITATED TO EVEN TOUCH IT.

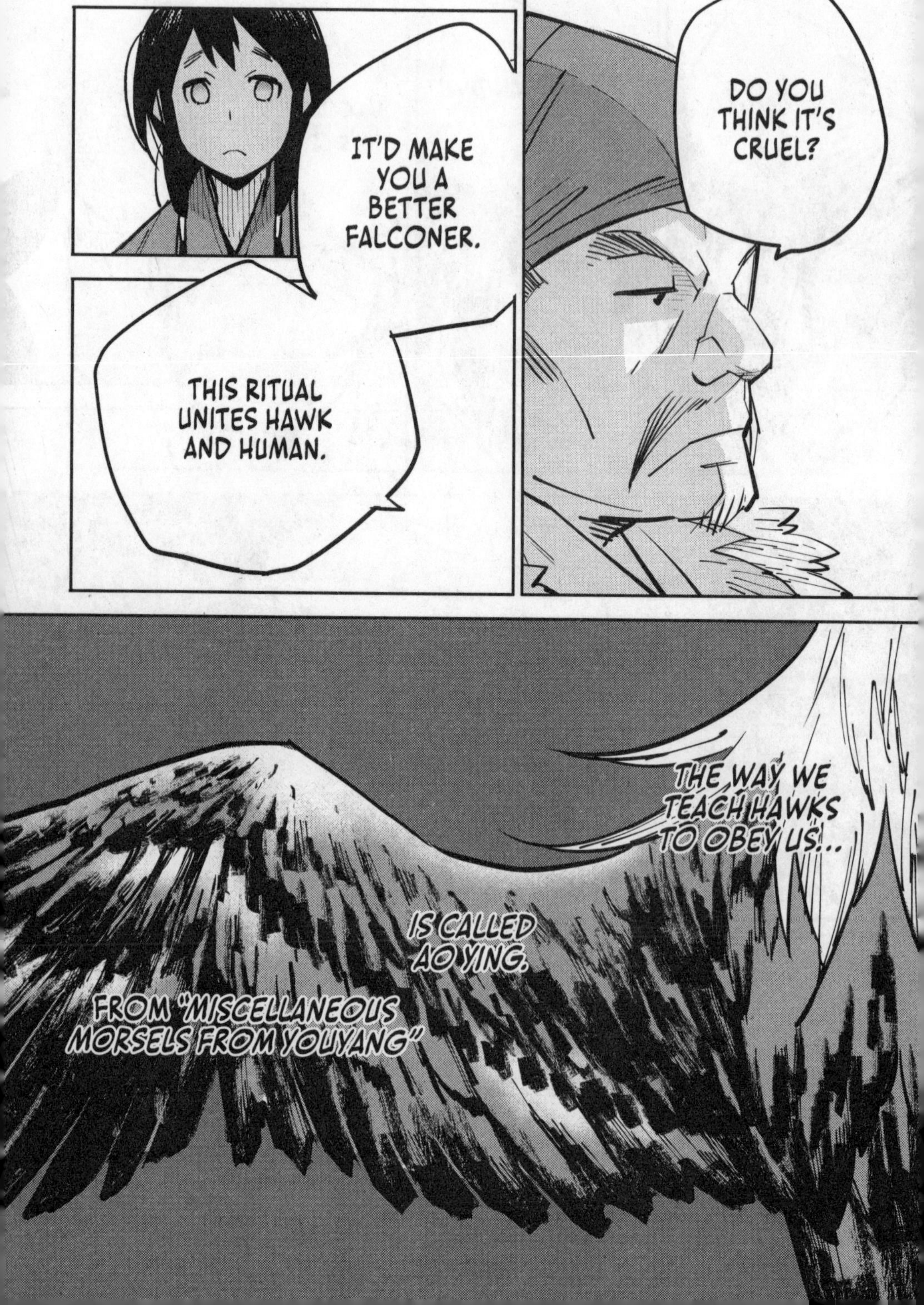
DO YOU THINK IT'S CRUEL?
IT'D MAKE YOU A BETTER FALCONER.
THIS RITUAL UNITES HAWK AND HUMAN.
THE WAY WE TEACH HAWKS TO OBEY US...
IS CALLED AO YING.
FROM "MISCELLANEOUS MORSELS FROM YOUYANG"

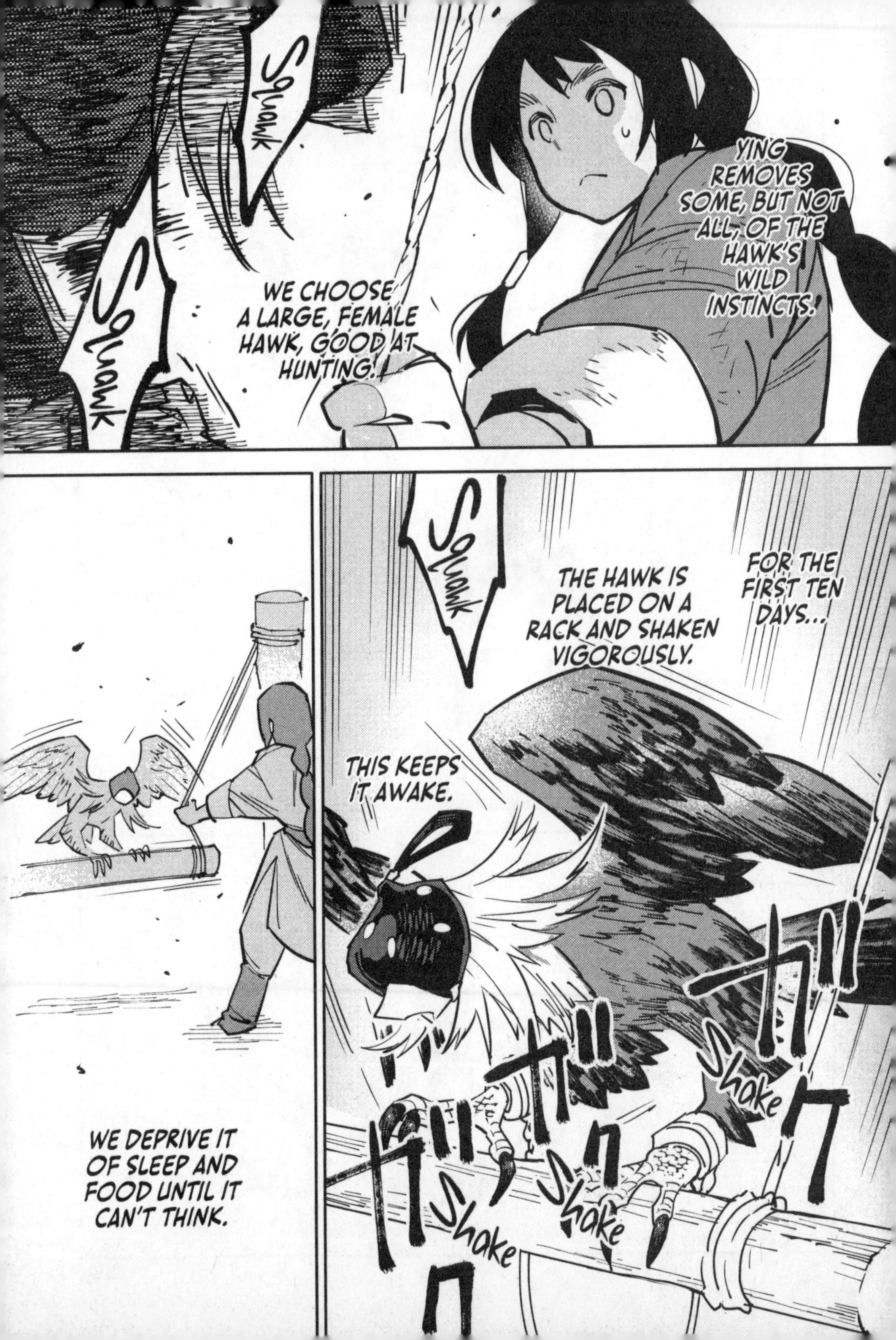
YING REMOVES SOME, BUT NOT ALL, OF THE HAWK'S WILD INSTINCTS.
WE CHOOSE A LARGE, FEMALE HAWK, GOOD AT HUNTING.
Squawk
Squawk
FOR THE FIRST TEN DAYS...
THE HAWK IS PLACED ON A RACK AND SHAKEN VIGOROUSLY.
Squawk
THIS KEEPS IT AWAKE.
Shake
Shake
Shake
WE DEPRIVE IT OF SLEEP AND FOOD UNTIL IT CAN'T THINK.

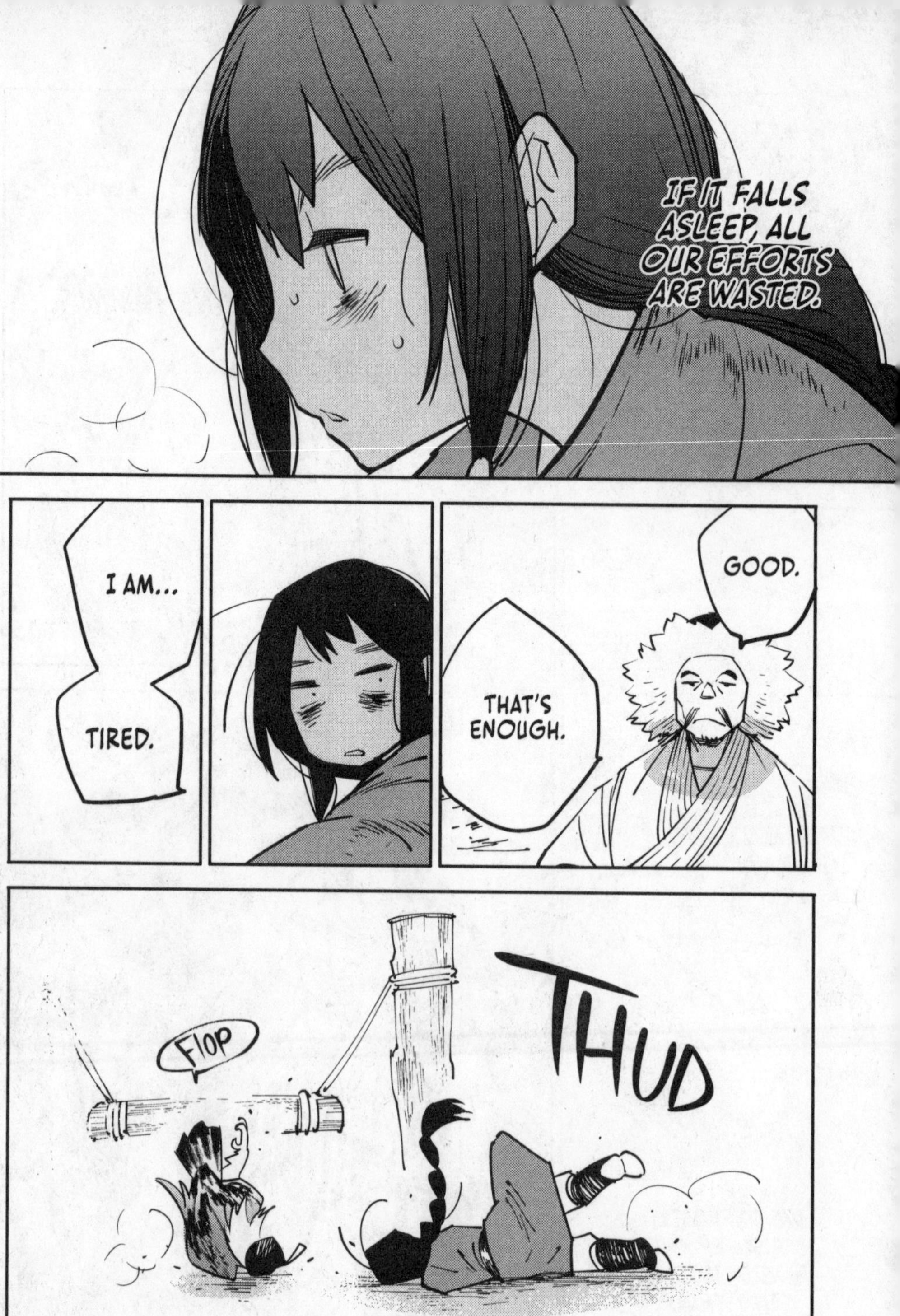
IF IT FALLS ASLEEP, ALL OUR EFFORTS ARE WASTED.
GOOD.
THAT'S ENOUGH.
I AM...
TIRED.
THUD
FLOP

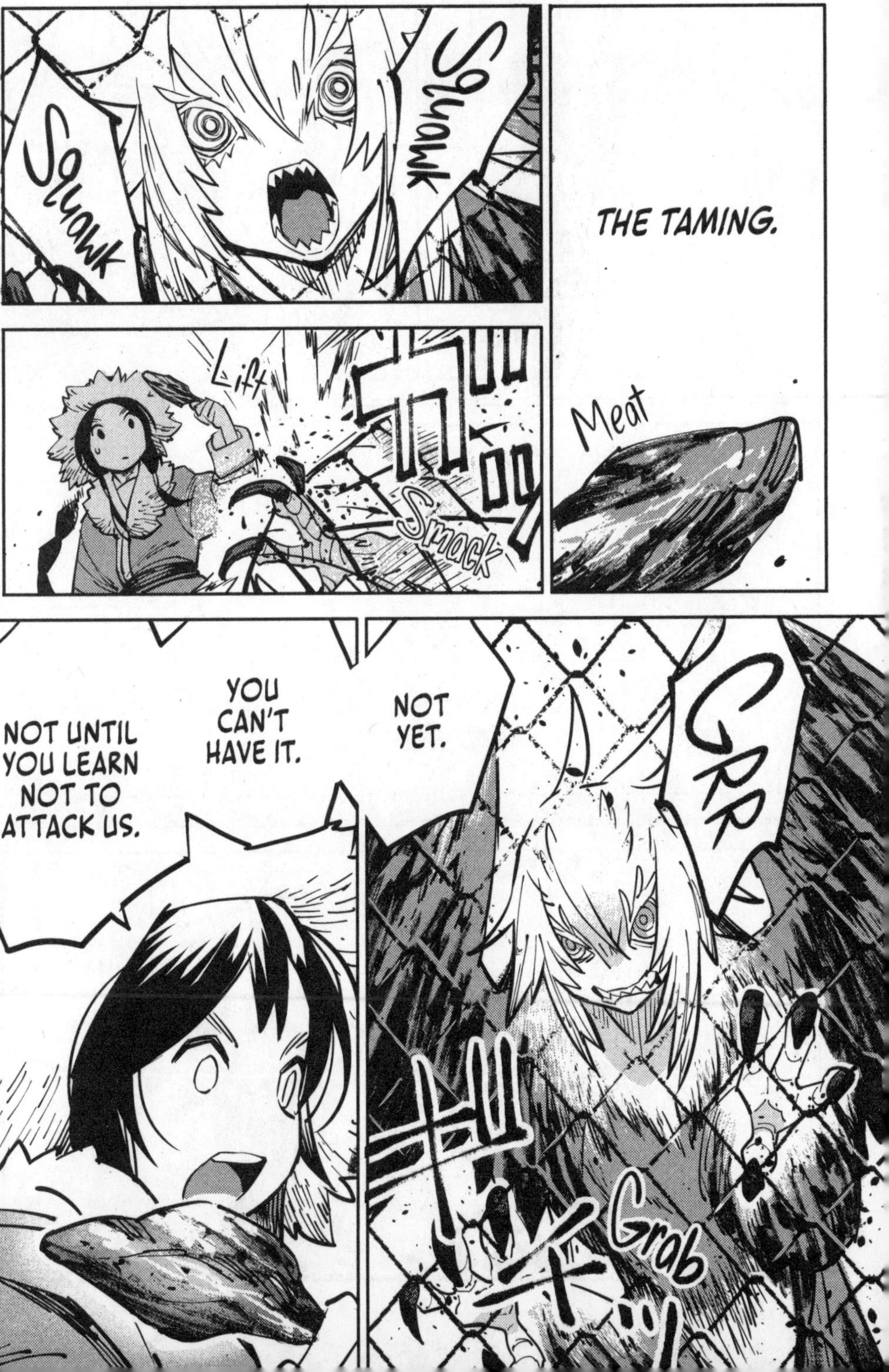
THE TAMING.
Meat
Squawk
Squawk
Lift
Smack
GRR
Grab
NOT YET.
YOU CAN'T HAVE IT.
NOT UNTIL YOU LEARN NOT TO ATTACK US.

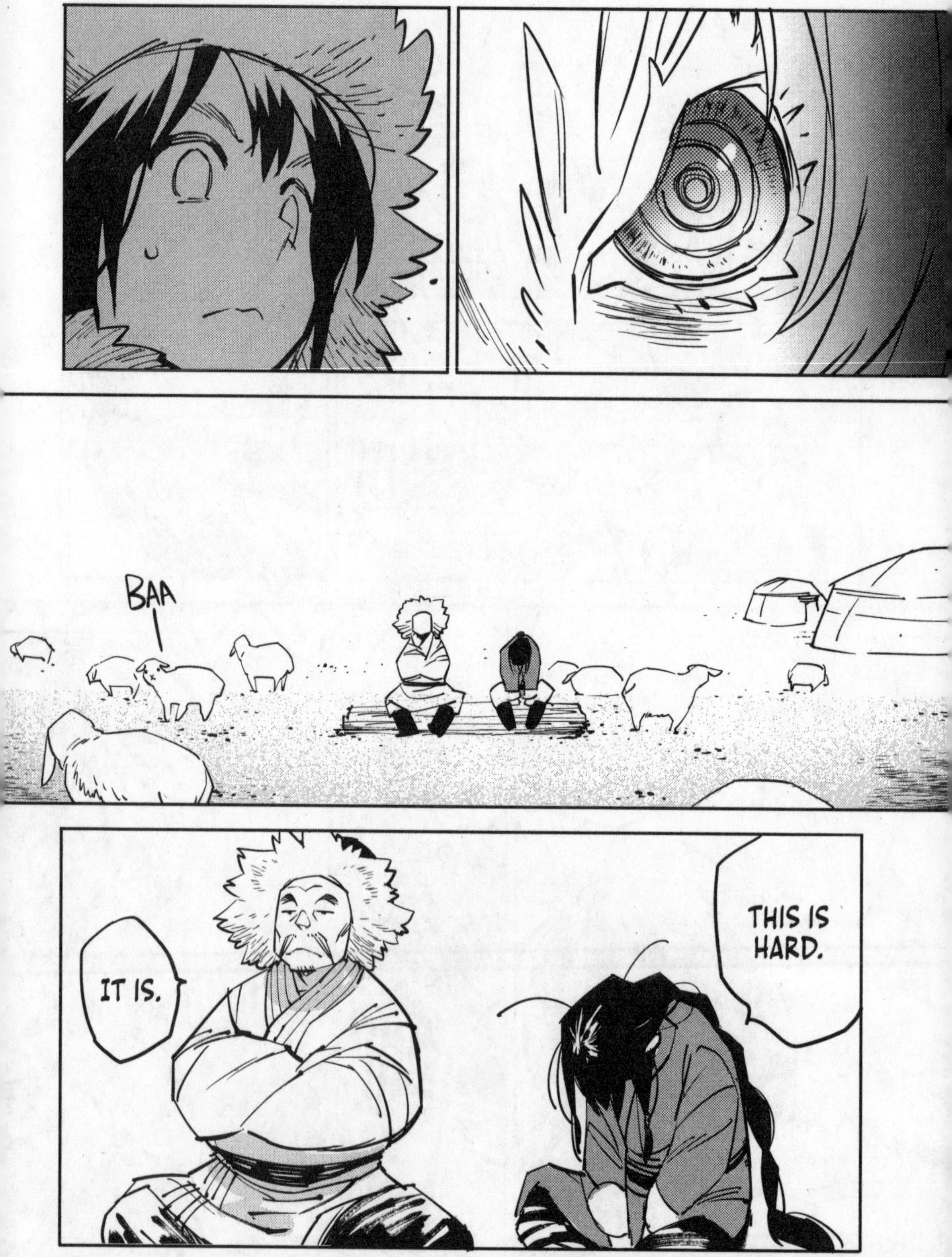
BAA
THIS IS HARD.
IT IS.

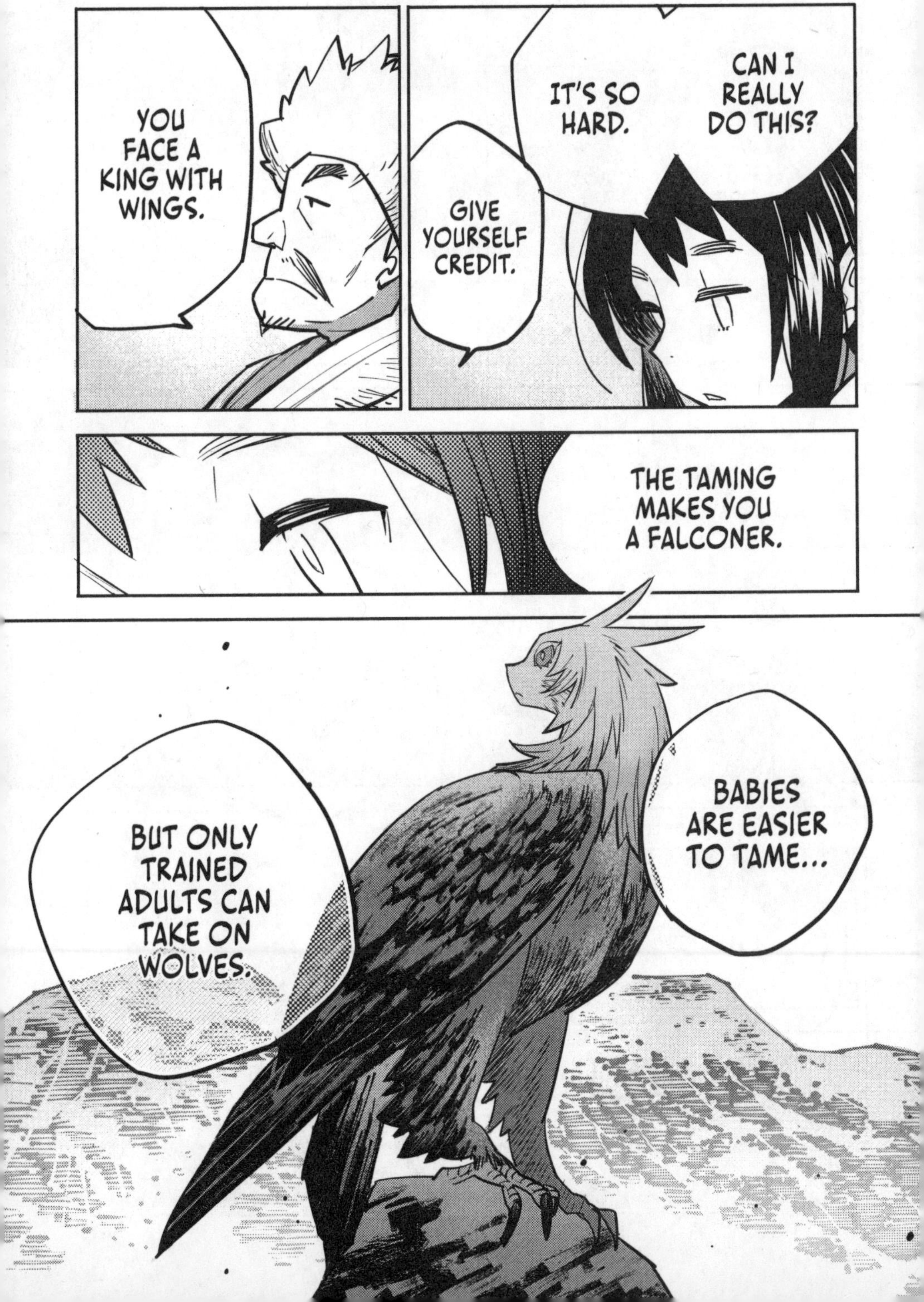
CAN I REALLY DO THIS?
IT'S SO HARD.
GIVE YOURSELF CREDIT.
YOU FACE A KING WITH WINGS.
THE TAMING MAKES YOU A FALCONER.
BABIES ARE EASIER TO TAME...
BUT ONLY TRAINED ADULTS CAN TAKE ON WOLVES.

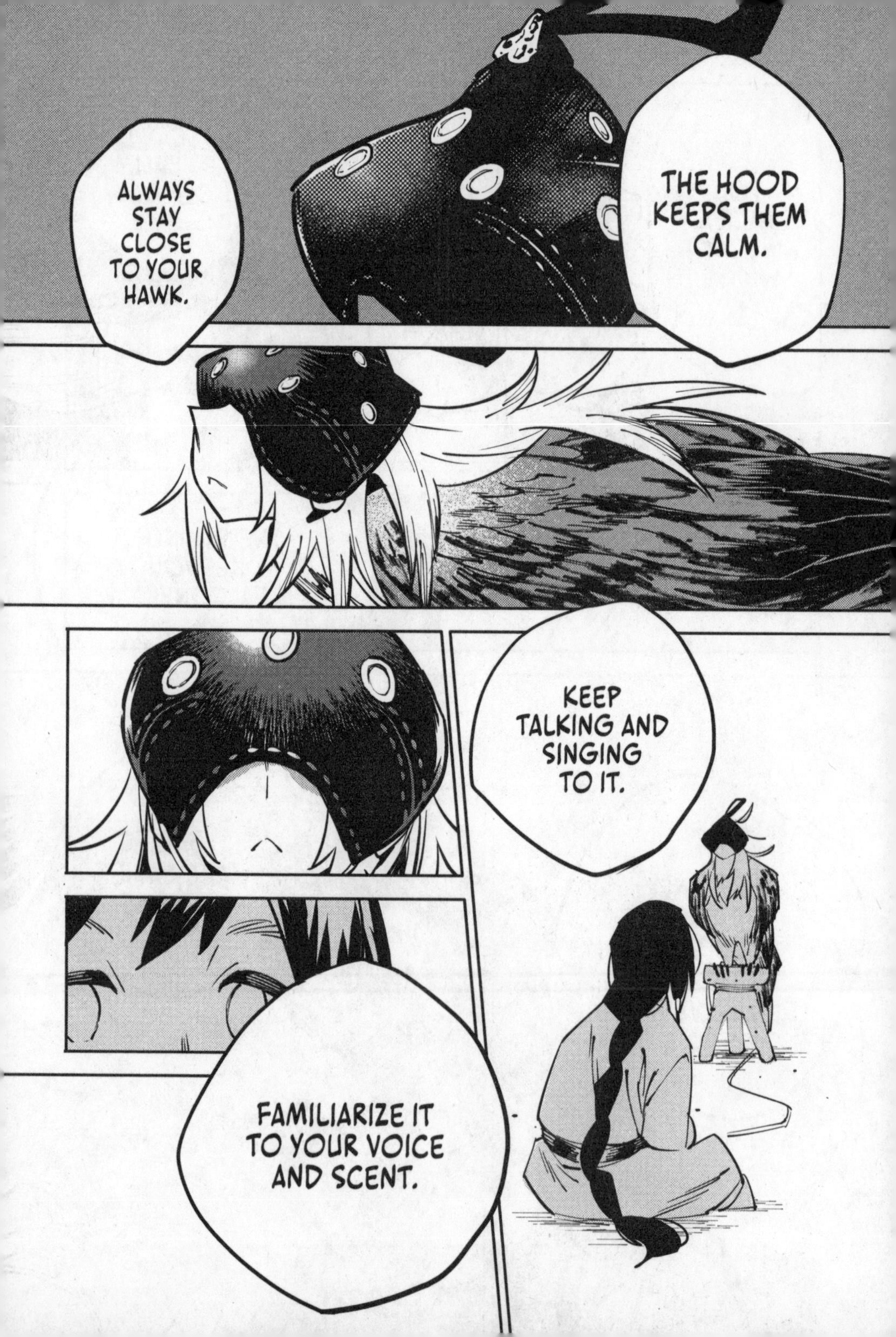
THE HOOD KEEPS THEM CALM.
ALWAYS STAY CLOSE TO YOUR HAWK.
KEEP TALKING AND SINGING TO IT.
FAMILIARIZE IT TO YOUR VOICE AND SCENT.

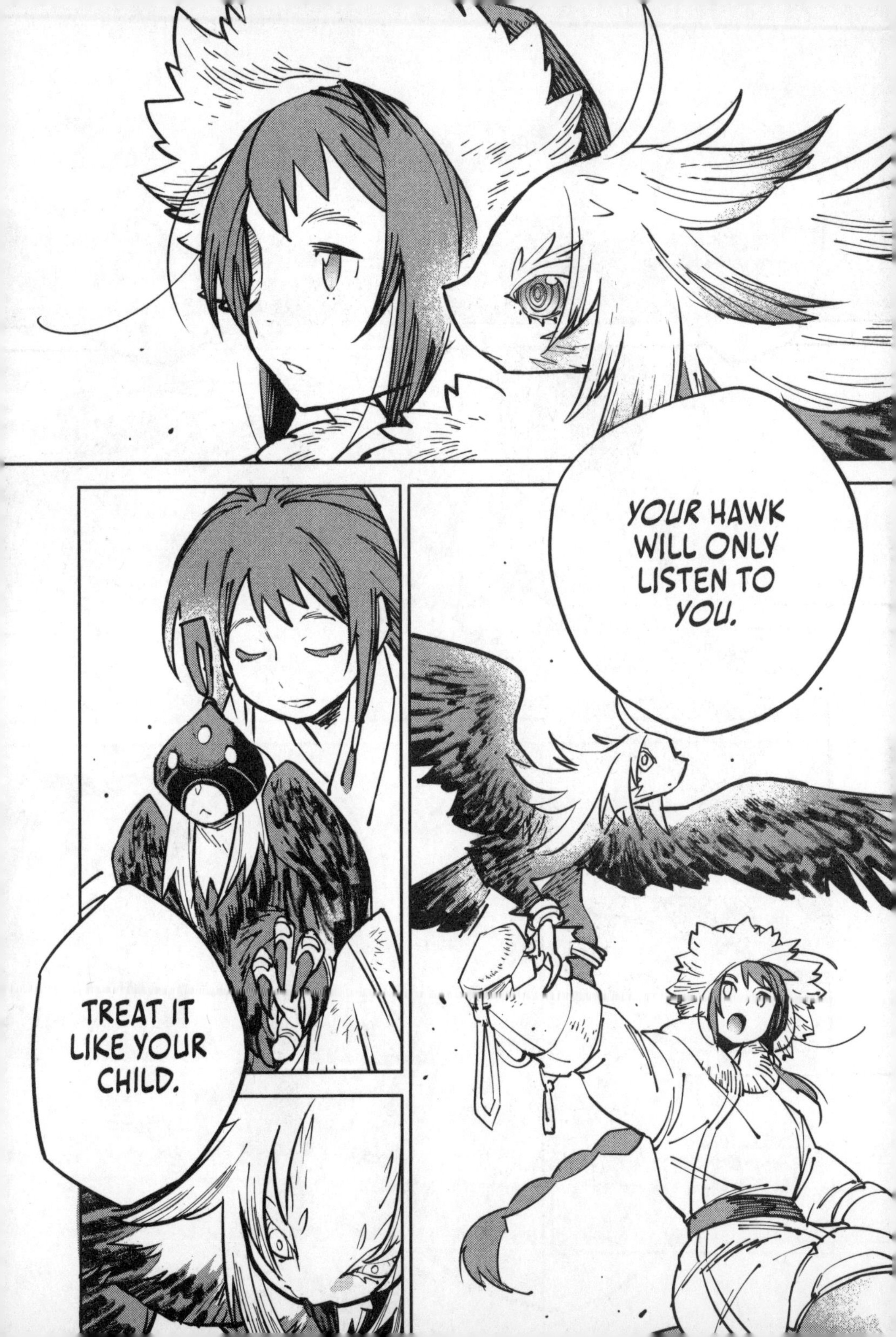
YOUR HAWK WILL ONLY LISTEN TO YOU.
TREAT IT LIKE YOUR CHILD.

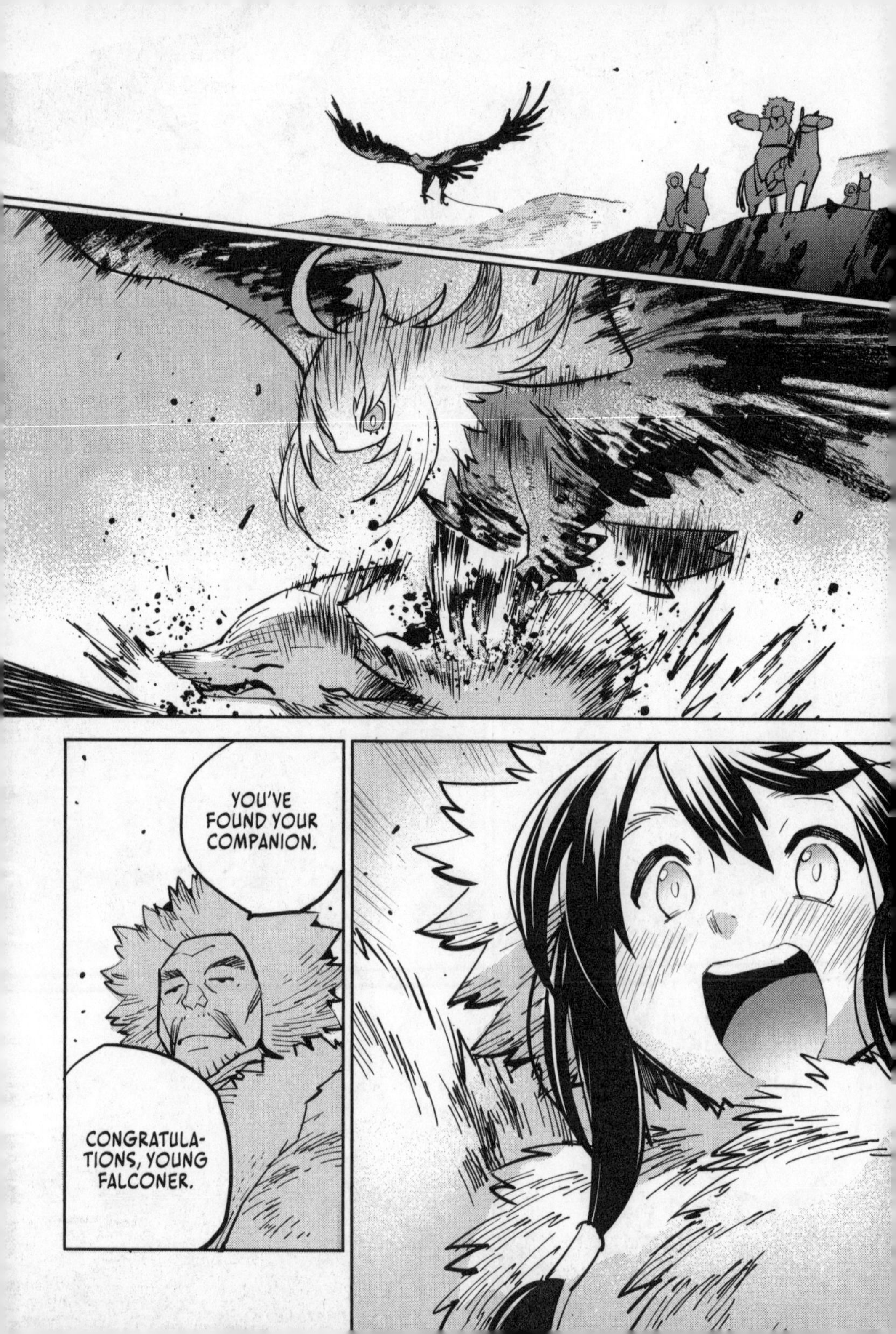
YOU'VE FOUND YOUR COMPANION.
CONGRATULA-TIONS, YOUNG FALCONER.

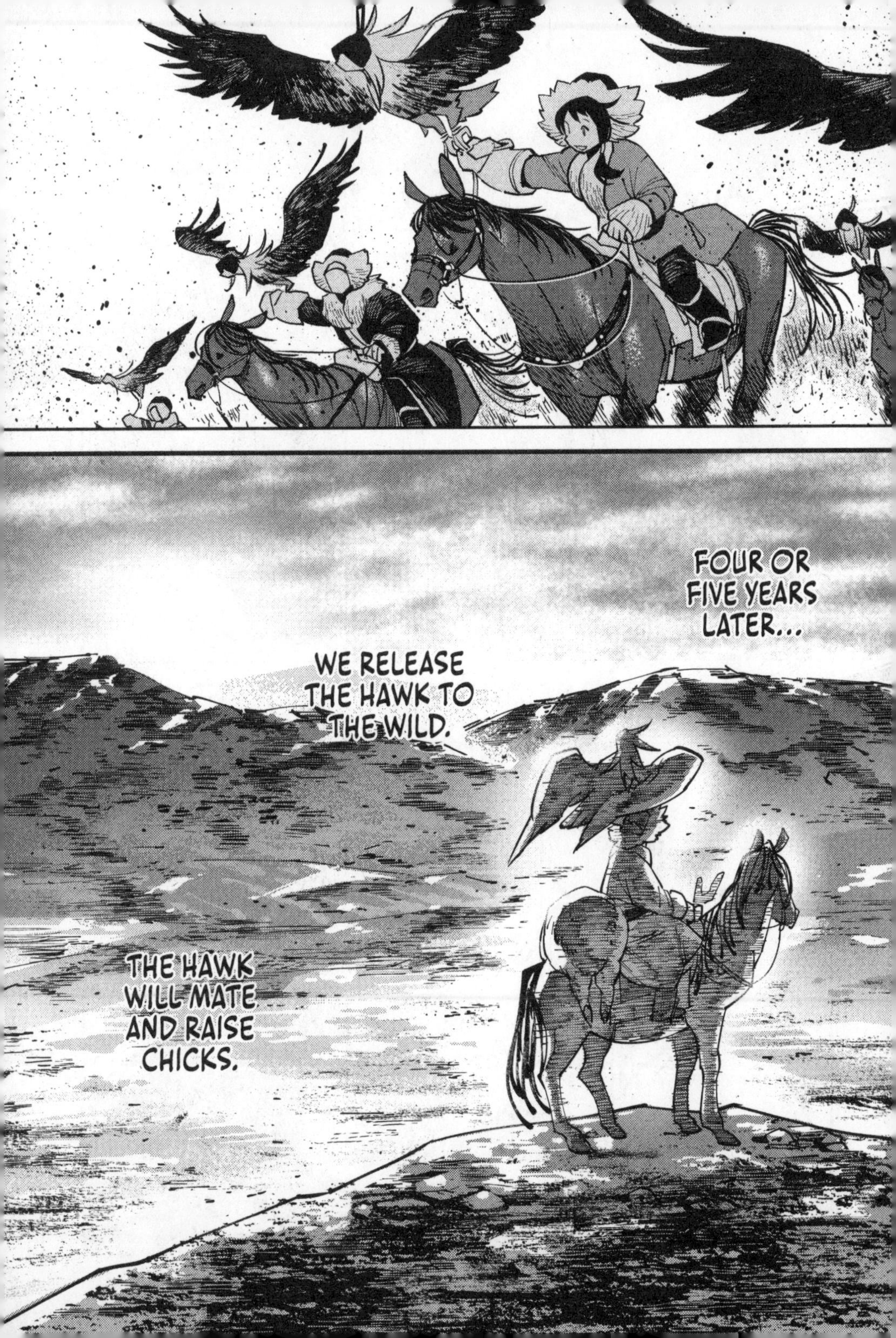
FOUR OR FIVE YEARS LATER...
WE RELEASE THE HAWK TO THE WILD.
THE HAWK WILL MATE AND RAISE CHICKS.

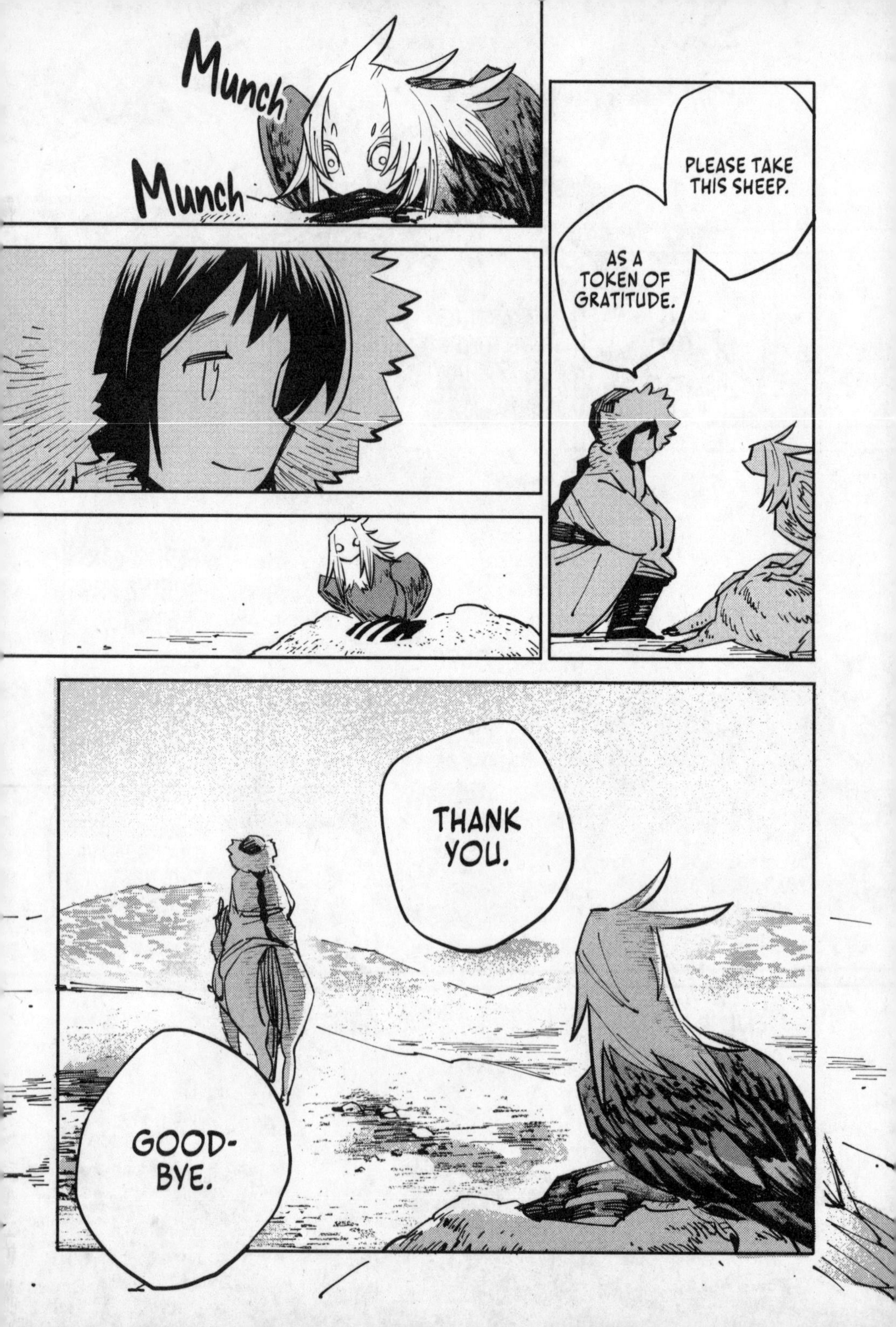
PLEASE TAKE THIS SHEEP.
AS A TOKEN OF GRATITUDE.
Munch
Munch
THANK YOU.
GOOD-BYE.

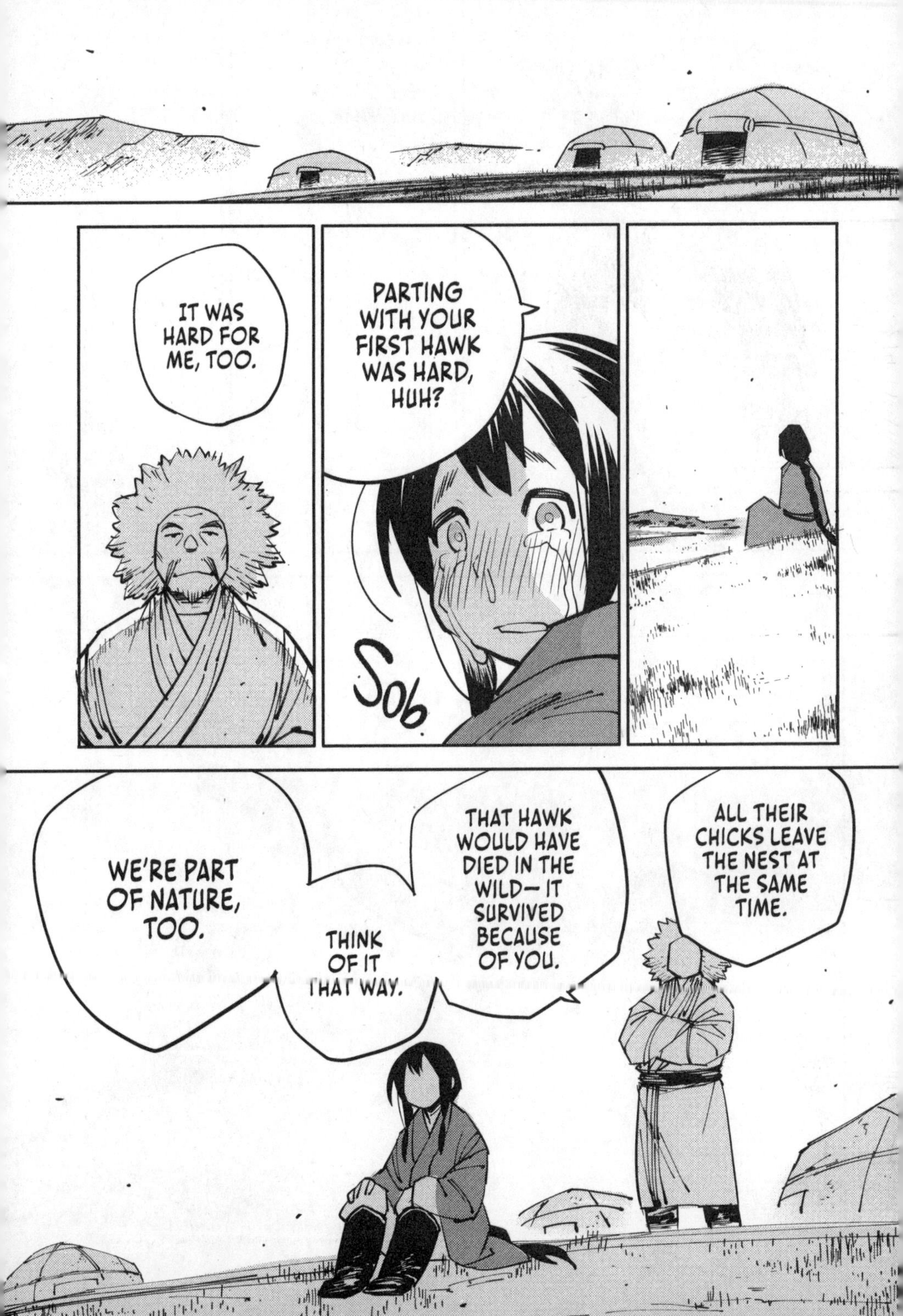
PARTING WITH YOUR FIRST HAWK WAS HARD, HUH?
Sob
IT WAS HARD FOR ME, TOO.
ALL THEIR CHICKS LEAVE THE NEST AT THE SAME TIME.
THAT HAWK WOULD HAVE DIED IN THE WILD— IT SURVIVED BECAUSE OF YOU.
THINK OF IT THAT WAY.
WE'RE PART OF NATURE, TOO.

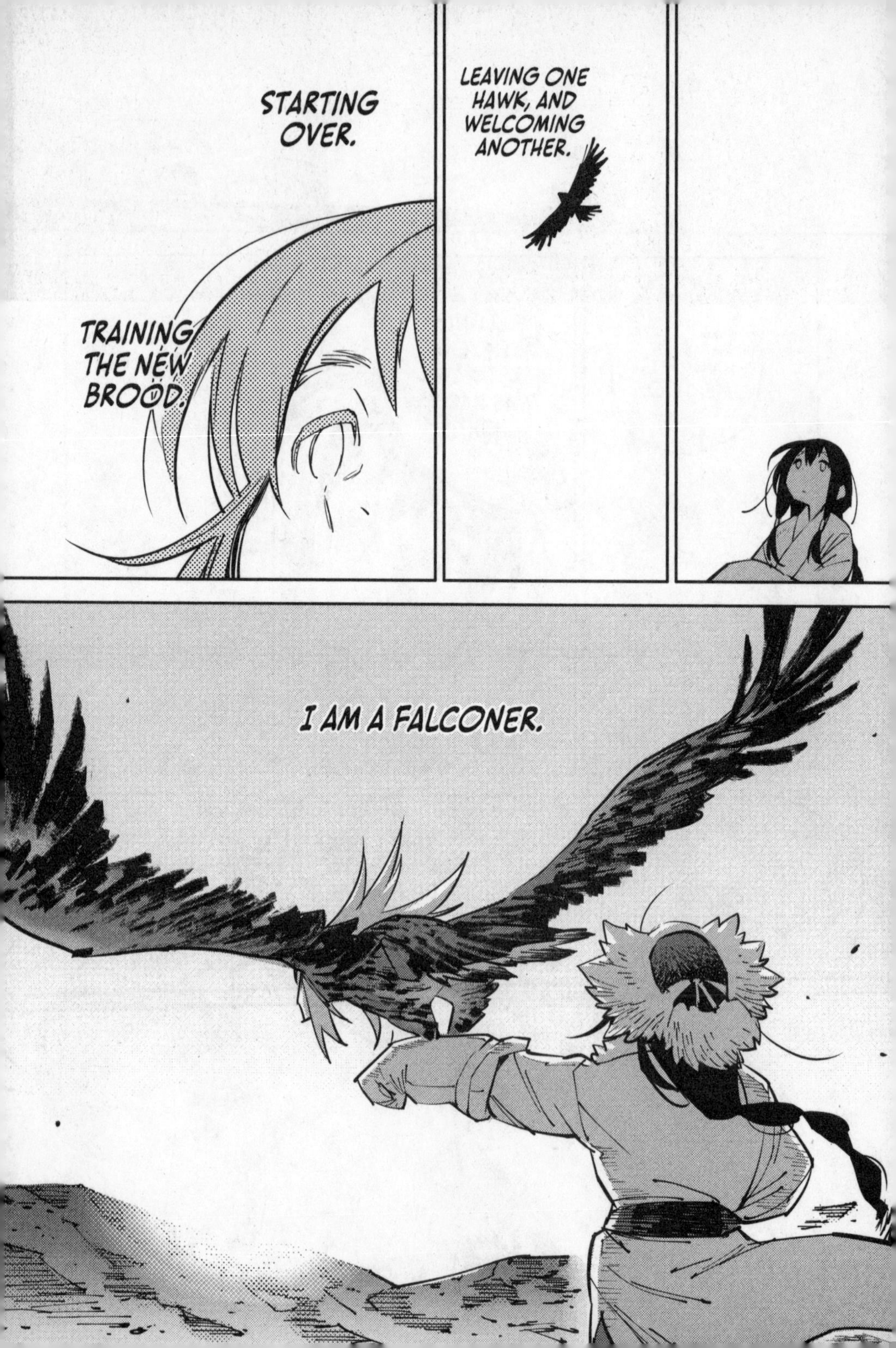
LEAVING ONE HAWK, AND WELCOMING ANOTHER.
STARTING OVER.
TRAINING THE NEW BROOD.
I AM A FALCONER.

Epilogue

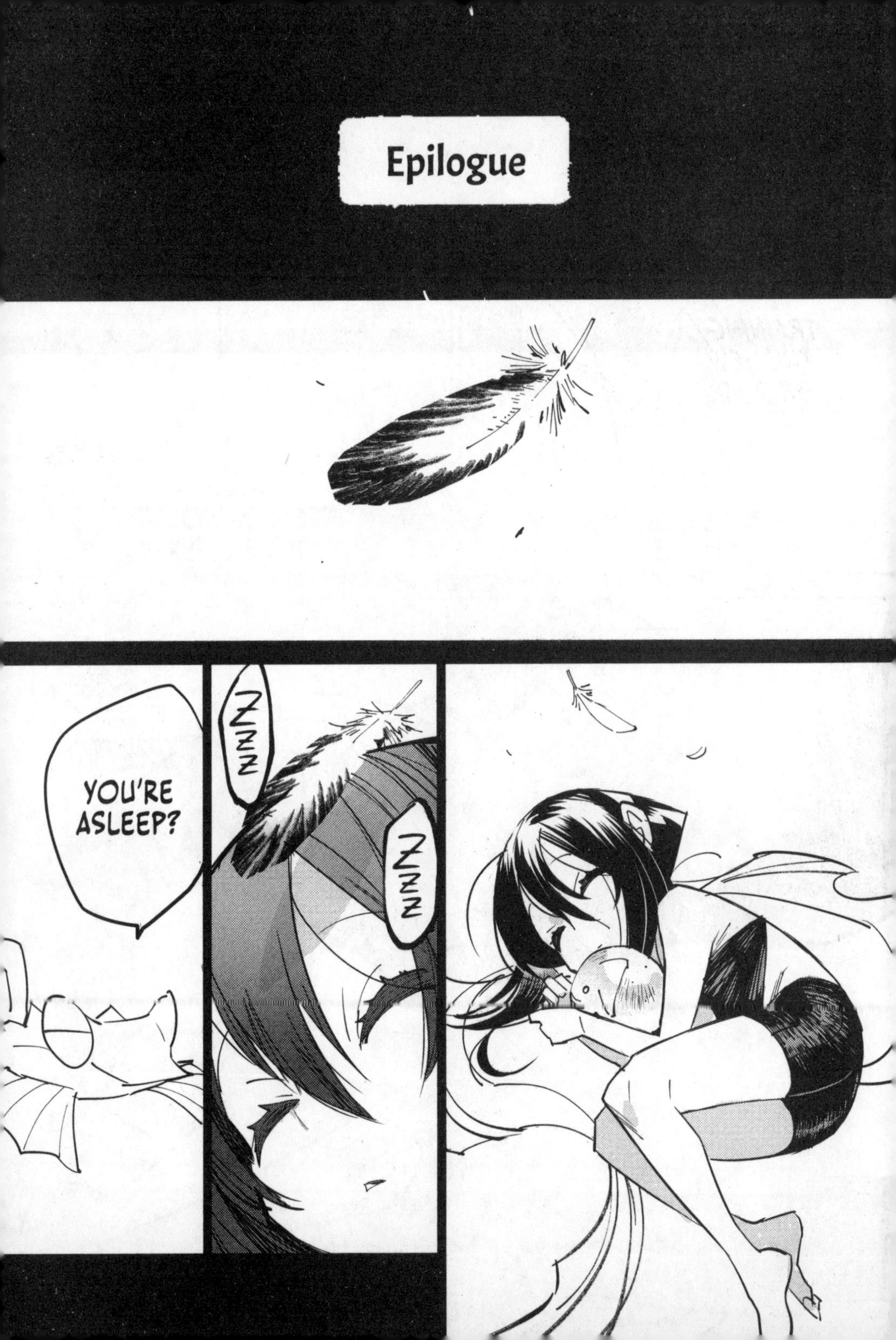
ZZZ
ZZZ
YOU'RE ASLEEP?

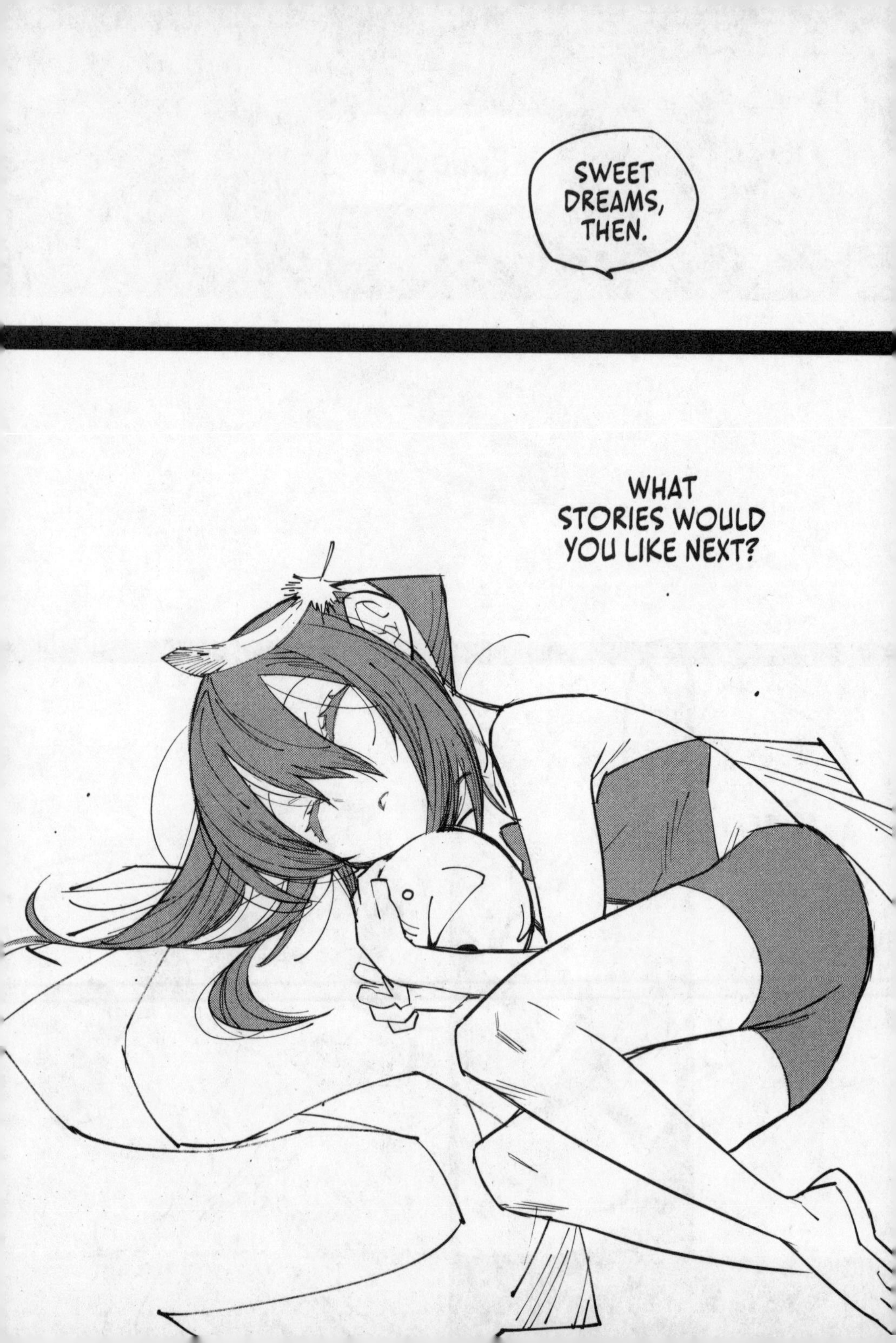
SWEET DREAMS, THEN.
WHAT STORIES WOULD YOU LIKE NEXT?

A Chinese Fantasy

The Dragon King's Daughter

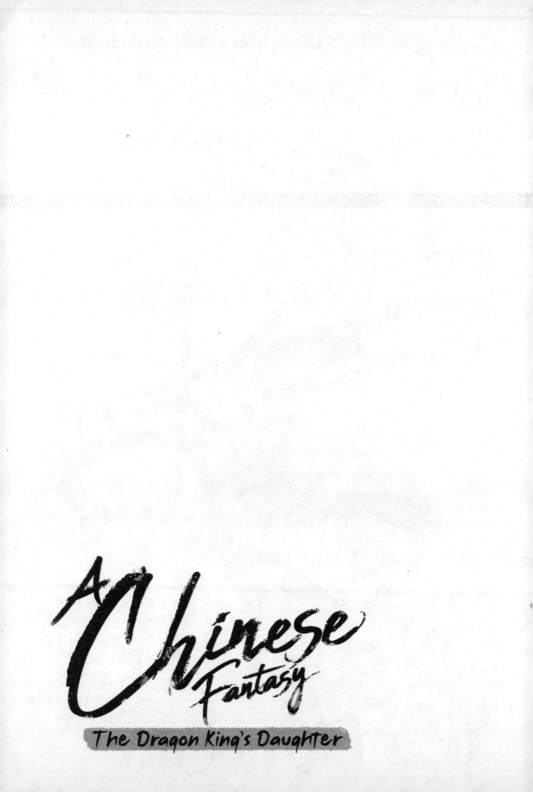

Dragon King's Daughter Character Guide

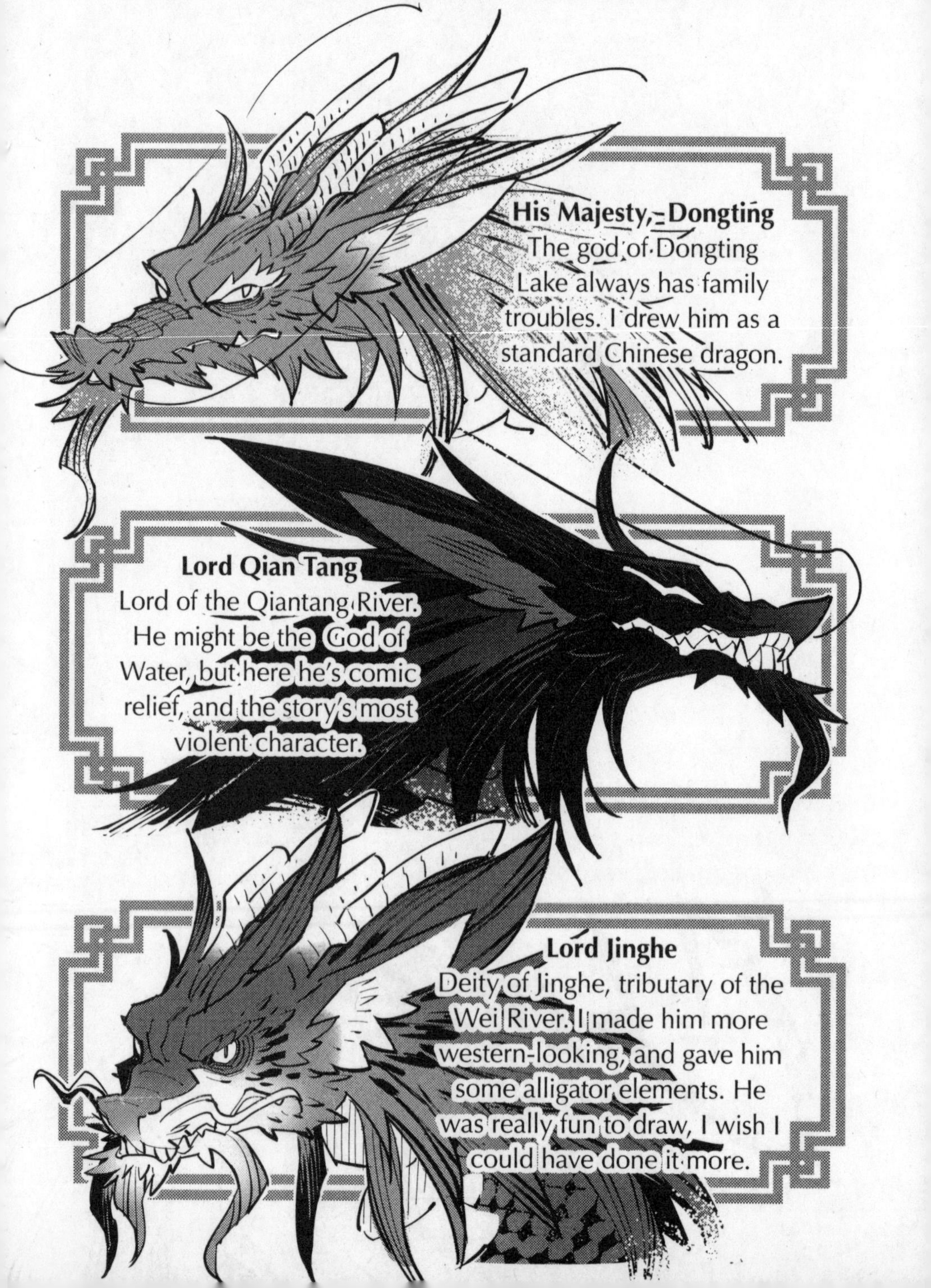
His Majesty, Dongting
The god of Dongting Lake always has family troubles. I drew him as a standard Chinese dragon.
Lord Qian Tang
Lord of the Qiantang River. He might be the God of Water, but here he's comic relief, and the story's most violent character.
Lord Jinghe
Deity of Jinghe, tributary of the Wei River. I made him more western-looking, and gave him some alligator elements. He was really fun to draw, I wish I could have done it more.